History of Logic and Semantics

History of Logic and Semantics

Studies on the Aristotelian and Terminist Traditions

Edited by

Paloma Pérez-Ilzarbe and María Cerezo

BRILL

LEIDEN | BOSTON

Originally published as Volume 53, No. 2-4 (2015) of Brill's journal *Vivarium*.

Library of Congress Control Number: 2016958234

Typeface for the Latin, Greek, and Cyrillic scripts: "Brill". See and download: brill.com/brill-typeface.

ISBN 978-90-04-32426-8 (paperback)
ISBN 978-90-04-32427-5 (e-book)

This book is printed on acid-free paper and produced in a sustainable manner.

Printed by Printforce, the Netherlands

Contents

In Memoriam

Angel d'Ors (1951-2012)

Vides ergo iam nihil nos locutione nisi ut doceamus appetere. The words that St Augustine addressed to his son and interlocutor Adeodatus in *De Magistro* contain a wonderful summary of the life of Angel d'Ors. However, the best image of his existence might perhaps be found in the dedication he made to his father that he included at the beginning of his brief commentary on a fragment of St Augustine's dialogue,[1] a dedication that for those of us who knew him seems like an autobiographical note, even if not consciously so:

> A mi padre,
> que me ayudó a comprender
> cuánta sabiduría y amor separan
> al 'responder' que se da
> del 'contestar' que se exhibe

---

* A version of this note was published in Spanish in *Anuario Filosófico* 46 (2013), 191-8.

1 Angel d'Ors, 'Sobre hablar y enseñar. Un comentario de texto a propósito del *De Magistro*', in *Cómo se comenta un texto filosófico*, ed. J.J. García Norro and R. Rodríguez (Madrid, 2007), 81-96.

To my father,
Who helped me to understand
The wisdom and love that separate
The 'answering' that is given
From the 'replying' that is exhibited.

To devote a lifetime to giving answers is not an easy task. First, it requires the wisdom to select the right interlocutors with whom to examine the relevant questions, that is, the questions that really deserve our attention. It requires both the wisdom to open a sincere and honest dialogue with them in order to search for the answers and the courage to give those answers when one truly believes they have been found. Finally, it requires a love of the truth, and a love of those to whom one wishes to convey that truth, by *giving* those answers, and by leaving the answers as a legacy when one departs.

Angel d'Ors was born in Santiago de Compostela on 25 January 1951 in the bosom of a family with a strong intellectual and academic tradition. He inherited the creative force of his father and grandfather, Alvaro d'Ors and Eugenio d'Ors respectively. He obtained his undergraduate degree and PhD in Philosophy at the University of Navarre in 1976 and 1981, respectively, and devoted his life to teaching and research first at the University of Navarre (1973-1991) and later at the Complutense University of Madrid (1991-2012).

Angel d'Ors was a philosopher, a logician, a historian, a medievalist, a hispanicist and a pedagogue. He practiced each of these professions with rigour and depth. From the beginning of his career he was drawn to the observation of the processes of change in which the history of logic was involved. He decided to devote himself to the study of these processes and to confronting the logical doctrines that he discovered in them, choosing medieval philosophers and, in particular, Hispanic philosophers as his main interlocutors. Although he initially studied the logical works of Spanish scholastic thinkers of the 15th and 16th centuries, in particular Diego Mas and Domingo de Soto, his attention turned to broader interests, such as Aristotle's work and his Greek and Latin commentators, and also towards the great scholastic philosophers. In his approach to medieval logicians, he set out to show the logical relevance of their doctrines and disputes, examining them in the light of contemporary symbolic logical methods.

His research centred on the history of the genres of the treatises of the *Logica Modernorum*, with particular attention to the complex development of the summulist tradition, and on the identification and biographical reconstruction of authors of manuscripts preserved in Spanish libraries and archives. He put forward a novel interpretation of the treatises *De obligationibus*, since he discovered the existence of a meta-dialogue that does not follow the rules of an obligational dialogue. He paid attention to many other specific topics in medieval logic and semantics, such as the theory of *proprietates terminorum*, the conception of hypothetical propositions, the *insolubilia*, and the treatises *De consequentiis*, always submitting his conclusions to the scrutiny of other researchers, by means of publications and participation in specialized academic events, such as for example the *European Symposia on Medieval Logic and Semantics*.

In his final years the horizon of his research expanded even more. On the one hand, he was exploring novel interpretations of Aristotelian doctrines, in particular those in the *Peri Hermeneias*. On the other, he paid considerable attention to logicians and philosophers of language of the 19th and 20th centuries, offering original analyses of the logical and semantic doctrines of Peirce, Frege, Russell, Moore, Wittgenstein, Quine and Kripke, some of which remain unpublished. In addition, he embarked upon some editing projects of the works of his grandfather, Eugenio d'Ors, in collaboration with his wife, Alicia García Navarro.

In his work he achieved a method of research that admirably combined both historical and systemic perspectives. His conviction that philosophical problems were generated in particular contexts, and that solutions to such problems were answers to questions about specific subjects, led him to pay detailed attention to the genesis and history of the semantic doctrines he explored, carefully analyzing the theoretical assumptions of these doctrines. But in so doing, he was not concerned about history itself, but about the theoretical value of the questions and answers whose histories he researched. In this way, he managed, in a novel and challenging manner, to give due consideration both to the doctrines and to those who put them forward.

The systematic rigour and precision with which he dealt with the issues was not at odds with discovery. He used to say that the principle that guided his research was one of "remaining attentive to surprises," and he attributed some of his achievements to such attention, for example his contribution to determining the identity of Peter of Spain. For him, some unexpected data, an unusual card found in a library, or a marginal remark with no clear relevance could turn into new questions, novel hypotheses and unexpected projects.

Although his character was reserved and discreet, when he was in a friendly and trusted environment he was not only cordial but also straightforward and warm, showing in his sincere and sober conversation, and in his attention to detail, his estimable human quality. As an indefatigable, hard working person and an enemy of haste, his way of researching was characterized by its diligence and honesty, shunning academic fashions and living with an intellectual integrity that was often incompatible with what was politically correct. He dedicated himself to his teaching duties, converting his classes into master lectures, never skimping on time or energy in his commitment to his students. When he taught, it was easy to perceive that he really enjoyed it, and it seemed that he was simply saying, as St Augustine said to Adeodatus: *Vides ergo iam nihil nos locutione nisi ut doceamus appetere*.[2]

María Cerezo

---

2 I would like to express my gratitude to Alicia García Navarro for access to some materials from Angel d'Ors' archives, which were very helpful in writing this tribute.

Complete Bibliography of Angel d'Ors

This Bibliography includes: A. Publications by Angel d'Ors in the field of Logic and Philosophy of Language; B. Editions of the work of Eugenio d'Ors; C. Some unpublished writings by Angel d'Ors.

1 Publications in Logic and Philosophy of Language

1977

[Review of] John Lyons et al., *Nuevos horizontes de la Lingüística* (Madrid, 1975), *Nuestro Tiempo* 272 (1977), 118-9.

[Review of] J.M. Bochenski, *Compendio de Lógica Matemática* (Madrid, 1976), *Anuario Filosófico* 10/2 (1977), 233-5.

[Review of] Pascual Martínez Freire, *Lógica Matemática. Primeras Lecciones* (Madrid, 1975), *Anuario Filosófico* 10/2 (1977), 245-7.

[Review of] Helmut Seiffert, *Introducción a la Lógica* (Barcelona, 1977), *Anuario Filosófico* 10/2 (1977), 259-62.

1981

'En torno a una figura de oposición de proposiciones hipotéticas. Condicional y consecuencia intrínseca', *Philosophica* 4 (1981), 155-67. [Also published in *Lógica, Epistemología y Teoría de la Ciencia*, ed. R. Fernández González (MEC, Madrid, 1981), 237-49].

1984

'Las "Summulae" de Domingo de Soto. Los límites de la regla "tollendo ponens"', *Anuario Filosófico* 16/1 (1984), 209-17.

'Los límites de la regla "tollendo ponens": Juan Versor y Lamberto del Monte', *Anuario Filosófico* 17/1 (1984), 9-26.

[Review of] Gonzalo Díaz Díaz, *Hombres y Documentos de la Filosofía Española* vol. I, A-B (Madrid, 1980); vol. II, C-D (Madrid, 1983), *Anuario Filosófico* 17/2 (1984), 164.

[Review of] Marc Richelle, *Skinner o el peligro Behaviorista* (Barcelona, 1981), *Anuario Filosófico* 17/2 (1984), 175-8.

1985

'La doctrina de las proposiciones hipotéticas en la "Logica" de Pedro de Castrovol', *Antonianum* 60 (1985), 120-59.

1986

(transl.), R.C. Jeffrey, *Lógica Formal. Su alcance y sus límites* [Spanish translation of R.C. Jeffrey, *Formal Logic. Its scope and limits*] (Eunsa, Pamplona, 1986 [2nd ed., 1999]).

'La doctrina de las proposiciones insolubles en las "Summulae" de Domingo de Soto', *Cuadernos Salmantinos de Filosofía* 13 (1986), 179-203.

1987

[Review of] Alexander Broadie, *Introduction to Medieval Logic* (Oxford, 1987), *Anuario Filosófico* 20/2 (1987), 194-9.

[Review of] Johannis de Oria, *Opera Logica. Summularum* volumen primum, ed. V. Muñoz Delgado (Madrid, 1987), *Anuario Filosófico* 20/2 (1987), 205-6.

[Review of] Petrus Hispanus, *Tractatus*, trad. M. Beuchot, (México, 1986), *Anuario Filosófico* 20/2 (1987), 210-1.

1988

'Sobre el tratado anónimo "De Arte Obligatoria" recogido en el MS. 306 del Merton College', *Philosophica* 11 (1988), 169-85.

'Sobre las "Obligationes" de Juan de Holanda', *Anuario Filosófico* 21/2 (1988), 33-70.

1989

[Review of] L.M. de Rijk, *Some Earlier Parisian Tracts on Distinctiones Sophismatum* (Nijmegen, 1988), *Anuario Filosófico* 22/1 (1989), 189-91.

[Review of] Paul of Venice, *Logica Magna*. Part II Fascicule 8, ed. E.J. Ashworth (Oxford-New York, 1988), *Anuario Filosófico* 22/2 (1989), 201-2.

1990

(ed., with I. Angelelli), *Estudios de Historia de la Lógica. Actas del II Simposio de Historia de la Lógica* (Eunate, Pamplona, 1990).

'La doctrina de las proposiciones insolubles en las "Dialecticae Introductiones" de Agustín de Sbarroya', in *Estudios de Historia de la Logica. Actas del II Simposio de Historia de la Lógica* (Eunate, Pamplona, 1990), 499-552.

'On Stump's interpretation of Burley's "De Obligationibus"', in *Knowledge and the Sciences in Medieval Philosophy. Proceedings of the Eighth International*

Congress of Medieval Philosophy (S.I.E.P.M.), Helsinki 24-29 August 1987, Vol. II ed. S. Knuuttila, R. Työrinoja and S. Ebbesen ([s.n.], Helsinki, 1990), 468-78.
'Ex impossibili quodlibet sequitur (Walter Burley)', *Archives d'Histoire Doctrinale et Littéraire du Moyen Âge* 57 (1990), 121-54.
[Review of] N. Kretzmann and B.E. Kretzmann, *The Sophismata of Richard Kilvington. Text Edition* (Oxford, 1990), and N. Kretzmann and B.E. Kretzmann, *The Sophismata of Richard Kilvington. Introduction, Translation and Commentary* (Cambridge, 1990), *Anuario Filosófico* 23/2 (1990), 183-4.
[Review of] Francisco Sanches, *That Nothing is known*, ed. E. Limbrick and D.F.S. Thomson (Cambridge, 1988), *Anuario Filosófico* 23/2 (1990), 190-1.

1991
'Tu scis regem sedere (Kilvington, S47[48])', *Anuario Filosófico* 24/1(1991), 49-74.
'Sobre las "Obligationes" de Richard Lavenham', *Archives d'Histoire doctrinale et Littéraire du Moyen Âge* 58 (1991), 253-78.
'De Mixta Suppositione', in *Meeting on Logic and Philosophy of Science-Encuentro de Lógica y Filosofía de la Ciencia. Madrid, 13-15 Noviembre 1991. Rudolf Carnap & Hans Reichenbach in memoriam. Comunicaciones* ([s.n.], Madrid, 1991), 73-81.
'Un problema de interpretación en el "De Obligationibus" de Walter Burley', *Revista de Filosofía* (Maracaibo) 15 (1991), 33-42.

1993
'Ex impossibili quodlibet sequitur (John Buridan)', in *Argumentationstheorie. Scholastische Forschungen zu den logischen und semantischen Regeln korrekten Folgerns*, ed. K. Jacobi (Brill, Leiden, 1993), 195-212.
'Hominis asinus / asinus hominis', in *Sophisms in Medieval Logic and Grammar*, ed. S. Read (Kluwer Academic Publishers, Dordrecht-Boston-London, 1993), 382-97.
'"Sortes non currit vel Sortes movetur" (Roger Swyneshed, Obligationes, §§137-138)', *Archives d'Histoire doctrinale et Littéraire du Moyen Âge* 60 (1993), 165-72.
'Función y argumento en el Begriffsschrift de G. Frege', in *I Congreso de la Sociedad de Lógica, Metodología y Filosofía de la Ciencia. Actas*, ed. E. Bustos et al. ([s.n.], Madrid, 1993), 51-4.

1994
(and Manuel García Clavel), 'Sobre las "Obligationes" de R. Fland. Antiqua et nova responsio', *Revista de Filosofía* (Madrid) 11 (1994), 51-88.

1995

'Utrum nomen significet rem vel passionem in anima (Antonio Andrés y Juan Duns Escoto)', *Archives d'Histoire doctrinale et Littéraire du Moyen Âge* 62 (1995), 7-35.

(and María Cerezo), 'Tractatus 5.54-5.5423. Sobre los llamados "enunciados de creencia" en el "Tractatus Logico-Philosophicus" de Ludwig Wittgenstein', *Anuario Filosófico* 28/2 (1995), 269-310.

'"Non erat veritas", "Non erit veritas". Sobre las pruebas anselmianas de la eternidad de la verdad', in *Verdad, percepción, inmortalidad /Wahrheit, Wahrnehmung, Unsterblichkeit*, ed. S. Castellote, (Facultad de Teología San Vicente Ferrer, Valencia, 1995), 201-14.

'Insolubles deónticos (Robert Holcot y Roger Roseth)', *Acta Philosophica* 4/2 (1995), 173-88.

1996

'Utrum propositio de futuro sit determinate vera vel falsa (Antonio Andrés and John Duns Scoto)', in *Studies on the History of Logic*, ed. I. Angelelli and M. Cerezo (Gruyter, Berlin-New York, 1996), 97-116.

(and María Cerezo), 'La concepción de la matemática en el Tractatus Logico-Philosophicus de Ludwig Wittgenstein', *Themata. Revista de Filosofía* 17 (1996), 267-88.

'Raimundo Lulio, Nicolás de Paz y la "Logica Parva"', *Documenti e Studi sulla tradizione filosofica medievale* 7 (1996), 115-30.

1997

'Petrus Hispanus O. P., Auctor Summularum', *Vivarium* 35/1 (1997), 21-71.

'"Insolubilia" in Some Medieval Theological Texts', in *Vestigia, Imagines, Verba. Semiotics and Logic in Medieval Theological Texts (XIIth–XIVth Century)*, ed. C. Marmo (Brepols, Turnhout, 1997), 133-50.

1998

'"Ex impossibili quodlibet sequitur" (Domingo Báñez)', *Medioevo* 24 (1998), 177-217.

2000

'"*Dubium proponitur*". Andrés Limos y la Doctrina de las Obligaciones', in *Medieval and Renaissance Logic in Spain*, ed. I. Angelelli and P. Pérez-Ilzarbe (Olms, Hildesheim-Zürich-New York, 2000), 225-49.

2001

'Petrus de Cruce Hispanus Portugalensis', *Analise* 22 (2001), 109-45.

'Petrus Hispanus O. P., Auctor Summularum (II). Further documents and problems', *Vivarium* 39/2 (2001), 209-54.

'Petrus Hispanus O. P., Auctor Summularum (I)', *Dicenda. Cuadernos de Filología hispánica* 19 (2001), 231-79.

2002

(transl.), G.E. Moore, *La naturaleza del juicio* [Spanish translation of G.E. Moore, *The Nature of Judgement*] (Encuentro, Madrid, 2002).

'Gometius Hispanus Ulixbonensis O. F. M. (†1513)', *Analise* 24 (2002), 69-118.

2003

'La naturaleza de la identidad y el problema del análisis del contenido en Über Sinn und Bedeutung (1892), de Frege. Un comentario de texto', *Analise* 25 (2003), 83-106.

'Petrus Hispanus O. P., Auctor Summularum (III). "Petrus Alfonsi" or "Petrus Ferrandi"?', *Vivarium* 41/2 (2003), 249-303.

2004

(ed., with J.M. Ansemil and E. Gallego), José F. Prida, *Teorías inseparables* (Trotta, Madrid, 2004).

'*Propositiones de modo loquendi inconsueto: De mixta suppositione*', in *Medieval Theories on Assertive and Non-assertive Language*, ed. A. Maierú and L. Valente (Olschki, Roma, 2004), 537-67.

2007

'Sobre hablar y enseñar. Un comentario de texto a propósito del "De Magistro"', in *Cómo se comenta un texto filosófico*, ed. J.J. García Norro and R. Rodríguez (Síntesis, Madrid, 2007), 81-96.

'*Conveniunt ergo Scotus et Thomas*... Los *Theoremata super universalia Porphyrii* de Jacobo de Naveros', *Documenti e Studi sulla tradizione filosofica medievale* 18 (2007), 501-29.

'Petrus Hispanus O. P., Auctor Summularum (II). Nuevos documentos y problemas', *Dicenda. Cuadernos de Filología hispánica* 25 (2007), 139-80.

2009

(ed., with E. Gallego), José F. Prida, *Lógica Matemática* (Marova, Madrid, 2009).

'El problema del sentido de las "expresiones de concepto" en la obra de Gottlob Frege. Un comentario de texto', *Themata. Revista de Filosofía* 41 (2009), 269-309.

'"Αἱ ὀρθαὶ οὐ συμπίπτουσι" (Aristóteles, *An. Post.*, 74a,4-74a,32)', *Documenti e Studi sulla tradizione filosofica medievale* 20 (2009), 23-56.

2010

'"*Omnis volens ipsum suum velle vult*". A propósito del *De libertate arbitrii* de San Anselmo', in *"Autotrascendimiento". Homenaje al catedrático de filosofía D. Ignacio Falgueras Salinas por su jubilación*, ed. J.A. García González and J.J. Padial (SPICUM, Málaga, 2010), 183-203.

2011

'*Quod probat sic quidam doctor...*', in *In umbra intelligentiae. Estudios en homenaje al Profesor Juan Cruz*, ed. A.L. González and M.I. Zorroza (Eunsa, Pamplona, 2011), 203-19.

(transl.) C.S. Peirce, 'Memoranda a propósito del silogismo aristotélico' [Annotated Spanish translation of C.S. Peirce, 'Memoranda Concerning the Aristotelean Syllogism' (1866), W 1.505-514; CP 2.794-806]. URL = http://www.unav.es/gep/PeirceMemoranda1866.pdf.

2013

'Logic in Salamanca in the Fifteenth Century. The *Tractatus Suppositionum Terminorum* by Master Franquera', *Vivarium* 51 (2013), 427-63. [Also published in E.P. Bos (ed.) in coll. with H.A.G. Braakhuis, W. Duba, C.H. Kneepkens and C. Schabel, *Medieval Supposition Theory Revisited* (Brill, Leiden, 2013), 427-63].

2015

'*Tu scis an de mentiente sit falsum Sortem esse illum*. On the Syncategorem "*an*"', *Vivarium* 53/2-4 (2015), 269-93. [Also published in this book].

'Petrus Hispanus O. P., Auctor Summularum (III). ¿"Petrus Alfonsi" o "Petrus Ferrandi"?', *Dicenda* 33 (2015), 35-89.

2 Other Publications: Editions of Eugenio d'Ors

1998

(with Alicia García Navarrro, eds.), Eugenio d'Ors, *Último glosario I. Helvecia y los lobos* (Comares, Granada, 1998).

(with Alicia García Navarrro, eds.), Eugenio d'Ors, *El secreto de la Filosofía* (Tecnos, Madrid, 1998).

(with Alicia García Navarrro, eds.), Eugenio d'Ors, *El valle de Josafat* (Espasa-Calpe, Madrid, 1998).

(with Alicia García Navarrro, eds.), Eugenio d'Ors, *Último glosario II. De la Ermita al Finisterre* (Comares, Granada, 1998).

1999

(with Alicia García Navarrro, eds.), Eugenio d'Ors, *Cézanne* (Acantilado, Barcelona, 1999).

(with Alicia García Navarrro, eds.), Eugenio d'Ors, *Diccionario filosófico portátil* (Criterio, Madrid, 1999).

2000

(with Alicia García Navarrro, eds.), Eugenio d'Ors, *Trilogía de la 'Residencia de Estudiantes'—De la Amistad y del Diálogo. Aprendizaje y Heroísmo. Grandeza y Servidumbre de la Inteligencia*—(Eunsa, Pamplona, 2000).

(with Alicia García Navarrro, eds.), Eugenio d'Ors, *Último glosario III. El cuadrivio itinerante* (Comares, Granada, 2000).

2001

(with Alicia García Navarrro, eds.), Eugenio d'Ors, *Pablo Picasso* (Acantilado, Barcelona, 2001).

(with Alicia García Navarrro, eds.), Eugenio d'Ors, *Flos Sophorum* (Eunsa, Pamplona, 2001).

2002

(with Alicia García Navarrro, eds.), Eugenio d'Ors, *Lo barroco*, New revised edition (Tecnos, Madrid, 2002).

(with Alicia García Navarrro, eds.), Eugenio d'Ors, *Último glosario IV. El designio y la ensalada* (Comares, Granada, 2002).

(with Alicia García Navarrro, eds.), Eugenio d'Ors, *Último glosario V. El guante impar* (Comares, Granada, 2002).

2003

(ed.), Eugenio d'Ors, *La civilización en la historia* (Criterio, Madrid, 2003).

2004

(with Alicia García Navarrro, eds.), Eugenio d'Ors, *Tres horas en el Museo del Prado* (Tecnos, Madrid, 2004).

2005

(ed.), Eugenio d'Ors, *Tina y la Guerra Grande* (Biblioteca Nueva, Madrid, 2005).

2006

(with Alicia García Navarrro, eds.), Eugenio d'Ors, *Paliques (1922-1925)*, vol. I (Áltera, Barcelona, 2006).
(with Alicia García Navarrro, eds.), Eugenio d'Ors, *Paliques (1926-1929)*, vol. II (Áltera, Barcelona, 2006).
(with Alicia García Navarrro, eds.), *Eugenio d'Ors, Teatro, títeres y toros. Exégesis lúdica (con una prórroga deportiva)* (Renacimiento, Sevilla, 2006).

2009

(ed.), Eugenio d'Ors, *Tres lecciones en el Museo del Prado de introducción a la crítica de arte* (Introd. Javier Olivares), New edition, revised and extended (Tecnos, Madrid, 2009).

3 Unpublished Writings

This section includes the items listed by Angel d'Ors himself in the last version of his CV: in addition to his unpublished dissertations, it contains the manuscripts that he intended to publish in the near future. Other unpublished manuscripts are not included.

La Lógica Proemial del Maestro Diego Mas, BA Dissertation, University of Navarra, Pamplona, 1976.
Las "Summulae" de Domingo de Soto, PhD Dissertation, University of Navarra, Pamplona, 1981.
'"οἱ δὲ ἄλλοι συνδέσμῳ εἷς / alie vero coniunctione une" (*Perihermeneias* 5, 17a, 8-26)'.
'Burley's *Insolubilia*. A revision'.
'Sobre "*Identity and Necessity*" de S. Kripke. Un comentario de texto'.
'Sobre "*Performative utterances*" de J. L. Austin. Un comentario de texto'.
'"Vuestra alteza comprende . . ." Leonhard Euler (1707-1783) ante la silogística'.
'"*Der Ochse vor dem neuen Tore*". A propósito de un inédito de Frege'.
'¿Dice o significa '*What is a speech act?*' qué es un acto de habla? Un comentario de texto'.

Introduction

Paloma Pérez-Ilzarbe and María Cerezo

This book was conceived as a memorial volume in honour of the philosopher and historian of logic Angel d'Ors (1951-2012). A number of his friends were glad to have this opportunity to pay homage to Angel's scholarly achievements and to express their thanks for his generous commitment to his colleagues.

From the beginning of his career, Angel d'Ors approached his studies of logic from a historical perspective, trying to understand the changes that this discipline underwent during its lengthy and complex evolution from Aristotle's *Organon* to the new logic of the 20th century. Two ideas underpinned his research: on the one hand, that narrating the history of logic involves describing diverse logical traditions, their development and spread, their mutual confrontation and change. On the other, that concrete people and books, with their particular stories, are the key agents responsible for this coming and going of ideas. The present volume aspires to reflect the amplitude and diversity of the work that Angel developed on these premises.

In the first place, Angel d'Ors paid particular attention to the medieval reception of ancient logic, and more specifically to the interpretation—often misinterpretation, in his opinion—of Aristotle's *Organon* in the works of scholastic logicians. The articles by Allan Bäck and José Miguel Gambra, on the fallacy of accident and on what *is in* a subject, respectively, pay tribute to this long-standing interest in Angel's research.

The problem of the relation between logic and language was one of the main concerns in Angel's approach to logic, a concern that shaped his involvement in the study of medieval and post-medieval logical traditions. Having this general problem in mind, he was often engaged in the investigation of very concrete technical questions, which he approached with his rigorous analytical mind. This is the approach adopted by Luisa Valente in her article on desire in Abelard's theory of sentences, and by María Cerezo in her study of paronymy in St Anselm's *De Grammatico*.

Angel d'Ors devoted special attention to the way the different logical doctrines of the *Logica Modernorum* developed. In particular, his colleagues acknowledge Angel's valuable contributions to the study of *insolubilia, consequentiae* and *obligationes*. The piece by Calvin Normore pays tribute to Angel's insightful reflections on the consequence relation, and the papers by E.J. Ashworth, Stephen Read and Mikko Yrjönsuuri are recognitions of his work on the theory of obligations.

 | DOI 10.1163/9789004324275_002

Angel combined his interest in strictly logical questions with a parallel dedication to purely historical research, which he considered essential to achieve a proper understanding of the complex processes of transformation of logical doctrines. He devoted much energy, on the one hand, to the cataloguing and edition of texts and their classification into literary genres, and, on the other, to the identification of authors and the study of the institutions to which they were linked. His contribution to our knowledge of the intellectual life of medieval and post-medieval Europe is undisputed. Angel's hitherto unpublished erudite study on the syncategorem *'an'* offers a wonderful example of this kind of historical research. The edition by Sten Ebbesen of an English sophism can be included under the same heading, and so can the careful survey of a collection of grammatical sophisms by C.H. Kneepkens and Joke Spruyt's analysis of the *Introductiones Montanae maiores*.

Finally, Angel was proudly aware of the importance of Spanish logicians at the last stage of the development of the Aristotelian-Scholastic tradition. He took the study and clarification of their role in this development as his own special duty and devoted particular attention to the role played by Spanish scholars in the transformation of the doctrines of the *Logica Modernorum*, from the first commentaries on Peter of Spain's *Tractatus* to the subtle post-medieval developments of these doctrines. In this context, Paloma Pérez-Ilzarbe follows up on Angel's interest in Fernando de Enzinas.

It is more than a happy coincidence that this memorial volume was first published in the journal where Angel d'Ors wanted his most esteemed contribution to the historiography of Spanish logic to be published: the three parts of his 'Petrus Hispanus O.P., Auctor Summularum' (1997, 2001, 2003), which, challenging the general consensus about the identity of Peter of Spain, revived a neglected discussion and opened new paths for future research. We are grateful to *Vivarium* for this opportunity.

It has not been possible for all of Angel's friends to participate in this volume, nor is it feasible to list them all. However, we would like to make two exceptions to this general rule. On the one hand, Angel d'Ors felt particularly tied to the international groups devoted to the study of medieval and post-medieval logic (originally driven forward by Professors L.M. de Rijk and Jan Pinborg, whom Angel held in high esteem). He maintained contact with these groups through the *European Symposia on Medieval Logic and Semantics*: his many colleagues in that forum join us in thankfully recognising Angel's intellectual merit and human qualities. On the other, we would also like to explicitly mention Angel d'Ors' special bonds with three colleagues. First, Angel shared with Jaime Nubiola a lasting interest in the work of C.S. Peirce, whom Angel considered to be 'the last logician of the syllogism' and hence an important figure in the history of logic. Encouraged by his friend and colleague, Angel d'Ors conceived the ambitious project of studying the development of the Peircean general theory of reasoning from a syllogistic perspective. Second, Miguel Pérez de Laborda was Angel's first doctoral student: they shared a passion for every challenging detail in Aristotle's theory of predication. Angel's certainty concerning the need to reinterpret the received version of Aristotelian logic was always present on his intellectual horizon. Finally, Angel d'Ors shared with Olga Weijers an eagerness to reconstruct with utmost accuracy the intellectual history linking texts and people in the network of the medieval traditions of thought. Angel's assiduous support for her work on the repertory of the Arts masters in Paris was evidence of his need to share knowledge—a need that drives every genuine researcher.

We would like to take this opportunity to thank the many colleagues and institutions that supported Angel's research in various ways: providing him access to sources, collaborating with him on research and editorial projects, inviting him to conferences, sharing manuscripts and editions with him, publishing his articles, and generally entering into fruitful dialogue and correspondence with him. Special mention has to be made of E.P. Bos, who in collaboration with others included the first posthumously published article of Angel d'Ors in 2013 in a special issue of *Vivarium*.

We also want to express our warmest thanks to Angel's wife, Alicia García Navarro, for having generously shared with us the Research Project prepared by Angel in 2011 and submitted for the public examination in which he obtained his position as Full Professor at the Complutense University of Madrid. This document, which was of great help when we were writing this Introduction, is an impressive testimony to Angel's wide range of interests, interests that he pursued with an astonishing depth and rigour.

How the Fallacy of Accident Got Its Name (and Lost It)

Allan Bäck

I offer an explanation of why the fallacy of "accident" was so called by Aristotle. By 'accident' here, Aristotle does not mean accidental predication but being *per accidens*. Understood in this way, the fallacy of accident can be analyzed in terms of the rules that Aristotle gives for being *per accidens*. I show that these rules handle the instances of that fallacy brought forward by Aristotle. The fallacy of accident then lost the original justification for its name in the late Greek period through the changes made to the fallacy: it was extended to terms of second intention like 'species'; it was construed syllogistically so that the paralogisms became invalid through not having a universal major premise. This approach dominated in the medieval period but has led to much confusion over the fallacy. I end by considering how to formulate Aristotle's original solution to the fallacy of accident in modern terms.

1 Aristotle's Account of the Fallacy of Accident

Aristotle considers the fallacy of accident to be one of the fallacies independent of language [*Soph. El.* 165b23-4]. It comes not from a mistake about language but from a mistake about what language signifies.[1] This suggests that for him the fallacy does not come about on account of some ambiguity in the expressions being used.

* An earlier version of this paper was presented at a conference at the Humboldt-Universität zu Berlin with the support of Excellence Cluster Topoi. I am grateful for comments from the audience.

1 Cf. Irène Rosier-Catach, 'La notion de *translatio*, le principe de compositionalité, et l'analyse de la prédication accidentelle chez Abélard', in *Langage, sciences, philosophie au XIIe siècle*, ed. J. Biard (Paris, 1999), 125-64: 137 "... secundum locutionem lorsque le mot possède plusiers acceptions pour lui-même et que le context en sélectionne une .... extra locutionem lorsque le context crée une signification nouvelle." So Peter Abelard, *Super Periermeneias, Logica 'Ingredientibus' III*, ed. C. Baeumker (Münster, 1933), 400, 29-37.

 | DOI 10.1163/9789004324275_003

He introduces the fallacy of accident as follows:

> Thus, there are fallacies by accident when it be thought right that whatever belongs to the object also belongs to the accident. For, since many things are accidental to the same thing, it is not necessary for all these to belong to all the predicates and of that of which they are predicated. [*Soph. El.* 166b28-32; my translation][2]

Aristotle is saying that the fallacy of accident occurs when what belongs to an accident and what belongs to its subject are confused. He offers a single solution: the fallacy occurs when it is "indeterminate" when a predicate of an accident must also belong to its subject:

> There is a single solution for all fallacies by accident. For since it is indeterminate when something must be said to belong with the object when it belongs with the accident, and in some cases it seems so and people say so, while in other cases they say that it is not necessary, so it must be said similarly for them all, when there has been a conclusion, that it is not necessary. [*Soph. El.* 179a26-31; my translation]

This does not offer much precise guidance as to how to solve the fallacy. Aristotle suggests also that this fallacy errs about the deduction and demonstration, when he is reducing all fallacies to ignorance of refutation. But once again he gives few details on how to solve this fallacy in his summary remarks:

> Fallacies that depend on accident are clear once deduction has been defined. For the same definition ought to hold good of refutation too, except that a mention of the contradictory is here added; for a refutation is a deduction of the contradictory. If, then, there is no deduction as regards an accident of anything, there is no refutation. For supposing, when these things are the case, that must necessarily be, and that is white, there is no necessity for it to be white on account of the deduction. So, if the triangle has its angles equal to two right angles, and it happens to be a figure, or a primitive or a principle, it is not proved that a figure or a principle or a primitive has this character. For the demonstration proves the point about it not *qua* figure or *qua* primitive, but qua triangle. [*Soph. El.* 168a34-168b4; trans. Pickard-Cambridge, *Complete Works*, 1: 284-5]

---

2 Sten Ebbesen, *Commentators and Commentaries on Aristotle's Sophistici Elenchi*, 3 vols. (Leiden, 1981) 1: 224, calls this description of the fallacy "no masterpiece of clarity."

Aristotle is saying that a demonstrative syllogism must have the primary subject as the subject in its conclusion. Thus, if the conclusion has as its predicate 'having its interior angles equal to two right angles' its subject must be 'triangle', and not 'isosceles triangle' or '[some] figure'. Otherwise the syllogism is not demonstrative but sophistical, as he says in the *Posterior Analytics* [74a23-30].[3] So from this passage we get the result that the fallacy of accident comes somehow from not using the subject primary for the predicate being asserted. Yet again we get few details—and a major puzzle: given that every triangle is a figure, and every triangle has its angles equal to two right angles, it does follow that some figure has its angles equal to two right angles. This conclusion may not be demonstrative, as the predicate holds of its subject neither universally nor primarily. Still, it is syllogistical.[4] Perhaps in this passage Aristotle is responding to a particular puzzle about demonstration. In any case, he does not give us much more than a clue on how to solve the fallacy of accident.

Moreover, a sound syllogism can have a universal conclusion without a primary subject as with

(1) Every figure is extended
Every triangle is a figure
Therefore every triangle is extended

So, unless Aristotle is imposing the stricter conditions of demonstration (of the cause [*An. Po.* I.13]) for validity, it is hard to see his point here.

A simpler way of taking this passage is to consider the syllogism

(2) A triangle is a figure
A triangle has its angles equal to two right angles
Therefore a figure has its angles equal to two right angles

Here the two extremes of the premises are combined somewhat in the manner of the paternal dog example (discussed below (5)), and the syllogism is invalid if the indefinite conclusion is taken universally instead of particularly. Saying that having its angles equal to two right angles holds *qua* triangle and

---

3 On the 'qua' locution and the primary, commensurately universal subject, see Allan Bäck, *On Reduplication* (Leiden, 1996), ch. 2.

4 Cf. (ps.) Alexander (Michael Ephesus), *In Sophisticos Elenchos Commentarium*, ed. M. Wallies (Berlin, 1898), 59,27-31; 60,6-19. He goes on, 59,35-7, somewhat implausibly, to say that "some figure" at 168b1 in the passage above indicates that the conclusion must be universal.

not *qua* figure would then amount to saying that the conclusion holds universally for triangle and not for figure. The fallacy of accident would then arise since it is being inferred that having its angles equal to two right angles holds for figure universally just because it happens in some cases that a figure is a triangle. Still, this interpretation too gives but a clue on how to solve the fallacy of accident in general. It is tempting to think that the fallacy comes from an indefinite proposition having two readings, the universal and the particular.[5] Yet Aristotle denies that the fallacy here is due to the language being used.

Perhaps looking at some examples will provide more clues. Aristotle gives examples like

(3) Coriscus is different from Socrates
Socrates is a man
Therefore, Coriscus is different from a man

(4) The one who is approaching is not known by me
Coriscus is the one who is approaching
Therefore, Coriscus is not known by me [but: I know Coriscus] [179b1-4]

(5) This dog is yours
This dog is a father
Therefore, this dog is your father [or: is a father of yours] [179b14-5]

Some of these paralogisms, particularly (3) and (5), may strike us as coming from ambiguity of terms like 'yours', just as (2) could be construed.[6] Yet Aristotle has said that they do not occur in virtue of the language used.[7] So consider, rather, these paralogisms in terms of their truth makers, the things making their assertions true: what makes the dog yours and what makes the dog a father is not what would make the dog your father. Now what makes the dog yours is a certain accidental circumstance of the dog, and likewise for what makes the dog a father. So the fallacy of accident would arise on account of certain relationships between accidents, which belong to substances.

5 Scott Schreiber, *Aristotle on False Reasoning* (Albany, 2003), 117, rejects this interpretation too.
6 A 'fallacy' is a type of logical mistake, while a 'paralogism' is an instance of a fallacy.
7 Although he does seem to admit at 179b38-180a7 that the fallacy of ambiguity occurs here too.

We then can see the point of Aristotle's remark: the fallacy of accident occurs when a predicate proved to hold of an accident is then inferred to hold of its substance—or *vice versa*, it would seem from the *Posterior Analytics* passage.

Moreover, note that most, if not all, of the examples given by Aristotle of the fallacy of accident have a reading of their conclusions according to which they turn out to be true, as Ockham notes.[8] Then no fallacy need result. For instance: (3) 'Coriscus is not known [recognized] by me [now]', (4) 'there is a man different from Coriscus', and (less plausibly) (5) 'you have a dog-father' might all be true. But then they might also be false. Aristotle might have meant at least this when he says that it is "indeterminate" whether or not the object has the feature of the accident. Still, note that, on the latter reading, even though the conclusion *might* be true, the fallacy would still occur, as the conclusion would not follow *necessarily* from the premises.

Furthermore, it is unlikely that Aristotle had in mind accidental predication when naming this fallacy 'the fallacy of accident'. For he shows no hint in his syllogistic that the rules of inference hold only for essential predications. Indeed, many of the examples that he offers there contain accidental predications.[9]

Again, if Aristotle barred accidental predications from syllogistic and demonstration, he would have no science. For Aristotle thinks that science deals with demonstrating the *propria*, the proper accidents, of the species, and of finding out its real definition, composed of genus and *differentia*. But, at least at times, Aristotle also holds that *propria* and *differentiae* are in accidental categories [*Cat.* 3a21-2; *Top.* 102a18-20].[10] Moreover, many of the objects of his sciences are accidents: numbers, shapes, moving things. So for Aristotle: no accidental predication, no science. Consequently, we must concede that Aristotle allows for syllogisms composed of accidental predications containing no fallacy.[11]

---

8 William of Ockham, *Expositio super libros Elenchorum* (*Opera Philosophica* 3), ed. Francesco Del Punta (St Bonaventure, NY, 1979), 231,37-42.

9 Likewise Louis André Dorion, trans. and comm., *Aristote: Les Réfutations Sophistiques* (Paris, 1995), 233, holds that 'accident' in fallacy of accident does not mean accident in the technical sense.

10 Allan Bäck, *Aristotle's Theory of Predication* (Leiden, 2000), 151-8.

11 As his own examples suggest, *pace* Schreiber, *Aristotle on False Reasoning*, 13. Joan Kung, 'Aristotle on Thises, Suches, and the Third Man Argument', *Phronesis* 26 (1981), 207-47: 221-2. Aristotle does not offer any logical rules for ten distinct logical types of *copulae*. Rather, 'is' has a basic but incomplete meaning that needs to be specified further. Those further determinations fall into the ten categories. Cf. *Soph. El.* 178b36-9a10 and Michael Frede and Günther Patzig, *Aristoteles "Metaphysik Z"*, 2 vols. (Munich, 1988), 2: 47.

But, then, what mistake is committed in the fallacy of accident? Why does Aristotle name it thus? Aristotle calls instances of this fallacy:

> οἱ παρὰ τὸ συμβεβηκὸς παραλογισμοί [166b28]

What does Aristotle's name of this fallacy mean? Literally it is a fallacy 'compared to the accident' or 'due to an accident'. This does not necessarily mean 'predicated accidentally'. Aristotle usually speaks of accidental predication as "λεγέται κατὰ συμβεβηκός" [*Int.* 21a8]. Aristotle uses 'κατά' typically to indicate predication; he does not use 'παρά' that way. So the name of the fallacy need not, and probably does not, signify accidental predication. Let me then propose another option.

2 The Antepredicamental Rule

The fallacy of accident might be, and has been, taken to be so named and to err on account of violating the antepredicamental rule. Aristotle says in the *Categories*, "whenever one thing is predicated of another as [said] of a subject (ὡς καθ' ὑποκειμένου), all things said of what is predicated will be said of the subject also" [1b10-2].[12] However, when an accident is the predicate, Aristotle says that the definition is never predicated, and the name "usually" is not either [2a27-24]. So Aristotle might be taken to be implying that the antepredicamental rule does not hold for accidental predication. For in such predication the fallacy of accident can occur.

This is the standard position held by the Greek commentators: the antepredicamental rule is valid only for essential predication.[13] E.g., they say that

12 Cf. *An. Pr.* 43b30-2; Alexander, *In Aristotelis Analyticorum Priorum Librum I Commentarium*, ed. M. Wallies (Berlin, 1883), 302,14-16; *Top.* 122b7-10; 154b6-12; *Phys.* 185a30-1: "All things are predicated of substance as of a subject."

13 Porphyry, *In Aristotelis Categorias Commentarium*, ed. A. Busse (Berlin, 1887), 81,7; Simplicius, *Aristotelis Categorias Commentarium*, ed. C. Kalbfleisch (Berlin, 1907), 51,30-1; 52,9-14; 82,9-11; Ammonius, *In Aristotelis Categorias Commentarius*, ed. A. Busse (Berlin, 1895), 31,1-12, and *De Interpretatione Commentarius*, ed. A Busse (Berlin, 1897), 89,27-36; Philoponus, *In Aristotelis Categorias Commentarium*, ed. Adolf Busse (Berlin, 1898), 38,29; Boethius, *In Categorias Aristotelis*, ed. Migne, PL 64: 175D-6D. However, Porphyry, *In Cat.* 113,17-25; 114,11-12; 124,6, hints at there being no fallacy when paronymous accidental terms are used; Simplicius, *In Cat.*, 54,8-12, reports that Andronicus et al. said that the antepredicamental rule holds for all predications—all predications of being *per se*, as I shall hold. Michael Wedin, 'The Strategy of Aristotle's *Categories*,' *Archiv für Geschichte*

(6) Socrates is white
White is the lightest color
Therefore Socrates is the lightest color

is invalid, as it has true premises and a false conclusion. They then take all such inferences to commit the fallacy of accident.[14] On this account the antepredicamental rule does not hold for 'accidental predication', and, when it is so used, the fallacy of accident occurs.

However, a difficulty arises with such examples like (6). Strictly speaking, the definition of 'white' is not 'the lightest color' but something like 'having the lightest color'.[15] But then replacing the name of the accident with its definition does seem to preserve truth. Then no fallacy occurs, for 'having the lightest color' is indeed predicated of Socrates. Yet Aristotle, on this interpretation, insists that in 'accidental predication', as in 'Socrates is white', the definition of 'white' cannot replace it, *salva veritate*, as Aristotle himself says. But it can. Aristotle thus appears silly. To be sure, Aristotle does seem to assume, or at any rate report the endoxic usage, that the definition of 'white' is 'the lightest color' [2a33-4]. But then he would be forgetting his distinction of paronyms at 1a12-5. Once again he would appear silly.

Elsewhere I have suggested the following solution.[16] Take the expression 'as of a *subject* [my emphasis]' to require that the subject terms used in the inference signify substances, or at least something substantive, explicitly or implicitly. Then we get

---

der Philosophie 79 (1997), 1-26: 14-16; Avicenna, *Al-Maqūlāt*, ed. G. Anawati, A. El-Ehwani, M. El-Khodeiri, and S. Zayed (Cairo, 1959), 26,11-6; 43,12-44,20. Ockham, *Expositio super libros Elenchorum*, ed. Del Punta, 234,100-9, and many others make this point explicitly.

14 It is not clear whether Aristotle himself would call such an example an instance of the fallacy of accident. He gives no example obviously like it when he discusses the fallacy of accident. Moreover, it seems to depend on taking 'white' ambiguously. But Aristotle says that ambiguity does not indicate the fallacy of accident [*Soph. El.* 179b38-180a3]—although, to be sure, the same argument can commit multiple fallacies. At best such examples are implied at *Soph. El.* 168a40-b3 and *An. Pr.* 1.36 and 38; Alexander, *In An. Pr.*, ed. Wallies, 356,28-357,16; 362,25-35; 374,16-19.

15 *Top.* 119a30. Aristotle was taken to define 'whiteness' thus. Cf. Alexander, *In Aristotelis Topicorum Libros Octo Commentaria*, ed. M. Wallies (Berlin, 1891), 427,1; 446,15; Ammonius, *In Cat.*, ed. Busse, 45,2; 40,13-14.

16 Bäck, *Aristotle's Theory of Predication*, 228-37.

(7) A white thing is a thing having the lightest color
Socrates is a white thing
Therefore Socrates is a thing having the lightest color

Here no fallacy results.[17] In contrast if we take the predicate not 'as of a subject' we get the fallacy (6). The mistake in (6) lies in how the middle term is being taken: in the minor premise as the *quale*, signified by an adjective, and in the major as the quality, as equivalent to 'whiteness'. So the two paronyms, whiteness and white, are being confused. The quality does not exist in its own but in a subject, ultimately, a substance. The mistake comes from an accident, a *quale*, being taken as a subject in its own right. Once its real subject is stated, as in (7), no fallacy occurs. However, if accidents are taken as subjects in their own right, fallacy can result, particularly when accidents are linked together without the glue of a substance to bind them—especially when subjects of the statements about them are taken from accidental categories (like 'the musical'). For instance, in 'white is P', the subject is 'white' [τὸ λευκόν], literally 'the white' or 'what is white'. 'What is white' could signify (1) a substance that happens to be white or (2) the *quale* itself, the white, abstracted from anything else, or (3) the quality itself, whiteness. In the second way, the fallacy of accident arises (and perhaps also the fallacy of ambiguity). (It could in the third way too, except that the paralogisms produced are not too persuasive or effective: most respondents would just say that 'Socrates is whiteness' is false.[18])

On this interpretation, the antepredicamental rule holds not merely for essential predication. To be sure, restricting it thus has the advantage of safely avoiding fallacy. Yet it also has the danger of invalidating other doctrines

17 Simplicius, *In Cat.*, ed. Kalbfleisch, 54,8-21, notes the problem that cases like (7) occasion no fallacy. He gives an example from Andronicus, but does not do much with it.

18 The solution of the Greek commentators is to take the third reading and to hold that 'white' in the premises is ambiguous. This makes the fallacy of accident one dependent on language. Cf. (ps.) Alexander, *In Soph. El.*, ed. Wallies, 59,21-3. Ebbesen, *Commentators and Commentaries on Aristotle's Sophistici Elenchi*, 1: 226. Ebbesen thinks that Blemmydes, a Byzantine commentator, is original (also on p. 331; on p. 330 Ebbesen says that his compendium is "no brilliant work") when he takes the problem with 'white' to signify either a white object ("a qualified object") or whiteness ("the quality"). Ebbesen suggests that this is perhaps what Porphyry means by the ranged and unranged (συγκατατεγμένος) predicate; cf. pp. 224, 229. Schreiber, *Aristotle on False Reasoning*, 116 cites the first two senses of 'essential' in *Posterior Analytics* 1.4 to explain what Aristotle means by 'the fallacy of accident'; he should have picked the third sense there, which concerns *being per accidens*.

central to Aristotle's thought. For consider Aristotle's fundamental syllogistic principle the *dictum de omni*:

> Now that one thing is in another as a whole and that one is predicated of all of another are the same. And we say that one term is predicated of all of another, whenever nothing can be found of which the other term cannot be asserted. [*An. Pr.* 24b26-30; my translation][19]

That rule allows transitivity of predication for all [respectable] predications, whether accidental or essential. Otherwise the syllogistic would not apply to predicates like 'is white'. But Aristotle clearly thinks that it does, if we judge from the examples of syllogisms that he in fact uses. Note that Aristotle uses the same phrase, 'predicate of' (κατηγορεῖσθαι κατά), in stating the *dictum de omni* as he does in stating the antepredicamental rule.[20] Likewise, the antepredicamental rule resembles the Barbara syllogism, the first form of the first figure: 'all A are B; all B are C; therefore all A are C' [*An. Pr.* 25b32-5].[21] To repeat, this syllogism is valid for other types of predication beside the essential.

Accordingly, although Aristotle is unclear, it is best to understand him not to restrict the antepredicamental rule to essential predication. Yet surely it does require some restriction to avoid fallacy and to account for the doctrine of the fallacy of accident.

In sum, the antepredicamental rule does have some relevance for fallacy of accident as tradition has it. Yet taking essential predication in its usual sense to provide a criterion for validity raises many other problems. Moreover, we have to beware moving too far away from the paralogisms of the fallacy of accident that Aristotle actually gives. So: back to Aristotle.

3 Accidental Predication versus Predication *Per Accidens*

It would help for us to be clear on what Aristotle means by 'accident' in the name of this fallacy. On the usual view, 'accident' is understood in the sense

19 Alexander, *In An. Pr.*, ed. Wallies, 53,19-21, takes 'of every' and 'in a whole' to state two different principles, but then concedes, 54,2-5, that they are the same.

20 Cf. Alexander, *In An. Pr.*, ed. Wallies, 24,29-30.

21 Simplicius, *In Cat.*, ed. Kalbfleisch, 52,7-9, sees the antepredicamental rule to be a Barbara syllogism. On the relation between the *dictum de omni* and the antepredicamental rule see Robin Smith, trans. and comm., *Prior Analytics* (Indianapolis, 1989), 111.

of 'accidental predication': what is not said of but is in a subject; the relationship holding when the predicate is not in the essence of the subject [*Cat.* 2; *An. Po.* I.4]. If we turn to *Metaphysics* V.7, however, we see that Aristotle has another, related sense of 'accident'. It is in this sense, I contend, that Aristotle names this fallacy "the fallacy of accident."

There Aristotle makes the distinction of being *per se* and being *per accidens*:

> Those are said to be *per se* in as many ways as the figures of the categories signify. Whatever the figures of predication signify are said to be *per se*: for 'be' signifies in as many ways as they are said. Thus since some predicates signify the what it is (τί ἐστιν; the substance), and others the *quale*, and others the *quantum*, and others the in-relation-to-which, and others acting or being acted upon, others the where, and others the when, 'be' signifies the same as each of these: for 'man is healthy' differs in no way from 'man heals', nor 'man is walking or is cutting' from man walks or cuts, and likewise for all the others. [*Metaph.* 1017a22-31, my translation]

This distinction needs to be understood not as the distinction between the 'is' of essential predication and the 'is' of accidental predication. For Aristotle is counting many accidental statements as statements of being *per se*.[22] He says that beings are said *per se* in as many ways as there are categories. He gives 'a man is healthy' and 'a man is walking' as examples of statements of being *per se*.

What then does Aristotle mean by 'being *per accidens*'? Aristotle says about being *per accidens*:

> Being is said sometimes *per accidens* ... when we say that the just one is musical and man is musical and the musical one is a man—resembling your saying that the musical one builds because it has happened to the builder to be musical or to the musical one to build (for that this is this signifies that this has happened to that)—and so too in the examples mentioned: for when we say a man is musical and the musical one is a

22 Franz Brentano, *Von der mannigfachen Bedeutung des Seienden nach Aristoteles* (Freiberg, 1862; repr. Hildesheim, 1960), 13; trans. R. George, as *On The Several Senses of Being in Aristotle* (Berkeley, 1975), 8. W.D. Ross, *Aristotle's Metaphysics*, 2 Vols. (Oxford, 1966), at *Metaph.* V.7, takes Aristotle to be distinguishing accidental from essential predication. Cf. Michael Frede, 'Categories in Aristotle', in *Essays in Ancient Philosophy* (Minneapolis, 1987), 41 ("Δ.7, a most obscure chapter").

> man, or the white is musical or this is white, in the first cases we say that both are accidental to the same thing, and in the latter that it has happened to a being, while with 'the musical is a man' [we are saying] that the musical has happened to this. (So too it is said that the not-white is, because that to which it is accidental is.) Thus those are said *per accidens* in this way either for the reason that both belong to the same being, or that it belongs to that being, or that that of which it is predicated, to which it belongs, is. [*Metaph.* 1017a7-22, my translation]

Here Aristotle is recognizing different sorts of being *per accidens*, but then assimilates them. Being is said *per accidens* 1) when an accident is predicated of a substance, or 2) when a substance is predicated of an accident, or 3) when one accident is predicated of another accident. Aristotle's examples for these three types of cases are 1) 'the man is musical', 2) 'the musical is a man', 3) 'the just is musical'.[23]

To be sure, all these cases of being *per accidens* have accidental predications. Still, being *per se* and being *per accidens* overlap. An accidental predication, like 'a man is musical' or, equally so, 'a man is walking', is an instance of something said to be both *per se* and *per accidens*. Being an accidental predication does not disqualify a sentence from making a claim of being *per se*. Although being *per accidens* is defined in terms of accidental predication, not all cases of accidental predication have to be read as being *per accidens*. So we have here a special understanding of 'accident'. Indeed Aristotle distinguishes these two senses of accident at *Posterior Analytics* 73b5-10. Let us see if it will serve to separate out the fallacious cases of inferences from accidental predication from the valid ones.

The basic idea is that what has being *per accidens* does not have being in its own right but through another.

But why then does Aristotle say that a man is walking holds also *per se*? It seems that one type of accidental predication is respectable and *per se*; the other is not.

Looking at another passage about accidental complexes helps to resolve this puzzle better. (Indeed later on in the Aristotelian tradition this passage

---

23 Aristotle does not give here the other possibility, that one of the two accidents may be an accident of a substantial subject, and the other an accident of the first accident, as he does elsewhere [*Int.* 21a9].

was thought to be discussing the fallacy of accident.[24]) In *On Interpretation* 11 Aristotle is discussing inferences like

(8) Socrates is white
Socrates is musical
Therefore Socrates is musical white

(8) has the same structure as (5), where the two predicates of the premises are put together in the conclusion. Aristotle rejects the inference on the following grounds:

> Of things predicated, and things they get predicated of, those which are said accidentally, either of the same thing or of one another, will not be one. For example, a man is white and musical, but 'musical' and 'white' are not one, because they are both accidental to the same thing. And even if it is true to say that the white is musical, 'musical white' will still not be one thing, for it is accidentally that the musical is white and so 'white musical' will not be one. [*Int.* 21a7-14; trans. Ackrill, *Complete Works*, 1: 33]

Again there is a respectable conclusion for (8): Socrates is a white musical thing. What is illegitimate is taking the two accidents to form a whole without the glue of an actually present substance (or substantial subject). Aristotle says that 'white musical' taken with it does not form a single thing. Here then is a case of being *per accidens* of the sort discussed in the *Metaphysics* passage. This is why Aristotle talks about 'combination' (σύνθεσις) of accidents in discussing the fallacy [*Soph. El.* 180a4].[25]

We can apply this insight to explain why 'a man is walking' or 'a man is musical' can make a statement of both being *per se* and being *per accidens*. Take its subject and predicate to form a complex: walking man. In one sense, this complex does signify a single thing: the human substance having the accident of walking. On the other hand, if the accident and the substance are taken as two independent things stuck together there as: the human substance plus the accident of walking or musicality, they do not. The usual, respectable and scientific way to read such a statement is to take it as forming a single thing. In the disreputable, sophistical way to read it is to take it as a mixture, a sum

24 Bäck, *On Reduplication*, Ch. 7 and 15.

25 Dorion, *Aristote: Les Réfutations Sophistiques*, 379 80, notes that some have found the connection perplexing.

of substance and accident.[26] Apart from the particular context it is unclear—'indeterminate'!—in which way to take such a statement. Such 'indeterminacy', Aristotle has said, marks the fallacy of accident.[27]

Thus the examples that Aristotle gives for the fallacy of accident fit what he says about being *per accidens*. (3) and (4) predicate an accident of an accident of the subject; (5), although a type not explicitly mentioned at *Metaphysics* v.7 (although it is in the *On Interpretation* passage), takes accidental predications to forge a connection between the accidents themselves. In all cases the attribute belongs to the accident and not to the logical subject. Fallacy arises because what holds of the accident considered by itself alone need not hold for its subject. The point is that, since being *per se* and being *per accidens* overlap, it is hard to tell when an assertion of the latter can be read also as an assertion of the former. Not all accidental predications lead to fallacy; only those that do not allow the transfer of features of the accident to its subject do. As Aristotle says, it is hard to tell—"indeterminate"—which accidents these are. Hence the fallacy of accident is a material fallacy, concerned with the content of the terms, and not a formal fallacy nor one arising from a mistake in language. Fallacy arises because what holds of the accident considered by itself alone need not hold for its subject.

Understanding the fallacy of accident to concern predication *per accidens* has the further merit of explaining why Aristotle says that the fallacy of the consequent is a part or branch of the fallacy of accident [*Soph. El.* 168b27; 169b6-7; 170a4-5]. Aristotle says that in the latter only one thing is involved, where in the former two are. To extrapolate examples from what he says: 'I know that what I am seeing is yellow; that yellow thing is honey; therefore I know that what I am seeing is honey' commits the fallacy of accident. 'The snow is something white; the swan is something white; therefore the snow is the swan' commits the fallacy of the consequent [168b28-35]. The fallacy of accident concerns the first two cases of being *per accidens* distinguished above, where only one subject is involved and there is some overlap with being *per se*, as with 'the man is walk-

26 Thus Alexander, *In Aristotelis Metaphysica Commentaria*, ed. M. Hayduck (Berlin, 1891), 290,17-21: "For (one) accident cannot be syllogized of (another) accident through a middle term, if the accident proved in the conclusion were not [said?] of those belonging *per se*, through an accident being taken as the middle term, as with 'Socrates walks; anything walking moves': for moving is in the essence of 'walks'. Therefore the contradiction does not hold for the same thing." The idea is to avoid *per accidens* syllogisms—and the fallacy of accident—by requiring that, when the minor premise has an accidental predication, the major premise must have an essential one. See too 288,33-289,12; 289,18-19.

27 Dorion, *Aristote: Les Réfutations Sophistiques*, 366.

ing'; the fallacy of the consequent concerns the third case, where one accident is predicated of another. Here the two accidents may have different subjects, and there is no overlap with being *per se*.

4 Later Greek Developments

The Greek commentators gave other instances of the fallacy of accident, notably ones involving terms not appearing in Aristotle's categories, later called those of second intention. E.g.,

(9) Socrates is man
Man is a species
Therefore Socrates is a species[28]

(9) does not fit the rules given for being *per accidens*. For the minor premise has an essential predication, while the major has one that, however it be classified, is not one of the usual, garden-variety (object language, first intention) accidental predication or of a statement *per accidens*. So what about this one?

I submit that Aristotle would not classify it as an instance of the fallacy of accident. (9) has no overlap of being *per se* and being *per accidens*. Rather, he might exclude such paralogisms as ill-formed, as 'species' is not a term signifying an object in the categories.[29] Aristotle tends to be interested only in terms of first intention, of terms that appear in the object language.

Perhaps such new paralogisms like (9) came to be classified under the fallacy of accident because the ancient (mis!) interpreters took the fallacy to concern accidental predication of any type whatsoever. One sign of this lies in the Greek commentators requiring the antepredicamental rule to apply only to essential predications, despite holding for cases like (7).[30]

---

28 E.g., Porphyry, *In Cat.*, ed. Busse, 80,32-81,2; Philoponus, *In Aristotelis Analytica Priora Commentarius*, ed. M. Wallies (Berlin, 1905), 325,27-326,4.

29 A reader of this paper has pointed out to me that at 168b1-4 Aristotle does bring up the example, 'a triangle is a principle', in discussing the fallacy of accident. Yet he doesn't use it very clearly in constructing a paralogism. The import of the example is puzzling; see my discussion of the passage above.

30 *Cat.* 1b10-2; Simplicius, *In Cat.*, ed. Kalbfleisch, 82,9-11; Porphyry, *In Cat.*, ed. Busse, 81,7; Ammonius, *In Cat.*, ed. Busse, 31,1-12; Philoponus, *In Cat.*, ed. Busse, 38,29; Allan Bäck, 'Philoponus on the Fallacy of Accident', *Ancient Philosophy* 7 (1987), 131-46: 139.

In any event, the fallacy of accident came to be extended to this new type of cases. As a result Aristotle's original solution would no longer cover all of its paralogisms, even if it did work on the original cases.

Thus Philoponus observes that a syllogism needs a universal major premise in order to be valid. Now instances of the fallacy of accident do not have a universal major premise. Hence they are invalid.[31] The mistake comes from taking the middle term particularly in the minor premise and universally in the major.

Philoponus' solution works better on some purported instances of the fallacy than on others. It does handle paralogisms of the new type. Consider (9) with a universal major premise:

(9') Every dog is a species
Fido is a dog
Therefore, Fido is a species

The major premise is either false or ill-formed. Hence the syllogism is not sound.

Again, consider (4) with a universal major premise:

(4') Everyone who is approaching is not known by me
Coriscus is the one who is approaching
Therefore, Coriscus is not known by me [179b1-4]

The syllogism would be valid but not sound, as the major premise is false.

Other examples like (3) and (5) do not fare as well. Yet these tended to be ignored after Aristotle—or relegated to other fallacies. Surely 'your(s)' is ambiguous in 'this dog is yours' and 'this dog is your father' [Cf. *Soph.El.* 179b38-180a7]. 'Being different from Socrates' seems to be an attribute worth discussing only for sophists. And so some said, like Aristotle [*Metaph.* 1004a34-b26].

But, above all, for the method even to have a chance of being applied to cases like (4) some account would have to be given of how to have a universal premise with a singular term as subject. For many instances of the fallacy of accident involve singular premises. In what sense is 'Coriscus is different from Socrates' universal or particular?

Philoponus takes the radical step of allowing quantification over singular terms. Accordingly he makes the fallacy of accident formal and not material: not having a universal major premise makes the syllogism invalid, regardless

31 Philoponus, *In An. Pr.*, ed. Wallies, 325,27-326,4.

of whether and how its terms are 'accidental'. He has some precedent, albeit an obscure one, for doing so in the text of Aristotle himself [*An. Pr.* I.33].[32] When I say 'every Socrates is a philosopher', I mean to take every individual Socrates. It may turn out that there is just one of these—but that is a matter of fact and not a matter of logical form.[33] Or we might read the universal quantification thus: everything named by 'Socrates' is a philosopher.

Jonathan Barnes endorses this doctrine of quantifying over singular terms in order to get this solution.[34] However, he prefers an account of such quantifying mentioned if not endorsed by Alexander: there is an individual form of, say, Socrates, of which only a single Socrates is an instance.[35]

The Greek commentators also used the doctrine of *On Interpretation* 11 to analyze the fallacy of accident. Aristotle considers inferences like

(10) Socrates is good
Socrates is a cobbler
Therefore Socrates is a good cobbler [*On Interpretation* 20b35-7]

This has similarities with the paternal dog example (5). In both cases Aristotle speaks of accidental connections along the lines sketched above. Moreover, a complex predicate like 'good cobbler' could be construed as 'good with respect to being a cobbler'[36] In this way the inference becomes: S is P, and S is M; therefore S is P *qua* M—and then the fallacy of accident could be taken as the converse of the next fallacy discussed by Aristotle, the fallacy of *secundum quid ad simpliciter* dealing with the inference 'S is P qua M; therefore S is P' [*Soph. El.* 166b37-8]. The Greek commentators did just that.[37]

---

32 See Bäck, 'Philoponus on the Fallacy of Accident'.

33 So too William of Ockham, *Summa Logicae* II.2.15-6, ed. P. Boehner, G. Gál, and S.F. Brown (St Bonaventure, NY, 1974). Also cf. Philoponus, *In An. Pr.*, ed. Wallies, 326,5-10; 20,30-21,5; Alexander, *In An. Pr.*, ed. Wallies, 350,35-351,19.

34 Jonathan Barnes, *Truth etc.* (Oxford, 2007), 150-5. Despite his pitch, vii-viii, for interest in the history of logic, especially its ancient history, it is amazing how completely he ignores medieval Aristotelian logicians.

35 Barnes, *Truth etc.*, 163. Cf. Alexander, *In An. Pr.*, ed. Wallies, 352,25-6; Philoponus, *In An. Pr.*, ed. Wallies, 326,6-10.

36 Bäck, *On Reduplication*, Ch. 3.

37 Ammonius, *In De Int.*, ed. Busse, 210,25-31; cf. 184,11-21; (ps.) Alexander, *In Soph. El.*, ed. Wallies, 41,8-10.

5 Medieval Developments

Medieval logicians followed these trends. By the time of the *Logica Modernorum*, paralogisms involving inferences of *secundum quid ad simpliciter* and *simpliciter ad secundum quid* were combined into the single fallacy of *secundum quid et simpliciter*.[38] Sometimes instead the fallacy of accident was taken as the converse of the fallacy of *secundum quid ad simpliciter*.[39]

Moreover, many medievals likewise followed the solution of the Greek commentators and came to hold also that a fallacy of accident committed a mistake concerning the distribution of the middle term or the universality of the major premise.[40] Generally the connection of the fallacy of accident to accidental predication was discarded—thus stimulating discussions on how to formulate the antepredicamental rule. Boethius himself has a clear example of a sound syllogism containing only accidental predications [*De Syllogismo Categorico* II.821C.]. Early commentaries on the *Sophistical Refutations* make this point and revert to something like being *per accidens*.[41] Thus in

(6) White is the lightest color
Socrates is white
Therefore, Socrates is the lightest color

'white' is taken '*disiunctim*', separately from its substance, in the major premise ('the [*quale*] white'), and '*coniunctim*', together with its substance, in the minor

38 *Fallacie Parvipontane*, in *Logica Modernorum*, ed. L.M. de Rijk (Assen, 1962), 1: 596-8; Bäck, *On Reduplication*, Ch. 5.

39 For this and a fuller and more sequential discussion of the medieval developments see Bäck, *On Reduplication*, Ch. 7, and 'The State of the Fallacy of Accident'; J.M. Gambra, 'Medieval Solutions to the Fallacy of Accident', in *Argumentationstheorie*, ed. K. Jacobi (Leiden, 1993), 431-50: 435-49.

40 Avicenna, *Al-Burhān*, ed. A. Affifi (Cairo, 1956), 45,14-46,1; 48,4-50,2; Peter of Spain, *Tractatus Called Afterwards Summule logicales* VII, §103, ed. L.M. de Rijk (Assen, 1972), 147,1.

41 Peter of Spain, *Tractatus* VII §103, ed. De Rijk, 146,12-26, saying that 'accident' here is not the usual one of the predicables but concerns *inesse* and not following necessarily; William of Sherwood, *Introductiones in Logicam*, ed., trans. and comm. H. Brands and C. Strub (Hamburg, 1995), 366-426: 194-8; trans. N. Kretzmann as *Introduction to Logic* (Minneapolis, 1966), 150-2. Sherwood is groping towards 'accident' in the sense of being *per accidens*, as opposed to being *per se*. Brands and Strub, nn. 269 and 270, make the distinction amount to having the same extension but different intensions.

('white thing').[42] On this view *fallacia accidentis dicatur fallacia medii* ("The fallacy of accident is called the fallacy of the middle [term]").[43] The middle term in the two premises has two different concepts or *rationes*.[44] This is a version of the doctrine of paronymy and being *per accidens* that I have located in Aristotle's own discussion. However, this view came to be discarded, on the grounds that many instances of the fallacy of accident, like (4), do not seem to have this problem.[45]

Following this tradition and (pseudo-)Alexander, Abelard takes the fallacy of accident, erroneously, as a mistake of language due to equivocation of the middle term in paralogisms like (9).[46] However, Abelard construes the predication in cases like (10) as accidental in a new way, so as to fuse the predicate with the copula. In this way, 'Homer is a poet' gets parsed as 'Homer poetizes'.[47] On the other hand, Graham Priest claims that Abelard had a view of numerical identity that is not transitive.[48] That would block the Coriscus fallacy, if the predications were taken as identity statements. Yet all this, I say, is becoming far removed from Aristotle's original fallacy.

After Abelard, in the thirteenth century, authors such as Albert the Great and Giles of Rome continued analyzing the fallacy of accident in conjunction with the fallacy of *secundum quid et simpliciter* and distinguished various modes of the fallacy.[49] Aquinas, likely drawing on his commentaries of Aristotle's works in his *De Fallaciis* and perhaps going back to the views before

42 *Summa Sophisticorum Elenchorum*, in *Logica Modernorum*, ed. De Rijk, 1: dist. 1, vol. 1, lib. 2, ch. 1, 357,5-14-32 on Magistri Jacobus and Albericus.

43 Albert the Great, *Liber I Elenchorum*, Tract. III.3 (Venice, 1632), 563 col. 1; 565 col. 2.

44 Peter of Spain, *Tractatus* VII §106, ed. De Rijk, 148. Cf. 157,1-8; William of Sherwood, *Introductiones*, ed. Brands-Strub, 390-410.

45 *Summa Sophisticorum Elenchorum*, ed. De Rijk, dist. 1, vol. 1, lib. 2, ch. 1, 358,5-9.

46 Rosier-Catach, 'La notion de *translatio*', 139; Gambra, 'Medieval Solutions to the Fallacy of Accident', 437-8.

47 John Marenbon, 'Abélard, le verbe 'être' et la prédication', in *Langage, sciences, philosophie au XIIe siècle*, ed. Biard, 199-216; Rosier-Catach, 'La notion de *translatio*', 145-6. They consider Abelard to be making an innovation here. Perhaps he invented it on his own, but the doctrine can be found already in Lycophron, as mentioned by Aristotle, *Physics* 185b27-30; cf. Bäck, *Aristotle's Theory of Predication*, 55.

48 Graham Priest, *One* (Oxford, 2014), 58 n. 6.

49 Bäck, *On Reduplication*, 181.8. Dafne Murè, '*Suppositum* between Logic and Metaphysics: Simon of Faversham and His Contemporaries (1270-1290)', *Vivarium* 51 (2013), 205-29: 216-8.

Abelard, may be the medieval with a solution closest to Aristotle's distinction of being *per se* and being *per accidens*.[50]

By the beginning of the fourteenth century the logical doctrine was fairly standardized. Ockham, for instance, states that this fallacy concerns 'accident' not in the usual sense but in the sense of being *per accidens* [*Summa Logicae*, III.4.11.4-7.]. Second, he embraces the doctrine that one specific cause of the fallacy lies in not having a universal major premise.[51] However, perhaps on account of cases like (4), he says that the generic mistake lies in violating the basic principles of syllogism, the *dicta de omni et de nullo* and not keeping the mode or time of statements in the argument the same.[52] Still, the fallacy does not occur on account of ambiguity in the middle term [*Summa Logicae* III.4.11.38-41]. Gambra claims that Ockham ends up concluding that the fallacy of accident comes from either a syllogistic mistake, as in (9), or from an opaque context, as in (4).[53]

When Ockham applies these doctrines to the standard examples of the fallacy of accident, he gets results that, at the least, Aristotle does not state explicitly. With a universal major premise, the example of the approaching Coriscus (4') occasions no invalid inference, although it likely has a false major premise, that everyone approaching is known by you [*Summa Logicae* III.4.11.65-7].

Ockham is also aware that singular terms might cause trouble for a syllogistic analysis. On his own theory they won't. He holds that 'every S is P' is true iff everything referred to by 'S' is referred to by 'P'.[54] Such a truth condition accommodates singular terms quantified universally—allowing for the context to fix the reference etc. For instance, there can be more than one person named 'Coriscus' or 'Socrates', while the proposition may intend to refer only to one human being.[55] (He himself is more concerned about inferences involving the singular terms used in discussing the Trinity [*Summa Logicae*, III.4.11.88ff.].)

---

50 Gambra, 'Medieval Solutions to the Fallacy of Accident', 438; cf. Gyula Klima, 'The Semantic Principles Underlying Saint Thomas Aquinas's Metaphysics of Being', *Medieval Philosophy and Theology* 5 (1996), 87-141. Following Busa, Klima, 95 n. 16, takes the *De Fallaciis* to be authentic.

51 Ockham, *Summa Logicae* III.4.11.66-9, ed. Boehner-Gál-Brown; Ockham, *Expositio super libros Elenchorum*, ed. Del Punta, II.9.1.32-3; II.9.4.292-305.

52 Ockham, *Expositio super libros Elenchorum*, ed. Del Punta, II.9.7.28-35; II.9.4.41-50. Here Ockham has a different analysis of the Coriscus example: if I know that every man is an animal it is not necessary that I know every proposition in which 'man' appears.

53 Gambra, 'Medieval Solutions to the Fallacy of Accident', 448-9.

54 See n. 42.

55 Already Simplicius, *In Cat.*, ed. Kalbfleisch, 29,3-4; 30,25-7 speaks of the two Ajaxes.

Ockham considers the paralogism of your paternal dog (4) to be an instance of the fallacy of the figure of speech.[56] However, he notes that similar inferences, like

(11) This is your father
Therefore this is yours

could be considered to commit the fallacy of *secundum quid ad simpliciter*.[57] He also notes that inferences like

(12) Socrates is an animal
Socrates is rational
Therefore Socrates is a rational animal

are valid, whereas those like

(13) Socrates is an animal
Socrates is a man
Therefore Socrates is a man animal

are invalid. These examples hark back to Aristotle's *On Interpretation* 11 and had already been incorporated into discussions of the fallacy of *secundum quid et simpliciter*, as Ockham himself states.[58] However he denies that the fallacy of accident and the fallacy of *secundum quid et* [N.B.] *simpliciter* are converses, because in the former the conclusion does not follow at all while in the latter it does, so long as the qualification be kept.[59] Still, he does admit the connection between these two fallacies.

Buridan takes similar positions. The fallacy of accident is so called because here 'accident' is taken for "a middle term that is not adequately disposed to

56 Ockham, *Summa Logicae* III-4, III.65-71, ed. Boehner-Gál-Brown, follows Philoponus, but also recognizes other mistakes; predicating accidents (III.16-8); ambiguity (III.251-2); the fallacy of figure of speech (III.189-90). Hester Gelber, 'The Fallacy of Accident and the *Dictum de omni*: Late Medieval Controversy over a Reciprocal Pair', *Vivarium* 25 (1987), 110-45: 116-19.

57 Ockham, *Summa Logicae* III.4.11.33-7; 168-76; 183-8, ed. Boehner-Gál-Brown. Cf. Ockham, *Expositio super libros Elenchorum*, ed. Del Punta, II.9.5.14-5; II.9.2.114-9.

58 Ockham, *Expositio super libros Elenchorum*, ed. Del Punta, II.9.5.28; Bäck, *On Reduplication*, Ch. 6.

59 Ockham, *Expositio super libros Elenchorum*, ed. Del Punta, II.9.16.68-77. Cf. Ockham, *Summa Logicae* III.4.11.46-8, ed. Boehner-Gál-Brown.

render the inference of a conclusion necessary." So it comes from "an illusion of syllogism."[60] He takes the Coriscus example to be valid, except for the opaque context created by 'know'.[61] Paralogisms like (7) having terms like 'species' do not commit the fallacy of accident. Rather they err in having two modes of supposition for 'man'.[62]

The analyses of authors such as Ockham and Buridan are sophisticated. Yet they do not explain the unity of the fallacy of accident as formulated by Aristotle. Instead, they reclassify some of the paralogisms and deny the fallacy of others. Perhaps they need to do this—but Aristotle's analysis has been abandoned.

Others took the fallacy of accident to be the converse of the fallacy of *secundum quid ad simpliciter*.[63] Later on writers such as John Versor did the reverse and analyzed the fallacy of *secundum quid ad simpliciter* as the converse of the fallacy of accident.[64] For instance, just as it does not follow from 'Coriscus, insofar as you see him at a distance, is not known by you' that Coriscus is not known by you, so too it does not follow from 'Coriscus is known by you' that Coriscus is known by you insofar as you see him at a distance.[65]

Whately and De Morgan inherited this tradition. In this way, the fallacy of *secundum quid ad simpliciter* became known as the fallacy of converse accident.[66] From there to the modern textbooks. They tend not to offer a general

60 Buridan, *Summulae* 7.4.1. trans. Klima (New Haven and London, 2001), 548-9.

61 Buridan, *Summulae* 7.4.1., trans. Klima, 550-1. Cf. Aristotle, *Soph. El.* 179b27-33.

62 Buridan, *Summulae* 7.4.1., trans. Klima, 550. Buridan is disagreeing with, e.g., Peter of Spain, *Tractatus* VII §102, 146,6-8. Cf. Gyula Klima, 'Socrates est species', in *Argumentationstheorie*, ed. Jacobi, 489-504: 473.

63 Domingo de Soto, *Summulae* IV.3 (Salamanca, 1554; reprint Hildesheim, 1980), 106r col. II-107r col. 1. Peter Tartaretus, *In Universam Philosophiam Opera Omnia* (Venice, 1621), 279, also analyzes the Coriscus example in a similar way under the fallacy of accident. So too Antoine Arnauld and Pierre Nicole, *La Logique*, ed. P. Clair and F. Girbal (Paris, 1970), III. xix.5, 254.

64 Bäck, *On Reduplication*, 425.

65 Domingo de Soto, *Summulae*, IV.3, ed. cit., 106r col. 2-107r col. 1; cf. *Sophistical Refutations* 168a30-b4. However, Ockham rejects such a reduplicative analysis at *Expositio super libros Elenchorum*, ed. Del Punta, II.9.2.90-99.

66 Richard Whately, *Elements of Logic* (London, 1826; many reprints), III.12: 177: "The other kind of ambiguity... the last case of Ambiguous middle that I shall notice is the *'fallacia accidentis'*, together with its converse, *'fallacia a dicto secundum quid ad dictum simpliciter'*; in each of which the middle Term is used, in one Premiss to signify something considered simply, in itself and in its essence; and in the other Premiss, so as to imply that its Accidents are taken into account with it: as in the well-known example, 'what is bought in the market is eaten; raw meat is bought in the market; therefore raw meat

method for determining which generalizations or particularizations are 'careless' and 'special', and which are not, and occasion no fallacy. The features are 'accidental', in the sense of 'accidental predication', but not all such features bring about the fallacy. Apparently we can figure out which occasion the fallacy so long as we pay attention and are not careless (in the spirit of the *Port-Royal Logic*, III.19.5). At any rate the main current analysis of the fallacy of accident does not offer a very formal method to avoid it.[67] The medieval analyses look more sophisticated. Yet the medieval focus on a syllogistic analysis loses sight of Aristotle's original fallacy.

6 A Modern Version of Aristotle's Solution

I have taken Aristotle to claim: the fallacy of accident occurs when transitivity or combination is allowed across predications of being *per accidens*, linking accident to accident.[68] Suppose I have given Aristotle's solution. Can we learn anything from it?

Consider a paralogism of the fallacy of accident, like the famous

(4) The one who is approaching is not known by me
Coriscus is the one who is approaching
Therefore, Coriscus is not known by me

All of its predications are accidental. We assume its premises to be true and its conclusion false.

In what follows, I shall consider instances of the fallacy of accident that have, or can be put into, the following form:

---

is eaten'." Auguste De Morgan, *Formal Logic* (London, 1926) (first published 1847), 291-2 (250-1). William Hamilton, *Lectures on Logic* (Boston, 1858), 326-7 follows De Morgan on this point. Cf. Antoine Arnauld and Pierre Nicole, *La logique*, ed. Clair and Girbal, III.xix.5, 254. Charles L. Hamblin, *Fallacies* (London, 1970), 30, is wrong in seeing this view to arise with De Morgan, or even Whately. It goes back at least to De Soto.

67 Douglas Walton, *A Pragmatic Theory of Fallacy* (Tuscaloosa, 1995), 53; 211; 254-5. Walton sees little use in the traditional fallacy of accident, although, at p. 53, he does like Aristotle's treatment of the converse fallacy of *secundum quid ad simpliciter*. Maurice Finocchiaro, 'Fallacies and the Evaluation of Reasoning', in idem, *Arguments about Arguments* (Cambridge, 2005), 109-27: 110-18.

68 So too Anibal Bueno, 'Aristotle, The Fallacy of Accident, and the Nature of Predication', *Journal of the History of Philosophy* 26 (1988), 5-24: 10-11.

(14) Φ is Ψ
Σ is Φ
Therefore Σ is Ψ

Cases like (5) work somewhat differently, but my main point will apply to them too.

In modern terms, some of these terms in Aristotle's paralogisms of accident would routinely be taken as singulars: as individual constants ('Coriscus') or definite descriptions ('the one who is approaching'); others are predicate functions ('known by me'). Yet, unlike Frege, Aristotle takes predicates of a subject and predicates of those predicates to be of the same logical type. The antepredicamental rule exemplifies this: it treats a predicate of a subject and a predicate of a predicate as having the same status.[69] I don't want to rehash this large issue here again but only to point out that, in formulating Aristotle's solution, we need to treat the terms in a paralogism of the fallacy of accident as being of the same logical type. We can do this in a modern way by taking them all as predicates or as individuals. Resolving this issue, i.e., which logical type of predication to use, won't affect the main point of my analysis; I am just trying to motivate and explain my notation. So I am proposing to treat the predications in a paralogism of accident as being of a single logical type—either (A) by taking all the terms as singular or (B) by taking them all as predicate functions.

Many later Aristotelians, such as Ockham and Buridan, took them in the latter way (B). Making all the terms predicates helps to make these paralogisms amenable to an Aristotelian syllogistic analysis. Then the particular statements would have the form, 'some Φ is Ψ', and the universal ones, 'every Φ is Ψ'. However, the result is that the paralogisms become less persuasive. When the major premise of (2) is taken particularly, the syllogism is invalid:

(4*) Someone who is approaching is not known by me
Coriscus is the one who is approaching
Therefore, Coriscus is not known by me

69 Ignacio Angelelli, *Studies on Gottlob Frege and Traditional Philosophy* (Dordrecht, 1967), 52-3; Nicholas Rescher, 'The Equivocality of Existence', in *Studies in Ontology, American Philosophy Quarterly*, Monograph, Vol. 12 (Oxford, 1978), 57-66: 58-9; Bäck, *Aristotle's Theory of Predication*, 178-85.

Suppose then we take it universally:

(4**) Everyone who is approaching is not known by me
Coriscus is the one who is approaching
Therefore, Coriscus is not known by me

Most of us would consider the major premise of (4**) false. Hence the paralogism does not entice many of us; we would reject it as unsound. Moreover, when the major premise has a singular term, in particular, a proper name, this approach will require quantification over singular terms to make the syllogism valid. As we have seen, those favoring this interpretation allow for this: for them, 'every Socrates is a philosopher' is well formed.[70] The fallacy of accident then becomes a syllogistic error: the major premise is either not universal or it is false, when taken universally.

A normal instance of the fallacy of accident for Aristotle has both predications singular. If we take the routine, modern symbolizations of these, we have nothing resembling a valid syllogism, which requires a universal major premise. But then the paralogisms just look silly. We can see then why Aristotle himself talked of sameness and difference in the fallacy of accident, and modern interpreters construe the propositions as making identity statements.[71] However, Aristotle does not use identity statements in his syllogistic, except perhaps by having a predicate like 'being the same as the one approaching'.[72]

---

70 *Prior Analytics* 1.33. Cf. David Hitchcock, 'Fallacies and Formal Logic in Aristotle', *History and Philosophy of Logic* 21 (2000), 207-21: 219.

71 E.g., Francis Pelletier, 'Sameness and Referential Opacity in Aristotle', *Noûs* 13/3 (1979), 283-311; Nicholas White, 'Aristotle on Sameness and Oneness', *Philosophical Review* 80 (1971), 177-97; Norman Dahl, 'Two Kinds of Essence in Aristotle', *Philosophical Review* 106 (1997), 233-65: 243; 255; Gareth Matthews, 'Accidental Unities', in *Language and Logos*, ed. M. Schofield and M. Nussbaum (Cambridge, 1982), 223-40; Frank Lewis, 'Accidental Sameness in Aristotle', *Philosophical Studies* 42 (1982), 1-36, 'Self-Knowledge in Aristotle', *Topoi* 15 (1996), 39-58: 42-3, and *Substance and Predication in Aristotle* (Cambridge, 1991).

72 Euclid uses 'equal' in stating mathematical propositions; Diophantus abbreviates it as: is. Carl Boyer, *A History of Mathematics*, Second Edition (Hoboken, NJ, 1991), 180-2. The earliest explicit use of the identity sign seems to have been by Richard Recorde, *The Whetstones of Witte* (London, 1557)—thanks to Christian Thiel and Ignacio Angelelli for pointing this out. Dorion, *Aristote: Les Réfutations Sophistiques*, 371-5 surveys the recent literature on identity and the fallacy of accident. Fred Sommers, 'Do We Need Identity?', *Journal of Philosophy* 66 (1969), 499-504 offers a method to have something isomorphic with the modern notion of identity in the traditional subject-predicate syllogistic.

So it becomes problematic to use the predicative option without extending Aristotle's theory.

Let me then turn to the other approach (A), of taking all the terms singularly.[73] This approach looks closer to Aristotle's text. He does say that the errors in this fallacy come from confusion over whether or not the subject and its accident are "the same thing" [*Soph. El.* 169b2-6; cf. 178b29-33]. He uses many singular terms in his instances of the fallacy. Then all the propositions in a paralogism like (4) might be read as having the form: 'Φ is the same as Ψ'. Accordingly, I am inclined to this reading, although I do not insist upon it.

To preserve Aristotle's approach we shall have to assume that we can have individuals in the various categories: dog, this white, that black... These individuals, and their universal types, are to be understood as beings, to be just what they are. So 'this white' signifies solely the *quale*, 'the white', a white thing, and nothing more. 'The one who is approaching' does not name a substance like Coriscus but just a 'thing', the mere *quale* in motion. Here I do not mean 'thing' to indicate an implicit presence of a substance; I do not insist here on the ontological dependence of all other beings on substance. For allowing for being *per accidens* lets an accident take on an existence of its own—sophistically so, as Aristotle remarks [*Metaph.* 1026b13-21]. In contrast, if this ontological dependence be required, we have being *per se* and not being *per accidens*.

When the terms are treated as singulars, the fallacy of accident has the following form:

(15) Φ is (the same as) Ψ
Σ is (the same as) Φ
Therefore Σ is (the same as) Ψ

Surely there are valid instances of this form! So what is Aristotle's general criterion for there occurring a fallacy of accident?

Take an accidental connection to be a contingent one and an essential connection to be a necessary one.[74] In modern modal semantics, then, to say that something has a property necessarily entails that it has it in all possible worlds; to say that it has one contingently entails that it has it in some possible worlds but not in others.

---

73 Aristotle does routinely allow for singular terms in syllogistic in exposition and in rhetorical contexts. Cf. *Rhet.* 1401b11-19.

74 Of some sort. Aristotle himself relates the accidental to chance, and the essential to the necessary.

The fallacy of accident comes from the premises being assertions of being *per accidens*.

So the fallacious inferences have the form

(15*) Φ is (the same as) Ψ *per accidens*
Σ is (the same as) Φ *per accidens*
Therefore Σ is Ψ *per accidens*[75]

To be *per accidens* requires (1) that the predications be accidental and (2) that the premises predicate an accident of an accident of a subject.

Construe (14) with accidental predications thus:

(16) Φ is Ψ in W_a, and Φ is not Ψ in some W_i [accessible to W_a]
Σ is Φ in W_a, and Σ is not Φ in some W_i [accessible to W_a]
Therefore Σ is Ψ in W_a, and Σ is not Ψ in some W_i [accessible to W_a]

To capture the second requirement, stipulate that in predication *per se* the subject carries the predications from one statement into the other statement, whereas in predication *per accidens* it does not. Consider again (15). When the premises are combined and taken to hold *per se*, the major premise, relative to the minor premise, becomes

Φ, which is (the same as) Σ, is (the same as) Ψ

when the terms are taken singularly (B). Likewise for the minor premise, relative to the major premise, although that is superfluous here. (If we take all the terms as predicates (A), we can capture this requirement by stipulating again that whatever predicates an individual has in one premise are to be reiterated in the other premise.)

In either way, the Coriscus example (4) then becomes

(17) The one who is approaching, who is Coriscus, is not known by me
Coriscus is the one who is approaching
Therefore, Coriscus is not known by me

75 It's not clear that the conclusion need be taken *per accidens* too, but let me do so.

The major premise becomes false: I know (or recognize) both the one approaching and Coriscus.

Nevertheless, we can still find a modern counterpart to the fallacy of accident thus construed in modal arguments:

(18) That white thing can be a swan
This dog can be a white thing
Therefore, this dog can be a swan

(19) This dog can be a white thing
This dog can be a black thing
Therefore, a white thing can be a black thing

Understand the modalities thus: 'this dog can be a white thing' holds that there is an individual dog in W_1 and an individual white in W_2, and that W_1 has access to W_2. So then, when we look at the white thing in W_2, all we see is that it is white, and *qua* white it has the possibility of being a swan in some world, say W_3. If the possibilities are transitive, so that W_1 has access to W_3, then the fallacy of accident results. The fallacy is avoided if the subjects are taken to carry their predicates with them: e.g., 'the white thing that is a dog can be a swan' is false. In effect, if a term like 'this dog' is taken to designate rigidly, no fallacy results; if non-rigidly, so as to designate a counterpart, fallacy may occur.

7 Conclusion

On this reconstruction, the fallacy of accident becomes a formal mistake of logical inference, about the access relations between one possible world and another: for instance, using the rules of the modal system T to make inferences in S5. It still has a material component: it must be stipulated just what predicates belong by necessity to the thing that is going from world to world.

This account makes the fallacy of accident far more interesting than the relics of it present in logic books today. Copi takes the fallacy of accident to occur by inferring a predication holding in general or for the most part to hold in specific unusual circumstances.[76] Again, Daniel Bonevac, following the *Port-Royal Logic*, defines an instance of the fallacy of accident to be an argument that "tries to justify its conclusion by treating as essential an accidental feature

76 Irving Copi and Carl Cohen, *Introduction to Logic*, Ninth Edition (New York, 1994), 125.

of something."[77] Such approaches follow the later treatment of the fallacy of accident, of involving accidental predication and not predication *per accidens*. These treatments, being vague, have little logical interest.[78]

The original treatment of Aristotle has more promise, as I hope my modern account of it suggests.

---

77 Daniel Bonevac, *The Art and Science of Logic* (Mountain View, CA, 1990), 84.

78 Finocchiaro, 'Fallacies and the Evaluation of Reasoning', 110-18 has a similarly low view of the accounts of fallacies in current textbooks.

To *Be in* a Subject and Accident

José Miguel Gambra

1 The Boethian Interpretation of *Cat.* 2 and 3, 1b10-15

In *Cat.* 2, 1a20-b9, Aristotle offers a well-known fourfold division of beings (τῶν ὄντων) based, on the one hand, on the distinction between what *is in* and *what is not in* a subject and, on the other, on the distinction between what *is said* and what *is not said* of a subject. In his commentary on the *Categories*, Boethius assimilates what *is said* and what *is not said* of a subject respectively with the universal and the particular, and what *is* and *is not* in a subject with the accident (understood as *accidens praedicamentalis*, which includes the nine non-substantial categories)[1] and what *is not* in a subject with the substance. These two assimilations are outlined on the famous square of Boethius where the Aristotelian division is replaced by another one that distinguishes between universal and particular substances, on the one hand, and universal and particular accidents, on the other.[2]

As much as this change of vocabulary has been almost universally accepted, it is still problematic. According to Boethius, what is able to be predicated of many (*aptum de pluribus praedicari*)[3] is a universal (it *is said* of a subject). On the contrary, what is not able to be predicated of any subject (*de nullo subiecto praedicatur*) is a particular (it *is not said* of a subject). The 'to be said' of a

---

1 Boethius, *In Categorias Aristotelis Commentaria*, in *Patrologia Latina*, ed. J.P. Migne, 217 vols. (Paris, 1841-1864) 64: 159-294, 169C. According to Bidez, in this work by Boethius virtually everything comes from Porphyry's commentary on the Categories; cf. Joseph Bidez, 'Boèce et Porphyre', *Comptes rendus des séances de l'Académie des Inscriptions et Belles-Lettres* 66 (1922), 346-50. Therefore, it is not surprising that his interpretation of the fourfold division in *Cat.* 2 agrees with that habitually given by the Neoplatonist, whose commentaries were also inspired by Porphyry's. Simplicius, for example, explains the division as follows: "since the goal [...] was about simple and generic expressions which signify simple and generic realities, [Aristotle] judged that before carrying out the division of them into the maximum number—that is to say, the division into ten, since it was not possible to discover more than ten—he should first undertake their division into the minimum number, to fewer than which it was impossible to compress them [...] These four things are substance, accident, the universal, and the particular" (Simplicius, *On Aristotle's Categories 1-4*, trans. Michael Chase [London, 2003], 58).

2 Boethius, *In Categorias Aristotelis Commentaria*, 175B and C.

3 Boethius, *In Categorias Aristotelis Commentaria*, 170B. Cf. 171A.

 | DOI 10.1163/9789004324275_004

subject is identified, then, with the ability to be the predicate in any sentence, either universal, particular or of any other kind. This interpretation of what 'is said of a subject' does not fit with the intention of *Cat.* 2 1a20-b9, where the logical or linguistic elements of the proposition are not explained, but rather the relations between beings that serve as the ontological basis for predication. In effect, the relation of *being said of* a subject is neither the predication nor the capacity to be predicated of a given subject, but rather the relation between the universal and its inferiors, meaning that these are the only ones that *fall under* (ὑπό)[4] the universal or, rather, those of which the universal in question can be essentially said.[5] Moreover, the identification in *Cat.* 2 of the 'to be said of a subject' with mere universality does not conform to the use of the same term in *Cat.* 5, 2a19, nor is it linked to the expression 'to be predicated as of a subject' appearing in *Cat.* 3, 1b10. Boethius himself understood that in those passages the latter expressions do not refer to any predication, but only to the essential[6] or synonymic predication.[7]

On the other hand, the identification of what *is in* a subject with the predicamental accident is not exempt from difficulties. From the systematic point of view, which does not pay attention to the chronology of the Aristotelian works, the distinction between the predicamental and the predicable accident is defensible,[8] as well as the connection between both uses of the word and the assimilation of what *is in* a subject with the accident and what *is not* with the substance. However, this does not correspond to the terminology used in the treatises of the *Organon* that nowadays are considered chronologically prior.

The term 'accident' (συμβεβηκός) appears rarely in the *Categories*, but very often in the *Topics*. In neither of these works is it used to designate the whole of what have been called the accidental, or not substantial, categories (*accidens praedicamentalis*). In general,[9] it can be said that the use of the noun

4 On this use of ὑπό, cf., e.g., *Top.* IV, 1, 120b20 and Hermann Bonitz, *Index Aristotelicus* (Graz, 1955) 795a34-50.

5 Against what is often said (cf., e.g., Bonitz, *Index Aristotelicus*, 798b40-55; James Duerlinger, 'Predication and Inherence in Aristotle's Categories', *Phronesis* 15 [1970] 175-203: 183), I understand that the relationship of *being said of* a subject is not a relation of predication, but that of subordination. The predication and its different types are based on the division of beings of *Cat.* 2, 1a20-b9, rather than vice versa.

6 Boethius, *In Categorias Aristotelis Commentaria*, 176A.

7 Boethius, *In Categorias Aristotelis Commentaria*, 184D.

8 Juan José García Norro and Rogelio Rovira, *Porfirio. Isagoge* (Barcelona, 2003), 96.

9 It has been argued that "accident" in Books II and III of the *Topics* and in the fallacy of accident discussion has the broad meaning of "predicate" with nothing more: Jacques

'accident' in the first treatises of the *Organon* corresponds to the definition that appears in *Top.* I, 5, 102b4, i.e., to what the scholastics usually call predicable accident. When you want to justify the use of that term to designate what falls under the non-substantial categories, you can only use later works and mainly the *Metaphysics.*[10]

Immediately after the aforementioned division of beings, Aristotle enunciates some rules, the first of which (what I will call *the transitivity of predication*) reads as follows:

> When one thing is predicated of another as of a subject (ὡς καθ' ὑποκειμένου), all that which is said of the predicate will also be said of the subject. Thus, 'man' is predicated of the individual man; but 'animal' is predicated of 'man'; it will, therefore, be predicable of the individual man also: for the individual man is both 'man' and 'animal'.[11]

Boethius understands that in this passage 'to be predicated as of a subject' (*praedicari de subjecto/ut de subiecto*)[12] is the same as essential predication (*in eo quod quid est*), "because it is said that only what is predicated *of a subject* is put in the substance and in the definition of anything else." So the predication ὡς καθ' ὑποκειμένου does not refer, then, to the mere predication of the universal, as might be expected, given the previous interpretation of the λέγεσθαι καθ' ὑποκειμένου in *Cat.* 2 as the ability to be predicated. Boethius also holds that the rule only applies to what is predicated essentially of the essential predicate, which adds a precision that is not explicitly contained in the Aristotelian rule, which only says that the rule applies to "all that which is said of the predicate."[13] Therefore, the rule comes to say that what is essentially

---

Brunschwig, *Aristote. Topiques*, 2 vols. (Paris 1967-2007), vol. 1, Int. XLV-LV; Gianni Serino, 'Para una interpretación unitaria de la doctrina de los predicables', *Anuario Filosófico* 35 (2002), 183-219. It is not a matter that directly affects what I intend to exhibit here.

10 Cf. L.M. de Rijk, *The Place of the Categories of Being in Aristotle's Philosophy* (Assen, 1952) c. 3, § 2.

11 *Cat.* 3, 1b10-15. Modified translation of E.M. Edghill in *The Works of Aristotle*, ed. W.D. Ross, vol. 1 (Oxford, 1928). Unless otherwise noted, translations are my own.

12 Boethius uses both expressions without distinction.

13 Cajetan expresses this very clearly: "ad intellectum istius regulae oportet concurrere duas praedicationes essentiales, licet Aristoteles primam tantum explicet" (Thomae de Vio Caietani *In Praedicabilia Porphirij, Praedicamenta, Postpraedicamenta & libros Posteriorum Analyticorum Aristotelis Commentaria* [Paris, 1572], 111-12).

predicated of a subject's essential predicate is predicated of that subject.[14] As a whole, the interpretation of this rule can be plausibly explained by the desire to clarify the limits where the transitivity of predication is valid, in order to avoid the fallacy of accident,[15] which I will discuss briefly at the end of the article.

But what immediately concerns us here is that Boethius, in line with this passage, divided predication into two classes: one is predication 'of a subject', or essential, and the other is predication by accident, which is not essential (*non in eo quod quid sit*).[16] The latter, the accidental one, is explicitly identified with the predication of what *is in* a subject, so it seems reasonable to

14 An interpretation that deviates from the commentary of Boethius commentary holds that the rule in question is merely the expression of the principle *dictum de omni*. Burley, e.g., maintains that the rule, generally understood, says: "quando alterum de altero praedicatur universaliter quotquot praedicatur de praedicato praedicatur et de subiecto [...] Sic non sequitur homo est animal et animal est asinus, ergo homo est asinus, quia asinus non praedicatur de animali universaliter" (Walter Burley, *Expositio super Artem Veterem Porphyrii et Aristotelis* [Venice, ca. 1476/78], 36). Soto judiciously rejects this interpretation: "Hic tamen sensus longe est ab intentione Aristotelis quia iste non fundatur in natura praedicati, sed in vi distributionis medii per artem syllogisticam" (Dominicus Soto, *In Porphyrii Isagogen, Aristotelis Categorias, librosque de Demonstratione Commentaria* [Venice, 1587; Frankfurt, 1967], 125D-E). Interpretations similar to Burley's have been maintained recently in Hester Goodenough Gelber, 'The Fallacy of Accident and the *dictum de omni*: Late Medieval Controversy over a Reciprocal Pair', *Vivarium* 25 (1987), 110-45: 110-14, and in Allan Bäck, *Aristotle's Theory of Predication* (Leiden, 2000), 238. On the fallacy of accident seen from this perspective, cf. also Aníbal A. Bueno, 'Aristotle, the Fallacy of Accident and the Nature of Predication', *Journal of the History of Philosophy* 26 (1988), 5-24; José Miguel Gambra, 'Medieval Solutions to the Sophism of accident', in *Argumentationstheorie*, ed. K. Jacobi (Leiden, 1993), 431-50: 434-5 and 446-9.

15 Cajetan recognizes this *expressis verbis*: "Notandum est hic, quod Aristoteles notanter appossuit in hac regula ly, ut de subiecto: quoniam absque illa particula regula ista est locus sophisticus fundatus fallaciam accidentis" (ed. cit., 111-12). In fact, Boethius' commentary on the rule ends noting that it does not apply to arguments of the type: 'Socrates est homo, homo est species, ergo Socrates est species', which the medievals often included among the sophisms due to the accident. Cf. José Miguel Gambra, 'The Fallacy of the Accident in Peter of Spain Tractatus and in Other Thirteenth-Century Works', in *Medieval and Renaissance Logic in Spain*, ed. I. Angelelli and P. Pérez-Ilzarbe (Hildesheim, 2000), 21-60: 33.

16 Boethius, *In Categorias*, 175D-6A. Boethius neglects the Aristotelian definition of predication by accident (*Top.* I, 5, 102b4) and redefines it as non-essential predication. So he can present this distinction as a complete division of predication. Here we leave aside this question.

understand that predication *of a subject*, or essential, is identified with the predication of what *is said of* a subject.[17]

Both Boethius' interpretation of the rule and his division of predication are held by Domingo de Soto, but he adds an explanation of how property and difference are included, in a way, within the predications by accident:

> Quia aliquid dici de aliquo apud Aristotelem quando addit ut de subiecto profecto idem designat quod dici de aliquo ut de quidditative inferiori, quod superiori capite adnotavimus. Quodcirca accidentia et propria passio praedicatur de subiecto, non ut de subiecto, sed ut in subiecto, et suo modo differentia quatenus praedicatur in quale admodum accidentis. Intelligitur ergo hic quando alterum de altero praedicatur, solum quidditative: ut de eodem praedicato sit haec regula, de quo fuit divisio secunda. Hoc supposito Boetius exponit sic: quando alterum de altero praedicatur ut de subiecto, id est quidditative, quicquid praedicatur itidem quidditative de praedicato, praedicatur et de subiecto.[18]

I understand that this Boethian division of predication, which Aristotle does not mention when he explains the transitivity rule, is in perfect harmony with his thought. The division of *Cat.* 2, 1a20-b9 is ontological insofar as it makes a distinction between various modes of being. However, it has a logical intention, as it seems to be devised to ground the predication relations that are viable between such sorts of beings. Suitable evidence for this is the recurring presence, in the early chapters of the *Categories*, of observations on expressions that "are said with combination"[19] and on the composition of true and false assertions[20] that, in short, come to say that assertions are constituted by the combination of things that fall under the categories.

It is not surprising, therefore, that Boethius, when commenting on the rule of transitivity, which deals with the predication of what *is said* of a subject, should have wanted to complete the catalogue of the possible predications by adding the predication about the subject of what *is in* that subject.[21] The first class includes all the predications that may be called descending within

17 Boethius does not say it enough clearly.

18 Dominicus Soto, *Summulae*, W. Risse ed. (Hildesheim 1980), 126.

19 *Cat.* 2, 1a16-19.

20 *Cat.* 4, 2a5-10.

21 Obviously, the notion of subject (ὑποκειμένον), as it is used in *Cat.* 2, 1a20-b9, is multiple since in the expression 'it is in a subject' the subject is always a substance, be it universal or particular. On the contrary, in the expression 'it is said of a subject' the subject is what

each category, because they express the attribution of genera to species or to individuals. The second, on the contrary, may be called transversal, because it occurs between the universals of the non-substantial categories and the substance.[22] On the other hand, it is not surprising that, having equated the predication about a subject of what *is said* of that subject with essential predication, he also wanted to equate the predication about a subject of what *is in* that subject with the accidental predication about the substance.

From these identifications, the former seems solid from the Aristotelian point of view, since the predication of what *is said* and the essential predication are characterized by predicating the logos.[23] The other identification also seems to be well grounded. Indeed, what *is in* a subject is identified with the things that belong to the non-substance categories, as we have previously seen. Moreover, *Top.* I, 9, which we cannot analyze here, states that when something belonging to other categories is predicated of a substance, then the predication is accidental.[24] It follows from the above that the things that *are in* a subject are predicated by accident of the substance. However, this conclusion seems to clash with what is said in *Cat.* 5, 2a19-34.

---

falls under something universal, and it will be a substance if this something is a substance, and it will not be a substance if this something is not.

22 Here I do not deal with predication among things belonging to non-substantial categories (cf., e.g., *Met.* V, 7, 1017a15 and *Cat.* 6, 5b1) nor with whether substance can be predicated of things belonging to non-substantial categories (cf., e.g., *Met.* V, 7, 1017a14 and *An. Post.* I, 22, 83a3).

23 The multiplicity of intertwined meanings that the notion of λόγος has is well known. In this text it means the definition (genus and difference), but it has a broader sense. For example, in *Top.* IV, 1, 121a17 it is said that the *being* and the *one*, which cannot be defined by genus and difference, have however a λόγος. So as not to ramble on unnecessarily, I will use generally the transliteration 'logos' (pl.: 'logoi'). The predication of the logos can be identified with essential predication. For instance, in *Cat.* 5, 3a17 it is said that when predicating second substances of first substances, the logos is being predicated, and in *Cat.* 5, 2b9 that those second substances (the genera and species of the substances) express *what* the subject *is*. In *Top.* I, 9, 103b27-35, this applies also to the predication of the universals of any category. According to the context, Aristotle designates essential predication in other ways. For example, in *Top.* IV, 1, 121a10 he uses the verb 'partake' (μετέχειν) and in *Cat.* 5, 3a 33-3b9 and *Top.* II, 2, 109b4 he calls it 'synonymic predication'.

24 Cf. *An. Post.* I, 22, 83a19-35; Richard Bodéüs, *Aristote. Catégories* (Paris, 2002) Int. LXXXV; José Miguel Gambra, 'La théorie aristoteliciènne de la différence dans les Topiques', *Philosophie Antique* 3 (2003), 21-56: 30-8 and Suzanne Mansion, 'Notes sur la doctrine des catégories dans les *Topiques*', in *Aristotle on Dialectic: the Topics*, ed. G.E.L. Owen (Oxford, 1968), 189-201: 198-200.

2 The Problem

Cat. 5, 2a19-34 considers the predication of what *is said of* a subject and of what *is in* a subject, indicating what is attributed to their subjects in each case. In summary, what it comes to say is that the predication of what *is said of* a subject (a universal) involves the name as well as the logos[25] being predicated of the subject (things below the universal), whereas in the predication of what *is in* a subject in most of the cases (ἐπὶ τῶν πλείστων) neither the name nor the logos is predicated of that subject (a substance), although 'in certain cases' (ἐπ' ἐνίων)[26] the name is indeed predicated.

For the name of something to be predicated of the subject means that it is attributed to it by means of the verb 'to be', because if something *is predicated* of a subject then that subject *is* the predicate.[27] According to this, the passage says, for example, that if something like man *is said of* a subject like Socrates (an individual man), then man *is predicated* of Socrates and Socrates *is* a man. But the name of things, like science, which *are in* a subject, like Socrates, generally cannot be predicated of this subject, because Socrates is not science. This does not prevent its being predicated on some occasions, however, because, for example, white *is in* a body and it is predicated of it since the body *is* white.[28]

If the beings that *are in* and those that *are said of* a subject are already different, depending on whether the name is predicated or not of their subjects, they will differ all the more due to the predication of their logos, since the predication of what *is said of* a subject entails the predication of it, whereas the predication of what *is in* a subject entails the impossibility of predicating the logos of such subject. Hence, if what *is said of* Socrates is predicated of him, his logos (rational man) will be predicated of him. However, even if the name of what *is in* Socrates is predicated of him, e.g., white, the logos of white will not be *predicated* of him.

This passage does not intend to set up a classification of predication modes (which would involve that both what *is in* and what *is said of* that subject are predicated of that subject), but only to examine if what *is in* and what *is said of* a subject are predicated of it. The reply to this is that there is, in fact, predica-

25 See above, n. 23.

26 *Cat.* 5, 3a16 uses the adverb ποτε (in some cases).

27 "If man were predicated [of the difference] it is evident that the difference would be man" (*Top.* VI, 6, 144b8). Furthermore, in the quoted text (2a24) and also in *Cat.* 3, 1b11-15 the expressions 'B is predicated (κατηγορεῖται) of A' and 'A is B' are used as equivalent.

28 I will deal with this problem and the difficulties it involves on several occasions. See especially pp. 184-5, 187-8 and 190-3.

tion of what *is said of* and what this entails is added. This predication is what is called in *Cat.* 1, 1a10 predication "as of a subject" (ὡς καθ' ὑποκειμένου). Instead, it is said that there is no predication of what *is in* a subject, save exceptionally. In fact, nowhere is it spoken of predication 'as in a subject' that would be parallel to predication 'as of a subject'. Considered this way, this paragraph seems to contradict almost directly the claim that the things that are in a subject are predicated of that subject (the substance).

3 Boethius and Soto on *Cat.* 5, 2a27-34

Boethius and those who followed him in identifying the predication of what *is in* a subject with accidental predication do not seem to be affected by this obvious difficulty. Boethius' commentary on *Cat.* 5, 2a27-34 is reduced to the following:

> Illorum uero quae sunt in subiecto aliquoties quidem neque nomen ipsum de subiecto dicitur. Nam uirtus in anima est sed uirtus de animo minime praedicatur; aliquoties autem denominatiue dicitur, ut grammatica, quoniam est in homine, denominatiue grammaticus a grammatica dicitur.
>
> Saepe autem ipsum nomen de subiecto praedicatur, ut quoniam album est in corpore, corpus album dicitur. Sed siue nomen non praedicetur, siue denominatiue dicatur siue proprio nomine praedicatio sit, definitio eius quod est in subiecto de proprio subiecto nunquam praedicabitur.[29]

When Boethius uses virtue as an example of cases in which the name of what *is in* is not predicated of the subject, he refers to an example that Aristotle presented in *Cat.* 8, 10b6-7, as a linguistic exception of what should be designated paronymously—that is, with a change in the flexion—but is not. Indeed, 'virtue' in Greek (ἀρετή) lacks the corresponding derived adjective, so, to say that someone has virtue, it is necessary to resort a word of another root, such as 'honest' (σπουδαῖος). The explanation of the case where neither the name nor the logos of what *is in* a subject is predicated of the substance, which is presented in the passage as the most frequent case (ἐπὶ τῶν πλείστων), is thus reduced to this example, which is exceptional for Aristotle.

29 Boethius, *In Categorias*, 185A-B.

In turn, the cases in which the name of what *is in* is predicated, exceptional or infrequent (ἐπ' ἐνίων) according to the passage in Aristotle, are divided into two: in one, the same name of what *is in* the subject is predicated of the subject; in the other, a derived name, or paronymous (*denominativus*), is predicated. The explanation of these two cases is found in Boethius' commentary on Aristotle's definition of the paronyms: for a term to be paronymous of another, three things are necessary: 'participation' in something by the thing (*re*), 'participation' in the name, and a *transfiguratio* (flexion of the name). If the latter is not met, such as when the same name of what *is in* the subject is predicated of it—e.g., when music (*musica*) *is in* a woman and '*musica*' (musician) is predicated of her—, then it is used homonymously. On the other hand, when between the name of what *is in* a subject and the one that is predicated of that same subject there is not only a participation of the term and of the thing, but also a *transfiguratio* of that name—e.g., when '*musicus*' (musician) is predicated of a male—, then the name is used paronymously.[30]

Boethius understands, therefore, that Aristotle's paragraph is devoted to explaining the predication of the terms that mean what *is in* and what *is said* of their subjects, according to the definitions of synonyms, homonyms and paronyms given in *Cat.* 1. After pointing out correctly that these things that are said of a subject are predicated synonymously,[31] he says that those that *are in* a subject are sometimes predicated paronymously, others homonymously and others not predicated, as in the case of virtue.

This analysis does not admit or resolve adequately the conflict between, on the one hand, predication by accident (which, according to Boethius himself, occurs between the things that are in a subject and the substance) and, on the other, this passage, which, in short, says that what *is in* the substance is not predicated of it, except in some cases in which only the name is predicated. Indeed, Boethius deviates from the text when he reduces to an exception the case in which neither the name nor the logos of what *is in* it is predicated of the substance, when according to Aristotle this is the most common case. In addition, the explanation of the case where the same name of what *is in* is predicated as an equivocal predication does not seem to have clear support in Aristotle. Finally, as we will see, he interprets wrongly the text of Aristotle when he understands that the paronymical predication is one of the cases in which the name of what is in the subject is predicated of it.

Domingo de Soto, despite following Boethius in the identification of the predication of what *is in* a subject with accidental predication, differs widely

30 Boethius, *In Categorias*, 167D-168C.

31 Boethius, *In Categorias*, 184D. Cf. above, n. 23.

from him in his explanation of *Cat.* 5, 2a27-39. His interpretation of the phrase about the predication of what *is in* a subject is based on the distinction between *abstract* and *concrete* terms, abundantly employed in medieval semantics.[32] In his opinion, this sentence, according to which neither the name nor the definition, or logos, of what *is in* the substance is predicated of it, refers only to the name taken *in abstracto* (e.g., 'whiteness'), because neither *whiteness* nor *disgregative color of vision* (the definition of whiteness) is predicated of Peter. Instead, the clause, according to which sometimes the name is predicated but not the definition, means that, when you take the name *in concreto* (e.g., white), the name is predicated but not the definition, because 'white' is predicated of the body, but disgregative of vision is not its definition.[33]

This solution assumes, first, that the concrete name (white) and the abstract one (whiteness) signify the same thing, but in a different manner.[34] This identification allows Soto to say that the name of the accident *white* (taken *in concreto*) is predicated of the body and that the name of the same accident (taken *in abstracto*) is not predicated of the body. This only enunciates a general rule valid for the names of any accident, but it does not explain why Aristotle says that the name of what *is in* the subject is predicated of it in some cases and not in others. Second, it also assumes that the predication of the definition does not mean only that it is predicated of the subject, but also that it is predicated *as a definition*.[35] This resolves the difficulty posed by the fact that, although 'disgregative of the vision' can be predicated of the body, this predication is not a predication of the definition of white, because the body is not *defined* as disgregative of vision. But this adds a condition to the predication of the definition or logos that is not in Aristotle's text.

32 A distinction remotely founded on some texts of Aristotle. On this and the medieval discussion on concrete accidental terms, cf. Sten Ebbesen, 'Concrete Accidental Terms: Late Thirteenth-Century Debates about Problems Relating to Such Terms as 'album' ', in *Topics in Latin Philosophy from the 12th-14th centuries. Collected Essays of S. Ebbesen* (Farnham, 2008) 109-51. Soto briefly addresses this distinction in the *Summulae* I, c. 7, ed. W. Risse (Hildesheim, 1980), 10v, and in *In Porphyrii Isagogen*, c. 1, 120I.

33 Soto, *In Porphyrii Isagogen*, 144L.

34 Soto, *Summulae* I, c. 7: "Album et albedo idem significant, sed diversimode: unus concretive et alter abstractive."

35 Soto, *In Porphyrii Isagogen*, 144K: "Notandum [...] quod praedicari secundum rationem est quod definitio praedicati sit definitio subiecti." 154I: "Haec corpus est disgregativum visus: hoc tamen non sufficit, ut album praedicetur ratione de corpore: sed requiritur quod definitio albi sit definitio corporis."

The explanation of Soto[36] manages to cleverly reduce problematic sentences concerning the predication of what *is in* the subject to two rules about the modes of signification of the terms. But it does so at the expense of admitting the two above assumptions that do not correspond with what is said in *Cat.* 5, 2a27-34.

The discordant interpretations of *Cat.* 5, 2a27-34, of which I have only presented an example that links the origins of medieval Aristotelianism with some of the best examples of Renaissance Scholasticism, reveal an obstacle that seems to have been in the way of interpreters of all eras. The paragraph in question hides not one, but several difficulties, which I will try to solve separately in what follows. The first refers to the name and asks how to reconcile the fact that what *is in* the subject (things of non-substance categories) is predicated by accident of the substance with the fact that nevertheless its name should not be predicated except in some cases.

4 What *Is in* Is Predicated as Accident, but Its Name Is Not Predicated

This problem arises when we try to explain how it is possible to predicate of the substance things from non-substance categories (what *is in* a subject), following the rule according to which only on some occasions can the name of such things be predicated. In the first place, it is noteworthy that the phrase in the passage that reads "with regard to those things which *are in* a subject, it is generally the case that their name is not predicated of the subject" does not deny that *being in* a subject could give way to a predication. It only points out that the names of the entities that are in a subject are not predicated of the substance.

In order to understand this, it is worth noting that Aristotle speaks about predication from various perspectives and that he uses different expressions for each of them. On the one hand, as we have seen, Aristotle sets up in *Cat.* 2 a classification of beings regarding the relations of *being* or not *in* a subject and *being said* or not of a subject. The terminology through which these distinctions are expressed is *fundamental* or *ontological*, since those relations occur between beings and they serve as a foundation for essential and accidental predication, but they are not in themselves modes of predication.[37]

---

36 Cajetan's interpretation (ed. cit., 125-7) is substantially identical to that of Soto.

37 *Pace* Bäck, *Aristotle's Theory of Predication*, 146. To this same fundamental or ontological level belongs the verb ὑπάρχειν (to belong), which is, however, broader than 'be in' or 'be

On the other hand, there are the *predications themselves*, as 'the man is grammatical', whose expression is characterized by resorting to the verb 'to be', and which belong to what we could call the *linguistic* level, which is different from the fundamental level. Phrases of this sort mean the composition of things, and the predicate in them expresses something about the subject.

Finally, a third perspective is that of *reflexive* or *metalinguistic* expressions that come to mean directly the linguistic or intellectual operation of predicating something of something, although indirectly they mean the same as the predications themselves. To that end, Aristotle uses the verbs κατηγορεῖν and also λέγειν in some of their accepted meanings.

Aristotle does not state this diversity of perspectives explicitly. However, he makes terminological observations here and there that allow for it. Thus, for instance, as we have seen, he points out that the use of κατηγορεῖν, characteristic of predication in a reflexive or metalinguistic sense, entails the predication itself by means of the verb 'to be'. He also states that one thing 'belonging' (ὑπάρχειν) to another does not involve that the former can be attributed to the latter through the verb 'to be':

> It does not suffice to show that whiteness or justice belong (ὑπάρχει λευκότης ἢ δικαιοσύνη) to someone in order to prove that *he is* white or just (λευκὸς ἢ δίκαιός ἐστιν).[38]

Now, the two rules on the predication of the name of what *is said of* and what *is in* the subject belong, in my view, to that same type of terminological observation about the transition from some levels of predication to others. Both of them link the expressions on the grounding of predication with the predications as such. They indicate that the terms used to express the grounding of predication can always be used in the predications as such, if what is predicated is a thing that is in a relation of *being said* in respect of its subject: if animal *is said of* man (that is, if man falls under animal), then animal is predicated of man, i.e., man *is* animal. In other words: one can move from 'being said of' at the fundamental level to the predication at the reflexive level, or to 'being', which is used in the predication as such. Instead, when a thing *is in* a substantial subject the same cannot be done, save for some exceptions, because

said of' a subject, for it comprises them both, and παρεῖναι, which is used with the same meaning as 'be in' (cf. *Top.* IV, 5, 126b13-33).

38 *Top.* II, 1, 109a22. The reason why we cannot go from *belonging* to attribution by means of the verb 'to be' is not the same as the one that prohibits going to that attribution from the *being in*. However, we will not discuss this now.

if science *is in* man, it doesn't amount to saying 'man is science' (predication level), nor is science predicated of man (reflexive level).

Viewed as an observation on the use of language in predication, what *Cat.* 5, 2a19-34 says on the possibility to predicate what *is in* of its subject does not imply that this cannot be attributed at all to the subject, but only that it is not predicated with the same term employed to say that one thing *is in* a subject, i.e., at the fundamental level. If that is so, what we must consider is how it is expressed, at the linguistic level (by means of the verb 'to be'), that the things that *are in* a subject are predicated accidentally of that subject. Aristotle's reply to this question is not found in this passage, but in the theory of paronymy that is defined at the beginning of the *Categories*.

Paronymous things are defined and exemplified there as follows: "Things are called paronymous which receive their name from something, but given a different flexion. Thus the grammarian from grammar, and the courageous man from courage."[39] Since paronymy is defined from the notion of flexion,[40] i.e., of the derivation of words from others, it seems that paronymy is no more than a linguistic observation. Since, moreover, the term 'paronym' is very rarely used by Aristotle, it is not surprising that some have maintained that it is a notion of minor importance in Aristotle's work.[41] However, I believe, like Bäck,[42] that, in spite of its limited use, paronymy has a remarkable importance in the *Organon* for it is used in relevant theories that refer to it more or less implicitly.

39 *Cat.* 1, 1a13.

40 Cf. *De Int.* 2, 16a32; 3, 16b16; *An. Pr.* 36, 48b40. Aristotle includes in the flexions the terms rising from the grammatical accidents of a term (for instance, gender, cases other than nominative, number, verb tenses other than present, etc.) as well as the terms with the same root as the original term, for instance, adverbs (Bonitz, *Index Aristotelicus*, 659a2-22; Brunschwig, *Aristote. Topiques*, 1: 25; Paul Slomkowski, *Aristotle's Topics* [Leiden, 1997], 152. Cf. Frédérique Ildefonse and Jean Lallot, *Aristote. Catégories* [Paris, 2002], 24). Here we only talk about the flexions as terms derived from others. However, there remains a certain ambiguity in the Aristotelian notion of flexion, which is not of great importance and which we cannot elucidate here. Aristotle does not use the distinction between root and desinence, but he maintains that different terms derived from other terms, also different from each other, can have the same flexion. So it is not clear if 'flexion' means the set of all those words, the desinence common to all of them or the transformation practiced on the original term that all of them have suffered similarly.

41 As Brunschwig has pointed out, *Aristote. Topiques*, 1: 140.

42 Bäck, *Aristotle's Theory of Predication*, 234.

Throughout the *Categories* paronymy is explicitly mentioned when dealing with relatives[43] and quality,[44] in both cases in order to distinguish the things that belong to each of these categories from what is designated paronymously from them.[45] In the *Topics* there are only two passages that mention paronymy.[46] Instead the notion of flexion appears abundantly, especially in the sections devoted to argumentation from *flexions* (πτώσεις) and *coordinates* (σύστοιχα), which are notions obviously related to paronymy. Generally speaking, the terms of a different root with the same desinence[47] belong to the same flexion and those terms that have the same root and different desinence are coordinated among themselves.[48] The Aristotelian theory of paronyms is not limited to these grammatical concepts but, on the contrary, it is a logical doctrine that explains why words sometimes match at their root and sometimes in their desinence.[49]

When looked at it closely, the notion of paronym in *Cat.* 1 is not, as it would seem, only a linguistic observation, for words are not paronyms but the things they designate.[50] And these things are not characterized by being given a name derived from another name, but by that name deriving from another thing's name. Paronymy, therefore, involves not only one thing's name and the name it derives from, but two names and two things.[51] This is endorsed by the examples given in the *Categories*: when a name has a paronym, this paronym always designates something different from that designated by the name it derives from. Thus 'white' (λευκός) is a paronymous name that designates

43 *Cat.* 7, 6b10-14.

44 *Cat.* 8, 10a26-b12.

45 *Cat.* 7, 6b12.

46 *Top.* II, 2 109a39-b12 and 4, 111a33-b11. We will discuss them later.

47 *Top.* II, 9, 114a33: "Flexions are, for instance, justly (δικαίως), bravely (ἀνδρείως), healthily (ὑγιεινῶς) and all that is formed in this way."

48 They are coordinates, for instance (*Top.* II, 9, 114a37), "justice (δικαιοσύνη), the just (δίκαιος), what is just (δίκαιον), justly (δικαίως)."

49 Aristotle uses these notions to justify arguments of the following type: "if justice is identical with bravery, the just will have to be identical with the brave, and justly with bravely" (*Top.* VII, 1, 151b31-34). We are not going to deal with them, but it is clear that the validity of this type of reasoning would be at least doubtful, if only founded on empirical observation of the similarity of roots or desinences in words. In reality these forms of argumentation, to which Aristotle devotes a large number of passages in the central books of the *Topics*, are implicitly founded on the theory of paronymy.

50 J.L. Ackrill, *Aristotle's Categories and De Interpretatione* (Oxford, 1963), 72-3.

51 Bodéüs, *Aristote. Catégories*, 76.

something qualified, a white man, by the name of a quality, which is 'whiteness' (λευκότης).[52]

On the other hand, the definition in question implies that paronyms are given the name of another thing but not vice-versa, because, for example, 'just' derives from 'justice' and not the other way around. The paronymic relation establishes an order between terms, unlike what happens with coordinates, which hold a symmetric relation between them ('justice' is coordinate with 'just' and vice-versa). This entails that there are terms that are not paronymous, that is, that there are things and terms from which paronyms arise and that they are not paronymous themselves. This also appears clearly in the examples of paronymy that Aristotle gives: grammarian and white are paronymous because they are designated from grammar and whiteness, which are not paronyms.[53]

Regarding the order of derivation of names, we should first ask why Aristotle decides that grammarian takes the name from grammar and not the other way around. The coincidence in these names' roots is not, in Aristotle's view, only the result of linguistic conventions. The conventional conception of language that Aristotle holds refers to the inherent connection between names and their meanings, but not to all connections between names of different things—which is, in his view, rational. The use of a name with a change in its desinence to designate something different from what is designated by the original term is not fortuitous or accidental, like pure homonymy, but it is due to a reason or foundation. This foundation, on the one hand, serves as a criterion to decide which terms are derived and which are not, and, on the other, it allows to judge, as it will be seen later, as to how everyday language has gaps and exceptions in the derivation of names. Then what does that foundation consist in?

Among the *topoi* of what is preferable, there is one that, although not explicitly using the notion of paronymy, is highly useful for responding to this question:

> In the second place, that which is essentially the thing in question (τὸ ὅπερ τόδε τι)[54] [is more desirable] than what is not included in its genus, e.g., justice (δικαιοσύνη) than a just man (τοῦ δικαίου); for the former falls within the genus good, whereas the other does not, and the former is essentially a good (ὅπερ ἀγαθόν), whereas the latter is not: for nothing is said to be essentially what a genus is if it does not happen to belong to

52 *Cat.* 8, 10a30. Cf. 7, 6b10. On 'white' and 'whiteness', cf. Bäck, *Aristotle's Theory of Predication*, 230.

53 *Cat.* 1, 1a14; *Cat.* 8, 10a30-2.

54 On this translation, cf. Brunschwig, *Aristote. Topiques*, 1: 154-5.

> this genus; e.g., the white man is not precisely what the color is. Likewise also in other cases.[55]

In my view, this text indirectly provides the criteria on which *the white* (the white man) is a paronym and *whiteness* is not.

Let us consider first the meaning of names that are not paronymous. Names, through the logos that is conventionally associated with them, signify the things in which that logos is essentially present. According to its mode of being, this logos (and the things signified) will belong to one or another category. We shall now examine the meaning of coordinated names, such as *justice* (δικαιοσύνη) and *the just* (τοῦ δικαίου). There is in them, on the one hand, a logos associated with the common root that will belong to one category, but, on the other, every one of the various terms of a series of coordinates will mean things from categories that are different from one another. For instance, 'justice' means a good that belongs to the category of quality, but the things signified by 'the just' are, unlike the former, substances (the just men). Now, the text comes to say that those things that fall essentially under the common logos of the root are the things signified by *original* terms (not paronyms), "for nothing is said to be essentially what a genus is if it does not happen to belong to this genus," as the passage says. However, the other things will not fall under the genus signified by the common root, for they belong to different categories and these will be the paronymous things whose names will be a flexion of those that are not.

On the other hand, paronyms, besides being included in a series of coordinates in virtue of their common root, are included in one and the same flexion with other terms of similar desinence, namely justly (δικαίως), bravely (ἀνδρείως), healthily (ὑγιεινῶς). In fact, Aristotle seems to understand that the desinence has a meaning on its own, which refers to the genus or category of the things that can be the subject of the paronymous term concerned.

He sometimes actually puts together the terms in flexions on solely morphological criteria: "flexions are, for instance, justly, bravely, healthily and all the terms formed in this way."[56] On other occasions this criterion rather seems to be semantic, like in *Top*. III, 3, 118a34, where he appears to admit that some flexions mean *uses*, others, *effect* and still others, *actions*. It is most interesting, however, that sometimes both criteria are joined, for instance in the following text:

---

55 *Top*. III, 1, 116a23-29. Modified translation of W.A. Pickard-Cambridge in *The Complete Works of Aristotle. The Revised Oxford Translation*, ed. Jonathan Barnes, vol. 1 (Princeton, NJ, 1991).

56 *Top*. II, 9, 114a33.

> If 'beneficial' (ὠφέλιμον) means 'productive of health' (use?), 'beneficially' (ὠφελίμως) means 'productively of health' (action?) and 'what has been beneficial (ὠφεληκὸς) means 'which has produced health' (effect?).[57]

From the above it would be sensible to derive that each ending has a special meaning (or *co-meaning*) that seems to point to the genus of things about which the terms with inflexions can be said, so that 'usefully' would be usefulness insofar as it *is in* the actions.[58]

In summary, the names of things from any category (be they the substance or not) that I have named 'original' are truly predicated on their own of the subjects that are their inferiors, that is, of the ones that fall under the same category as the logos associated with the name, but they are not truly predicated of things belonging to other categories. This is why it is true to say that an individual man is man or animal and also that grammar is science. By contrast, the terms whose root means something that falls under the non-substantial categories (what *is in* the substance) cannot normally be predicated themselves of the substance.[59] Rather, what can be predicated of the substance are their paronyms, that is, their flexions, which will have the co-meaningful desinence either of the category or of the genus of the subject. That is why it is said that what is predicated of man is 'scientist', not 'science', although science *is in* him.

The above explains the observation contained in *Cat.* 5, 2a19-34 about the predication of the name of beings that, according to the *Cat.* 2 division, *are in* a subject: insofar as, in this ontological division, the examples of names that are used to designate the things that *are in* a subject are designated as they *are in* it, and not as they are predicated of it, they designate them as belonging to its corresponding category and therefore without any changes in the flexion. That is why they cannot be predicated of the substance. This does not prevent its flexion from being predicated of them in the way I have pointed out.

Within the linguistic field of predication of the names of non-substantial categories, we still have to explain the exception according to which "there is

---

57 *Top.* VI, 10, 148a10.

58 This meaning of inflexion itself is seen somehow more clearly in the *Sophistic Refutations*, where there are examples according to which a flexion sometimes can mean (σημαίνειν) a grammatical gender, for instance, the neuter, and sometimes a kind of object, for instance, instruments: "but this (τοῦτο), although it is its job to signify the neuter it often means some other gender [...]. On the other hand, for the masculine and feminine, flexions are all different whereas for the neuter some are and others are not [...]. The names that end in 'on' are the only ones that denominate instruments" (*Soph. Ref.* 14, 173b28-174a1). Cf. Louis-André Dorion, *Aristote. Les refutations sophistiques* (Paris, 1995), 316-17.

59 Or of things from other categories different from those of the things they derive from.

nothing in certain cases to prevent us from predicating the name of the subject [...]. For instance, 'white', which is in a body, is predicated of this subject, for a body is called white."[60] Aristotle's theory of paronyms and their predication, which I have introduced, seems to be founded in the observation of everyday language and sets up a rule applicable to this language, which is the one used in dialectical disputes. Aristotle is well aware that ordinary language is full of irregularities and exceptions. When dealing with qualities, he distinguishes between these and the things qualified, which are said paronymously from them, and then he devotes a long paragraph to remarking insistently that the paronymic relation between a quality and the qualified thing depends on linguistic conventions, which have numerous exceptions. One of those exceptions occurs because there is no name for some qualities, so it is not possible to designate paronymously what is qualified through such qualities:

> There are some cases, however, in which, as the quality under consideration has no name, it is impossible to designate paronymously from them. For instance, the name given to the runner or boxer, who is so called in virtue of an inborn capacity, is not said paronymously from any quality.[61]

Another exception is that even when there is a name established for the quality, the qualified is not expressed paronymously from the corresponding quality, but from another term.[62] To these exceptions we should add the one that appears in the quoted passage: there are occasions in which the same term used at the fundamental level is predicated of the subject without any changes in the flexion, that is, without paronymy. This is what happens with 'white', which can be used with the fundamental terminology (white *is in* the body) as well as with the predication terminology (the body *is* white).[63] This is, in fact, plainly, an exception. Now we are to examine why the logos of what *is in* the subject is not predicated of it.

---

60 *Cat.* 5, 2a29-31.

61 *Cat.* 8, 10a33-b1. Modified translation of Edghill.

62 *Cat.* 8, 10b5-9. Something similar, but not exactly the same, happens with the names of the reciprocal of the relatives (*Cat.* 7, 7a5-22).

63 Curiously, Aristotle seems to admit somewhere else that the non-paronymous original term of 'white' (λευκός) is 'whiteness' (λευκότης), and not the same term 'white'. Cf. *Cat.* 8, 10a30 and *Top.* II, 1, 109a23. However, this is not an objection, since language seems to allow either of the two terms to that effect.

5 The Logos of What *Is in* Is Not Predicated of the Subject Either

The first difficulty this involves is, on the one hand, that the 'being in' is the grounding of a type of predication in which the predicate should express something of the subject by means of a name, since predication always entails that something is said of the subject. What is expressed of the subject in the predication of what *is said of* the subject is that it has a common form as the constituting element of its being. In other words, what *is said* of the subject is its whole essence or part of it. According to this, it is easy to understand that, in the second part of the observation on what *is said* of a subject, Aristotle should point out that it is its logos that is predicated and not only the name. However, if we consider the observation about what *is in* a subject the following question arises: which logos is predicated of the subject in the predication that is grounded on the *being in* relation? This predication is, as we know, accidental predication, and in it the name, save exceptions, is a term derived from the name of what *is in* the subject, that is, a paronym of it. In view of this, the above question can be posed as follows: what does the predicate express about the subject in accidental predication, i.e., in the predication of a paronymous name derived from the name of something which *is in* this subject?

The answer is to be sought in the theory of paronyms and of the coordinates and flexions. As I have pointed out before, the paronyms of a term have a logos that coincides, to a certain extent, with the logos of the original term, but it is not exactly the same, since it adds the meaning of the flexion concerned in each case. Moreover, paronyms have as definition, genus, and difference, paronyms (or terms with flexion) derived from the definitions, genera and differences of what is designated by the original term. Thus, for instance,

> if destruction is the dissolution of substance, likewise, destroying is diluting of the substance [...] and if the destructive is the dissolutive of the substance, destruction will also be the dissolution of the substance.[64]

---

64 *Top.* VII, 3, 155b31. In general, Aristotle says that paying attention to flexions and coordinates "it is necessary that the genera accompany the genera and definitions accompany definitions" (155b25). It could be objected that there should exist genera, differences and definitions of the paronyms other than the genera, differences and definitions of original names, because if for each term contained in a category there are flexioned or paronymous terms and each one of them has genera distinct from the originals, it would seem that the number of supreme genera, or categories, would grow excessively. For instance *just* would belong to the genus of the *virtuous*, and going further to the category of the *qualified*. And this category would be neither that of the substance nor of the quality but that of the things designated by means of the paronyms of qualities. Aristotle does not

The result is clear, therefore, that in accidental predications the logos attributed to the subject is not the one of what *is in* the subject, but the logos of the paronym. Aristotle says that if the soul "moves in accordance with some of the species [of movement], it is evident that it moves." Through this he comes to exemplify a law according to which when a species of a genus is attributed paronymously, i.e., by accident, then that genus is also predicated paronymously. Indeed, if it is said of the soul that it 'is generated' (γίγνεσθαι)—a term paronym of 'genesis' (γένεσις), which means one of the species of the movement genus (κίνησις)—then it is said of the soul that 'it moves' (κινεῖσθαι), i.e., a paronym of that genus.[65]

This theory, in my view perfectly in accordance with the texts, not only enables the explanation of laws like the one I have just mentioned, but also of other passages in the *Topics* that assume that the definition or logos of what is said by accident should also be possible to be said of the subject. One of the most evident of these passages is the following:

> Another *topos* is to make definitions (λόγος) both of the accident and of its subject, either of both separately or else of one of them, and then look and see if something that is not true has been taken as true. Thus, e.g., to see if it is possible to wrong a god, ask what is to wrong? For if it is to damage deliberately, it is evident that a god cannot be wronged: for it is impossible that a god should be damaged.[66]

According to this argumentative procedure, to refute an accidental predication we can replace the predicate with its logos to verify if the falsity of that predication is made evident. Now, if it were impossible for the logos of the accident to be said of the subject, it would always be not-true to say of the subject what is contained in the logos of the predicate, and this passage[67] would not make sense.

consider the above question, but if an objection were made to it he would probably reply that derivation is a linguistic fact that concerns the use of terms in predication but does not change the category they belong to if considered in isolation. In fact, in the list of categories (*Cat.* 4) that divides the terms without composition with which assertions are formed, the examples include paronymous terms like 'grammarian'. Cf. Soto, *In Porphyrii Isagogen*, 174I-L.

65 Cf. *Top.* II, 4, 111a33-b11.

66 *Top.* II, 2, 109b30-5.

67 Cf. also *Top.* II, 7, 113a24-32.

We have yet to clarify the exception according to which the name of what *is in* a subject is sometimes predicated of it, although not even then is its logos predicated. Which logos is the one predicated in such cases? The answer is found in the observation made before, according to which the possibility to use the same name of what *is in* the subject as predicate in the accidental predications is a linguistic exception to the paronymy rule. Such an exception does not affect the logos that is not subject to language conventions. Therefore the logos attributed in those accidental predications is that of the term that would have had to be a paronym of what *is in* the subject. Thus, white (τὸ λευκόν) *is in* the body, and, as an exception, 'white' is predicated of this subject "since it is said of a body that it is white."[68] However, since color (χρῶμα) is the genus of white (i.e., a part of its logos), what is predicated of the body, *in which is* the white, is not 'color' but 'being colored' (κεχρῶσθαι),[69] which is paronymous of the white genus.[70]

6 Last Observations. The Transitivity Rule

The observations contained in *Cat.* 5, 2a9-34 and the theory of predication of paronyms are 'bridge theories'. The former goes from the ontological grounding of predication to the consideration of its linguistic expression, and the latter follows the reverse path. The first one uses the terminology of the distinction between beings that *are in* and those that *are said* of a subject, or rather the categories theory, to show that such terminology cannot be used indiscriminately in predication within the linguistic level or the reflexive level. The second one departs from an empirical observation on the flexions of terms, and the manner they are predicated, to establish a rule on predication grounded on the ontological theory of classification of beings. Both theories, precisely due to their bridging character, only appear sporadically in Aristotle's logical works. Both coincide on the properly logical distinction of accidental predication and essential predication and, in general, they only reappear in the field of logic to set up links between the reflexive or logical level of predication with its ontological grounding or with its linguistic expression. Thus, in *Top.* II 2, 109b3-12, Aristotle points out that the use of paronymic predication in everyday language is a sign of predication by accident. Also, he says, when dealing

68 *Cat.* 5, 2a32.

69 *Top.* V, 5, 134a23-4.

70 *Top.* II, 2, 109a38.

with the predication of genus in *Top.* IV, 6, 127b1-4, that if something is said *to be in* the subject, then it is not its genus.

These observations provide the key to resolving the limits within which a law we could call transitivity of what is essentially attributed to the predicate should be valid. According to this, the essential attributes of the predicate are also predicated of the subject. This law, as we shall see, is not universally valid. It is on the relation of *being said of a subject* that appears in the ontological classification of *Cat.* 2 that essential predication is grounded. According to this type of predication, attributed to the subject are the name and the content or logos of what *is said* of it. For these predications the transitivity law of essential predication is always valid: what is essentially predicated of the essential predicate is predicated of the subject. Aristotle sometimes enunciates this law with fundamental terminology, as in *Cat.* 3, when he says: "whenever something is predicated of something else *as of its subject* (ὡς καθ' ὑποκειμένου), all that is said of what is predicated will be said of the subject,"[71] and other times using the various modes of essential predication:[72] "It is necessary that the definitions of the genera be predicated of the species and of the things which partake of the species."[73]

In its turn, the relation of 'being in a subject' grounds accidental predication in which the name and the logos of the paronym of what *is in* the subject is normally predicated of it, although with the exceptions we have seen. The fact that in this case the transitivity law should be valid of what is essentially predicated of the accidental predicate is much less clear. As I have pointed out before, in a normal case (that is, when the accident is a paronym) it seems that the transitivity is valid, for the essential predicates of the accident (which are also paronyms in the sense I have indicated) are predicated of the subject. On the other hand, Aristotle states in the *Sophistic Refutations* that "it is not necessary that what is true of the accident should also be true of the thing" (*Soph. Ref.* 24, 179a34). It seems, therefore, that transitivity is not a logical law when it is applied to a predication by accident. In fact, some authors, like Alexander of Aphrodisias,[74] have rightly thought that on the example given in *Cat.* 5, 2a31 a sophistic reasoning can be construed that illustrates how transitivity is not valid in the case of the accident:

---

71 *Cat.* 3, 1b10.

72 Which would belong to what I have called *reflexive terminology*.

73 *Top.* IV, 2, 122b9; cf. IV, 2, 122a31-b6 and IV, 1, 121a10-19.

74 Alexander Aphrodisiensis, *In Aristotelis Sophisticos Elenchos*, ed. M. Wallies (Berlin, 1898), 38, 8. Cf. Louis-André Dorion, *Aristote. Les refutations sophistiques*, 233-5.

Socrates is white,
the white is a color,
then Socrates is a color

As this discourse adopts the form of the transitivity law, and it has true premises and a false conclusion, it is clear that transitivity would not be valid if the first premise were an accidental predication. This seems to contradict what I said above. But this is not the case: Aristotle does not say that the essential attribute of the accident is *never* predicated of the subject, but that *it is not necessary* that it be predicated. In other words: it is not enough that a predicate is essentially said of the accident of a subject to conclude that the predicate is said of the subject. This leaves the possibility open for distinguishing when it is predicated and when it is not. Now, in my view, the above considerations allow us to conclude that the transitivity law is invalid only in the exceptional case that the name of what *is in* a subject *is said of* that subject, that is, when the accidental predicate is not designated by a paronym, but by the same name of what is in the subject.[75] In this case, if an essential predication of what *is in* the subject is taken as the second premise, instead of the essential predication of what should have been designated by a paronym, the reasoning is invalid. In fact, the final example[76] in the passage quoted above illustrates precisely this possibility: if the second premise had been 'the white is colored', it would be valid to conclude that 'Socrates is colored'.

7 Conclusion

I have tried to show, from the texts of Aristotle, how confusing phrases in *Cat.* 5, 2a27-34 do not contradict the idea that what *is in* a subject is predicated by accident of the substance. To do so, I have analyzed somewhat thoroughly the theory of paronyms, whose importance in Aristotelian semantics is much greater than appears at first sight. Among other things, thanks to this theory, the limits that separate the transitivity of predication from the fallacy of accident are determined more precisely than in the rule in *Cat.* 3, 1b10.

It is not possible to compare these results with the solutions offered by Boethius and by the Renaissance Scholastics mentioned at the beginning, but

75 Bäck, *Aristotle's Theory of Predication*, 237, gives an almost correct solution to this problem, but does not properly interpret the rule of *Cat.* 3, 1b10, because he thinks that καθ' ὑποκειμένου "would signify paronymy."

76 *Cat.* 5, 2a31.

the differences in the interpretation of 2a27-34 are evident. Many other issues discussed by medieval logicians are related to what is stated here: for example, the significance of concrete accidental terms, their belonging to the categories or the interpretation of the rule of transitivity and its relationship with the sophism of accident. Nor is it possible to examine these here, but the above perhaps is useful for determining whether they reflect the thought of Aristotle or depend on sources and developments that are beyond it.

Anselm of Canterbury's Theory of Meaning: Analysis of Some Semantic Distinctions in *De Grammatico*

María Cerezo

The dialogue *De Grammatico*, written by Anselm of Canterbury (1033-1109), has received little attention, due most likely to its complexity.[1] The work includes a conception of paronymy according to which a paronym signifies a quality and is appellative of a substance. The received interpretation of the dialogue was offered by Desmond Paul Henry in 1964,[2] but the more recent research of Alain Galonnier, Marilyn McCord Adams, John Marenbon, Peter King and Peter Boschung has brought fresh issues to light, revealing the importance of Anselmian doctrines in the dialogue.[3]

I have chosen to study *De Grammatico* on this occasion because Angel d'Ors considered that work and its doctrines significant and encouraged me to read

1 For an analysis of the reasons why St Anselm's place in the history of logic has been overlooked, cf. Sara Uckelman, 'The Reception of Saint Anselm's Logic in the Twentieth and Twenty-First Centuries', in *Saint Anselm of Canterbury and His Legacy*, ed. G.E.M. Gasper and I. Logan (Toronto, 2012), 405-26.

2 Desmond Paul Henry, *The* De Grammatico *of St. Anselm: The Theory of Paronymy* (Notre Dame, 1964).

3 Alain Galonnier, '(Au sujet) de Grammarien', in *Le Grammarien; De la vérité; la liberté du choix; la chute du diable: Anselme de Cantorbéry*, ed. A. Galonnier, M. Corbin and R. de Ravinel (Paris, 1986), 25-49; idem, 'Le *De Grammatico* et l'origine de la théorie des proprietés des termes', in *Gilbert de Poitiers et ses Contemporains: aux Origines de la Logica Modernorum*, ed. J. Jolivet and A. de Libera (Naples, 1987), 353-75; idem, 'Sur quelques aspects annonciateurs de la littérature sophismatique dans le *De grammatico*', in *Anselm: Aosta, Bec and Canterbury: Papers in Commemoration of the Nine-Hundredth Anniversary of Anselm's Enthronement as Archbishop, 25 September 1093*, ed. D.E. Luscombe and G. Evans (Sheffield, 1996), 209-28; Marilyn McCord Adams, 'Re-reading *De Grammatico*, or Anselm's Introduction to Aristotle's *Categories*', *Documenti e studi sulla tradizione filosofica medievale* 11 (2000), 83-112; John Marenbon, 'Some Semantic Problems in Anselm's *De grammatico*', in *Latin Culture in the Eleventh Century*, ed. M. Herren, C. McDonough and R. Arthur (Turnhout, 2002), 73-86; Peter King, 'Anselm's Philosophy of Language', in *The Cambridge Companion to Anselm*, ed. B. Davies and B. Leftow (Cambridge, 2004), 84-110; Peter Boschung, *From a Topical Point of View: Dialectic in Anselm of Canterbury's* De Grammatico (Leiden, 2006). Cf. also Guilherme Wyllie, 'Signification et forme logique dans le *De grammatico* d'Anselme de Cantorbéry', in *Anselm of Canterbury (1033-1109): Philosophical Theology and Ethics*, ed. R.H. Pich (Porto Alegre, 2011), 111-18.

 | DOI 10.1163/9789004324275_005

the dialogue carefully. Angel d'Ors himself focused on other Anselmian works at the beginning of his career and toward the end of his life,[4] but he never actually wrote a paper on *De Grammatico*. However, some handwritten notes in his volume of Anselm's *Complete Works* show that he read and thought through the dialogue on several occasions. There are at least four different sets of notes, written at different times. In what follows, I have taken these notes into account, and I have been inspired by his comments on the contents of particular chapters. Nevertheless, the notes are very sketchy and it is not easy to reconstruct his interpretation of *De Grammatico*. Although this contribution is therefore my own reflection on Anselm's semantic doctrines, I must express my debt to Angel d'Ors' notes and what I have understood of his analysis, in particular, his attention to the different distinctions dealt with in the second section of this article.[5]

One could study *De Grammatico* from different perspectives, expressed in four different questions: what are the doctrines *out of which* the contents of the dialogue are developed (its sources, 'out-of-what-question'); *what* are the contents themselves (the doctrines, 'what-question'); *why* were they developed (its immediate motivation, 'why-question'), and *for what* was it written (the purpose, 'for-what-question').[6] Broadly speaking, the dialogue can be causally analysed, correlating the four questions with the four Aristotelian causes, material, formal, efficient and final, respectively, although the main focus of this paper is on the second question, regarding the contents of the dialogue

---

4 Angel d'Ors, ' 'Non erat veritas', 'Non erit veritas'. Sobre las pruebas anselmianas de la eternidad de la verdad', in *Verdad, percepción, inmortalidad/Wahrheit, Wahrnehmung, Unsterblichkeit*, ed. S. Castellote (Valencia, 1995), 201-14; Angel d'Ors, '«*Omnis volens ipsum suum velle vult*». A propósito del *De libertate arbitrii* de San Anselmo', in *"Autotrascendimiento". Homenaje al catedrático de filosofía D. Ignacio Falgueras Salinas por su jubilación*, ed. J.A. García González and J.J. Padial (Málaga, 2010), 183-203.

5 My thanks are also due to Alicia García Navarro, the wife of Angel d'Ors, for allowing me to use his materials for my work. I also want to thank Alfonso García Marqués, Paloma Pérez-Ilzarbe, Lucía Rodríguez and two anonymous referees for their useful comments.

6 Of course, there are other important questions, for example on the date of composition of the dialogue and the influence of the Anselmian doctrines on later logical and semantic theories. According to Henry, *The* De Grammatico *of St. Anselm*, 1-2, the dialogue was written between 1060 and 1078, but new research has dated it to the early 1080s; cf. Osmund Lewry, 'Boethian Logic in the Medieval West', in *Boethius: His Life, Thought, and Influence*, ed. M. Gibson (Oxford, 1981), 90-134; R. Sharpe, 'Anselm as Author: Publishing in the Late Eleventh Century', *Journal of Medieval Latin* 19 (2009), 1-87. Galonnier has defended the view that Anselm's dialogue contains doctrines that anticipate 12th-century logic and semantics (see references in note 1). For some doubts about this claim, see Boschung, *From a Topical Point of View*, 72-6.

(the doctrines). In section 1, I will use the questions to raise four crucial issues that Anselm attempts to resolve in the dialogue (DG-issues).

Section 1 introduces the dialogue, presents the questions and DG-issues and briefly discusses the strengths and weaknesses of some previous works on *De Grammatico*. Section 2 presents the contents of the dialogue, offering an interpretation of the oppositions that appear in different arguments in the work: *dicitur in eo quod quale/dicitur in eo quod quid, esse ut in subiecto/non ut in subiecto, significare/appellare, significare ut unum/non ut unum* and *significare per se/per aliud*, and the role that these distinctions have in Anselm's theory of language. This interpretation allows for a presentation of Anselm's resolution of the four DG-issues in section 3.

1 Four Issues in *De Grammatico*

The topic of the dialogue is paronymy, that is, the linguistic phenomenon in which thing A is named by means of word B formed derivatively out of a different word C that in turn names a further thing D. A courageous man (A) is named by means of 'courageous' (B), which is formed out of 'courage' (C), which in turn names the quality of courage (D) (cf. *Categories* 1, 1a13-15). Anselm's example is *grammaticus*, one who knows *grammatica*, and who can thus be named by means of '*grammaticus*', which is formed derivatively out of '*grammatica*'.[7]

Anselm addresses the topic of paronymy by raising a question in the first chapter of the dialogue: whether *grammaticus* is a substance or a quality ('*De 'grammatico' peto ut me certum facias utrum sit substantia an qualitas*'). I consider this to be one of the four DG-issues, and will refer to it as 'the initial DG-issue' (DG I, 145, 4-6).[8] The issue expresses an ongoing debate between the Priscian grammatical and Aristotelian dialectical traditions[9] and serves

7 Given the difficulties in translating '*grammaticus*' into English, I will use the Latin words '*grammaticus*' and '*grammatica*' to mean 'knowing or skilled in the use of language' and 'grammar or knowledge or skill to use language', respectively.

8 To quote or refer to *De Grammatico*, I will use DG followed by the chapter of the dialogue and the pages and lines of Schmitt's edition: Anselm of Canterbury, '*De Grammatico*', in *S. Anselmi Cantuariensis Archiepiscopi Opera Omnia*, vol. 1, ed. F.S. Schmitt (Stuttgart–Bad Cannstatt, 1968), 145-68.

9 For a useful reflection on this issue, cf. Sten Ebbesen, 'The Traditions of Ancient Logic-cum-Grammar in the Middle Ages—What's the Problem?, *Vivarium* 45 (2007), 136-52.

Anselm as the immediate motivation (why-question) to develop his theory of language. The initial DG-issue is about reality, since the question concerns the *res* signified by '*grammaticus*', namely, whether it *is* a substance or a quality.

In the dialogue, Anselm shows that *grammaticus* is both a substance and a quality. His strategy in answering this way is to have recourse precisely to the theory of signification (*multiplicity* of *things* signified and *multiplicity* of *ways* of signifying) in order to solve the apparent conflict in the possibility that *grammaticus* is both a substance and a quality. If '*grammaticus*' signifies more than one thing, then each of the things signified can differ in kind (substance and quality). But if this is the solution, then how can one word signify more than one thing, and how does the signifying relation occur in this case? This I consider 'the central DG-issue', which also includes the question about the definition of '*grammaticus*' (DG IX, 154, 7-10; XIII, 157, 16; XIV, 159, 18-24).

The central DG-issue, therefore, can be analysed in four DG-questions: (a) what does '*grammaticus*' signify? (b) what does '*grammaticus*' express? (c) what can *grammaticus* be predicated of? (d) how is *grammaticus* predicated of the subjects of which it can be predicated? Question (a) is not only about the things signified by '*grammaticus*', but also about the manners in which it signifies them. Question (b) is about the definition of '*grammaticus*'. Questions (c) and (d) reflect the two important issues about predication when a predicate is confronted: the subjects of which it can be predicated and the mode of predication.

The precise answers to the DG-questions will come in section 3, once the dialogue has been reviewed in detail in section 2, but it will be easier to understand the dialogue if the general features of Anselm's framework are presented now. Anselm's answer to the central DG-issue is that '*grammaticus*' is *significativum grammaticae* (it signifies a quality, *grammatica*) and *appellativum hominis* (it appellates a substance, *homo*), and that the definition of *grammaticus* is *sciens grammaticam*, and it thus does not include *homo* in its definition. There are then two different signifying relations between language and the world according to the two different functions of language, to present or indicate the things of the world (*appellare*) and to express what something is (*significare*): the term '*homo*' indicates or appellates a substance (*homo*) and expresses what that substance is (*homo, animal rationale*), and the term '*grammaticus*' indicates or presents a substance (*homo*) and expresses what that substance is (*grammaticus*). Notice that there are two different senses of '*is*' here: what a substance is because of its essence (definition) and what a thing is because of the qualities (or other accidents) that are present in it. Thus '*homo est animal rationale*' and '*homo est grammaticus*' express two different forms of predication (*dicitur in eo quod quid* and *dicitur in eo quod quale*, respectively). Since '*grammaticus*' appellates or indicates something (*homo*) that it does not signify or express, it is necessary to account for the manner in which appellation takes place. The explanation lies in the distinction between *significatio per se* and *significatio per aliud*. Finally, given that '*grammaticus*' signifies more than one thing, the question about how the things signified by it relate to each other arises, and the distinction between *significare ut unum* and *significare non ut unum* accounts for the different ways in which multiple things signified by one term can relate to each other.

The third DG-issue concerns the scope of the Aristotelian doctrine of the *Categories* ('the *Categories* DG-issue', DG XVII, 162, 16-19), and arises because of the way in which Anselm argues for the claim not only that '*grammaticus*' signifies *per se* a quality, but also that *grammaticus* is a quality. Finally, the fourth DG-issue is about the possibility that *grammaticus* belongs to two categories, quality and having ('the *habere* DG-issue', XIX, 164, 28-29). These two issues show the importance of the *Categories* among the sources of *De Grammatico* (out-of-what-question).

It is rather strange that Anselm devoted a dialogue to a fairly technical semantic problem that is not directly related to the rest of his theological work, for which the problem's resolution does not appear to be essential. Scholarship on *De Grammatico* has aimed at clarifying the role and sense of the dialogue in the context of Anselm's philosophy and theology, developing readings of *De Grammatico* in which either its sources, immediate motivation or purpose is stressed, which gives rise to rather insufficient or not completely accurate interpretations of the doctrines. Received interpretations read *De Grammatico* from a particular perspective determined by one of the four questions indicated above.

Henry is a paradigmatic example. He reads the dialogue as an attempt to reply to the initial DG-issue. Henry thus focuses on the immediate motivation of the dialogue, the why-question, and develops an interpretation according to which Anselm aims at reconciling the Priscian grammatical and Aristotelian dialectical traditions. In order to do so, he presents Anselm as deploying an artificial language to account for phrases such as these:

(1) *Grammaticus est grammatica*
(2) *Grammaticus est qualitas*

(1) is nonsensical according to the grammatical tradition, but it expresses a theoretical truth in the dialectical tradition, as does (2). Henry applies Leśniewski's

calculus to elucidate Anselm's logical and semantic doctrines, and in particular he proposes a multi-layered interpretation of the copula (*est*) that allows an interpretation of the copula in (1) as a higher-order functor whose arguments are predicative expressions.

Adams and Boschung have reacted to Henry's interpretation of the dialogue, rejecting his recourse to Leśniewski's formal apparatus. I think that their revision of Henry's enterprise is correct, for the following reasons in particular: (i) Henry thinks that his formalization renders Anselm's proposal more nominalist, but this is a reason to avoid such formalization, since Anselm's doctrines commit him to a realist conception (subsection 2.8); (ii) Leśniewski's formalization entails an extensional reduction of predicates, which is alien to Anselm's doctrines; and (iii) Henry's interpretation gives priority to the difference between grammatical and logical form over the differences between signification and appellation, and between *significatio per se* and *significatio per aliud*, which are Anselm's real concerns in the dialogue (B 281-302).[10] But neither Adams nor Boschung has paid attention to what lies at the heart of Henry's presentation, namely, a conception of qualities and their linguistic expressions as unsaturated or incomplete entities and expressions. This point is crucial in Henry's interpretation and explains why the methodological tool he deploys to account for theoretical truths (and reconcile grammarians with dialectics) is unsatisfactory. This point will be explored in subsection 2.5.

Adams is a paradigmatic example of a scholar who approaches *De Grammatico* from the out-of-what-question perspective. She claims that "*De Grammatico* is Anselm's own distinctive introduction to Aristotle's *Categories*,"[11] despite her acknowledgment that, as an introduction, it is a fragmentary work since only a few ideas from the *Categories* are presented.[12] Adams is correct, however, in indicating Aristotle as the crucial source, since the *Categories* is the only work cited in the dialogue, and two of the DG-issues relate directly to this Aristotelian work (the *Categories* DG-issue and the *habere* DG-issue).[13]

---

10 Since I will be referring quite often to Boschung's interpretation (Boschung, *From a Topical Point of View*), I will refer to his book using B followed by the page numbers. Boschung's review of Henry is inspired by Adams', which contains further details; see Adams, 'Re-reading *De Grammatico*', 90-105.

11 Adams, 'Re-reading *De Grammatico*', 84.

12 Adams, 'Re-reading *De Grammatico*', 112.

13 For a very detailed exposition of the sources of *De Grammatico*, in addition to the *Categories*, see B 22-31, 161-222, 310. Boschung's presentation of Augustine's *De Magistro* as a source of Anselm's theories is particularly illuminating.

What was the dialogue written *for*? Anselm answered this question in the preface to *De Veritate*, where he says that *De Grammatico* should be considered an introduction to dialectics (*non inutilem, ut puto introducendis ad dialecticam, cuius initium est De Grammatico*). Boschung's interpretation is an example of a reading offered from the perspective of the what-for-question. He thinks that to properly understand the contents of the dialogue it is crucial to focus on the inferential context in which they are introduced and on the methodology Anselm employs to deal with fallacies.[14] I agree with Boschung that Anselm presents his ideas and argues for them by means of the analysis of sophistical arguments of syllogistic form, as will be shown in the way I present Anselm's distinctions in this paper. In order to show their sophistical form, Anselm analyses their premises and conclusions, clarifying the sense of their parts, subjects and predicates. And, crucially, this clarification is via an analysis of the signification of those terms (different kinds of terms and different modes of signification) and the diverse forms of predication. However, the semantic doctrines that Anselm defends, which are properly speaking the contents of the dialogue, are not dependent in an essential way on the way and inferential contexts in which they are introduced.

The interpretation put forward here will concentrate on the contents of *De Grammatico* themselves (what-question), focusing directly on the four DG-issues presented above. Most interpreters have focused on the problem of elucidating how Anselm's distinctions between *significare* and *appellare* and between *significatio per se* and *significatio per aliud* solve the initial DG-issue: *grammaticus* is a substance and a quality because the term '*grammaticus*' relates to the world in two ways, signifying *per se* a quality, *grammatica*, and appellating and signifying *per aliud* a substance, *homo*.

The received view prior to Adams' and Boschung's work was that there is no difference between *appellare* and *significatio per aliud*.[15] But recent research has offered a better understanding of Anselm's proposal, distinguishing the two concepts. However, in spite of the important advances offered by Boschung's interpretation, which is the most extensive, there are still several points on which it is not accurate or complete.

---

14 Boschung claims that the dialogue intends to introduce a specific new methodology to deal with fallacies; the discussion of this point goes beyond the scope of the present article.

15 Even the two concepts are considered to be synonymous in Sten Ebbesen, 'Language, Medieval Theories of', in *Routledge Encyclopedia of Philosophy*, version 1.0 (London-New York, 1998), 157.

First, Boschung's interpretation, like others, presents the semantic doctrines as if Anselm were introducing and defining both the distinction between *significatio per se* and *significatio per aliud* and the distinction between *significare* and *appellare* (see, for example, B 247). However, I do not think that Anselm's intention is to introduce and define the second of these distinctions in the dialogue, but rather that the distinction is inherited from his predecessors.[16] The difference between *appellare* and *significare* is presupposed and used rather than proposed or theoretically defined; and as will be seen, part of the problem of interpreting the fragment where Anselm makes reference to the appellative use of names comes from reading the text as a definition. This point will be dealt with in subsection 2.5.

Second, Boschung grounds the difference between *significare* and *appellare* on the relation of predication in a way that goes beyond Anselm's dialogue. Boschung says that "in such a linguistic expression, used to express appellation, the predicate is said of [i.e., appellates] that for which the name in subject position stands" (B 247), and later he says that "while Anselm does not define the term 'appellation' with respect to predication, appellation can only be expressed, and thus considered in discourse, in the context of predication" (B 247). In my interpretation of Anselm's semantic doctrines, in subsections 2.1-2.5, I will try to show that it is understanding, rather than predication, that grounds appellation, even if appellation makes the relation of predication possible when the *esse* of what is expressed by the subject is not the same as the *esse* of what is expressed by the predicate.

Finally, one of the main points of Boschung's interpretation is his analysis of the *habere* DG-issue. In a nutshell, Boschung wrongly claims that '*grammaticus*' is defined as *habens grammaticam*, and that it signifies *per se* not only the quality but also the inherence of the quality in the substance (the inherence of *grammatica* in *homo*), and he thinks that this is why Anselm holds that '*grammaticus*' signifies *per se habere*, in addition to signifying *per se qualitas* (*grammatica*). This interpretation of the *habere* DG-issue will be challenged in subsection 2.9.

Let us now turn to a detailed exposition of the contents of *De Grammatico* with a view to responding to the four issues in section 3.

---

16 Boschung has interesting suggestions on this point, indicating Augustine as the source of inspiration: B 172-80, in particular, 178-80, and 247.

2 Exposition of the Contents of the *De Grammatico*

The dialogue begins by raising the initial DG-issue, whether *grammaticus* is a substance or a quality, and presenting arguments supporting the two alternatives. First, that *grammaticus* is a substance is proven by means of the following syllogism:

A1. (1) *Omnis grammaticus ⟨est⟩ homo*
(2) *Omnis homo ⟨est⟩ substantia*
(3) *⟨Omnis⟩ grammaticus ⟨est⟩ substantia* (DG I, 145, 14-15)

Second, that *grammaticus* is a quality is shown by the authority of the philosophers (DG I, 146, 1-3; *Categories* 4, 1b25-2a4).

As we have seen, the initial DG-issue concerns the *thing* signified by the term '*grammaticus*', but in the course of the dialogue Anselm introduces three further orders: the order of intellection (understanding or apprehending a certain intelligible content), the order of signification and definition and, finally, the order of predication as different from the order of intellection. These three orders display the semantic framework necessary to show Anselm's solution to the initial issue at the level of signification.

2.1. Esse grammatici non est esse hominis: *From the Order of Reality to the Orders of Intellection and Signification (chapters 1-5, 8)*

The orders of intellection and signification are introduced by discussing some sophistical syllogisms:

A2. (1) *Nullus grammaticus potest intelligi sine grammatica*
(2) *Omnis homo potest intelligi sine grammatica*
(3) *Nullus grammaticus est homo* (DG II, 146, 21-23)

A3. (1) *Omne animal potest intelligi praeter rationalitatem*
(2) *Nullus homo potest intelligi praeter rationalitatem*
(3) *Nullus homo ⟨est⟩ animal* (DG III, 147, 9-16)

A4. (1) *Omnis homo potest intelligi homo sine grammatica*
(2) *Nullus grammaticus potest intelligi grammaticus sine grammatica*
(DG IV, 148, 27-28)

To show that something is wrong in A2, Anselm presents A3, which is similar to A2[17] and whose conclusion is obviously false. The order of signification is then introduced: A3 is preceded by a question about what the name '*animal*' signifies, where the answer is *substantia animata sensibilis* (DG III, 147, 1-23.21). The definition of '*animal*' accounts for premise (1) in A3. Finally, in A4 Anselm presents the correct form of the premises of A2, showing that there is no middle term and, therefore, that nothing follows from them.[18]

By introducing the order of intellection, Anselm separates the *subject* (thing, a '*this*') and *what* is understood of that subject (and therefore *signified* by the corresponding sign). Premises (1) and (2) of A2 contain, respectively, the case in which the subject and what is understood are not separable (*grammaticus-grammatica*) and that in which they are separable (*homo-grammatica*). But note crucially here that, in the two corrected premises offered in A4, the subject (*homo, grammaticus*) appears reduplicated expressing with the second occurrence what is understood. Anselm introduces the modes of intellection (*modi intelligendi*), and in this way establishes that intellection is intellection of a *quidditas*, intellection of *what* something is, and not a mere intellection of *that* thing, of the *subject*.

This difference between *what is understood* and *the thing or entity that is so understood* is at the root of the difference between the two functions of language, expressive and indicative, which in turn correspond to the two different signification relations of linguistic entities, *significare* and *appellare*. Terms signify *what is understood*, and by signifying what is understood they also appellate (name) the *thing so understood*. As we shall see, even if in many cases terms signify and appellate the same entity ('*homo*' signifies a substance and appellates it), paronymous or denominative terms are characteristically those terms in which what is appellated by the word is not what is signified by it, but something different. Not until the later chapters in the dialogue will the complexity of the semantic relations that Anselm envisages be appreciated.

17 Since '*sine*' and '*praeter*' are different types of words and have different semantics, it is not clear how A3 is similar to A2. I think, however, that Anselm uses them in the same way, since premise (2) of A3 appears in a new syllogism in chapter 7 and is formulated as '*nullus homo potest intelligi sine rationalitate*' (DG VII, 151, 1-2; see also another analogous occurrence in DG VII, 151, 32-3). In fact, Boschung replaces '*praeter*' with '*sine*' in his presentation (B 317) and Henry translates '*sine*' and '*praeter*' as 'without', ignoring any semantic difference.

18 There are further sophistical syllogisms in *De Grammatico*, but I will pay attention only to a selection of them. For a more complete presentation, see Henry's and Boschung's books (see notes 2 and 3 above).

Let us return to the discussion of the syllogisms. Premises (1) and (2) in A4 allow the construction of a new syllogism in which the conclusion does follow from the premises. Since from (1) and (2) in A4, (1) and (2) in A5 follow, it is possible to conclude that *esse grammatici non est esse hominis*:

A5. (1) *Esse hominis non indiget grammatica*
(2) *Esse grammatici indiget grammatica*
(3) *Esse grammatici non est esse hominis* (DG V, 149, 19-28)

Anselm finishes chapter 5 by contrasting the conclusions of A2 and A5, and by stressing the difference between *grammaticum non esse hominem*, which does not follow given the sophistical character of A2, and *esse grammatici non est esse hominis*, which is true. This difference is important, since it allows the difference between predication and identity to be shown: from the difference between *esse grammatici* and *esse hominis*, it follows that *grammaticus non est idem quod homo* (they do not have the same definition), but not that *grammaticum non esse hominem* (DG V, 149, 30-33). This distinction is crucial because it grounds the difference between the two kinds of 'is' of predication presented previously: what a substance is because of its essence (definition) and what a thing is because of the qualities (or other accidents) that are present in it.

Now let us turn to the order of predication.

2.2. Dicitur in eo quod quale/dicitur in eo quod quid: *From the Order of Intellection and Signification to the Order of Predication (chapters 6, 10)*

The discussion of new syllogisms allows Anselm to introduce the order of predication:

A6. (1) *Omnis grammaticus dicitur in eo quod quale*
(2) *Nullus homo dicitur in eo quod quale*
(3) *Nullus homo ⟨est⟩ grammaticus* (DG VI, 150, 4-6)

A7. (1) *Omne rationale dicitur in eo quod quale*
(2) *Nullus homo dicitur in eo quod quale*
(3) *Nullus homo ⟨est⟩ rationalis* (DG VI, 150, 7-9)

A8. (1) *Omnis grammaticus dicitur grammaticus in eo quod quale*
(2) *Nullus homo dicitur homo in eo quod quale* (DG VI, 150, 13-14)

As in the case of intellection, in order to show that something is wrong in A6, Anselm presents A7, which is similar to A6, and whose conclusion is obviously false. In A8, Anselm presents the correct forms of the premises of A6, showing that there is no middle term and, therefore, nothing follows from them.

As in the previous case (A2-A5), Anselm also claims that from (1) and (2) in A8 it does not follow that *nullus grammaticus praedicatur de homine* (DG VI, 150, 14-17), but that *essentia hominis non est essentia grammatici*, and, again, that there is no identity between the two: *homo non est idem quod grammaticus* (DG VI, 150, 22-30).[19] As in the case of intellection, now in the two corrected premises offered in A8 the subject also ('*grammaticus*', '*homo*') appears reduplicated in the second occurrence expressing what is predicated of the subject. This allows the separation of the thing of which something is predicated (subject) and what is predicated of that thing (predicate).

The separation of what is predicated from that of which it is predicated allows us to predicate of a subject a predicate that expresses (signifies) something that is present in the subject, even if they do not have the same *esse* (*dicitur in eo quod quale*). Later, in chapter 10, Anselm presents another relation of predication that accounts for the case in which what is said of a subject is what that subject is (*dicitur in eo quod quid*). It is then possible to distinguish the case in which what is predicated is that a *quality* is present in the subject (*in eo quod quale*) from the case in which what is predicated is *what* the subject is (*in eo quod quid*). Different predications are thus made possible: *homo dicitur homo in eo quod quid, homo dicitur grammaticus in eo quod quale, grammaticus dicitur grammaticus in eo quod quale, grammaticus dicitur homo in eo quod quid*. We shall see later that this allows Anselm to answer the question about how *grammaticus* is predicated of the subjects of which it can be predicated (see subsection 2.4 and section 3).

Two considerations are important. First, if we look at '*grammaticus*' in the proposition '*grammaticus dicitur homo in eo quod quid*', we observe that it has an indicative function: to present (appellate) the subject of which *homo* is predicated; *homo* expresses what the thing appellated by *grammaticus* is. Second, it is important to avoid confusion between this distinction (*dicitur in eo quod quale/dicitur in eo quod quid*) and the distinction between accidental and essential predication. Essential predication is when the predicate

---

19 In chapter 6 of the *Monologion*, Anselm distinguishes between *essentia, esse* and *ens*, and compares the relations among them to the relations between *lux, lucere* and *lucens*, respectively. *Essentia* is that in virtue of which something (*ens*) is what it is (*esse*). In the context of *De Grammatico*, that in virtue of which *homo* is *homo* is different from that in virtue of which *grammaticus* is *grammaticus*. See Tetsuro Shimizu, 'Word and *Esse* in Anselm and Abelard', in *Anselm and Abelard: Investigations and Juxtapositions*, ed. G.E.M. Gasper and H. Kohlenberger (Toronto, 2006), 179-95.

expresses something that is necessary for the subject to be what it is, and to be so understood; it expresses something that is not separable from the subject. Accidental predication expresses something that, being present in a subject, is separable from it. Every predication *in eo quod quid* is essential predication, but not all predication in *eo quod quale* is accidental predication: *homo* and *knowledge* are essentially and *in eo quod quid* predicable of *Socrates* and *grammar*, respectively; *rationalis* is essentially and *in eo quod quale* predicable of *homo*; and *grammaticus* is accidentally and *in eo quod quale* predicable of *homo*. The distinction between essential and accidental predication will be elaborated later in terms of intellection, by recourse to quantification on *modi intelligendi* (see next subsection).

Finally, in chapters 5 and 6, Anselm defends the view that propositions can be interpreted in different ways. The proposition '*nullus grammaticus* ⟨*est*⟩ *homo*' is false when it is interpreted in the standard way. But the proposition can be interpreted in another way, as a negative identity statement (*grammaticus non est idem quod homo*), and in that sense the proposition is true (DG V, 149, 30-33). Similarly, the proposition '*nullus homo* ⟨*est*⟩ *grammaticus*' is false when it is interpreted in the standard way. But again the proposition can be interpreted in another way, as a negative identity statement (*homo non est idem quod grammaticus*), and in that sense the proposition is true (DG VI, 150, 23-24). The multiplicity of ways in which a proposition can be interpreted is important, since this, together with the multiplicity of modes of signification, will provide an Anselmian solution to the problem of the formation of nonsensical phrases in later chapters.

2.3. Aliquo modo intelligi/quolibet modo intelligi: *Quantification on* modi intelligendi (*chapter 7*)

In chapter 7, Anselm displays a new sophistical argument (A9):

A9. (1) *Nullus homo potest intelligi sine rationalitate*
(2) *Omnis lapis potest intelligi sine rationalitate*
(3) *Nullus lapis* ⟨*est*⟩ *homo* (DG VII, 151, 1-4)

Anselm intends to contrast (3) in A9 with (3) in A2 ('*nullus grammaticus est homo*'). As we have seen, although on a plausible standard interpretation this proposition is false, it can be true if the proposition is interpreted as stating that *esse grammatici* is not the same as *esse hominis*. But '*nullus lapis* ⟨*est*⟩ *homo*' is true in the two senses in which it can be interpreted. In order to show this, Anselm has recourse to quantification on *modi intelligendi*, as in (A10):

A10. (1) *Nullus homo potest aliquo modo intelligi sine rationalitate*
(2) *Omnis lapis quolibet modo potest intelligi sine rationalitate*
(3) *Nullus lapis aliquo modo est homo* (DG VII, 151, 32-152, 1)

Anselm contrasts '*nullus homo potest aliquo modo intelligi sine rationalitate*', which is true, with '*nullus grammaticus intelligi valet aliquo modo sine grammatica*' and '*omnis homo valet quolibet modo intelligi sine grammatica*', which are false. At this point, it is important to pay attention to the reasons that Anselm offers to account for the falsity of these two propositions: that *omnis qui grammaticus est, potest intelligi homo sine grammatica* and that *nullus homo potest intelligi grammaticus sine grammatica* (DG VII, 152, 3-6). By having recourse to quantification on *modi intelligendi*, Anselm can account for the difference between intellection of the essence of something (*homo—quolibet modo—rationalitate, lapis—nullo modo—rationalitate, grammaticus—quolibet modo—grammatica*), intellection of the substance or the subject, the '*this*' (*omnis qui grammaticus est*) and intellection of the accident (*homo—aliquo modo—grammatica*). The three intellections are present in *omnis qui grammaticus est* (substance), *potest intelligi homo* (essence) *sine grammatica* (accident).

2.4. Sunt in subiecto/non sunt in subiecto: *Different* modi essendi *and Different* res significata (*chapters 9, 10*)

In chapter 9, Anselm considers a further argument (A11) in which the Aristotelian distinction between things that are present in a subject and things that are not present in a subject (*Categories* 2, 1a20-b3) is used in order to derive *nullus grammaticus homo*.

A11. (1) *Aristoteles ostendit grammaticum eorum esse quae sunt in subiecto*
(2) *Nullus homo est in subiecto*
(3) *Nullus grammaticus* ⟨*est*⟩ *homo* (DG IX, 154, 1-2)

But *Aristoteles dicit et quendam hominem, et hominem et animal grammaticum* (DG IX, 154, 4-5; *Categories* 5, 3a1-6), which would not make sense if (3) in A11 followed from premises (1) and (2). The way to solve this difficulty is to have recourse to multiple signification: although in reality one thing cannot be a substance and a quality, a word can signify more than one thing, so that one of them can be a substance and the other a quality.

In this chapter, then, Anselm offers his reply to the initial DG-issue by making the separation between the order of language and the order of reality explicit, and making a complex relation between the linguistic entities and the things signified by them possible. In particular, '*grammaticus*' signifies *hominem* and *grammaticam* (DG IX, 154, 7-11), and that is why *grammaticus* is a substance and is not present in a subject *secundum hominem*, and *grammaticus* is a quality and is present in a subject *secundum grammaticam*.

Since *grammaticus* is a substance and is not present in a subject *secundum hominem*, *grammaticus* is a substance in every sense in which *homo* is a substance: it is a primary substance and a secondary substance. In reply to the first series of objections raised by a disciple aiming to show that *grammaticus* is not a substance because it is neither a primary substance (because *grammaticus dicitur de pluribus, quod primae non est*) nor a secondary substance (because *grammaticus nec est genus aut species nec dicitur in eo quod quid*), Anselm insists that, since *grammaticus* signifies *homo*, *grammaticus est homo* and, *secundum hominem*, *grammaticus* has all of the characteristics of primary and secondary substance (DG X, 155, 6-12).

Once the multiplicity of things signified by '*grammaticus*' is introduced in chapter 10, the central chapters of the dialogue are devoted to articulating what the relations between the word and the thing signified are. It is here that the difference between *significare* and *appellare* comes to light, even if it has been grounded on the multiplicity of modes of intellection (expressed by what the term signifies) of a thing (which is appellated). The term '*grammaticus*' signifies *grammatica* and appellates *homo*, and *usus loquendi* provides the criterion to establish which of the two *res significata* is appellated. This point will be dealt with later (subsection 2.5).

In addition to the problem of appellation, the problem of the signification of '*grammaticus*' gives rise to the question of its definition (subsection 2.6) and to the question of how appellation can take place, that is, how '*grammaticus*' can indicate or bring a substance into the discourse, if it signifies a quality. This gives rise to Anselm's notion of *significatio per aliud* (subsection 2.7).

2.5. Significare ut unum/significare non ut unum; significare per se/per aliud; significative/appellative: *Different* modi significandi (*chapters 11, 12*)

Since '*grammaticus*' has a twofold signification, speaking and understanding of language takes place according to these two significations.[20] Anselm then considers two other objections to the duality of things signified by '*grammaticus*'. The first stems from the fact that acceptance of such duality (that

20 DG XI, 155, 17-18: "A grammatico significari diversa, et secundum ea loquendum intelligendumque de grammatico."

'*grammaticus*' signifies *homo* and *grammatica*) allows for expressions such as '*utilis scientia est grammaticus*' and '*bene scit homo iste grammaticum*', but these expressions are not usually spoken. In other words, if '*grammaticus*' signifies a quality, then these two expressions should be accepted, but they are not used when speakers say things in the everyday use of language (*usus loquendi*) (DG XI, 156, 5-8). This objection and the way in which Anselm deals with it will be reviewed later, but now we will consider the second objection, which serves as the immediate motivation for the crucial semantic distinctions that Anselm employs.

The second objection arises by comparing the signification of '*homo*' and '*grammaticus*': if *grammaticus* is a substance and a quality because it signifies *homo* and *grammatica*, *homo* should also be a substance and a quality, since '*homo*' also signifies a multiplicity: the substance with the properties (*differentiis*) that *sunt in homine*, such as *sensibilitas* and *mortalitas* (DG XI, 156, 15-20).

Anselm introduces the opposition between *significare ut unum* and *significare non ut unum* to account for two different ways in which terms signify when they signify a multiplicity of things, and in particular to account for the different ways in which '*homo*' signifies a substance and its *differentia*, and '*grammaticus*' signifies *hominem* and *grammaticam* (DG XII, 156, 24-30). A term ('*homo*') signifies *ut unum* when it signifies *in the same manner* the various parts of the thing signified (*substantiam* and *differentias*). If this does not occur, if a term ('*grammaticus*') signifies *in different manners* the multiple things signified (*hominem* and *grammaticam*), it signifies *non ut unum*. Anselm explains why '*homo*' signifies *ut unum* in terms of the relation between the things signified, that is, between the *substantia* and its *differentiae: substantia* is the cause of the *differentiae* and they require and depend on it. And since these conditions are not satisfied in the case of *grammaticus*, '*grammaticus*' signifies *non ut unum*, because it signifies *grammatica* and *homo* in a different manner: *grammaticam per se et hominem per aliud significat* (DG XII, 157, 1-2).

It is crucial to note that the explanation of why a term signifies the multiple things signified by the term in the same manner or in different manners lies in the relation between those things: the things signified by '*homo*' (substance and *differentiae*) relate in a manner different from the way in which the multiple things signified by '*grammaticus*' (substance and quality) do. The term '*homo*', in signifying *per se homo*, also signifies *per se* and appellates those *differentiae* because the combination of the parts of *homo* results in an inseparable unity. As a result, '*homo*' is *significativum et appellativum substantiae* (DG XII, 156, 32-33). The things signified by '*grammaticus*', however, do not form an inseparable unity (*grammatica* does not require *homo*), and therefore each part is signified differently. At this point of the dialogue, Anselm associates the fact that a multiplicity of things signified does not result in a unity with the fact that two different manners of signification are involved. But, as we shall see later, this association is contingent. A term can also signify *non ut unum* a multiplicity of things that do not result in a unity, and this requires two signifying relations, but these relations do not have to differ in the manner they signify. This point will be re-examined in subsection 2.9.

At this point we can dwell on two issues on which previous interpretations of the dialogue can be revised. The first is Henry's formalization. In section 1, we saw that Adams and Boschung correctly criticized Henry's reading. I would now like to revise what I consider to be the root of Henry's confusion. Henry grounds his multi-layered interpretation of the copula (*est*) as a higher-order functor whose arguments are predicative expressions on a peculiar reading of the reasons given by Anselm to explain the inseparability of *homo* and its *differentiae*. In DG XII, 156, 27-29, Anselm says: *Substantia principalem locum tenet, quoniam est causa aliorum et habens ea, non ut indigens illis sed ut se indigentia.* Henry translates this sentence as follows: "substance is the chief feature, as the ground and possessor of the others, and this not in the sense that it is incomplete without them, but rather that they are incomplete without it."[21] In the text Anselm seems to be invoking the Aristotelian distinction between things that *sunt in subiecto* and those that *non sunt in subiecto*, and the ontological dependence of the former on the latter (they require the substance to exist). But the translation of '*indigens*' as 'incomplete' introduces the idea that *differentiae* are unsaturated and should be expressed by functional expressions. I think that this idea is alien to Anselm, as it is to Aristotle. The conflation between 'A *est in subiecto* B' and 'A is completed by B' is at the root of Henry's confusion.

The second issue concerns the definition of appellation. In DG 12, 157, 1-6, Anselm says: *Grammaticus vero non significat hominem et grammaticam ut unum, sed grammaticam per se et hominem per aliud significat. Et hoc nomen quamvis sit appellativum hominis, non tamen proprie dicitur eius significativum; et licet sit significativum grammaticae, non tamen est eius appellativum. Appellativum autem nomen cuiuslibet rei nunc dico, quo res ipsa usu loquendi appellatur.* Scholars have read and translated this text as if Anselm were offering a definition of appellation in the last sentence ('A' is appellative of x iff x is called [appellated] 'A' according to accepted usage in everyday language). It is not surprising that this reading has caused some perplexity. First, the definition appears to be circular, and, second, this reading does not fit Anselm's

21 Henry, *The* De Grammatico *of St. Anselm*, 64.

'*albus equus*' example, in which '*albus*' appellates *equus*, according to Anselm, since '*albus*' is not what horses are called in everyday language (see subsection 2.7 below).[22]

I do not think that the text presents any difficulty when it is properly read in its context. Anselm explains what '*grammaticus*' is significative and appellative of after he has claimed that '*homo*' is *significativum et appellativum substantiae* (DG XII, 156, 32-33). The sentence '*appellativum autem nomen cuiuslibet rei nunc dico, quo res ipsa usu loquendi appellatur*' must be read not as a definition, but as a criterion for establishing which of the two *res significata* by '*grammaticus*' is the one signified and which is the one appellated, and *usus loquendi* shows us that paronymous terms such as '*grammaticus*' are used in ordinary language to indicate a substance (*res ipsa*). And it is precisely because paronymous terms are appellative of what they are not significative of that *significatio per aliud* is necessary (subsection 2.7).

The first objection raised by expressions such as '*utilis scientia est grammaticus*' and '*bene scit homo iste grammaticum*' can now be addressed. Recall that the objection was that speakers do not use these expressions in the ordinary use of language. Anselm's reply is clear: speakers regularly use language to indicate things, and therefore the way of signifying that is involved is the appellative. As a result, it is no surprise that '*utilis scientia est grammaticus*' and '*bene scit homo iste grammaticum*' are not used in everyday language, because '*grammaticum*' appellates and signifies *per aliud homo*.

In previous parts of the dialogue (chapters 5 and 6), Anselm had already directed our attention to the fact that propositions can be interpreted in different ways. Expressions such as '*utilis scientia est grammaticus*' and '*bene scit homo iste grammaticum*' could be considered further examples of this phenomenon; they could be interpreted in two ways according to the two manners of signification of '*grammaticus*', and *usus loquendi* shows that speaking and understanding of language takes place according to the *appellative* manner of signification.

2.6. Grammaticus est sciens grammaticam: *Definition of* grammaticus (*chapter 13*)

Given that '*grammaticus*' signifies *homo* and *grammatica*, and it signifies them in different ways, defining (expressing what is signified by) '*grammaticus*' is difficult. According to Anselm, the definition of '*grammaticus*' is *sciens grammaticam*. Anselm argues for this definition by showing the difficulties of a definition that would include the two things that are signified by '*grammaticus*':

22 King, 'Anselm's Philosophy of Language,' n. 25.

homo sciens grammaticam. In particular, his arguments are offered to establish that *homo* is not included in the definition of '*grammaticus*'.

We will focus here on three of the arguments that Anselm offers.[23] The first is that, if the definition of '*grammaticus*' were *homo sciens grammaticam*, then *grammatica* would not be an accident of *homo*, but a substantial *differentia*, *homo* would be a *genus* and *grammaticus* would be a *species*.[24] But *grammatica* is an accident, since it is not part of the essence of *homo* and its absence does not entail the corruption of the subject (DG XIII, 157, 19-22).

Second, Anselm considers the hypothesis that there is a rational animal other than *homo* that knows grammar (*sciens grammaticam*). Since everyone who knows grammar is *grammaticus*, he concludes that there is *quidam non-homo grammaticus*, and therefore that the definition of '*grammaticus*' does not include *homo*. He then explains why *homo* appears to be included by appealing to the fact that *grammatica soli homini accidit* (DG XIII, 157, 30-158, 12). *Grammatica* is separable from *homo*, even if it always happens to be (contingently) combined with it.

The third argument is that, if the definition of '*grammaticus*' included *homo*, then it would give rise to *nugatio* when predicated together with *homo*, as happens, for example, in *Socrates est homo animal*.[25] Anselm presents this argument in the form of the infinite regress to which such predications would lead if *grammaticus* included *homo*, since '*grammaticus*' could be replaced in '*Socrates est homo grammaticus*' by '*homo sciens grammaticam*', resulting in '*Socrates est homo homo sciens grammaticam*', which in turn could be turned into '*Socrates est homo homo grammaticus*', and this into '*Socrates est homo homo homo sciens grammaticam*', and so on. But in the case of *grammaticus*, it is possible and adequate to predicate it as in *Socrates est homo grammaticus*.

Boschung has addressed the issue of the definition of '*grammaticus*' and defends the view that Anselm considered *habens grammaticam* a plausible and better definition of *grammaticus* than *sciens grammaticam*, given that in the last part of the dialogue Anselm claims that '*grammaticus*' signifies *habentem disciplinam* (DG XIX, 164, 24-25; B 97). Boschung speculates that Anselm switched to this definition at the end of the dialogue due to a desire to generalize to other paronyms ('*albus*' defined as *habens albedinem*). However, I

---

23 See Henry, *The* De Grammatico *of St. Anselm*, 16-17.

24 DG XIII, 157, 24-5: "Non est igitur grammatica accidens sed substantialis differentia, et est homo genus, et grammaticus species."

25 See Sten Ebbesen, 'The Present King of France Wears Hypothetical Shoes with Categorical Laces', in *Topics in Latin Philosophy from the 12th-14th Centuries. Collected Essays of Sten Ebbesen. Volume 2* (Farnham, 2009), 15-30 (originally published in *Medioevo* in 1981).

think that Anselm's first argument against the inclusion of *homo* in the definition of *grammaticus* blocks Boschung's reading, because *disciplinam* or *grammaticam* is not related to *habere* as a *substantialis differentia* relates to *genus*. In fact, as we shall see later (subsection 2.9), this is one of the reasons why Anselm, in chapter 20, denies that '*grammaticus*' signifies *ut unum habere* and *grammatica*.[26]

2.7. Significare per se/significare per aliud *Elaborated* (*chapters 14, 15*)

Since the definition of '*grammaticus*' is *sciens grammaticam* and it does not include *homo*, Anselm has to account for how a term can appellate something not included in its signification. This problem (*quomodo grammaticus non significativum eius quod aliquo modo significat, aut quomodo sit appellativum eius cuius significativum non est*; DG XIV, 160, 1-3) is the motivation for an elaboration of the distinction *significare per se/significare per aliud*, in which the difference lies in how terms present the thing signified.

A term ('*homo*', '*grammatica*') signifies *per se* the thing signified if the name on its own is able to present to the mind what it appellates. A term ('*grammaticus*') signifies *per aliud* the thing signified if the name alone is not sufficient to present to the mind what it appellates. Thus '*grammaticus*' signifies *homo per aliud*, because what '*grammaticus*' signifies *per se* does not suffice to present *homo* to the mind. Here Anselm opposes indicating or appellating by understanding the definition of a term to indicating or appellating by other means, such as, for example, some contextual knowledge that is provided by experience (*per visum*) or some knowledge that is provided by the repeated experience of an association of what is signified *per se* and what is appellated (*quia expertus sum*).

Anselm illustrates his view with the example of the white horse. The word '*albus*', on its own, presents the essence of this colour to the mind, but further knowledge is needed in order to determine that a horse is appellated. However, if a white horse and a black ox are seen together and we are asked to hit the white, the term 'white' ('*albus*') will present the horse to the mind, and therefore, in this context, white signifies *per aliud* and appellates the horse. Two considerations are important to grasp the scope of Anselm's view. First, in this particular case, the context of the utterance is necessary for appellation of the horse to occur, since it is *per visum* that the relevant knowledge is provided. Yet, the second, more important consideration concerns what kind of knowledge is needed: that whiteness is present in the horse: *Sed quoniam scio albedinem esse*

26 Furthermore, it is difficult to discern how recourse to *habere* would help to generalise the analysis to all the categories: how could, say, place be so analysed?

in equo, et hoc per aliud quam per nomen albi, velut per visum: intellecta albedine per hoc nomen, intelligo equum per hoc quod albedinem scio esse in equo, id est per aliud quam per nomen albi, quo tamen equus appellatur (DG XIV, 160, 32-161, 4). It is, therefore, the combination of a thing *non ut in subiecto* with what is *in subiecto* that grounds the appellative relation of paronyms.

As we have seen, Anselm also considers the case in which knowledge is provided by the repeated experience of an association of what is signified *per se* and what is appellated (*quia expertus sum*). His example is of a surface or body appellated by the term '*albus*' (DG XIV, 160, 12-13). And it is not difficult to imagine that this is also the case for '*grammaticus*', for which the apparent inclusion of *homo* in its definition is explained by the contingent fact that *grammatica soli homini accidit.*

Finally, Anselm defends a distinction between signification *substantialis* and signification *accidentalis* that corresponds to that between signification *per se* and *per aliud*: signification *substantialis* is what makes *voces* to be *significative*, and this is signification *per se*, and signification *accidentalis* is the signification that *voces* happen to have because of other reasons, that is, *per aliud* (DG XV, 161, 14-18).

2.8. *Aristotle's Intention in the* Categories *According to Anselm* (*chapter 16-18*)

Once Anselm has established that '*grammaticus*' signifies *per se grammaticam*, he questions whether this is a sufficient condition for *grammaticus* to be a quality. There are two reasons why he doubts it. First, the question 'what is *grammaticus*?' is not adequately answered by saying that it is a quality. Second, and more interestingly, there is a sense in which *homo solus*, that is, *sine grammatica*, is *grammaticus*. Although '*grammaticus*' appellates *homo* insofar as *grammatica* is present in it, that in which *grammatica* is present (*homo*) is different from what is present in it. *Homo solus* indeed est *habens grammaticam.* And since *grammaticus* appellates the substance, it appellates *homo solus*, that is, *sine grammatica* (DG XVI, 162, 3-12).

The chapter is important because the objection necessitates an explanation of the sense in which *grammaticus* is a quality in terms of what Aristotle says in that *Categories*, thus raising the *Categories* DG-issue. In addition, it introduces the idea that *grammaticus est habens grammaticam*, which makes Anselm confront the *habere* DG-issue in the last chapters of the dialogue (see subsection 2.9).

Anselm answers the objection by invoking Aristotle's *Categories: Cum vero dicitur quia grammaticus est qualitas: non recte nisi secundum tractatum Aristotelis De categoriis dicitur* (DG XVI, 162, 12-14). Aristotle's primary concern in the treatise was not about reality, but about language; his intention was neither to show what the things are nor to determine the things appellated by different *voces*, but the things *quarum significativae sint*, and indirectly to show *quid sint res* because *voces non significant nisi res* (DG XVII, 162, 23-26). Thus the reason why *grammaticus* is a quality is simply that the term '*grammaticus*' signifies a quality, but in signifying a quality the term shows what the thing signified is (DG XVII, 163, 7-8).

2.9. Grammaticus significat habere et qualitas: Significare ut unum/non ut unum *Revisited* (*chapters 19-21*)

Anselm ends the dialogue by addressing the *habere* DG-issue. He compares '*armatus*' and '*grammaticus*' in the sense that the two signify *having something* (*arma/grammatica*). But then, if *grammaticus* is a quality because it signifies having a quality, *armatus* should also be a substance since it signifies having a substance (*arma*). Similarly, if *armatus* is a having (*habere*) because it signifies *habens arma*, *grammaticus* should also be a having since it signifies *habens disciplinam*. Therefore, *armatus* belongs to the categories of having and substance, and *grammaticus* to the categories of quality and having.

Anselm's answer is similar to the response he gives to the question whether *grammaticus* is a substance and a quality. Anselm claims that the thing signified by '*grammaticus*' or the thing signified by '*albus*', like that signified by '*armatus*', can only belong to one category (DG XIX, 164,30-165,1), but insofar as the word can signify more than one thing it can belong to more than one category (*habere* and *qualitas*). In explaining his answer, Anselm makes use of the conceptual tools introduced previously, the distinction between *significare ut unum/significare non ut unum*. *Voces* that signify *non ut unum* can belong to different categories because they signify several things (DG XIX, 165, 5-7). '*Grammaticus*' and '*albus*' signify *non ut unum* a quality and a having (*grammatica et habere, albedo et habere*). But in this case, the difference between the two signifying relations is not a difference in the manner of signifying (*per se/per aliud*), since '*grammaticus*' and '*albus*' signify *per aliud* and appellate a substance.

In order for a term to signify *ut unum* a multiplicity of things signified, it is necessary that the combination of those parts results in an inseparable unity, and then, of course, the term signifies those parts *in the same manner*, since it signifies the unity. This was the case with '*homo*', which signifies substance and its *differentiae per se et ut unum*. If the combination of those parts does not result in such unity, then the term signifies *non ut unum* a multiplicity of things. The manner in which it signifies depends on whether the term by itself suffices for presenting to the mind the thing signified: '*grammaticus*' suffices for presenting *grammatica* to the mind, but not for presenting *homo*;

and '*grammaticus*' suffices for presenting *habere* because it signifies *habentem disciplinam* (DG XIX, 164, 25). In this way, Anselm manages to differentiate *grammaticus* not only from *homo*, but also from *grammatica*, since only '*grammaticus*', but not '*grammatica*', signifies *non ut unum* a quality and a having.

Why do the things signified by '*albus*' ('*grammaticus*') not constitute an inseparable unity? According to Anselm, there are three ways in which relations between things constitute such unities: composition between parts of the same category that results in a whole (animal results from body and soul), convenience between *genus* and *differentiae* that results in the *species*, and relation between the species and the collection of properties that results in the individual (*homo* and a collection of accidents result in Plato). In the case of *grammaticus* and *albus*, quality and having do not relate to each other resulting in a unity according to either of these ways, and therefore they do not signify them *ut unum* (DG XX, 166, 2-10).

One of the specific features of Boschung's interpretation is his analysis of the *habere* DG-issue. I agree with him that the fact that '*grammaticus*' signifies *per se* a quality and a having allows distinguishing '*grammaticus*' from '*grammatica*', but my interpretation of Anselm on this differs from his on a crucial point. Boschung thinks that this duality in Anselm's signification theory is due to the fact that '*grammaticus*' includes in its signification the inhering accident (the quality *grammatica*) and its inherence in a substance (where he thinks *habere* expresses such inherence); in his words: "... the denominative name signifies, on Anselm's view, the inhering quality without the substance inhered in, which leaves inherence and the quality as the *per se* significate" (B 280). But the way in which Anselm presents his view points in a different direction: *grammaticus* is compared with *armatus*, in that the former signifies *habere disciplinam* in the same sense as the second signifies *habere arma*. Having is one of the Aristotelian categories, and things belonging to this category (*armatus*, shod) are things that *sunt in subiecto*. In other words, in the *Categories*, *habere* is also an accident that inheres in a substance, and therefore it cannot signify inherence. What Boschung refers to as 'inherence' or 'participation' is the relation of being present in a subject that any category has with respect to substance, which is not present in a subject. But this is what is expressed by means of the copula '*est*' in predication, and not what is expressed by the fact that a word has a paronymous form.

My interpretation of the *habere* DG-issue can be verified by a number of facts. First, Anselm explicitly raises the question whether *grammaticus* can belong to more than one category: *Vellem ergo a te doceri utrum unum aliquid possit esse diversorum praedicamentorum* (DG XIX, 164, 28-29), and therefore he conceives of *habere* as one of the Aristotelian categories. Second, there is an assymmetry between *sciens grammaticam* and *habens grammaticam*. In the case of the former, *sciens* relates to *grammaticam* as genus to species (*grammatica* is a species of knowledge), thus giving rise to an inseparable unity. But *habens* does not relate to *grammaticam* in this way, as Anselm explicitly says when he says that '*grammaticus*' signifies *non ut unum grammaticam* and *habere*. This is crucial, because it shows that *habens grammaticam* is not properly speaking the definition of '*grammaticus*', and therefore that *habere* is not part of its signification in the sense defended by Boschung. Finally, Boschung's interpretation renders the comparison with *armatus* meaningless. Anselm's point is that '*armatus*' signifies *per se habens arma*, and thus it signifies *per se habere* and *arma*. But since *arma* is a substance, it does not make sense to think of *habere* as the relation of inherence, because substances do not inhere in other substances.

Anselm finishes his dialogue by bringing to light what is at the heart of the difference between *significare* and *appellare* and between *significare per se* and *significare per aliud*. To account for the signification of language, it is necessary to pay attention, on the one hand, to how real things are understood (*modi intellegendi*), and, on the other, to how the *esse* of those things is manifested through language. Every substance is many things according to the different things that are present in it. In understanding reality, *one* of those things is understood; terms signify what is so understood, but they serve to name the thing (substance) understood. Since *homo* is *grammaticus*, it can be understood as *grammaticus*. The term '*grammaticus*' signifies, then, what is understood of *homo* (*sciens grammaticam*), but it serves to name (appellate) *homo*.

3 Answers to the Four Issues

What is the answer to the initial issue (whether *grammaticus* is a substance or a quality)? In reality, *grammaticus* can be only *one thing*, and therefore the answer to the initial issue seems to require that it is either a substance or a quality, but not both. But since the name '*grammaticus*' can signify two different things, by signifying in different ways, there is no problem in defending the position that *grammaticus is* a substance and *is* also a quality.

To solve the central issue, the four questions encompassed in it must be answered. Question (a) concerned the signification of '*grammaticus*'. Anselm defends the view that '*grammaticus*' signifies two things, and that it signifies them *non ut unum*, but it signifies *per se* a quality (*grammatica*) and *per aliud* it is appellative of a substance (*homo*). The answer to question (b) (what does '*grammaticus*' express?) is *sciens grammaticam*, which is the definition of '*grammaticus*', and which does not include *homo*.

Question (c) (of what can *grammaticus* be predicated?) is answered, according to the authority of Aristotle, as follows: *grammaticus* can be predicated of the individual (*prima substantia*) (*Socrates est grammaticus*), and also of its *species* and *genus* (*homo est grammaticus* and *animal est grammaticum*). Finally, the answer to question (d) (how is *grammaticus* predicated of the subjects of which it can be predicated?) is that *grammaticus* is always predicated *in eo quod quale* (while *homo* is predicated *in eo quod quid*). Anselm has thus grounded such predications in the fact that '*grammaticus*' appellates *homo* (and that is why it can be predicated of *Socrates*, *homo* and *animal*) and it signifies *grammatica* (and that is why it is predicated *in eo quod quale*).

The third issue concerned the significance of the *Categories*, and Anselm claims that Aristotle was concerned directly with the signification *per se* of the words. Finally, he defends the view that *grammaticus* can belong to two categories, quality and having, because it signifies them *non ut unum*.

Regarding the theory of signification that Anselm defends in the dialogue, I think that the three distinctions between *significare ut unum/significare non ut unum, significare/appellare, significare per se/significare per aliud* are different since they respond to different issues and difficulties. In fact, attention to what different terms signify allows one to establish that those distinctions are separate. Non-paronymous terms signify *per se et ut unum et appellant* what they signify, even if there is some multiplicity in the thing signified: '*homo*' signifies *per se et ut unum et appellat* a substance with its *differentiae* (*homo, rationalitas*). In the case of paronyms, however, there is a multiplicity of things signified that are not signified in the same manner. If '*grammaticus*' and '*albus*' are compared, on the one hand, with '*homo*', then '*grammaticus*' signifies *non ut unum* a quality (*grammatica*) and a substance (*homo*), and it signifies *per se* that quality (*grammatica*) and it signifies *per aliud* and appellates that substance (*homo*); if we compare '*grammaticus*' with '*albus*', the difference is only in the way in which signification *per aliud* takes place: for the former, by means of knowledge acquired through regular experience; for the latter, it might sometimes require occasional experience provided by the context of the utterance.

In addition, '*grammaticus*' and '*albus*' can also be compared with '*grammatica*' and '*albedo*', and while the latter *only* signify a quality *per se*, '*grammaticus*' and '*albus*' signify *non ut unum* and *per se* a quality (*grammatica, albedo*) and a having (*habere*), and, in addition, as we have seen, they signify *per aliud et appellant* a substance (*homo* or whatever substance in which the quality is present). Finally, '*grammaticus*' signifies *per se et ut unum sciens grammaticam*, since this is its definition: *grammatica* relates to knowledge as species to genus, but the word '*grammaticus*' does appellate the subject in which such knowledge is present (*homo*).

Anselm's solution to the problem of paronymy lies in looking back to the things signified and making the complexity involved in such things explicit (combinations of things that are not present in something with things that are present in something), employing a theory of signification that encompasses in the complexity of the signification relation the complexity of the thing signified: '*grammaticus*' signifies *non ut unum* the thing signified (the combination of *homo* and *grammatica*); it signifies *per se* but *non ut unum grammaticam* and *habere*, and it signifies *per aliud* and appellates *homo*.

The initial DG-issue was a question about the *esse* of what is signified by a sign, but concealing the mediation of the sign and its signifying relation, and the multiple signification of that sign. Anselm shows that, to account for the signification of signs, it is necessary to pay attention, on the one hand, to how intellection of reality takes place, and, on the other, to how the *esse* of real things is manifested in language. Anselm realizes that a thing is necessarily 'many things', since many things are *in a subject*. Intellection is always of *one* of those things, and terms signify what is understood in each case, but they are used to name the thing that is so understood. Language manifests *esse*, and it does so through the mediation of intellection. But the conditions of language are different from the conditions of *esse* and different also from the conditions of intellection.

Aliquid amplius audire desiderat: Desire in Abelard's Theory of Incomplete and Non-Assertive Complete Sentences

Luisa Valente

In the last forty years researchers have paid considerable attention to Peter Abelard's theory of sentences.[1] In this article I would like to concentrate on a special aspect of this topic, i.e., the role played by the notion of desire[2] in

1 On Abelard's theory of the complete sentence see in particular Irène Rosier-Catach, 'Les discussions sur le signifié des propositions chez Abélard et ses contemporains', in *Medieval Theories on Assertive and Non-Assertive Language. Acts of the 14th European Symposium on Medieval Logic and Semantics*, ed. A. Maierù and L. Valente (Florence, 2004), 1-34. See also Klaus Jacobi, 'Die Semantik sprachlicher Ausdrücke, Ausdrucksfolgen und Aussagen in Abailards Kommentar zu *Peri Hermeneias*', *Medioevo* 7 (1981), 41-89; Klaus Jacobi, Christian Strube, and Peter King, 'From *intellectus verus/falsus* to the *dictum propositionis*: The Semantics of Peter Abelard and his Circle', *Vivarium* 34 (1996), 15-40; Kevin Guilfoy, 'Peter Abelard's Two Theories of the Proposition', in *Medieval Theories*, 36-57; John Marenbon, '*Dicta*, Assertion and Speech Acts: Abelard and some Modern Interpreters', in *Medieval Theories*, 59-80; Martin Lenz, 'Peculiar Perfection: Peter Abelard on Propositional Attitudes', *Journal of the History of Philosophy* 43 (2005), 377-86; idem, 'Are Thoughts and Sentences Compositional? A Controversy between Abelard and a Pupil of Alberic on the Reconciliation of Ancient Theses on Mind and Language', *Vivarium* 45 (2007), 169-88; Christopher Martin, '*De Interpretatione* 5-8: Aristotle, Boethius, and Abaelard on Propositionality', in *Methods and Methodologies: Aristotelian Logic East and West, 500-1500*, ed. M. Cameron and J. Marenbon (Leiden, 2011), 207-28. For more in general on the medieval analysis of the semantics of propositions (in particular within logic and theology), see Gabriel Nuchelmans, *Theories of the Proposition. Ancient and Medieval Conceptions of the Bearers of Truth and Falsity* (Amsterdam, 1973); Irène Rosier-Catach, *La parole comme acte. Sur la grammaire et la sémantique au XIIIe siècle* (Paris, 1994); eadem, 'Speech Acts and Intentional Meaning in the Medieval Philosophy of Language', *Bulletin de Philosophie Médiévale* 52 (2010), 55-80; Costantino Marmo, 'Una semantica del verbo nella grammatica e nella teologia tra XII e XIII secolo', in *Medieval Theories*, 185-206; Christoph Kann, 'Assertive and non-Assertive Sentences. Classifications of the *oratio perfecta* in the Thirteenth Century', in *Medieval Theories*, 245-57; Fabrizio Amerini, '*Tommaso d'Aquino, il* desiderium *e la logica*', in *Il desiderio nel Medioevo. Atti del convegno Il desiderio nel pensiero medievale*, ed. A. Palazzo (Rome, 2014), 207-22.

2 According to the Stoics desire (*epithumia*) is one of the four fundamental passions or movements of the human soul, the others being fear, pleasure and pain. Latin medieval thinkers had access to this classification through Cicero, who, in his *Tusculanae Disputationes* (e.g., 4,11,22; 3,11,25; 4,6,11; 4,7,14), lists *libido* and *laetitia, metus* and *aegritudo* as the four *pertur-*

 | DOI 10.1163/9789004324275_006

Abelard's descriptions of incomplete sentences (*imperfectae orationes*) and of non-assertive complete sentences (*non enuntiativae orationes*).[3] Incomplete and non-assertive sentences are treated in Abelard's *Dialectica* (ca. 1104-1116) as well as in his *Commentary on Perihermeneias* (part of the collection of commentaries usually called *Logica Ingredientibus*: 1118-1120).[4] In both texts Abelard's starting points are Aristotle's *De interpretatione* and the two Boethian

---

bationes or *affectiones animi*. See Alessandro Garcea, 'Le passioni presso gli antichi: un percorso attraverso le *Tusculanae Disputationes* di Cicerone', in *Passioni, emozioni, affetti*, ed. C. Bazzanella and P. Kobau (Milan, 2002), 1-18. On emotions in Abelard, see Simo Knuuttila, *Emotions in Ancient and Medieval World* (Oxford, 2006), 180-1 and 206-9. On the central function of love in Abelard's thought as well as in the thought of Heloise, see Étienne Gilson, *Héloïse et Abélard* (Paris, 1938; second edition, 1948); Richard E. Weingart, *The Logic of Divine Love. A Critical Analysis of the Soteriology of Peter Abelard* (Oxford, 1970); Matthias Perkams, *Liebe als Zentralbegriff der Ethik nach Peter Abaelard* (Münster, 2001); see also Silvana Vecchio, 'Il piacere da Abelardo a Tommaso', in *Piacere e dolore. Materiali per una storia delle passioni nel medioevo*, ed. S. Vecchio and C. Casagrande (Florence, 2009), 66-86: 67-71. On the role of desire in Abelard's anthropology and theology, see Luisa Valente, 'Il desiderio di filosofia nel pensiero filosofico e teologico di Pietro Abelardo', in *Il desiderio nel Medioevo*, 185-206.

3 'Sentence' is not a completely satisfactory translation for *oratio* and *logos* since—as will be clear in the following pages—the term *oratio* is sometimes also used by Abelard to refer to a combination of verbal expressions that is not a sentence in the usual meaning of this term, i.e., as a composition of (at least) a subject term and a predicate term. If we take this into account, sentences are just a subset of *orationes*: I am grateful to an anonymous reviewer for calling my attention to this point (and in general for her/his attentive reading and remarks). To be more precise, *oratio* should therefore be translated by 'phrase' or 'expression', as suggested by Christopher Martin, '*De Interpretatione* 5-8'; idem, 'A Note on the Attribution of the Literal Glosses in Paris, BnF, lat. 13368 to Peter Abelard', in *Arts du langage et théologie aux confins des XIe et XIIe siècle*, ed. I. Rosier-Catach (Turnhout, 2011), 606-46: 624-6; idem, '"What An Ugly Child": Abelard on Translation, Figurative Language, and Logic', *Vivarium* 49 (2011), 26-49. Nevertheless, I prefer to use mainly 'sentence', since it is common in the secondary literature and in most cases it makes acceptable sense, while both 'phrase' and 'expression' risk being too generic and ambiguous.

4 The *Dialectica* has long been considered a late work of Abelard, but a dating at least before 1121 has been proposed by Constant J. Mews, 'On Dating the Works of Peter Abelard', *AHDLMA* 52 (1985), 73-134, reprinted in idem, *Abelard and His Legacy* (Aldershot, 2001), and is now generally accepted. On this topic see John Marenbon, *The Philosophy of Peter Abelard* (Cambridge, 1997), 40-3; idem, '*Dicta*, Assertion and Speech Acts', 59; idem, 'Logic at the Turn of Twelfth Century: a Synthesis', in *Arts du langage et théologie aux confins des XIe et XIIe siècle*, ed. Rosier-Catach, 181-217: 200; Anne Grondeux and Irène Rosier-Catach, 'Les *Glosulae super Priscianum* et leur tradition', in *Arts du langage et théologie aux confins des XIe et XIIe siècle*, 107-79: 154. For the dating of Abelard's *Commentary on Perihermeneias*, see Marenbon, *The Philosophy of Peter Abelard*, 46.

commentaries on it. Nevertheless, as Irène Rosier-Catach has shown in detail,[5] Abelard develops his theories concerning sentences using input that stems from the tradition of grammar (Priscian and his medieval commentators) and from Augustine. One of the peculiarities of Abelard's analysis of incomplete and non-assertive sentences is his use of the notion of desire: in both *Dialectica* and *Glosses on Peri hermeneias* the terms *desiderium* and *desiderare* move to the foreground side by side with other related terms, more common in the logical and grammatical tradition, like *optatio* and *optare, expectatio* and *expectare, suspensio* and *suspendi.* In this article I will try to show how Abelard applies the notion of desire in this context. But first of all we should consider how Aristotle and Boethius treat the different classes of non-enunctiative sentences.

1 Complete and Incomplete, Assertive and Non-Assertive Sentences in Aristotle's *De interpretatione* and Boethius' Commentaries

At the only point in *De interpretatione* where Aristotle mentions non-assertive sentences, he just mentions in passing prayer (*deprecatio*) as an example of such sentences. Aristotle states that all kinds of sentences express their meaning according to institution (*secundum placitum*) and while assertive sentences (*enuntiativae orationes*) are either true or false, non-assertive sentences (*non enuntiativae orationes*) are neither true nor false. Therefore, non-assertive sentences do not pertain to the domain covered by *De interpretatione* and must be left to the consideration of the poet or of the rhetorician:

> Est autem oratio omnis quidem significativa [...] secundum placitum; enuntiativa vero non omnis, sed in qua verum vel falsum inest; non autem in omnibus, ut deprecatio oratio quidem est, sed neque vera neque falsa. Et ceterae quidem relinquantur (rhetoricae enim vel poeticae

5 Irène Rosier-Catach, 'Abélard et les grammairiens, sur la définition du verbe et la notion d'inhérence', in *La tradition vive, sur la définition des textes en l'honneur de Louis Holtz*, ed. P. Larded (Turnhout, 2003), 143-59; eadem, 'Priscien, Boèce, les *Glosulae in Priscianum*, Abélard: les enjeux des discussions autour de la notion de consignification', *Histoire, Épistémologie, Langage* 25 (2003), 55-84; eadem, 'Abélard et les grammairiens, sur le verbe substantif et la prédication', *Vivarium* 41 (2003), 175-248; eadem, 'Les discussions sur le signifié des propositions chez Abélard et ses contemporains'; Grondeux – Rosier-Catach, 'Les *Glosulae super Prisicanum* et leur tradition'.

> convenientior consideratio est; enuntiativa vero praesentis considerationis est).[6]

As we can see, Aristotle does not show any particular interest in non-assertive sentences, and in any case, referring to them, he does not use any term concerning the realm of desire nor of other emotions or affections of the soul.

Boethius says something more about non-assertive sentences. In the introduction to his first commentary on *De interpretatione*, he first of all defines assertion (*enuntiatio*) as the kind of sentence that says what is true or what is false. The assertive sentence (*enuntiativa oratio*), writes Boethius, is a species of the genus 'sentence' (*oratio*), while the sentence is in turn a species of the genus 'interpretation' (*interpretatio*). By *interpretatio* Boethius means something like 'meaningful verbal expression', and as a larger genus it entails isolated nouns and verbs, as well as sentences. As an example of a non-assertive sentence, Boethius employs the imperative sentence "Give me the book!" ("Da mihi codicem!"). One should not be surprised, says Boethius, that in Aristotle's *De interpretatione*, despite the title, we find only assertive sentences. Aristotle in fact used the name of the genus (*interpretatio*) in order to refer to just one subspecies of it, i.e., assertion (*simplex enuntiativa oratio*) and its parts (nouns and verbs):

> interpretatio namque est nomen et verbum, interpretatio etiam est huiusmodi oratio: 'omnis homo animal est'. sed in hac verum falsumque auditor intellegit. haec enim oratio quae dicit 'omnis homo animal est' vera vel falsa est. interpretatio quoque est etiam huiusmodi oratio: 'da mihi codicem', in qua verum falsumque nullus inveniat. etenim 'da mihi codicem' neque verum esse poterit neque falsum. quocirca quoniam de his solis orationibus in quibus verum falsumque reperitur, quas enuntiationes vel propositiones vocamus, quae interpretationes sunt, disputaturus est quoniamque de nominibus illis verbisque dicendum est, quid sint quamque vim in significatione retineant, recte librum de interpretatione signavit. nec hoc nos turbet, quod sunt quaedam interpretationes, de quibus in hoc libro non tractet. tamquam enim si quis de homine disputans titulum operis de animali posuisset, quamquam non de omni animali, tamen quoniam de aliquo disputaturus esset, recte de animali libro nomen imponeret: ita nunc licet non de omni interpretatione pertractet,

6 Aristoteles, *De interpretatione* 17a1-5, tr. Boethii, ed. L. Minio-Paluello (Bruges-Paris, 1965) (AL II), 8,6-12. On Aristotle's and Boethius' theories of assertive sentences compared with that of Peter Abelard, see Martin, '*De Interpretatione* 5-8'.

tamen quoniam de una quae est enuntiatio et de nominibus et verbis, quae interpretationes simplices sunt, dicendum erat, a communi et generali vocabulum libri de interpretatione conposuit. est autem intentio de simplici enuntiativa oratione disserere.[7]

A little bit further on, while commenting on the first lines of Aristotle's treatise, Boethius divides the genus 'sentence' (*oratio*) into its five differences (*differentiae*), i.e., prayer (*deprecativa oratio*), imperative, interrogative, vocative, and assertive sentences:

> In principio, inquit, huius sermonis, qui de enuntiatione instituitur, constituere id est definire oportet, quid nomen sit, quid verbum. haec enim (ut dictum est) omnem coniungere orationem valent. quae oratio aliarum genus est orationum. sunt autem principales quinque orationum differentiae. est autem prima oratio 'deprecativa', ut 'Iuppiter omnipotens, precibus si flecteris ullis'; secunda 'imperativa' ut 'Suggere tela mihi'; tertia 'interrogativa' ut 'Quo te, Moeri, pedes?' quarta 'vocativa' ut 'Huc ades, o Meliboee!' quinta 'enuntiativa', in qua verum inesse falsumque perspicitur. huius autem duae sunt species, una adfirmatio, altera negatio. adfirmatio est ut 'homo animal est', negatio ut 'homo animal non est'.[8]

Later, commenting on the passage we have seen before where Aristotle refers in passing to prayer (*deprecatio*), Boethius mentions the affections of the soul (*adfectus*) in the context of a list of types of non-assertive sentences. Nevertheless, Boethius maintains Aristotle's exclusive focus on assertive sentences as those sentences that state truth or falsity. Boethius in fact remarks that Aristotle mentioned prayer not so much because he was interested in it but rather because he clearly wanted to focus just on enunciative sentences. The other kinds of sentences, says Boethius, are left to the poets and the orators, who use them in order to imitate or arouse or elicit emotions ("ad imitandos vel ad movendos adfectus"). Philosophers, on the contrary, have to consider just truth and falsity; therefore they have to consider just assertive sentences. The list of the non-assertive kinds of sentences given by Boethius in this passage has prayer (*deprecativa oratio*), optative sentences (*optativa oratio*), vocative, and imperative sentences:

---

7 Boethius, *Commentarii in Librum Aristotelis Peri ermeneias*, prima editio, ed. C. Meiser (Leipzig, 1877), 33,7-34,3. Cf. Rosier-Catach, 'Priscien, Boèce, les *Glosulae in Priscianum*, Abélard', 62-3.

8 Boethius, *Commentarii in Librum Aristotelis Peri ermeneias*, prima editio, 35,7-21.

> "Enuntiativa vero non omnis, sed illa in qua verum vel falsum inest, non autem in omnibus, ut deprecatio oratio quidem est, sed neque vera, neque falsa." Orationis (ut supra iam diximus) multae sunt species. est enim oratio prima optativa, ut 'Utinam tibi istam mentem di inmortales duint!' secunda vocativa, ut 'Heus tu', tertia imperativa, ut 'Cape, da hoc Dorcio', quarta deprecativa, ut 'Iuppiter omnipotens' et reliqua, quinta enuntiativa, ut 'dies est, dies non est'. sed in hac sola specie orationis veritas et falsitas inest, in illis vero ceteris minime. volens autem Aristoteles ostendere multas esse orationes et non omnem orationem esse enuntiativam hoc addidit: "deprecatio oratio quidem est, sed neque vera neque falsa." etenim deprecatio in orationis speciebus ponitur, sed nulla in ea veritatis natura falsitatisque cognoscitur. "Et ceterae quidem relinquantur: rhetoricae enim vel poeticae convenientior consideratio est; enuntiativa vero praesentis est speculationis." Deprecativam, inquit, et optativam et vocativam atque imperativam poetis atque oratoribus relinquamus. illis enim vel ad imitandos[9] vel ad movendos adfectus ceterae orationis species adsumuntur. nos vero philosophi, quibus veritatis et falsitatis discretio curae est, de illa sola oratione tractamus in qua utrumlibet horum possit agnosci. in enuntiatione vero aut veritas inest aut falsitas. quocirca nos quoque de enuntiatione tractemus.[10]

Boethius' analysis becomes richer in his second commentary on *De interpretatione*. In the introductory section, the Roman philosopher briefly describes the difference between complete and incomplete sentences, and this description is particularly relevant from our point of view. In fact, Boethius here defines incomplete sentences as those that leave the soul of the listener in a psychological condition of expectation and doubt: "auditoris animus aliquid plenius/ ultra expectat audire," "intellectus pendet ac titubat." Even if Boethius does not mention desire, he takes a step in the direction of involving the addressee's emotions in the description of not-yet-complete sentences. Anyway, Boethius does not insist on this point and he quickly switches to complete sentences. He gives one example for each type of complete sentences (prayer [*deprecativa oratio*], imperative, interrogative, vocative, and assertive sentences), most of the examples being extracted from Virgil's *Aeneid*, and eventually he follows Aristotle's intention of considering just the simple assertive sentence (*enuntiatio*) and its elements (nouns and verbs):

---

9 *Mss.* mitigandos, inuitandos, inmutandos. PL immittendos.

10 Boethius, *Commentarii in Librum Aristotelis Peri ermeneias*, prima editio, 70,24-72,2.

> orationum vero aliae sunt perfectae, aliae inperfectae. perfectae sunt ex quibus plene id quod dicitur valet intellegi, inperfectae in quibus aliquid adhuc plenius animus exspectat audire, ut est 'Socrates cum Platone'. nullo enim addito orationis intellectus pendet ac titubat et auditor aliquid ultra exspectat audire. perfectarum vero orationum partes quinque sunt: deprecativa ut 'Iuppiter omnipotens, precibus si flecteris ullis, Da deinde auxilium, pater, atque haec omina firma', imperativa ut 'Vade age, nate, voca zephyros et labere pennis', interrogativa ut 'Dic mihi, Damoeta, cuium pecus an Meliboei?' vocativa ⟨ut⟩ 'O pater, o hominum rerumque aeterna potestas', enuntiativa, in qua veritas vel falsitas invenitur, ut 'Principio arboribus varia est natura serendis'. huius autem duae partes sunt. est namque et simplex oratio enuntiativa et conposita. simplex ut 'dies est, lucet'; conposita ut 'si dies est, lux est'. in hoc igitur libro Aristoteles de enuntiativa simplici oratione disputat et de eius elementis, nomine scilicet atque verbo.[11]

Later, commenting on the *De interpretatione*'s section on the sentence (*oratio*), Boethius defines first of all complete sentences as those that transmit a complete semantic unity of information ("complent expediuntque sententiam") and incomplete as those that do not ("sententiam non expedit"); then he gives another list of the different kinds of complete sentences that is quite similar to the preceding one (the examples are different, although they also come from Virgil); and finally he makes an interesting remark about the fact that some people say that there may be in fact many more than five species of complete sentences. In any case, Boethius writes, this does not interest philosophers, who have to investigate just assertive sentences:

> Species quidem orationis multae sunt, sed eas varie partiuntur. at vero Peripatetici quinque partibus omnes species orationis ac membra distribuunt. orationis autem species dicimus perfectae, non eius quae imperfecta est. perfectas autem voco eas quae complent expediuntque sententiam. et sit nobis hoc modo divisio: sit oratio genus: orationis aliud est imperfectum, quod sententiam non expedit, ut si dicam 'Plato in lycio', aliud vero perfectum. perfectae autem orationis alia est deprecativa, ut 'Adsit laetitiae Bacchus dator'; alia imperativa, ut 'Accipe daque fidem'; alia interrogativa, ut 'Quo te, Moeri, pedes? an quo via ducit?' alia vocativa, ut 'O qui res hominumque deumque Aeternis regis imperiis';

11 Boethius, *Commentarii in Librum Aristotelis Peri ermeneias*, secunda editio, ed. C. Meiser (Leipzig, 1880), 8,30-9,20.

> alia enuntiativa, ut 'dies est' et 'dies non est'. in hac sola, quae est enuntiativa, veri falsive natura perspicitur. in ceteris enim neque veritas neque falsitas invenitur. et multi quidem plures species esse dicunt perfectae orationis, alii autem innumeras earum differentias produnt, sed nihil ad nos. cunctae enim species orationis aut oratoribus adcommodatae sunt aut poetis, sola enuntiativa philosophis.[12]

Another list of kinds of complete sentences, without a particular analysis of the different types, can be found in Boethius' *De syllogismo categorico*, where the author nevertheless indirectly affirms that there may be more than five kinds of complete sentences, since he writes that the division in five types is 'the shortest one' (*angustissima*):

> Sunt uero species orationis in angustissima diuisione quinque. Interrogatiua [...] Imperatiua [...] Optatiua uel deprecatiua [...] Vocativa [...] Enuntiatiua [...] Enuntiatiua uero sola aut uerum aut falsum continet.[13]

Even if Boethius refers to the listener's state of mind (*expectat, titubat*) in his descriptions of incomplete sentences, we do not find a particular interest in non-assertive language nor in the role of emotions in the linguistic phenomena in Aristotle's or Boethius' reflections on these topics. If we now move to read Abelard's treatments of sentences, we find a quite different situation.

2 The Distinction Between Complete and Incomplete Sentences in Abelard's *Dialectica*

In the chapter of Peter Abelard's *Dialectica* concerning the difference between complete and incomplete sentences, the notion of desire plays an important role from two points of view. On the one hand, Abelard writes that incomplete sentences produce in the listener's soul a 'desire' for more information. On the other, Abelard considers desire as one of the different 'affects of the mind' (*affectus animi*) according to which the speaker can 'show' (*demonstrare*) or

12 Boethius, *Commentarii in Librum Aristotelis Peri ermeneias*, secunda editio, 95,8-96,1.

13 Boethius, *De syllogismo categorico*, PL 64, 797B-C. Similar dry divisions of the types of complete sentences occur in the subsequent logic tradition, especially in treatises of the 11th and 12th centuries. Cf. *Ars Emmerana*, in L.M. de Rijk, *Logica Modernorum* II-2 (Assen, 1967), 151,28-9; *Dialectica Monacensis*, ivi, 467,25-8.

'propose' (*proponere*) an identical semantic content, constituting different kinds of complete sentences.

When Abelard explains how he interprets the notions of completeness or incompleteness of sentences (*orationum perfectio* vs *imperfectio*), he states that he means by complete sentence (*perfecta oratio*) a grammatically correct sequence of verbal signs that also 'show' a complete sense (*perfecta sensus demonstratio*). Therefore, a complete sentence, writes Abelard, is something similar to what the grammarian Priscian calls *constructio*.[14] As has been remarked,[15] Abelard points here to the two levels involved in the completeness of sentences: the grammatical and the semantic one. Correspondingly, an incomplete sentence is a sentence that can be grammatically correct, but does not produce a complete sense in the intellect of the listener. A non-complete sentence like 'running man', says Abelard, is grammatically correct (there is a *competens substantiui et adiectiui constructio*), but it leaves the soul of the listener unsatisfied and desiring to hear something more ("aliquid amplius audire desiderat") in order to reach 'the completeness of the sense' ("ut ad perfectionem sensus perveniat"). The listener may, for example, be expecting to know whether that man who runs is here, or whether he is doing something else: therefore, the listener is 'waiting for' and 'desiring' the verb 'is' or another verb that could be adequate in the given context. The verb, adds Abelard, is in fact the key to the semantic completeness of sentences. This is why the different complete sentences are classified and denominated as enunciative, imperative etc., according to the (moods of the) verbs that they entail:

> Orationum autem hae quidem 'perfectae' sunt, illae uero 'imperfectae'. Perfectas autem illas dico quas Priscianus 'constructiones' appellat, quarum uidelicet et partium recta est ordinatio et perfecta sensus demon-

---

14 In fact, Priscianus says that we have a complete sentence (*perfecta oratio*) when somebody understands (*comprehensio*) a well-ordered connection of words (*constructio* or *ordinatio*). See Priscianus, *Institutiones grammaticae*, ed. M. Hertz, 2 vol. (Leipzig, 1855-1888; reprint Hildesheim-New York, 1981), XVII, II, 108,5-10: "In supra dictis igitur de singulis vocibus dictionum, ut poscebat earum ratio, tractavimus; nunc autem dicemus de ordinatione earum, quae solet fieri ad constructionem orationis perfectae, quam admodum necessariam ad auctorum expositionem omnium diligentissime debemus inquirere, quod, quemadmodum literae apte coeuntes faciunt syllabas et syllabae dictiones, sic et dictiones orationem"; 108,23-109,3: "est enim oratio comprehensio dictionum aptissime ordinatarum, quomodo syllaba comprehensio literarum aptissime coniunctarum; et quomodo ex syllabarum coniunctione dictio, sic etiam ex dictionum coniunctione perfecta oratio constat."

15 See Rosier-Catach, 'Les discussions sur le signifié des propositions', 5-9.

> stratio, ut: '*homo currit*'. Imperfecta autem est quae in dispositione dictionum competenti imperfectum sensum demonstrat, ut: '*homo currens*'. Competens enim est substantivi et adiectivi constructio, cum ad eumdem casum, ad idem genus et eumdem numerum copulantur. Sed nondum in eis completa est sensus perfectio. Adhuc enim praemissa oratione prolata *suspensus audientis animus aliquid amplius audire desiderat, ut ad perfectionem sensus perveniat,* ueluti '*est*', aut aliquod aliud competens verbum. Praeter verbum namque nulla est sensus perfectio. Unde et omnes fere species perfectarum orationum ex verbis suis nominantur, ut *enuntiativa, imperativa* et aliae, quas in divisione perfectae orationis apponemus.[16]

Abelard goes on to explain that the semantic completeness of the sense in a sentence depends on the verb, since it is only through a conjugated verb that, by a sentence, the speaker 'demonstrates, according to the different affects of his soul' the inherence of something in something else. Thus 'demonstrating' or 'proposing' the inherence of something in something else according to one affect of the speaker's soul is, according to Abelard's *Dialectica*, what produces the completeness of the sense of a sentence.[17] Here the second sense of desire mentioned above is taken into account: desire is one of the affections of the soul according to which a speaker can 'propose' or 'demonstrate' the inherence of something in something else by using a complete sentence. Abelard gives two examples, that of injunction and that of desire. If we say "Come to me!" or "Oh would you come to me . . . ," we 'propose' in both cases the inherence of the action of coming in the person we are talking to.[18] Nevertheless, in the first instance we propose this inherence in the mood of injunction and in the second in the mood of desire:

> Perfectio itaque sensus maxime pendere dinoscitur in verbis, quibus solis alicuius ad aliquid inhaerentia[m] secundum varios affectus animi demonstratur; praeter quam quidem inhaerentiam orationis perfectio non subsistit. Cum enim dico: 'ueni ad me' vel 'utinam venires ad me', quodammodo inhaerentiam ueniendi ad me propono secundum iussum

16 Abelard, *Dialectica*, ed. L.M. de Rijk (Assen, 1970), 148,19-32 (my italics).

17 Abelard's theory according to which a complete sentence is a demonstration of the inherence of something in something else develops ideas contained in the *Glosulae super Priscianum*. See Rosier-Catach, 'Abélard et les grammairiens', 147-58.

18 Lenz, 'Peculiar perfection', 384, understands that in this text the inherence of the action of coming concerns the speaker, but in my opinion this is a mistake.

> meum uel desiderium meum, in eo scilicet quod iubeo illi ut uenire ei cohaereat, vel desidero, id est ut ipse ueniat.[19]

We have the mood of desire—*optativus*—when we 'propose' an inherence (*inhaerentia* or *cohaerentia*) of an action in one subject or more, and we intend to communicate, instead of the effective taking place of this inherence, the fact that we (the speaker[s]) *would like it to be the case.* Peter Abelard devotes particular attention to the desiderative mood, remarking that the desiderative mood is very close to the indicative mood, the mood of assertive sentences, and therefore also of inferences (*consequentiae*). It often happens, writes Peter Abelard, that we use the desiderative mood instead of the indicative mood in conclusive inferences, as when we say, "If you were here you would see him." This composite proposition may be considered a consequence as much as the parallel proposition with the indicative mood, "If you have been here, you have seen it":

> Unde et saepe in consequentiis verba optativi modi vim enuntiativi tenent, veluti cum ita propono:
> *'Si fuisses hic, vidisses eum'*:
> tam bene enim haec consequentia dici potest sicut ea quae ex enuntiationibus iungitur hoc modo:
> *'Si fuisti hic, vidisti eum'*:
> Unde et cum quidam de illa assumunt ac concludunt, partes eius in enuntiationes resolvunt, sic:
> *'Sed fuisti hic; quare uidisti eum'*
> uel ita: *'Sed non vidisti; quare non fuisti'*.[20]

If we compare these quotations from Abelard's *Dialectica* with the corresponding texts from Aristotle's *De interpretatione* and from Boethius' commentaries on it (see above), we can see in which directions Abelard deepens and develops their analysis. We have seen that Aristotle and Boethius, while describing the difference between *perfecta* and *imperfecta oratio*, hardly mention

19 Abelard, *Dialectica*, ed. De Rijk, 149,20-6. The idea according to which complete sentences are those that satisfy the expectation and desire of the listeners in my opinion is not refuted in the *Logica Ingredientibus*, as asserted by Lenz, 'Peculiar perfection', 384-5, and idem, 'Are Thoughts and Sentences Compositional?', 177, but it continues to play an important role in this more mature work as well (see below).

20 Abelard, *Dialectica*, ed. De Rijk, 149,26-37.

non-assertive sentences, and that desire does not appear at all in their considerations on this topic, even if Boethius writes of *expectatio* and *suspensio* as the state of mind proper to those who hear an incomplete sentence. In his *Dialectica*, Abelard first of all interprets in terms of desire the particular kind of expectation that is produced in the listener when hearing an incomplete sentence. Second, he introduces within the logical context of the analysis of complete sentences the grammatical distinction of the moods of the verbs as expressions of the different affects of the souls. Third, he gives to non-assertive sentences, and in particular to injunctions and desiderative sentences, the dignity of being objects of reflection on their own. These peculiarities of Abelard's approach to incomplete and non-assertive sentences are even more prominent in his *Glossae super Peri hermeneias*.

3 The Wish for More Information by Who Hears an Incomplete Sentence According to Abelard's *Glossae super Peri hermeneias*

In his *Glossae super Peri hermeneias* Peter Abelard refines his analysis of incomplete sentences. While in the *Dialectica* his analysis is centred on the idea of the complete sentence as the result of an act of demonstration—according to different affections of the soul—of an inherence of something in something else, now Abelard also introduces the idea of the completeness of the sentence in relation to its strength (*vis*) and purpose (*causa inventionis*). In order to really distinguish complete from incomplete sentences, writes Abelard, the semantic content is not relevant, since a sentence like 'Socrates reads' has the same semantic content as expressions like 'Socrates reading', or 'Socrates runs' as 'Socrates running'. But 'Socrates reads' or 'Socrates runs' are complete since they reach the goal they have been invented for: that of making the soul of the listener 'tranquil',[21] while 'Socrates running' or 'Socrates reading'

21 On the differences between the *Dialectica* and the *Logica Ingredientibus* concerning the theory of the completness of sentences, see Rosier-Catach, 'Les discussions sur le signifié des propositions' (she considers that the difference is not substantial); Guilfoy, 'Peter Abelard's Two Theories' (he stresses this difference); Marenbon, '*Dicta*, Assertion and Speech Acts'. On the compositional character of sentences according to Abelard, see also Jacobi-Strube-King, 'From *intellectus verus/falsus*', and Irène Rosier-Catach, 'La notion de *translatio*, le principe de compositionalité, et l'analyse de la prédication accidentelle chez Abélard', in *Langage, sciences, philosophie au XIIe siècle*, ed. J. Biard (Paris, 1999), 125-64; Lenz, 'Are Thoughts and Sentences Compositional?'.

are incomplete and do not reach their goal: by hearing them the soul of the listener is kept "suspended" and "*wishing* to hear something more" ("suspensum reddit auditorem, ut aliquid amplius audire desideret"). The reason for this is that these incomplete sentences, as well as nouns and verbs as such, do not have as their goal that of generating an intellection in the soul of the listener. The fact that they nevertheless engender an intellection is a sort of secondary effect: they are invented and instituted in order to produce a complete sentence by composing with other words. According to Abelard, all words and sequences of words have been instituted so that they signify something *even if* we take them alone; only for some of them (the complete sentences), signifying something when taken alone *is actually their goal*.

Consequently, in his *Glossae* Abelard analyses the special kind of desire that is proper to the listener of an incomplete sentence in order to distinguish it from the generic desire for more information, which can also be provoked by a complete sentence. Of course, Abelard notes, when we listen to the complete and enunciative 'Socrates reads' we may wish to know what Socrates is reading, and also when we hear 'Socrates is running' we may wish to know where he is running. But the desire for more information produced in the soul of the listener by an incomplete sentence is not the same kind of desire that can be provoked by complete sentences like these. The desire for more information experienced by the listener of an incomplete sentence, which interests Abelard here, is strictly connected with the ability and purpose (*vis* and *institutio* or *causa inventionis*) of incomplete sentences to combine with other words in order to become complete sentences. As we have seen, 'Socrates running' is an incomplete sentence since, even if it produces an intellection in the soul of the listener, it has not been instituted in order to generate this intellection, but in order to combine with other words and sentences. This is why one who hears or reads this expression (i.e., the incomplete sentence 'Socrates running'), knowing that it has not been instituted in order to signify alone, *expects and desires another word with which it can be combined*, and he also expects this other word to be coherent with the reason or purpose for its institution (its *causa inventionis*). Therefore, Abelard concludes, a sentence will be said to be complete only in relation to the cause or reason of its invention. We will not call complete some sentences just because they produce an intellection in the soul of the listener, since incomplete sentences also satisfy the Aristotelian criterion of producing an intellection in the listener. We will consider complete the sentence that produces an intellection in the soul of the listener only *if this is its goal*. Those sentences are incomplete that leave the soul of the listener suspended and desiring to hear something more in order to receive a complete sentence, because of their own institution and goal:

> Nos autem perfectionem orationis non iuxta perfectionem significationis pensamus, quod uidelicet significatiuum huius perfectum est, illius imperfectum. Nam 'Socratem legere' quae imperfecta est idem penitus significat quod 'Socrates legit' et 'Socrates currens' eundem habet intellectum quem <habet> 'Socrates currit' et per se etiam dicta eandem animi conceptionem facit quam 'Socrates currit'; non tamen perfecta dicitur, sicut illa, quippe suspensum reddit auditorem, ut aliquid amplius audire desideret. [5] Sed et similiter dicetur, quod 'Socrates currit' suspendit auditorem et 'Socrates legit', ut uidelicet adhuc audire desideret, quid legat uel quo currat uel qualiter; similiter 'Homo currit', ut uidelicet ambigamus, quis homo currat uel utrum omnis uel quidam. [6] Si quis autem dicat, quod dum dicitur 'Socrates currit' non suspenditur animus auditoris de eo quod ad demonstrationem orationis pertinet, similiter dico, cum dicitur 'Socrates currens', non suspendi auditorem de eo quod ad intellectum orationis pertinet, quia totum ostendit quod debet. [7] Accipimus itaque perfectionem orationis secundum uim et institutionem ipsius, quia, cum omnes uoces [etiam] impositae ad significandum sint institutae, et quaedam ex eis per se etiam prolatae significationem habent, sicut nomina et uerba nec non etiam orationes imperfectae, licet ita sint inuentae, ut per se quoque significent, non tamen propter hoc, sed magis, ut appositae aliis constructionem implerent. Aliud est autem ita inuentas esse uoces, ut in se hoc habeant, aliud propter hoc inuentas esse. Quantum ergo ad causam inuentionis imperfecta est oratio 'Socrates currens', quia, licet et intellectum constituat per se etiam prolata, non propter hoc, ut per se hoc faceret, instituta fuit, sed cum aliis uocibus iuncta. [8] Vnde et ille qui audit eam proferri et scit eam non esse inuentam propter hoc, ut simpliciter proferretur, aliam exspectat uocem, cum qua ex causa inuentionis suae habeat poni, ut 'ambulat' uel 'est' et similia. Vnde perfectam orationem dicimus, quae integram constitutionem habet secundum causam institutionis orationum, sicut ista 'Socrates currit'. Haec enim instituta fuit non solum ut intellectum generaret, sed propter hoc etiam, ut per se dicta id faceret; aliae uero non, quaecumque imperfectae dicuntur.[22]

As we can see, expecting and desiring are fundamental elements in the linguistic act both in Abelard's *Dialectica* and in his *Glossae super Peri hermeneias*. On the pragmatic level, expecting and desiring are the sentiments of the addressee during the process of receiving the linguistic message, i.e., while the message is

---

22 Abelard, *Glossae super Peri hermeneias*, ed. K. Jacobi and K. Strub (Turnhout, 2010), 148,22-149,56.

changing step by step from incomplete to complete. On the descriptive level, Abelard describes the goals and potentialities of isolated nouns and verbs as well as of incomplete sentences such as those that produce by their nature expectation and desire for more information in the addressees. It is clear, then, that Abelard's interpreting the intrinsic desire for more information in the listener's soul as a sign of a (still) incomplete sentence is strictly connected with his pragmatic, compositional and temporal representation of linguistic communication. According to this analysis, the meaning of a sentence is the final result of a series of successive moments of attention ("aliqua per successionem *attendit*"), expectation for, combination (*coniunctio*), or disjunction (*disiunctio*) of separated parts of information (*intellectae res*). The series of partial moments that ends up in constituting a sentence is unified by the continuity of the same intention and the same mental act.[23] This is explicitly said both in the *Glossae super Peri hermeneias* and in the *De intellectibus* (1122-1126):

> Sunt itaque tres actiones in intellectu propositionis, intellectus scilicet partium, coniunctio uel disiunctio intellectarum rerum.[24]

> Sicut enim qui loquitur et dicit *homo ambulat* per plures progreditur significatiuas dictiones, ita qui audit ex singulis dictionibus proprios colligendo intellectus procedit. Primum quidem hominem intelligendo, cum uidelicet audit *homo* quod ad significandum hominem institutum est; postea ambulationem, cum audit *ambulat*, eam insuper homini copulando.[25]

> Vna autem est coniunctio, uel diuisio, siue disiunctio intellectus per quam animus continue, ex uno mentis impulsu, progreditur et una dirigitur intentione, per quam ei quod primum intellectum est aliquid coniungendo uel disiungendo, uel inter ipsum et aliud disiungendo, cursum quodammodo inceptum sine interruptione consummet. Tunc autem unam huiusmodi coniunctionem animus habet, cum sic aliqua per successionem attendit, ut ea sic inuicem aptet, ut per ea discurrendo unam conficiat entiam [var. essentiam], et insuper quotienscumque ad uim unius affirmationis quocumque modo aliqua inuicem colligat, siue per predicationem scilicet, siue per conditionis uel temporis coniunctionem,

23 See Rosier-Catach, 'Les discussions sur le signifié des propositions', 23-5.

24 Abelard, *Glossae super Peri hermeneias*, ed. Jacobi-Strub, 78,224-6. For other texts in this line see Rosier-Catach, 'Les discussions sur le signifié des propositions'.

25 Abelard, *De intellectibus*, ed. P. Morin (Paris, 1994), par. 32: 46.

> uel quolibet alio modo, dum hoc uidelicet […] uno mentis impulsu continue fiat.[26]

Even if in these texts the verb *desidero* does not appear, nevertheless its presence in the *Dialectica*'s and *Glossae*'s descriptions of incomplete sentences seem to me justified by this dynamic representation of language as a process where human beings come in touch with each other in time and through their souls, their acts of attention (*attendit*), their intentions (*una intentione*) and the force of their minds (*mentis impulsus*). It is not surprising, then, if the subjective, psychological, and pragmatic notion of desiring enters Abelard's description of sentences even though it is absent in Aristotle's and Boethius' parallel descriptions, since his approach to logic is less formal than theirs and less exclusively centred on assertions. To some extent, in Abelard's description of incomplete sentences in his *Glossae super Peri hermeneias*, desire becomes a part of the metalanguage of logic. Boethius' description of the state of mind of the listener of an incomplete sentence as one of *expectatio* and *titubatio* (see above) may have given Abelard a push in this direction. Another suggestion could have come to Abelard from the field of grammar. In his *Institutiones grammaticae*, Priscian uses the verb *desiderare* as synonymous with *egere* to mean the demanding or expecting of something by something else within the language as a formal system, e.g., of a certain part of the discourse by an incomplete sentence in order for it become complete:

> Ergo si tollas nomen aut verbum, deficiet oratio, desiderans vel nomen vel verbum, ut si dicam 'idem lapsus heu hodie concidit' vel 'idem homo lapsus heu hodie'; sin substrahas adverbium, non omnino deficiet oratio, ut 'idem homo lapsus heu concidit'.[27]

---

26 Abelard, *De intellectibus*, ed. Morin, par. 47-8: 52-4.

27 Priscianus, *Institutiones grammaticae* XVII, 12-16, ed. Hertz, II, 116,13-16. See also ivi, XIII, 31, II, 20,30: "[…] qualitatem, quam desiderat nomen"; XVIII, 18, II, 119,4-6: "additio pronominis discretionem aliquam desiderat alterius personae, ut 'ego lego, tu scribis' "; XVII, 32, II, 129,10-11: "[…] cum pronomine adiunctum tò 'quis' nomen desiderat sibi reddi: 'qui est ille?' "; XVII, 83, II, 154,24-155, 4. See also the 12th-century commentary on Priscian *Notae Dunelmenses*, MS Durham, Cathedral Library c. IV. 29, f. 53va: "[…] ex adiunctione participiorum cum prima uel secunda uerbi persona sequitur etiam nominum adiunctio cum eisdem personis. Vbicumque enim sit adiectiuum, ad perfectionem constructionis desiderat substantiuum […]." Ivi, f. 176va: "[…] 'suum' relatiuum est pronomen naturaliter, ideo ex natura suae inuentionis aliquid semper desiderat sibi addi ad quod referatur." I would like to thank I. Rosier-Catach and A. Grondeux, who allowed me to use their transcription of this text. Concerning *Notae Dunelmenses*, see Grondeux and Rosier-Catach,

The difference is that for Abelard the subject of the action of desiring involved in the description of incomplete sentences is not a formal part of the system of language (e.g., nouns or verbs), as in Priscian's *Institutiones*, but one of the two pragmatic actors of this system, the addressee. That is, in Abelard's considerations it is not the still incomplete sentence that 'desires' the missing part, as is the case with Priscian, but the person who receives (the first parts of) the message and wants it to become complete. Therefore, if we compare Abelard with Priscian on this point, we recognise in Abelard a stronger focus on the pragmatic level of language, e.g., in his stressing the active roles of the speakers and addresses, with their different emotions, intentions, and acts of attention. An influence on Peter Abelard's theory of sentences from Augustine's interest in the interior and psychological, as well as in the pragmatic, relational and 'intentional' elements within linguistic communication, is also evident, as I. Rosier-Catach has demonstrated.[28] The notion of *attentio*, in particular, which Abelard uses intensively in the *Glossae* while describing the real process of communicating by language,[29] very likely has an Augustinian origin. Concerning the notion of desire, probably it is not possible to find a unique or even a predominant source for Abelard's use of it, but it surely plays an important role in the writings of Augustine and in Boethius' *Philosophiae consolatio*.

4 Desire and Classification of Complete Sentences in the *Dialectica*

Peter Abelard's deepening of Aristotle's and Boethius' theories about sentences is also evident if we consider his classifications of types of complete sentences. Aristotle, as we have seen, mentions prayer just in passing and focuses only on assertive sentences. Like Aristotle, Boethius does not pay much attention

'Les *Glosulae super Priscianum* et leur tradition'; Irène Rosier-Catach, 'Priscian on Divine Ideas and Mental Conceptions: The Discussions in the *Glosulae in Priscianum*, the *Notae Dunelmenses*, William of Champeaux and Abelard', *Vivarium* 45 (2007), 219-37.

28 Rosier-Catach, 'Les discussions sur le signifié des propositions', 19-21, considers the role of memory, attention and expectation in some texts of Augustine's *De musica* and *Confessiones* concerning the perception of time. On Augustine as a source for Abelard's ethics and theology, see Tobias Georges, 'Die Verwurzelung von Abelards Ethik im Denken Augustins', *Archa Verbi* 3 (2006), 9-30.

29 See the texts mentioned by Rosier-Catach, 'Les discussions sur le signifié des propositions', passim. In particular Abelard, *Glossae super Peri hermeneias*, I, 103-8, ed. Jacobi-Strub, 56-7, where *attentio* or *attendo* occur on almost every line in the context of the discussion of the question whether it is possibile that a true sentence produces a false concept ("Utrum ulla propositio uera falsum intellectum generet").

to non-assertive complete sentences (*oratio non enuntiativa*): he mentions a certain number of types of non-assertive sentences, proposing different lists, some of which include prayers and optative sentences, but he does not expand on the subject, quickly switching to considering just assertions. Abelard, as usual, has Boethius' commentaries as his starting point, but very soon he follows his own way: he enlarges Boethius' lists, underlines the fact that his own largest list could be even more extended, clarifies the relations between the different types of non-assertive complete sentences, and, most important, seems to be genuinely interested in their semantics, which is strongly connected to the realm of affects.

In the *Dialectica*, Abelard lists and briefly defines five types of complete sentences: assertions and interrogative sentences, prayers, and imperative and desiderative sentences. If we compare Abelard's analysis with those of Aristotle and Boethius, we notice first of all the clear distinction between the optative sentence and the prayer (*deprecativa oratio*); the use the adjective *desiderativa* instead of the Boethian *optativa* to qualify the optative sentence (*desiderativa oratio*); and, finally, that, while all of Boethius' lists consider the vocative sentence as a distinct type of complete sentence, here Abelard does not agree with this position (but he will change his mind; see below):

> Harum igitur orationum quae perfectae sunt, aliae sunt 'enuntiativae', aliae 'interrogativae', aliae 'deprecativae', aliae 'imperativae', aliae 'desiderativae'. Enuntiativam autem eam Aristoteles definit quae enuntiat aliquid de aliquo uel aliquid ab aliquo, ut sunt illae quae affirmant praedicatum de subiecto vel negant, hoc modo: 'Socrates est homo', uel 'non est homo'. Interrogativa autem est per quam interrogamus hoc modo: 'quis' vel 'qualis' vel 'quid est Socrates?' Deprecativa autem, per quam deprecamur, sic: 'adesto Deus'. Imperativa, per quam imperamus, ut 'accipe codicem'. Desiderativa, ⟨per⟩ quam nostrum exprimimus votum, veluti cum dicimus: 'osculetur me amica'. Addunt autem quidam sextam speciem, 'vocatiuam' scilicet orationem. Sed mihi quidem vocatio non videtur diversam speciem a suprapositis procreare, quae quidem vocatio omnibus aequaliter potest apponi.[30]

The most relevant difference between Abelard and Boethius on this topic consists in Abelard's deepening the analysis of non-assertive complete sentences. In fact, in his descriptions of non-assertive sentences, Abelard stresses the role

30 Abelard, *Dialectica*, ed. De Rijk, 151,6-19.

played by the speaker with his subjectivity and especially with his different emotions:

> Nec mireris idem verbum secundum diversos affectus animi diversas orationes reddere, modo scilicet imperativam, quando sola imperatio attenditur, modo etiam deprecativam, quando deprecationem, nunc quoque desiderativam, quando desiderationem intelligimus, ut, cum dico: 'festinet amica', hanc vel imperativam vel deprecativam vel desiderativam secundum varios animi affectus, ut dictum est, proferre possunt. Indicativo quoque verbo saepe pro imperativo utimur; veluti cum in praeceptis Legis dicitur: "Non occides, non maechaberis" etc. Cum enim haec ad omnes dicta sint, si affirmative intelligeretur, falsum saepe inveniretur.[31]

Going much further in his analysis than Boethius, Abelard remarks that the same sequence of words, though phonetically, grammatically, and semantically identical, may be considered a complete sentence of different kinds (desiderative, imperative etc.), depending on which of the different affects of the soul is the object of the speaker's 'attention' (*attenditur*) or 'intelligence' (*intelligimus*) when it is pronounced (*proferri*). The sentence "May my friend hurry here!" ("Festinet amica"), e.g., is an imperative sentence if, while I pronounce it, I concentrate my attention on the affect of injunction; a desiderative sentence if I concentrate my attention on desire; and a prayer if I concentrate my attention on the sentiment of praying—where it seems also that according to Abelard the same sentence could belong at the same time to the three classes, imperative sentence, optative sentence, and prayer, if I felt the three emotions simultaneously. Abelard also underlines a sort of flexibility in the connection between the grammatical classification of the moods of the verbs and the logical classification of the different types of complete sentences. The indicative mood, e.g., which is proper to assertive sentences, is quite often used instead of the imperative mood, as in the case of the commandments of the Law. If we considered the indicative mood as an unequivocal sign of assertive sentences, then the commandments of the Law would be evidently false, since they concern everybody, but not everybody respects them.

31 Abelard, *Dialectica*, ed. De Rijk, 152,17-26.

5 Desire in the Classification of Complete Sentences in the *Glossae super Peri hermeneias*

In contrast to what he had done in his *Dialectica*, in the *Logica Ingredientibus* Peter Abelard considers the vocative sentence as one type of the *perfectae orationes*, and he now has a list of six species that includes assertions, imperative sentences, vocative sentences, prayers, desiderative sentences (*desiderativa oratio*), and interrogative sentences:

> Sunt autem sex species perfectarum orationum, quas Boethius distinguit, enuntiatiua scilicet, imperatiua, uocatiua, deprecatiua, desideratiua, interrogatiua.[32]

Abelard justifies the difference between his own list of six items and Boethius' list of five by remarking that in the list of his treatise on categorical syllogisms Boethius had put the "oratio optativa, idest desiderativa" and the prayer (*deprecativa*) into the same category when they are actually different:

> Ipse tamen sub uno membro in unam speciem duas coniungit in Categoricis, optatiuam, id est desideratiuam, et deprecatiuam, et ita quinque dicit, cum tamen singulae ab inuicem differant.[33]

Keeping the desiderative sentences separate from prayers, as well as Abelard's general interest in the role of emotions, and especially that of desire, could be once again the result of suggestions inspired by the grammatical tradition. Priscian, e.g., in his *Institutiones grammaticae*, writes of the indicative, imperative, optative (*optativus*), subjunctive, and infinitive moods of the verbs as inclinations (*inclinationes*) of the soul that are expressive (*demonstrantes*) of its affections (*affectus*) and that are in turn manifested by different declinations of the verbs:

> Modi sunt diversae inclinationes animi, varios eius affectus demonstrantes. sunt autem quinque: indicativus sive definitivus, imperativus, optativus, subiunctivus, infinitus.[34]

32 Abelard, *Glossae super Peri hermeneias*, ed. Jacobi-Strub, 149,57-9.

33 Abelard, *Glossae super Peri hermeneias*, ed. Jacobi-Strub, 149, 59-62.

34 Priscianus, *Institutiones grammaticae*, VIII, 63, ed. Hertz, I, 421,17-19.

> Modi sunt [...] diversae inclinationes animi, quas varia consequitur declinatio verbi.[35]

This passage gave rise to important discussions in the medieval tradition. The *Glosulae in Priscianum*[36] discuss at length the question whether we should interpret Priscian's assertion that the moods are the affections of the soul as a *realis diffinitio* or a *vocalis diffinitio*. Did Priscian mean that the moods are real modifications in the soul, or that they are vocal signs signifying modifications in the soul?[37] Another 12th-century commentary on Priscian, the *Notae Dunelmenses*, asserts that here Priscian uses figuratively the name of what is signified (i.e., the inclinations of the soul) instead of the name of the sign (the moods as vocal signs of the inclinations in the soul).[38] Since it has been proven that these grammatical texts reflect a teaching reality that Abelard knew and with which he was in contact,[39] we can also imagine that Abelard's interest in the mood of desire and in general in the role of the affections of the soul in the pragmatics of language could, to a certain extent,

---

35 Priscianus, *Institutiones grammaticae*, VIII, 67, ed. Hertz, I, 423,22-5; XVIII, 139-150,270-6. Priscian's description of the moods of the verb in connection with the 'inclinations of the soul' seems to have a Stoic origin. On the moods of the verbs in Priscian and in general in the tradition of Greek and Latin grammar, see Gualtiero Calboli, 'Les modes chez Priscien (GL 3, 235.16-267.5)', in *Priscien. Transmission et refondation de la grammaire de l'Antiquité aux Modernes*, ed. M. Baratin, B. Colombat, and L. Holtz (Turnhout, 2009), 315-29.

36 This is a commentary on the *Institutiones grammaticae* that was begun in the first decade of the 12th century and was written in more subsequent phases in the circle of William of Champeaux. On the *Glosulae in Priscianum* see *Arts du langage et théologie aux confins des XIe et XIIe siècle*, ed. Rosier-Catach, which describes the state of the research on this text at the moment of its publication.

37 *Glosulae in Priscianum*, MSS Metz, Bibliothèque municipale 209 (248), f. 62rb, Köln, Dombibliothek B. 201, f. 36ra: "Duae hic uidentur esse diffinitiones modorum, una realis, altera uocalis. Realis est: MODI SUNT INCLINATIONES, idest applicationes ANIMI, idest fundatae in animo [...]. Possunt autem praemissae diffinitiones pro una accipi ⟨id est⟩ uocali, ut sic dicatur: MODI SUNT DIUERSAE INCLINATIONES ANIMI, idest uoces ostendentes animum inclinari ad diuersa dicuntur modi." I would like to thank Eleonora Lorenzetti for allowing me to use her transcription of this text.

38 *Notae Dunelmenses*, MS Durham, Cathedral Library c. IV. 29, ff. 1v-216, f. 11rb "[...] etiamsi [...] uocet ipsas uoces uerbales inclinationes animi, figuratiue tamen hoc facit, nomen scilicet significati dans significanti. Videtur enim hic reuera agere de uocibus uerbalibus, quas uocat 'modos' [...]. Et quod secundum uocem definiat modos, ostendit sequens diuisio, quae est SVNT AVTEM QVINQVE INDICATIVVS etc."

39 See Rosier-Catach, 'Les *Glosulae super Priscianum* et leur tradition', passim, and the articles by Irène Rosier-Catach mentioned above, n. 5.

depend on them. In any case, Abelard's use of the term *desiderativa* instead of Boethius' *optativa* (*oratio*) could be Abelard's development of a suggestion derived from Priscian and the grammatical tradition. The ancient grammarian used the adjective *optativus* to designate the optative mood of the verb,[40] but nevertheless at times he wrote of a special class of *desiderativa vel inquisitiva verba* like *quaero, expecto, desidero*,[41] or of the derivative verbs *video* > *viso* and *capio* > *capesso* as *verba desiderativa*.[42] The same can be said of Priscian's medieval commentators who wrote the *Notae Dunelmenses*.[43]

As in the case of Abelard's treatment of incomplete sentences, the same deepening of Abelard's attention to the role of the speaker's subjectivity and emotions can be noticed in the *Glossae*'s analysis of the different kinds of complete sentences. Sometimes, Abelard explains in specifying what he had already written in his *Dialectica*, by using the same word, and notably the same verb, we produce (*facimus*) two complete sentences belonging to two different types according to two different affects of the soul (*affectus animi*). "Socrates, come!" e.g., may be an imperative sentence or a prayer depending on which emotion I have the intention (*intendo*) to pronounce it with:

> Et notandum, quod eodem uerbo et deprecatiuam facimus et imperatiuam secundum diuersos affectus animi. Cum enim dico 'Socrates adesto', si imperando uerbum proferre intendo, imperatiuam facio, quod si deprecando, deprecatiuam.[44]

This example clearly shows Abelard's idea that the complete meaning of a sentence is manifested not only by the combination of the partial semantic contents signified by its parts (i.e., its terms and their connections), but also by the expression of the emotional modality with which this combination is perceived by the speaker ("si imperando proferre intendo, imperativam facio").[45] Using

---

40 Priscianus, *Institutiones grammaticae*, VIII, 76, ed. Hertz, I, 431,10-18; X, 46, 535,9-11; XVIII, 140, II, 274,7-10.

41 Priscianus, *Institutiones grammaticae*, XVIII, 146, ed. Hertz, II, 274,6-10; 274,23-275,6.

42 Priscianus, *Institutiones grammaticae*, VIII, 76, ed. Hertz, I, 431,10-18; X, 46, I, 535,9-11. Similar *verba desiderativa* can be found also in Ps. Augustine's *Regulae*, ed. H. Hagan (Leipzig, 1868, reprint Hildesheim-New York, 1981), 496-524, 516,16.

43 See e.g. MS Durham, Cathedral Library c. IV. 29, ff. 47ra-b and 100rb.

44 Abelard, *Glossae super Peri hermeneias*, ed. Jacobi-Strub, 149,63-6.

45 See Jacobi-Strub-King, 'From *intellectus verus/falsus*', 18-21. Lenz, 'Are Thoughts and Sentences Compositional?', passim, writes for Abelard of 'attitudes', different from the 'propositional content' and similar to the 'propositional attitude' in contemporary logic and linguistics. In fact, under this respect Abelard's position seems to particularly recall

a verb that means desire, Abelard writes, is not sufficient to render a sentence a desiderative one: the sentence also has to be expressed with the corresponding affective modality. "Oh would the king come!" ("Vtinam rex veniret") and "I wish the king to come" ("Opto, ut rex veniat"), for example, have the same meaning ("idem intelligitur," "eundum intellectum generet"): the inherence of the coming in the king, and the same *innuitio*, i.e., indirect information:[46] the speaker's will that this should happen. But the two sentences, even if they have the same semantic content, are different in their 'mood': the second one has the 'mood of assertion' (*enuntiandi modus*), i.e., that of 'proposing' that things are or are not the way we assert, and is therefore an enunciation (*propositio*); the first one does not have it, and therefore it is not an enunciation. Even if Abelard does not say it, from what we read afterwards about desiderative sentences (see below) it is obvious that in his opinion in the first sentence ("Utinam rex veniret") the speaker expresses through the adverb *utinam* the inclination of desiring, and consequently the sentence is desiderative.[47] Abelard then proceeds by presenting another example, "Socrates, come!" ("Veni Socrates"): I can pronounce this sentence as an injunction or a prayer (*imperando vel deprecando*), and consequently the listener will understand (*intellectu capitur*) that (an affect corresponding to) an injunction or prayer is in me as speaker. Therefore, Abelard concludes, it is more convenient to say that some sentences are assertive sentences (*enuntiationes, id est propositiones*) because they possess the mode of truth and falsity (*modus enuntiandi*) than because of their content (*secundum intellectum*):

> Attende etiam huiusmodi species perfectarum orationum intellectibus non differre. Cum enim dico 'Vtinam rex ueniret', idem intelligitur, ac

---

John Austin's 'illocutionary force'; see John Austin, *How to Do Things with Words* (Oxford, 1962).

46 This notion has been used by Thierry of Chartres in the context of the discussion of theological language. See Luisa Valente, *Logique et théologie. Les écoles parisiennes entre 1150 et 1220* (Paris, 2008), 152-5.

47 We can see here something similar to the difference between signifying *per modum affectus* and signifying *per modum conceptus*, or between *actus exercitus* and *actus significatus*, a difference that is used by later grammarians especially within the analysis of interjections: interjections signify according to the mode of affection, other parts of the speech according to the mode of concept. See Rosier-Catach, *La parole comme acte*, in particular ch. 2 and 5; eadem, 'Discussions médiévales sur l'expression des affects', in *Le sujet des émotions au Moyen Âge*, ed. D. Boquet and P. Nagy (Paris, 2008), 201-23: 206-8; eadem, 'Speech acts and Intentional Meaning', 56-60. See also Kann, 'Assertive and non-Assertive Sentences'.

> si diceretur 'Opto, ut rex ueniat', et in utraque innuo uoluntatem inesse mihi de aduentu regis. Non tamen haec propositio est sicut illa, quia licet et eundem intellectum generet non habet enuntiationis modum, ut uidelicet esse uel non esse proponat. Similiter cum dico imperando uel deprecando 'Veni Socrates', imperium esse mihi uel deprecationem intellectu capitur. Unde secundum modum enuntiandi magis enuntiationes, id est propositiones, conuenit dici quam secundum intellectum.[48]

In his *Glossae super Peri hermeneias* Abelard devotes special attention to 'desiderative' sentences (*desiderativae orationes*). Among all types of complete sentences, Abelard remarks, desiderative sentences are those that most approach assertions ("ad uim enuntiationis optatiua uerba accedere"). This is true to such an extent that they often are confused with assertions and are even inserted in a chain of conclusive reasoning (*consequentia*)—a topic he had already touched on in his *Dialectica* (see above):

> Nota autem maxime ad uim enuntiationis optatiua uerba accedere, ut si dicam 'Mallem habere tunicam quam paenulam' uel 'Libentius uescerer carne quam piscibus' uel 'Vtinam rex ueniret' et respondeat is qui audit uerum esse quod dico uel falsum. Vnde etiam de optatiuis orationibus sicut de propositionibus consequentias componere solemus hoc modo: "Si fuisses hic, frater meus non fuisset mortuus" uel "Si idem esset caecitas et caecum esse, utraque de eodem praedicarentur" [...] ac si ita dicatur: 'Si sunt idem, praedicantur de eodem', et cum dicitur 'Mallem comedere quam ieiunare,' 'mallem' idem ualet quod 'malo'.[49]

The need to express the mood is particularly relevant in the case of desiderative sentences, since pronouncing a desiderative verb is not sufficient, writes Abelard, for obtaining a complete and desiderative sentence. In fact, it is also necessary to express the speaker's will or desire by a 'demonstration of wish' (*demonstratio optationis*), which is, e.g., a 'voluntative' adverb or an optatively conjugated desiderative verb.[50] "That the king come" ("Rex veniret") alone is not a complete sentence, while "Oh, would the king come!" ("Utinam rex

48 Abelard, *Glossae super Peri hermeneias*, ed. Jacobi-Strub, 150,84-151,93.

49 Abelard, *Glossae super Peri hermeneias*, ed. Jacobi-Strub, 151,94-106. For the examples see Io 11,21; Aristotle, *Categoriae*, 19a39-41.

50 See Nuchelmans, *Theories of the Proposition*, 148-9. This idea is similar to the later difference between signifying *per modum affectus* or *per modum conceptus*, about which see above, n. 47.

veniret") and "I would like the king to come" ("Vellem ut rex ueniret") as well as "I would gladly come" ("Libenter ego uenirem") are. Such words as 'Oh', 'gladly' or 'I would like' make it clear that there is a special will for what is signified by the sentence in the person who is speaking or writing (*demonstrare/designare/exprimere optationem/voluntatem*), and therefore these words render the sentences complete *and* desiderative. Desiderative and imperative moods are different in this respect, since optatively conjugated verbs need something else, e.g., a desiderative adverb or an optatively conjugated desiderative verb like *vellem*, in order to express the will of the speaker and so to render a sentence complete and desiderative, while imperatively conjugated verbs do not need such an adjunction. In other words, the *causa inventionis* of the desiderative mood in the verb is that of building up a complete sentence expressing a will present in the speaker not on its own (*per se*) but through an adjunction of the sign of will (*voluntatis designativum*); differently, the *causa inventionis* of the imperative mood in the verb is that of designating *imperium* also *per se*:

> Attende etiam, quod optatiua uerba sine demonstratione optationis prolata perfectionem orationis habere non uidentur. Non enim ita per se dicitur 'Rex ueniret' sicut 'Utinam rex ueniret', 'Vellem ut rex ueniret', uel 'Libenter ego uenirem'. Nam quia 'utinam' et 'libenter' et 'uellem' uoluntatis quae mihi coniungitur designatiua sunt, perfectam orationem reddunt. Si quis autem optatiuum uerbum per se etiam dictum dicat designare optationem sicut imperatiuum imperationem, negamus, sed potius ideo dici optatiuum, quia ad eam constructionem inuentum est proprie, ubi uoluntas exprimenda est uoluntatiuo aduerbio ei adiuncto, ut 'Utinam currerem'.[51]

Once again, it is possible that Priscian influenced Abelard on this point, since the great grammarian wrote something very similar in his description of the *modus optativus*:

> Tertius [sc. modus] est optativus, qui quamvis et temporibus et personis perfectior videatur esse imperativo, tamen eget adverbio optandi, ut plenum significet sensum.[52]

In the following text of the *Glossae*, Abelard remarks once again that sometimes desiderative verbs are not used in order to express an affection of the

51 Abelard, *Glossae super Peri hermeneias*, ed. Jacobi-Strub, 151,108-52,117.

52 Priscianus, *Institutiones grammaticae*, VIII, 68, ed. Hertz, 424,8-10.

soul (desire or will), but just according to the enuntiative modality. Thus when we say 'I would like to run' and we mean 'I will run', we are communicating an intellection, not expressing a will. In this case, according to Abelard, the sentence is complete, but it is not a desiderative sentence. If we want to use the verb *vellem* according to its real *causa inventionis*, i.e., in order to express, and not just to communicate our wish, we have to add an adverb and say 'Oh, how I would like to run!'. The desiderative verb, if it is taken as a desiderative verb and not in an assertive mood, does not produce a complete sentence if there is no adverb added to it:

> Si uero dicamus 'Vellem currere' pro 'Volo currere', perfecta est oratio. Si uero in ui illa ponam 'uellem' ⟨in⟩ qua inuentum est, optatiuum apponendum est 'utinam', ut perfecta sit oratio et dicamus 'Vtinam uellem currere'. Adeo autem liquet sine 'utinam' optatiuum uerbum non facere perfectionem orationis, quia nec sine eo declinatur.[53]

Finally, Abelard gives another list of types of complete sentences, each connected to a different emotion. This list is much longer than those given by Boethius and also longer than the one given by Abelard himself on the preceding occasions. Abelard mentions as his source Apuleius (who in his *Peri hermeneias* enumerates eighteen kinds of complete sentences)[54] and hypothesizes that we could add even more types:

> Videntur autem plures esse species perfectarum orationum praeter sex supra dictas, licet eas Boethius non ponat. Est enim oratio admiratiua sicut 'O mirum ineffabilem', uel oratiua ut 'Eia pugnemus', uel dehortatiua siue prohibitiua ut 'Ne pugnemus'. Sicut enim hortamur uel imperamus,

53 Abelard, *Glossae super Peri hermeneias*, ed. Jacobi-Strub, 152,117-22. It seems that there is a contradiction between this text, where sentences like "vellem currere" are said to be complete but non-desiderative, and the preceding one, where the sentence "vellem ut rex veniret" is given as an example of a complete sentence since vellem is *designativum voluntatis* and renders the sentence a complete and desiderative one.

54 See Apuleius, *Peri hermeneias* (Opera III), ed. P. Thomas (Stuttgart, 1970), 176,4-177,2: "sed cum disseramus oratione, cuius variae species sunt, ut imperandi mandandi succensendi optandi vovendi irascendi odiendi invidendi favendi miserandi admirandi contemnendi obiurgandi paenitendi deplorandi tum voluptatem afferendi tum metum incutiendi, in quibus oratoris excellentis est lata anguste, angusta late, vulgata decenter, nova usitate, usitata nove ***, extenuare magna, maxima e minimis posse efficere aliaque id genus plurima: est una inter has ad propositum potissima [...] quam [...] dicetur propositio." Cf. *Introductiones Montanae minores*, ed. De Rijk, *Logica Modernorum* II-2, 18,17-20.

ita dehortamur uel prohibemus, et pleraeque fortasse aliae esse possunt orationes perfectae praeter supra positas, unde Apuleius in Peri hermeneias suis multas perfectarum orationum species computat.[55]

6 Conclusion

Peter Abelard seems to consider logic as the discipline of verbal communication in a broader sense, and not just as the science of assertions and deductive reasoning. If we take this into account, it is easier to understand that for him desire is a key notion in logic. Many facts testify to this approach in Abelard's considerations of sentences. Following a different path than Aristotle and Boethius, Abelard reflects at length on incomplete sentences as well as on the various kinds of non-assertive complete sentences. Abelard's analysis of such sentences is much more subtle than Aristotle's and Boethius', and while considering them he underlines the role of desiring in language at different levels. Desire plays a deep, structural role in Abelard's descriptions of the compositional way in which the linguistic message is received, changing step by step from incomplete to complete, a process in which other affections or states of mind are involved besides desire, like expectation, doubt, but also intention, and attention. According to Abelard, the person who receives the incomplete message (e.g., 'Socrates' or 'Socrates legens') not only is in a state of mind of suspense, but also desires to obtain further information through other words since he knows that the purpose of such words or sequences of words (their *causa inventionis*) is to combine with other words in order to form a complete sentence. On the other hand, the expression of the speaker's attention to his inner affections renders the same semantic content a different complete sentence, like an injunction or an expression of hope and desire. If for Abelard the words' 'strength' (*vis*) or the 'reason for instituting them' (their *causa inventionis*) is that of calming the soul of the listener, according to the clear description "Constituit enim qui dicit intellectum, et qui audit quiescit" (Aristotle, *Peri hermeneias*, 16b20), for the Magister Palatinus this calming down has the form of satisfying a desire in the souls of the people who are communicating, a desire that is not just for sharing knowledge, but also for emotional participation.

55 Abelard, *Glossae super Peri hermeneias*, ed. Jacobi-Strub, 152,123-30.

The *Introductiones Montanae maiores*: A Student's Guide to Logic

Joke Spruyt

Logic throughout the Middle Ages was not merely a theoretical enterprise, but always had a practical component; as such it resembles skills training, as we would call it today. In recent years scholars have uncovered evidence suggesting that quite a few of the medieval works of logic that we are now familiar with were written for students relatively early in their academic careers, probably covering the final years of what we now call secondary school. When we read the medieval material, we should take this background into account.

Featuring prominently among the many topics that Angel d'Ors investigated is the theory of *Obligationes*. The origins of this highly formalised kind of academic disputation can partly be traced back to the 12th century, the period during which several logico-theological schools were active.[1] In the works of the 12th-century schools, the tracts on logic incorporated theoretical insights and discursive practice in an interesting way. Besides the tracts on *instantiae* per se, other treatises originating from roughly the same period also made abundant use of counterarguments (*oppositiones*) as a means to clarify and then to ultimately embrace or reject a thesis at issue.[2] As it would seem, the purpose of this practice was not only to analyse the meaning of specific sample-expressions featuring in object-language, but also to highlight the ins and outs of logico-linguistic lore. Later on, as we know, in *syncategoremata*-treatises, *sophismata*-collections and so-called *sophistaria*-treatises, propositions similar to the ones we find in the early works were to be discussed in a far more systematic way, again, to show pupils the ropes of doing logic and, more specifically, to show them what tools they could use to argue in a coherent manner.

One of the treatises dating from the earlier period is a tract that has been called the *Introductiones Montanae maiores* (hereafter cited as *IMM*), or the Great Introduction (to logic) of the School of Sainte Geneviève (a school dominated by master Alberic of Paris), found in the manuscript Paris, BnF lat. 15141,

1 For an extensive list of the literature (including the works of Angel d'Ors), see the *Bibliography of* obligationes *Literature*, compiled by Sara L. Uckelman, Tilburg Center for Logic and Philosophy of Science, September 28, 2012 (http://lyrawww.uvt.nl/~sluckelman/latex/obbib/obbib.pdf).

2 Cf. Yukio Iwakuma, '*Instantiae*: An Introduction to a Twelfth Century Technique of Argumentation', *Argumentation* 1 (1987), 437-53.

 | DOI 10.1163/9789004324275_007

ff. 47ra-104rb.[3] The first part of this treatise (ff. 47ra-63ra), identified by De Rijk as a *reportatio*, was presumably written during Alberic's lifetime, whereas the remainder of the tract, which is somewhat different in style and tone, must have been compiled later.[4]

The tract deals with all the items of logic that were discussed during that period (*vox, nomen, verbum, oratio, propositio, locus, syllogismus*). It presents the traditional topics by first providing definitions and descriptions of standard logico-semantic and -syntactic lore, and then elaborates on these matters by delving into counterarguments and producing solutions to the problems that these counterarguments address. The learning material (which starts off with an account of 'vox') is presented, as is stated in the text, in the form of a *disputatio*.[5]

For starters I shall look into the tract's way of dealing with some of the basic concepts featuring in the handbooks on dialectics of its time.[6]

1 How the Jargon Is Taught in the *IMM*: Some Examples

1.1 *Introducing 'Vox'*

True to tradition, the *Introductiones* first discusses the standard description of 'vox'.[7] The point of departure is Boethius' definition, "a *vox* is a percussion of air by the tongue that is emitted by a living being via the tongue though parts of the throat (that are called the windpipe)" (*vox est percussio aeris per linguam, que per quasdam partes gutturis* (*que arterie vocantur*) *ab animali profertur*). To this definition the text presents a counterargument, saying that if such were the definition of 'vox', then it would follow that every word is a percussion, on the grounds of the following syllogism:

---

3 Dr E.P. Bos and I are currently preparing an edition of the text.

4 L.M. de Rijk, 'Some new Evidence on Twelfth Century Logic. Alberic and the School of Mont Ste Geneviève (Montani)', *Vivarium* 4 (1966), 1-57.

5 *IMM*, Paris, BnF lat. 15141 (hereafter cited as *IMM*), f. 47ra: "Sed quoniam Introductionum ordo a voce sumpsit initium, hec quoque disputatio ab eadem ducat exordium."

6 Concepts discussed in those handbooks pertained not only to logic per se, but to semantics and grammar as well.

7 For an elaborate discussion of the notion of 'vox' in the *IMM*, see E.P. Bos, 'La théorie de la signification de la "vox significativa ad placitum" dans les *Introductiones Montanae Maiores*', in *Gilbert de Poitiers et ses contemporains*, ed. J. Jolivet and A. de Libera (Naples, 1987), 73-90: 83-86.

every percussion of air by the tongue is a percussion;
now a word is a percussion of air etc.;
therefore every word is a percussion.

This argument would seem to be justified by a specific rule of argumentation, to the effect that if something is said of a subject universally, and in turn that subject-expression applies to yet another something universally, then the first predicate is said of the ultimate subject universally.[8] However, as the text mentions, not everybody is happy with this outcome, and the way out would be to suggest that while the rule referred to is valid, it does not apply in this case, because the expression 'percussion' has changed its meaning along the way. In the expression 'every percussion of air is a percussion', 'percussion' indicates part of an activity, but in 'every word is a percussion of air', the expression 'percussion' indicates that to which a word owes its being.[9] The *IMM* agrees with this analysis and therefore the syllogism just brought forward is not valid.[10]

1.2 *On the Division between* voces significativae *and* voces non-significativae

The next item our tract goes into is the division between *voces significativae* and *voces non-significativae*. To help people understand this division and

8 *IMM*, f. 47ra: "Omnis percussio aeris per linguam etc. est percussio; sed omnis vox, ut dictum est, ⟨est⟩ percussio aeris etc.; igitur omnis vox est percussio. Sillogismus videtur esse in primo modo prime figure constitutus secundum regulam hanc: Si aliquid predicatur de aliquo universaliter et subiectum predicatur de aliquo universaliter, primum predicatum predicatur de ultimo subiecto universaliter."

9 *IMM*, f. 47ra: "Sed quidam, nolentes vocem percussionem esse concedere, determinant sillogismum presentem hoc modo quod enim in prima subicitur, in secunda minime predicari aiunt. Quia cum dicitur 'omnis percussio aeris etc. est percussio', proprie tenetur hic terminus 'percussio' significans quandam actionis partem; sed cum assumitur 'omnis vox est percussio aeris ⟨etc.⟩', non predicatur aliqua actio de voce, sed 'habens esse per aeris percussionem' de voce enuntiatur."

10 *IMM*, f. 47rb: "Hinc apparet quod iste paralogismus est qui* [*quod *P*] in his potest proponi hoc modo: omnis percussio est actio; sed omnis vox est percussio; ergo omnis vox est actio. Namque, ut dictum est, hoc nomen 'percussio' equivocum est, et aliud in prima subicitur et in secunda predicatur. Quare non sequitur." We are reminded here of the idea that universals are simply emissions of sounds ('flatus vocis'), but the argument is simply an example of a fallacy brought on by equivocation. Our author's stance suggests that he does not hold a vocalist position.

realise that it is appropriate, it would be useful if it were clarified what exactly the expression 'significativum' means. But instead of doing that, the tract simply starts off by giving a rather odd objection against the division, more specifically against the claim that the division is sufficient. The argument runs as follows. If the claim were sufficient, then whatever is contained under that which is divided should also be contained under one of the dividing categories, and the other way round. Now the universal 'signifying word' or the universal '[the] word Socrates' is contained under that which is divided. Hence it should be contained under either one of the dividing categories. But it is not, because neither is every signifying word significative or non-significative, nor is every word Socrates significative or non-significative, and yet every word Socrates is a word.[11]

From the response reported in the tract we can gather that the counterargument springs from a very basic misunderstanding of the expression 'whatever' (*quicquid*) featuring in the rule 'whatever is contained under that which is divided... (etc.)'. Later on in the Middle Ages this expression will come to be classified as a syncategorematic word and feature prominently in a number of *sophismata*. It can be difficult to interpret an expression containing the distributive word 'quicquid', because it is not clear what exactly the expression distributes. The author of the *IMM*, however, thinks that the opposition to the definition is impertinent, and explains that the word 'whatever' featuring in this particular case cannot apply to universals, but pertains to individuals only. For if it were to apply to universals, then many other kinds of divisions would fall short as well. For instance, the dividing description 'of animal, some are rational, others are non-rational' would also fail, because the universal 'mortal animal' is contained in what is divided, but does not fall under any one of the dividing categories. (This would imply that 'animal' should be taken as applying to individual animals.)[12]

---

11 *IMM*, f. 47rb: "De hac divisione queritur utrum sit sufficiens et per opposita. Si sufficiens est, tunc quicquid continetur sub diviso, et sub aliquo dividentium, et econverso. Sed hoc universale 'vox signifans*' [*significativa *P*] vel hoc universale 'vox Socrates' continetur sub illo diviso. Ergo sub aliquo dividentium continetur. Sed sub nullo dividentium eorum continetur, quia neque omnis vox significans est vox significativa vel non-significativa, similiter nec omnis vox Socrates est significativa vel non significativa; tamen omnis vox Socrates est vox."

12 *IMM*, f. 47rb: "Verum tamen est quod illud* [*illum *P*] 'quicquid' non comprehendit universalia, sed tantum singularia, ut dicatur 'quicquid continetur sub diviso' etc., idest quodcumque singulare. Quare non est obiectio. Nisi enim hoc dicamus, habemus in multis divisionibus hoc idem falsum; ut cum dicitur 'animalium aliud* [*alium *P*] rationale, aliud* [*alium *P*] irrationale', potest dici quod non sit sufficiens secundum illud, quia hoc

The text continues with another opposition against the division between significative and non-significative words, relating to the question whether or not the division is by way of opposites (*per opposita*). If so, then if a specific item were to fall under one of the dividing categories, then it would not fall under the other. The text discusses a possible counter-instance, i.e., of 'rex': the division is not one of opposites, because in that case they would not be said of the same individual. But the case of 'rex' seems to be an exception, because of that word we can say that it is both significative and non-significative. It is significative in the case of 'rex' occurring as such, but not when it occurs in 'sorex'.[13] And ultimately this would imply that the word 'rex' is both significative and non-significative.[14]

The remainder of the discussion sheds some light on how the division can apply *per opposita*. While one can agree that the word 'rex' is both significative and non-significative, it does not follow that therefore two opposites are applied to one and the same individual thing. The only way we can agree with the conclusion is if we take the expression 'the same word' in 'the same word is significative and non-significative' as a species, but not as something numerically the same, or as an *essentia*[15] *prolationis*.[16] So the distinction only applies *per opposita* to a particular occurrence, in our example 'rex'.

---

universale 'animal mortale' sub diviso continetur nec sub aliquo dividentium eius. Unde manifestum est illud 'quicquid' ad individua esse intelligendum, et non ad universalia."

13 *IMM*, f. 47va: "Rursus* [* rursum *P*], illa divisio per opposita fieri non videtur, quia si per opposita fieret, dividentia nec de se nec de aliquo individuo predicarentur. Sed quod de eodem individuo predicantur, hoc modo posse probari videtur: hec vox 'rex' est nomen; ergo hec vox 'rex' est significativa (*a parte* locus); et hec vox 'rex' est vox non-significativa, quia omnis pars nominis est vox non-significativa; sed hec vox 'rex' est pars nominis, quia ⟨pars⟩ huius nominis 'sorex'; ergo hec vox 'rex' est non-significativa. Quare 'non-significativum' et 'significativum' de eodem individuo predicantur, quia de hac voce 'rex'. (…) Quiddam enim quod est hec vox 'rex' est significativum* [*significativa *P*], quia est nomen, et quoddam quod est hec vox 'rex' est non-significativum* [*non significativa *P*]."

14 *IMM*, f. 47va: "Quare 'non-significativum' et 'significativum' de eodem individuo predicantur, quia de hac voce 'rex'."

15 The use of the word 'essentia' here, as is common in the 12th century, amounts to something like a particular 'occurrence' (the entity, so to speak). Bos mentions Tweedale's explanation of the word as 'thing' (cf. Bos, 'La théorie de la signification', 82).

16 *IMM*, f. 47va: "Sed si ex hoc concedimus 'hec vox "rex" est significativa et hec vox "rex" est non-significativa', quid inferatur?—(an) 'ergo eadem vox est significativa et non-significativa?' Potest concedi, quia eadem secundum speciem sed non secundum numerum neque secundum prolationis essentiam. (…) //f. 47vb// Quare* [*quia *P*] alia prolationis essentia, non specie sed numero, est finalis pars huius nominis 'sorex' et hoc nomen 'rex'."

A final point worth mentioning concerns the nature of significative utterances, a topic that also featured in early 12th-century commentaries on Aristotle's *De interpretatione*.[17] Apparently one way to understand the label 'significative' was as that which is actually significative. Our author disagrees with this interpretation, however, because if people who are not familiar with the language, or people who are asleep, were to utter significative words, then those very utterances would not signify (i.e., be actually significative). Nor will it do to say, as some do, that 'significative' amounts to 'that which could signify', because the utterance 'sida' could signify if someone were to impose it for anything, yet it is not significative. The Anonymous himself then explains that 'significative' is an indication of something that has the ability to signify by "a common or proper institution,"[18] which amounts to its being accepted as an expression in a language.

1.3 *On the Division between* nomen *and* verbum

As we have seen, the tract distinguishes between taking an utterance as a species and as an *essentia prolationis*. Bos already suggested that the notion of *essentia* is not entirely straightforward.[19] To find out more, it is useful to turn to the tract's discussion of the notions of *nomen, verbum* and *oratio*. One of the questions put forward is whether the division between these three kinds of significative words (*voces significativae*) is by way of opposites.[20] The following counterargument is presented:

> the word 'canis' (here to be translated as 'dog' or 'you are singing') is a noun;
> and the same *essentia* is a verb;
> therefore some noun is a verb.

---

17 Cf. Margaret Cameron, 'What's in a Name? Students of William Champeaux on the *vox significativa*', *Bochumer Philosophisches Jahrbuch für Antike und Mittelalter* 9 (2004), 93-114, esp. 100-1.

18 *IMM*, f. 48ra: "Quidam alii exponunt 'significativum', idest 'quod significat in actu'. Sed mentiuntur, cum quedam quoque voces significative prolate a nescientibus et a dormientibus non significent. Vel aliter dicunt alii 'significativum', idest 'quod possit significare'. Sed male dicunt, quia hec vox 'sida' potest significare si imponeretur cuidam rei, non tamen est significativum. Nos autem exponimus 'significativum', idest aptum natum* [*naturali *P*] institutione communi vel propria ad significandum."

19 Cf. Bos, 'La théorie de la signification', 83.

20 *IMM*, f. 49rb: "De predicta divisione, scilicet vox significativa ad placitum aliud nomen, aliud verbum, aliud oratio, ⟨queritur utrum sit per opposita⟩."

Before offering his own solution, the author of the *IMM* goes through a number of possible responses to this argument. The first response reports the viewpoint of people who would say that a noun is not a verb because it is not in virtue of its having the function of a verb that something is a noun. By analogy one could also reject the following type of syllogism:

> Socrates is sitting;
> Socrates is speaking;
> therefore someone who is sitting is speaking.

This particular syllogism fails because it is not in virtue of someone's sitting that he is speaking.[21] (Obviously the conclusion should be more or less understood here as saying that by the very fact that someone is sitting, he is speaking; the syllogism would certainly be valid if we were talking about two particular things one and the same person happened to be doing at the same time.) Yet it is clear, the argument proceeds, that the noun and the verb 'canis' are the same *essentia*. For supposing it were to be uttered by someone who did not understand, then in that case the person in question would either be uttering both (i.e., both noun and verb), or he would not be uttering anything, for there would be no more reason why he should be uttering a noun than a verb, because he does not understand either one of them.[22]

The main point of this argument is clear enough: by simply judging from the appearance of a single word, one cannot decide whether it is a noun or a verb. So any single occurrence (*essentia*) of the expression 'canis' can be either a noun or a verb. What is odd, though, is that it can both be a noun and a verb at the same time, and that this could be the case is illustrated with the example of someone who is saying something but has no idea of what he is saying. Apparently the speaker's role in establishing any kind of meaning of an expression of a particular utterance is completely disregarded. It would be better to simply say that a word cannot be identified at all as a noun or a verb

21 *IMM*, f. 49rb: "'Canis', hec vox est nomen, et illa eadem essentia est verbum. Ergo quoddam nomen est verbum. [...] Quidam tamen nituntur determinare, sensum concedentes, dicentes nomen non esse verbum quia non ex officio verbi nomen aliquod est. Eadem quoque ratione negare possent omnes sillogismos huiusmodi, 'Socrates est sedens; et Socrates est loquens; ergo quidam sedens est loquens'. Non enim ex eo quod sedens est, loquens est; quare nulla ratio est qua sillogismus esse dicatur."

22 *IMM*, f. 49rb: "Sed quod 'canis' in eadem essentia sit nomen et verbum apparet ex hoc quod si proferatur a non intelligente, aut utrumque profert aut nichil, cum nulla ratio sit quare magis proferat nomen quam verbum, cum nullum eorum intelligat."

(or whatever), or indeed as a word even, if the utterer is clueless. (Of course, as we have seen, the Anonymous does include this analysis as a possibility.)

The second argument simply brings forward a seemingly valid syllogism:

> everything that is a noun is a noun;
> now some verb is that which is a noun;
> therefore some verb is a noun.[23]

The next, somewhat circular argument leads to a similar conclusion by way of the *locus a parte*: if something is said of a part, it is also said of the whole in a particular way. The case at issue is the following. The word 'canis' is a verb. So some noun is a verb. And if the definitions of a noun and a verb are combined, when we say that some word that is significative by convention with time is a word significative by convention without time, the items themselves to which these definitions apply would also be mutually said of each other.[24]

The *IMM* eventually accepts not only that a verb is a noun, but also that the two *universalia*, being a noun and being a verb, can reside in one and the same individual thing. Consequently Aristotle's division between noun and verb should not be considered as applying to the *essentiae* of the relevant expressions, but instead it concerns their distinct functions respectively: it is by virtue of its function that a certain word (which by its appearance could be considered a noun or a verb) is a noun or a verb.[25] No more is said about the function of these expressions. By comparison, Abelard's account of the nature of noun and verb is far more explicit: they are not distinct in their *significatio*,

---

23 *IMM*, f. 49rb: "Iterum, probatur hoc idem sillogismo necessario: omne id quod est nomen est nomen; sed quoddam verbum est id quod est nomen; ergo quoddam verbum est* [*quod est *add. P*] nomen."

24 *IMM*, f. 49rb: "Iterum. 'Canis', hec vox est verbum. Ergo quoddam nomen est verbum. Locus *a parte*. Regula: *Si aliquid predicatur de parte, et de toto par⟨ticulariter⟩*. Et quia diffinitiones nominis et verbi coniunguntur, cum 'quedam vox significativa' dicimus 'ad placitum cum tempore est vox significativa ad placitum //f. 49va// sine tempore', ipsa quoque diffinita, scilicet nomen et verbum, de se invicem predicantur."

25 *IMM*, f. 49vb: "Quare verbum nomen esse concedimus, et in eodem individuo ista duo universalia nomen et verbum esse concedimus. Quare predictam divisionem non ut essentias vocum dividere proposuit Aristotiles [cf. Aristoteles, *De int.* 1, 16a1], sed* [*scilicet *P*] ut officia eorum esse diversa demonstraret et in suis officiis segregata esse ostenderet. Et dixit, 'vox alia nomen, alia verbum', non alia in essentia, sed ex alio officio nomen et ex alio officio verbum."

but what distinguishes a verb from a noun is that the former not only signifies, but also asserts that something is the case.[26]

To return to the question what is meant by *essentia* in the text, it would be safe to say, I think, that the distinction between *universale* and *essentia* of a word coincides with what later became known as that between type and token of an expression respectively. A token can be roughly circumscribed as a spatio-temporal occurrence of a word, whereas the type in this connection would be the same word as taken independently of any singular occurrence.[27] In the view of the *IMM*, the characteristics of a token word as such do not tell us whether it is, or can be, a noun or a verb; one needs to consider the context to see what function the word performs in an utterance.

So far I hope to have given some insight into the treatise's way of handling the basic ingredients of logic that were discussed during this time, and at the same time to have shown some of its theoretical starting points. More can be said about the treatise's approach to the elements of logical arguments,[28] but I shall leave this topic and turn to some of the tract's positions on the validity of logical arguments. First I shall say something about the different types of proposition to highlight some interesting items featuring in the discussions, and then I shall continue with an analysis of the tract's exposition of the logical relationships between propositions.

2 The *IMM* on Propositions

After a quite elaborate discussion on the proposition in general,[29] the *IMM* comes to talk about the division between the universal and the particular proposition. The origins of this division are to be found in Aristotle's *De interpretatione*, and more specifically in Boethius' commentary on that work. Most likely every student would have been familiar with the division, but the Anonymous will explain the use of the expressions 'universal' and so on in this connection later on. For now the tract simply addresses the question whether or not the

26 Cf. Petrus Abaelardus, *Dialectica*, ed. L.M. de Rijk (Assen, 1956), 149,2-27.

27 Incidentally, this distinction is also used in a variety of ways, and the explanations that are given are not always helpful either. See, e.g., Linda Wetzel, 'Types and Tokens', *The Stanford Encyclopedia of Philosophy* (Spring 2011 Edition), E.N. Zalta, ed., URL = <http://plato.stanford.edu/archives/spr2011/entries/types-tokens/>.

28 For more details, see Bos, 'La théorie de la signification', passim.

29 See the discussion in Bos, 'La théorie de la signification', 86-8.

division between universal and particular proposition is by way of opposites.[30] Once again, we find an opposition. If the division were by way of opposites, then no singular proposition would be indefinite. Yet there is a counterexample, namely the proposition '(a) lion lives' (*leo vivit*), which is both singular and indefinite.[31] The Anonymous explains that the division under discussion is in fact by way of opposites, and in this connection he once again makes use of the distinction he made earlier between the *essentia* and *officium* of an expression. However, the division does not cover the *essentiae* of the expressions, that is the tokens, such that one and the same indefinite token of a word should not also be singular. Instead the nouns 'singular' and 'indefinite' (and 'universal') apply to different functions. In conclusion the Anonymous says that we can accept that an indefinite (i.e., that token of a word which is indefinite) is singular, but we must reject the claim that a singular *significatio* of a word, or that in virtue of which the word is singular, is indefinite.[32] From this explanation it appears that a singular *significatio* includes its function as a singular.

In a subsequent section the *IMM* goes into an interesting problem about the label 'universal proposition', viz. whether or not this label is applicable in two particular cases.[33] The first problematic sentence brought forward is 'every chimaera is opinable'.[34] The dilemma is that if you accept that the label 'universal proposition' does not apply to it, then that would mean that it does not have a universal subject; but if you concede that it does (i.e., if you accept that it does

30 *IMM*, f. 55ra: "De oppositione huius divisionis, scilicet propositionum alia universalis, alia singularis etc., queritur utrum sit per opposita."

31 *IMM*, f. 55ra: "Si concedatur per opposita esse, concluditur: ergo nulla singularis erit indefinita* [*infinitiva *P*], et in aliis similiter. Probatur tamen quod quedam singularis est indefinita* [*infinitiva *P*], ut 'leo vivit'; et eadem est indefinita; ergo quedam singularis est indefinita* [infinitiva *P*]."

32 *IMM*, f. 55ra: "Concedimus quod hec divisio non est per oppositas essentias vocum, quod illa essentia que est indefinita illa eadem non sit singularis, ut sepe iam diximus. Non est inconveniens si non sint huiusmodi divisiones que sunt in nominibus secunde impositionis per oppositas essentias, cum nomina ipsa non essentias, sed officia denotare habeant* [*habent *P*], et divisiones ille non essentiarum, sed officiorum esse proponuntur; quare dividimus illam singularem propositionem. Si dicatur 'indefinita (illa essentia vocis que est indefinita) est singularis', concedimus; si vero dicatur quod significatio singularis sit indefinita* [*indefinite *P*], vel ex eo officio quo est singularis, sit indefinita, falsum ⟨est⟩."

33 These cases are also looked into in Bos, 'La théorie de la signification', 88-9.

34 It is interesting that in this case the discussion is about 'omnis chimaera'. The usual topic of debate is the question whether or not the expression 'chimaera est opinabilis' implies 'chimaera est'.

have a universal subject), then it follows that chimaera is a universal subject, because there is no other subject than that.[35]

The Anonymous replies that the argument just put forward is sophistic, and is brought on by a fallacy of equivocation in connection with the expression 'universal subject'. Let us consider the gist of the argument in detail. The conclusion, that chimaera is a universal subject, does not follow. We can accept that 'the proposition has a universal subject', but not that 'a universal subject is what the proposition has'. In these two propositions the expression 'universal subject' has a different meaning. When we say, 'the universal proposition "every chimaera is opinable" has a universal subject', in that sentence the expression 'universal subject' means 'that which is understood as universal'; in the second sentence, 'the universal subject chimaera is what the proposition "every chimaera is opinable" has', the label 'universal subject' is to be identified with 'that which is applicable to many things'. In sum, just as the expression 'man' signifies man, but not any determinate one, likewise the expression 'chimaera' signifies chimaera, but not any determinate one.[36]

The beginning of the author's reply proceeds in a way similar to Abelard's in his argument against one of his opponents on the issue of universals. In this particular argument Abelard makes use of the distinction between 'genus est vox' ('a genus is a word') and 'vox est genus' ('a word is a genus'). The former sentence is true, but the latter is false. In the former, the subject matter of the sentence is some material entity that happens to be a genus, but in the latter what is said is that an articulated sound as such is a genus, which is false. In fact, in the context of his discussion of universals, Abelard mentions the example of the chimaera, pointing out that in response to the question,

35 *IMM*, f. 55va: "Queritur de ista descriptione utrum conveniat huic propositioni, 'omnis chimera est opinabilis', 'nullus hircocervus disputat'. Si conceditur quod eis non conveniat, infertur: ergo non habet universale subiectum etc.; et si habet universale subiectum, cum nullum alium habeat* [*habet *P*] nisi 'chimeram', 'chimera* [*chimeram *P*]' est universale subiectum."

36 *IMM*, f. 55va: "Sed non sequitur. Quamvis enim concedimus quod habet universale subiectum, non tamen universale subiectum est quod habet propositio predicta. Et est *equivocationis* sophisma. Equivoce enim accipitur hoc nomen 'universale' cum dicitur 'hec propositio "omnis chimera est opinabilis" habet universale subiectum'. In prima enim 'universale' significat 'id quod ut universale intelligitur'. Cum enim dicimus '"omnis chimera est opinabilis", hec propositio habet universale subiectum', non intelligitur quod habet aptum predicari de pluribus subiectum, sed habet subiectum universale, idest habet subiectum ut universale significatum. Quemadmodum hoc nomen 'homo' significat hominem ita quod nullum determinate, sic hoc nomen 'chimera' significat chimeram, nullam chimeram determinans."

'What are you thinking?' (*quid intelligis*), you can truly answer, 'I am thinking a chimaera' (*chimaeram intelligo*); this is to say that, although there is no *thing* to be thought, you are still thinking something.[37] As we know, later on in the Middle Ages a similar issue is raised in analyses of sentences like 'papam percussi' ('the pope I have hit') and 'percussi papam' ('I have hit the pope').[38]

While the IMM's way of dealing with the sample sentence 'every chimaera is opinable' (*omnis chimaera est opinabilis*) indeed reminds us of some of Abelard's teachings, it is not nearly as refined. The only thing the Anonymous seems to claim is that the expression 'chimaera' has *significatio*, and that, moreover, it can be combined with the universal sign 'every' in such a way that the proposition it features in makes sense. Furthermore, the quantifier 'every' can be conjoined with some expression that is understood as a universal but cannot be applied to many individual things (in this case to something that cannot exist anyway). More evidence of the same perspective is the author's rejection of the inference, 'every animal is rational or irrational; therefore Socrates is rational or irrational'.[39] So what is meant by a universal proposition then is a proposition of which the subject is understood as a universal. Yet the Anonymous seems to confuse discrete entities and universal concepts, a distinction to which Abelard was particularly sensitive.

So far we have looked at a few distinctions leading up to an account of propositions in logical arguments. In the next section I shall pay attention to some of the IMM's arguments surrounding logical relationships.

---

37 For a detailed analysis of Abelard's line of reasoning here, see L.M. de Rijk, 'The Semantical Impact of Abailard's Solution of the Problem of Universals', in *Petrus Abaelardus (1079-1142). Person, Werk und Wirkung*, ed. R. Thomas, Jean Jolivet, D.E. Luscombe, and L.M. de Rijk (Trier, 1980), 139-51; L.M. de Rijk, 'Abailard's Semantic Views in the Light of Later Developments', in *English Logic and Semantics from the End of the Twelfth Century to the Time of Ockham and Burleigh. Acts of the 4th European Symposium on Medieval Logic and Semantics* (Leiden-Nijmegen, 1979), ed. H.A.G. Braakhuis, C.H. Kneepkens, and L.M. de Rijk (Nijmegen, 1981), 1-58. Both articles were reprinted in L.M. de Rijk, *Through Language to Reality. Studies in Medieval Semantics and Metaphysics*, ed. E.P. Bos (Northampton, 1989), nos. III and VI.

38 See L.M. de Rijk, 'Semantics and Ontology. An Assessment of Medieval Terminism', *Vivarium* 51 (2013), 13-59, esp. 46.

39 IMM, f. 52vb: "Hoc tamen scire hic sufficiat quod in illis in quibus alterum determinate inest non est concedenda huiusmodi disiunctio—ut dicatur 'Socrates irrationalis vel rationalis est', vel 'animalis omne est rationale vel irrationale animal'; immo nullum animal est rationale vel irrationale. Concedimus tamen omne animal esse vel rationale vel irrationale."

3 On Logical Relationships

After having spoken about contrary and subcontrary propositions, the *IMM* turns to the relationship of contradictories. The tract starts with one characteristic of contradictory propositions, saying that the nature of contradictories is such that it is always necessary that one is true and the other is false.[40] But then a counterexample is brought forward: if this were the case, then of the two propositions, 'Socrates is sitting' and 'Socrates is not sitting', it is necessary that one is true and the other is false. But that is not true, because of neither one it is necessary that it is true or false. Hence the description of contradictories is incorrect.[41]

In his solution to this difficulty, the Anonymous points out that the description of contradictory opposites can be taken in different ways. If we are talking about things (in the sense of states of affairs), then the description is in fact false, meaning that of all contradictories one would necessarily be true and the other would necessarily be false. But obviously neither one of the sample sentences is necessarily true or necessarily false.[42] On the other hand, if the description is not understood as concerning particular things, but the sense of the proposition, then one of the two contradictories 'Socrates is sitting' and 'Socrates is not sitting' is true and the other is false. The sense of the description then amounts to saying that the entire proposition 'that one of the two is true' is necessary. For it is at least possible for one of them to be true, and likewise for the other one to be false. The expression 'it is necessary', then, does not entail that one of the two is not contingently false.[43] Later on in the text

---

40 *IMM*, f. 57vb: "Natura igitur contradictoriarum talis est quod semper necesse est unam esse veram et alteram esse falsam."

41 *IMM*, f. 57vb: "Sed si omnium contradictoriarum necesse est unam esse veram et alteram falsam esse, tunc istarum duarum, scilicet 'Socrates sedet', 'Socrates non sedet', necesse est unam esse veram et alteram esse falsam. Sed hec falsa est, quia neutram istarum necesse est esse veram vel falsam. Falsum ergo est quod omnium contradictoriarum necesse sit unam esse veram et alteram esse falsam."

42 *IMM*, f. 57vb: "Ad quod dicimus quod propositio ista multiplex est. Exposita enim de rebus falsa est, ut dicamus 'necesse est omnium contradictoriarum unam esse veram et alteram falsam', idest de omnibus contradictoriis una illarum est vera necessario, et altera sit falsa necessario. De nulla namque istarum 'Socrates sedet', 'Socrates non sedet' est verum quod ipsa sit vera necessario, et altera falsa necessario, quia neque ista 'Socrates sedet', neque ista 'Socrates non sedet'."

43 *IMM*, f. 57vb: "Exposita de sensu enuntiationis ut loquamur non ⟨de⟩ contradictoriis, sed de sensu huius propositionis: 'una istarum contradictoriarum "Socrates sedet", "Socrates non sedet" est vera, et altera est falsa'. Et sit sensus talis: 'necesse est unam istarum esse

(see below, in an example of conversion) this distinction will be explained in terms of an exposition *per compositionem* or *per divisionem*.[44]

In the section on contradictories another issue comes up, which is evidence of the Anonymous' hostility towards some of Abelard's alleged positions. The question addressed is whether or not the two sentences 'every antlered man is an animal', and 'some antlered man is not an animal' are contradictory opposites.[45] The first response brought forward by the Anonymous denies that they are, for two reasons. For one thing, the two propositions are false. Besides, neither of the two is significative of one sense, that is to say, both sentences posit two things: the proposition 'every man who is antlered is an animal' asserts both that some man is antlered and that this very man is an animal, and likewise the proposition 'some man who is antlered is not an animal' asserts that some man is antlered and is not an animal.[46] Although strictly speaking the exposition of the two sentences under discussion does not seem entirely correct, the virtual opponent's point is evident: both sentences, in his view, entail the position that there is some man with antlers.

However, this is exactly what the treatise objects to, as is evidenced in the Anonymous' attack on an account he attributes to Abelard. For the latter, the Anonymous claims, the negative particle in the denial applies to the entire proposition that comes after it; and this forces him, according to our author, to accept propositions like 'it is not the case that there are eight days since they have shed their antlers', and many other absurdities.[47] In his final words on

---

veram', idest necessarium est quod ista proponit unam istarum esse veram. Minime enim contingere potest quod hoc non sit verum, unam istarum esse veram; similiter, 'altera istarum est falsa', quod ista dicit, necessarium est; non enim ponit quod altera cum est falsa contingenter, est vera necessario."

44 The *IMM* continues with some remarks about the proposition 'necesse est contradictoriarum omnium unam esse veram et alteram esse falsam', which was to become a frequently discussed *sophisma* in later treatises.

45 *IMM*, f. 58ra: "Queritur utrum sint iste contradictorie: 'omnis homo cornutus est animal', 'quidam homo cornutus non est animal'."

46 *IMM*, f. 58ra: "Dicimus eas contradictorias non esse, quia ambe false sunt. Neque sunt unius sensus significative. Utraque enim facit positionem, ut ista 'omnis homo qui est cornutus, est animal' ponit hominem quendam esse cornutum et ipsum esse animal; similiter ista 'quidam homo qui est cornutus, non est animal' ponit ⟨hominem⟩ quendam esse cornutum et non esse animal."

47 *IMM*, f. 58ra: "Quidam, ut m⟨agister⟩ P⟨etrus⟩, in talibus sic putant assignandas esse contradictorias, ut 'non' (negativa particula) in negatione ante totam propositionem ponatur, hoc modo: 'non omnis homo qui est cornutus, est animal'. A simili oportet eos concedere quod non sunt octo dies quod cornua amiserunt, et multa absurda huic consimilia."

the issue, the Anonymous states that it makes no difference where you put the negative particle, and he emphasises yet again that in the case at issue there is no contradiction, because both sentences are false to begin with and have more than one sense as well.[48] A similar analysis is given of the two sentences 'a chimaera within three days will ride to Rome' and 'a chimaera within three days will not ride to Rome'; again there is no contradiction because the two sentences are false and do not have one sense either.[49]

Finally, again against the supposed view of Abelard, the Anonymous argues that the two sentences 'every phoenix is an animal' and 'some phoenix is not an animal' are in fact contradictory opposites. Contrary to Abelard, who supposedly thinks that both propositions are false (because there is only one phoenix), the Anonymous says that the sentence 'every phoenix is an animal' is true. To begin with, phoenix is a species of animal. Furthermore, the use of the expression 'every' in the construction 'every phoenix' does not imply the existence of more than one phoenix, as indeed neither does the expression 'every man' in the sentence 'every man is running'. In the words of the Anonymous, "the word 'every' posited in the subject is not a noun, nor does it signify any multitude or any other subject-thing, but instead it consignifies universally [...], that is, nothing of the subject of which the predicate is not said."[50] As Iwakuma states, the subject term combined with the expression 'every' is considered a species-term.[51] Apparently, the expression 'phoenix', of

48 *IMM*, f. 58ra: "Nos vero dicimus quod* [*quia *P*], sive negativa particula preponatur sive interponatur, semper tales propositiones false sunt; neque eisdem assignande sunt contradictorie quia sunt unius sensus. Et nota nulla⟨m⟩ propositionem esse unius sensus que habet hoc nomen 'quod' preter subiunctivum cum 'est' iunctum, ut apparet in predicta propositione."

49 *IMM*, f. 58ra: "Dicimus eas non habere contradictorias, quia non sunt unius sensus. Sed utreque false sunt simul, quia utraque ponit chimeram equitaturam Romam, sed una ante tres dies equitaturam ⟨et altera non ante tres dies equitaturam eam⟩ proponit."

50 *IMM*, f. 58rb: "Respondemus igitur opinioni* [*oppositioni *P*] illi, ex qua illa falsa sententia initium traxit, ut negaret predictas propositiones contradictorias esse, scilicet* [*secundum *P*] huic 'hoc nomen "omnis" in subiecto positum multitudinem subiectorum colligit, ut "omnis homo currit" multos homines currere demonstrat'. Huic false opinioni* [*oppositioni *P*] contradicimus, dicentes hoc nomen 'omnis' in subiecto positum non esse nomen, et nullius multitudinis significativum nec alicuius rei alteri subiecte, sed consignificat* [*cum significat *P*] universaliter, ut ait Aristotiles, idest significat quod nichil est subiecti ad quod predicatum non dicatur."

51 Yukio Iwakuma, 'Alberic of Paris on Mont Ste Geneviève against Peter Abelard', in *Logic and Language in the Middle Ages*, ed. J. Leth Fink, H. Hansen and A.M. Mora-Márquez (Leiden, 2012), 27-47: 33.

which we know that only one exists, should be taken as a warning sign to interpret the expression 'every' in a species-related way.

This way of interpreting such universal expressions is not uncommon later on in the Middle Ages either. Peter of Spain, for instance, rejects the inference 'every man is of necessity an animal; therefore Socrates is of necessity an animal', precisely because in the antecedent the expressions 'man' and 'animal' are species-terms, whereas in the consequent one is talking about individuals. (Peter's view in this matter is not entirely consistent, however, for he does accept the inference 'every man is an animal; therefore Socrates is an animal', and, moreover, he says that in conjunction with the *syncategorema* 'de necessitate', the subject terms supposit for past present and future instances, i.e., individuals.)

Another sample expression worth mentioning in connection with the requirements for a contradiction is the pair 'Socrates will perhaps sleep tomorrow' and 'Socrates will perhaps not sleep tomorrow'. Of course, for those two to qualify as contradictories at all, they would first and foremost have to be propositions. As appears from the Anonymous' response, the difficulty addressed here does not have to do with future contingents, but points towards the issue of how to deal with expressions featuring in opaque contexts. On the assumption that the two sentences under discussion are uttered by different people, what they express are actually different doubts. Taken in this way, the utterances (by different people) have different senses and are not really propositions at all; they simply express different doubts. So in that sense there is no contradiction either. On the other hand, 'perhaps' could also be taken as expressing something contingent, in which case the two utterances would be propositions.[52] The tract does not in this context decide whether or not on this interpretation the proposition is true or false.[53]

52 IMM, f. 58ra: "Adhuc queritur de istis, utrum sint contradictorie 'Socrates cras forsitan dormiet' et 'Socrates forsitan non dormiet cras'. Et dicimus quod non sunt contradictorie, quia non sunt propositiones. //f. 58rb// A diversis sunt prolate, ⟨et⟩ secundum diversos proponentes diversa habent significare, ut ista 'Socrates forsitan cras dormiet' prolata a Platone significat Platonem dubitare de Socrate, utrum dormiet cras. Possumus tamen dicere has voces esse propositiones, ut 'forsitan' non dubitationem, sed contingens significet, velut* [*et *add. P*] fiat sensus talis 'Socrates forsitan cras dormiet', idest contingenter dormiet."

53 Bos discusses a number of possible characteristics of a proposition and also gives examples of problematic cases brought forward and analysed in the IMM; see Bos, 'La théorie de la signification', 86-9.

Another kind of logical relationship dealt with in the *IMM* is that of conversion. The question is raised whether or not conversion can be applied to propositions about the past and/or future. The tract considers the objection that it cannot, which is argued for by a counterexample (a seemingly absurd conversion). The following is false: 'no old man was a boy'; therefore the following is false: 'no boy was an old man'.[54] The Anonymous rejects this argument. The proposition 'no old man was a boy' is false, and this can be inferred from the false proposition 'no boy was an old man'. The proposition 'no boy was an old man' is proven to be false because its contradictory opposite, 'some boy was an old man', is true (for example, if we are talking about Methuselah, who lived for a very long time).[55] The author also notes that the sentences can be analysed *per divisionem* and *per compositionem*. In the former sense both of them are false, and in the latter they are true.[56] As De Rijk has noted, the kind of problem addressed in this particular example later on inspired people like John Buridan to come up with the idea of an expression sometimes having *appellatio formae*.[57]

A final example of a logical relationship that is quite extensively dealt with in the *IMM* is the rule *a toto per remotionem*, which runs: whatever is removed from a universal universally is also removed of any of its parts (*quicquid removetur a toto universali universaliter, et a parte sua qualibet*). There is one particular

54 *IMM*, f. 59ra: "Obicitur. Ista est falsa 'nullus senex fuit puer'; ergo ista est falsa 'nullus puer fuit senex', quam quidam decepti vera⟨m⟩ esse putant. Et ideo neque in preterito, neque in futuro conversiones aliqualiter fieri putant." (From the response [see note 55, below], it would appear that it might be better to read the sample as "ista est falsa 'nullus puer fuit senex'; ergo ista est falsa 'nullus senex fuit puer'." The problematic sentence 'puer fuit senex' was a famous example of Abelard's.)

55 *IMM*, f. 59ra: "Unde conversionem in illis concedimus. Et falsam istam 'nullus senex fuit puer' dicimus, et ex ista 'nullus puer fuit senex' falsa, falsam esse istam 'nullus senex fuit puer' inferri concedimus. Et quod ista sit falsa probatur ex hoc quod sua contradictoria, scilicet 'quidam puer fuit senex', vera esse probatur, hoc modo: 'Metusalam fuit senex; ergo quidam puer fuit senex', vel 'ille puer qui vixit per centum annos fuit senex' (locus *a parte*) vel 'ille homo qui ortus est in tempore David, fuit senex; ergo quidam puer fuit senex'."

56 *IMM*, f. 59ra: "Possunt enim exponi per divisionem et compositionem. ⟨In compositione⟩ false erunt; in divisione vere, ut dicamus 'quidam puer fuit senex', idest 'ille homo in quo pueritia fuit, in eodem senectus fuit', quia in Socrate. Sed non in quo pueritia fuit, in eodem simul senectus esse potuit. Sicut 'quoddam album fuit nigrum': non quod simul fuit album et nigrum, sed quoniam istud quod album fuit, //f. 60ra// aliquando fuit nigrum."

57 For the literature, see above, n. 38.

counterargument that had apparently raised quite a stir, as appears from the parade of masters reported to have voiced an opinion on it. The debate is also useful to look at in order to see the differences of opinion among the schools of the time.

The inference under discussion is the following: no stone or silver has been made by Socrates; therefore no stone or silver statue has been made by Socrates.[58] The Anonymous' response to this so-called opposition is that it has no bearing on the subject under discussion, because he by no means takes a stone statue to be a 'subjective part of stone'.[59] Abelard in particular is vehemently attacked. The Anonymous may have taken his cue from the *Dialectica*, where Abelard talks about the categories *facere* and *pati*, and the sequence *si fit, non est*.[60] But the underlying motive for Abelard to object to the inference is that the antecedent reads that no stone is brought to being a stone by an activity of Socrates, whereas the consequent says that no statue is brought to being a statue by an activity of Socrates. And so, our author ridicules, he claims that no body is made by Socrates, yet a statue and a house are made by Socrates.[61] Indeed, Abelard clearly makes a distinction between the creating and compiling: creation can be carried out by the Creator only, whereas it is up to man to compile something out of an entity that has been created.[62]

Next master Alberic's position is introduced. The master opposes the inference by saying that by the activity of Socrates bone and iron are conjoined, and from these two elements one body is made, viz. a knife. This body did not exist yesterday, and it was made by none other than a man, because it was not produced by nature. And because Socrates is the only one to produce this body, therefore Socrates has made this body, because it was made, and was made by

58 IMM, f. 69rb: "Item obicitur: nullus lapis fit a Socrate vel nullum argentum; ergo nulla statua lapidea vel argentea fit a Socrate."

59 IMM, f. 69rb: "Hec et huiusmodi non sunt oppositiones secundum sententiam quam tenemus. Minime namque statuam lapideam concedimus esse lapidis partem subiectivam."

60 Cf. Petrus Abaelardus, *Dialectica*, ed. De Rijk, 106,35-107,11.

61 IMM, f. 62rb: "M⟨agister⟩ P⟨etrus⟩ vero nimium in huiusmodi oppositionis solutione ut suam falsitatem defenderet, laborabat; et dicebat quod illud quod in prima ⟨pro⟩positione removetur, non removetur in secunda, quod, quando dicimus 'nullus lapis fit a Socrate', vis subiecti redundat in predicatum, et est sensus talis: nullus lapis operatione Socratis promovetur in esse lapidis. Illud vero non potest removeri a statua, ut dicatur* [*diceretur *P*] 'nulla statua operatione Socratis movetur in esse statue'. Et sic, semper referendo predicatum subiecto, dicebat quod nullum corpus fit a Socrate, tamen statua et domus fit a Socrate."

62 Cf. Petrus Abaelardus, *Dialectica*, ed. De Rijk, 417.

no one else.[63] After repeating his own position, the Anonymous gives a final blow to Abelard, accusing him of having to grant that Abelard himself and the queen of France and he himself and Mount Apennine were one body, because he could not accept that this body did not exist yesterday.[64]

4 Concluding Remarks

As Bos has already correctly surmised, the *IMM* is not a unified treatise.[65] It does not give us any elaborate theory on logic and it does not explain the common lore in a very systematic way either. Its *modus operandi* is to present a thesis, to point out the implications of such a thesis by analysing counterarguments either ascribed to real masters or to virtual debaters, and then to provide solutions to the arguments in question. The context of the work is evidently educational: students are supposed to learn several things at the same time, such as the standard ways of defining and describing the properties, functions and behaviours of linguistic expressions, and what the current definitions and descriptions entail. But they also learn how to frame arguments, or how to refute them, by being confronted with all kinds of examples.

The tract is an important witness of the teachings of the 12th century. It gives us evidence of the rivalry among different schools in Paris; the author's favourite target is Abelard, whose views on a particular issue are usually rejected with reference to Alberic of Paris' teachings. The *IMM* is also a rich source for the study of the practice of teaching logic during that period. While it may not be a very original treatise, it does include many discussions of the existing vocabulary used in logic, and it also brings up quite a few instances of problematic propositions that inspired later logicians to delve into them more deeply and to make more refined distinctions.

---

63 *IMM*, f. 62rb: "Huic m⟨agister⟩ Al⟨bericus⟩ opponit sic. Per operationem Socratis os et ferrum coniunguntur, et ex illis duobus efficitur unum corpus, scilicet cultellus. Istud corpus non fuit heri, neque factum est ab alio nisi ab homine, cum non sit opus nature. Et cum nullius operatione hoc corpus sit factum nisi Socratis, Socrates igitur hoc corpus fecit, cum factum sit, et a nullo alio ⟨factum est⟩."

64 For more details about this particular argument, see Christopher J. Martin, 'Abelard on Logic', in *The Cambridge Companion to Abelard*, ed. J.F. Brower and K. Guilfoy (Cambridge, 2004), 158-99: 198, n. 68.

65 See Bos, 'La théorie de la signification', 89.

Tu scis an de mentiente sit falsum Sortem esse illum: On the Syncategorem '*an*'

Angel d'Ors

1 Introduction. Genres of Treatises: '*Syncategoremata*', '*Abstractiones*', '*Sophismata*' and '*Sophistaria sive Distinctiones*'

Logical analyses of the syncategorem '*an*' can be found in several genres of 13th-century treatises on logic ('*Syncategoremata*', '*Abstractiones*', '*Sophismata*', and '*Sophistaria sive Distinctiones*'). Within each genre of treatises, these logical analyses bear distinctive characteristics. This invites one to reflect on the nature of these 'genres' and their defining characteristics,[1] even if a study of this syncategorem on its own does not allow us to draw definitive conclusions on the matter.

An overview of the distinctive characteristics of the analyses of the syncategorem '*an*' in different genres of treatises yields four provisional conclusions: i) it is possible to find 'logical criteria', as well as 'formal features' related to them, that indeed allow us to speak of different genres of treatises; ii) nevertheless, complex processes of transformation and convergence affected treatises in each genre during the 13th century, and, owing to these changes, a majority of the known works are, to varying extents, of a mixed nature, hence the fact that only in a few exceptional cases is it possible to label a work as a pure example of one genre; iii) the titles by which these treatises have come to be known do not always reveal their distinctive features or, therefore, the genre

* Note of the Editors: This text was read at the 16th European Symposium on Medieval Logic and Semantics held in Udine, Italy, in September 2006. It is a short (cut out) version of a longer paper written in Spanish, which at present remains unpublished. The editors have employed the text that was presented at the conference and added the footnotes and the concluding section, taken from the full Spanish version.

1 On the nature and characteristics of these genres, see H.A.G. Braakhuis, *De 13de eeuwse traktaten over syncathegorematische termen*, Deel I, Inleidende studie (Meppel, 1979); Norman Kretzmann, '*Syncategoremata, exponibilia, sophismata*', in *The Cambridge History of Later Medieval Philosophy*, ed. N. Kretzmann, A. Kenny, and J. Pinborg (Cambridge, 1982), 211-45; Alain de Libera, 'La littérature des *abstractiones* et la tradition logique d'Oxford', in *The Rise of British Logic*, ed. P.O. Lewry (Toronto, 1985), 63-114; L.M. de Rijk, *Some Earlier Parisian Tracts on Distinctiones Sophismatum* (Nijmegen, 1988), IX-XI.

 | DOI 10.1163/9789004324275_008

to which they belong; and iv) the criteria used so far to define these genres do not seem to be the most adequate.

When attempting to define the characteristics of the different genres of logic treatises, the 'analysis of sophisms' has generally been regarded as the 'common matter' of all genres, whereas the 'differentiating forms' were thought to arise from the different 'classification criteria' of the sophisms, with a view to their logical analysis. Besides, sophisms have been considered to be 'propositions' with an ambiguous meaning, which originates from the fact that they contain a term that may serve different functions or have several meanings. Seen from this angle, L.M. de Rijk proposed a classification of the treatises in three genres, based on whether their principal matter be 'sophisms' proper ('*Sophismata*'), or the 'syncategorems' operating in the sophisms ('*Syncategoremata*'), or the 'distinctions' whereby these sophisms can be solved ('*Sophistaria sive Distinctiones*').[2] This criterion might in principle seem adequate for a characterisation of '*Syncategoremata*' and '*Sophistaria sive Distinctiones*', but it does not seem to be satisfactory towards a characterisation of '*Sophismata*': can a classification of sophisms proper have any meaning if these are seen as propositions, without considering the intervening syncategorems or the distinctions that solve them? And the '*Abstractiones*', which

2 De Rijk, *Some Earlier Parisian Tracts*, X-XI: "The literary genre covering this sort of scholastic writings, is threefold: 1. the tracts on *syncategoremata*, which classify the precise meaning of a number of syncategorematic words, the ways in which they are used ambiguously; and they discuss current grammatical, semantic and logical rules related to these words and, finally, deal with special sophismata and the (attempted) solutions to them; 2. the *sophismata* collections, where the *sophismata* themselves are the primary objects of discussion, although each of them is typical of a special difficulty concerning special ambiguous terms or phrases; 3. the so-called *Sophistariae*, the tracts on *sophismata* which, unlike the *Sophismata* collections, take the usual solutions (in fact, *distinctiones* concerning the ambiguous expression involved) as their starting-points. To be sure, the borderlines between the three genres are rather fuzzy, [...]. For this reason I shall use the name *Sophistaria* for those special tracts on the solutions to sophismata which do not focus on the sophismata themselves (as is the case with the *Sophismata* collections) nor the syncategorematic and other ambiguous expressions as such (as do the *Syncategoreumata* and other special tracts of the kind) but rather on the different *distinctiones* rules for the solution to all kinds of semantic ambiguities illustrated by (well-known) sophismata. So the *distinctiones* treatises have the discussion of the *distinctiones* as their main theme and framework, and adduce *sophismata* to illustrate their use or lack of use [...] To be sure, from the doctrinal point of view they are quite similar with (and frequently run parallel to) tracts of syncategoreumata or those on special sophisms. To my knowledge the tracts on distinctiones called *Sophistariae* disappear (as an individual genre) at the beginning of the fourteenth century."

A. de Libera has regarded as a specific genre,[3] seem to be left out. Furthermore, some treatises belonging to these genres do not pay any attention whatsoever to sophisms, which makes it impossible to consider the latter as the common matter of all genres.

It seems to me that it would be better to consider '*syncategoremata*' as the common matter when attempting to characterise the different genres, assigning a subordinate role to the sophisms in which they feature. Also, it seems convenient to consider sophisms as inferences or argumentations, rather than as propositions, or, even better, as sets of two arguments, one backing the truth and one the falsity of a proposition (which can then be considered to be the defining element of the sophism).[4] One of such argumentations (either the one for truth or the one for falsity) must be regarded as sophistic, and its 'solution' involves identifying it and finding the cause of its delusory appearance.

From this point of view, a few points can be made: first, syncategorems have a meaning (or fulfill a function) that must be analysed; second, propositions with syncategorems are governed by a set of logical rules that must be formulated; third, the breaking of these rules begets sophisms of several types that seem to contradict these rules; and fourth, their delusory character has a cause that must be elucidated, resorting to the appropriate distinctions when necessary. Thus, four elements ('*syncategoremata*', 'logical rules', 'sophisms', and 'solutions') provide the basis for us to characterise four different genres of treatises, depending on which of these four is the main focus of attention.

The first two genres of treatises, dealing with the analysis of syncategorems and the formulation of rules, seem to be of a predominantly theoretical nature, whereas treatises of the last two genres are mostly practical. The differences between the former and the latter are probably related to the different roles they played within the Arts curriculum. The first two genres also share a common 'organisation' given by the ordering of syncategorems, which varied in different periods, universities, schools, or authors, whereas the characteristics of the 'organisation' of the other two genres of treatises seem to be less stable, making it more difficult to define them in an accurate and distinct way.

If we are to abandon an *a priori* characterisation of the genres of treatises (which is based on an analysis of the different tasks that logical analysis may involve) for a more in-depth study of the characteristics of the logic treatises

3 See de Libera, 'La littérature des abstractiones', 71.

4 See Angel d'Ors, '*Dubium proponitur.* Andres Limos and the Treatise on Obligations', in *Medieval and Renaissance Logic in Spain*, ed. I. Angellelli and P. Pérez-Ilzarbe (Hildesheim, 2000), 225-49: 226-8.

known to us, it can be said that, indeed, there are treatises focusing mostly on the meaning of syncategorems (at least, regarding the analysis of the syncategorem '*an*')—the most paradigmatic example could be Iohannes Pagus' *Syncategoremata* (partially edited by H.A.G. Braakhuis)[5]—as well as others in which the main concern is the formulation of the logical rules regulating the inferences with propositions involving these syncategorems—the paradigmatic examples could be the *Abstractiones* written by Richard Rufus (which are being edited by M. Sirridge and P. Streveler) or those by Herveus Raucus (edited by A. de Libera).[6] Therefore, if the titles of these works were to be used in naming the genres of which they are exponents, one might advance that the defining feature of '*Syncategoremata*' as a genre[7] is the inquiry into the meaning of syncategorems, which takes the form of a series of '*quaestiones*'. Similarly, in the genre of '*Abstractiones*' the main interest is the formulation of logical rules regulating the inferences in which syncategorems are involved, and this is approached by formulating a series of rules, usually illustrated with the relevant sophisms.

There are also treatises of the genres characterised above as practical (focusing on sophisms, rather than on the meaning of the syncategorems they contain or on the logical rules regulating their use); these also have distinctive features, although they are more difficult to characterise in an overarching way. They could be considered as examples of a single broader genre, '*Sophismata*',[8] but, although I have been able to study just a few treatises of this genre discussing the syncategorem '*an*', their characteristic features seem to allow us to distinguish between not two species (as would fit the four-fold division we have been using), but three, although a study of other syncategorems might call for more.

One of these species is clearly indebted to the genre of '*Abstractiones*' and comprises works that can be considered to be excerpts of those. The

5 Braakhuis, *De 13de eeuwse traktaten*, 184-246.

6 Alain de Libera, 'Les *Abstractiones* d'Hervé le Sophiste (Hervaeus Sophista)', *Archives d'Histoire Doctrinale et Littéraire du Moyen Âge* 52 (1986), 162-230.

7 On treatises of this genre, see H.A.G. Braakhuis, 'English Tracts on Syncategorematic Terms from Robert Bacon to Walter Burley', in *English Logic and Semantics from the End of the Twelfth Century to the Time of Ockham and Burleigh*, ed. H.A.G. Braakhuis, C.H. Kneepkens, and L.M. de Rijk (Nijmegen, 1981), 131-65.

8 On treatises of this genre, see Martin Grabmann, *Die Sophismataliteratur des 12. und 13. Jahrhunderts mit Textausgabe eines Sophisma des Boetius von Dacien* (Münster, 1940); Alain de Libera, 'La littérature des *Sophismata* dans la tradition terministe parisienne de la seconde moitié du XIIIe siècle', in *The Editing of Theological and Philosophical Texts from the Middle Ages*, ed. M. Asztalos (Stockholm, 1986), 213-44.

paradigmatic example might be the *Summa Sophismatum Disputabilium sive Abstractiones Venetae* (edited by S. Ebbesen, M. Sirridge, and P. Streveler),[9] clearly indebted to Richard Rufus' *Abstractiones*. Such works contain sophisms contravening a given rule, accompanied by the 'solutions' found in the same treatises. Works of the second species deal in an overarching way with diverse sophisms that have a proposition in common, but which break different rules in each case. These treatises are also somehow subordinated to '*Abstractiones*', but in these the backbone of the examination of sophisms is the proposition they have in common, rather than the rules governing them. The typical example of this sub-genre is the work which S. Ebbesen has named *Anonymus Catacheus* (Paris, BnF lat. 3572, unpublished). Syncategorems are the organising criterion of the treatises in these first two species. Lastly, the third species is indebted to Aristotle's *De sophisticis elenchis* and not to the *Abstractiones*: sophisms are classified (or, at least, examined) from the point of view of the fallacy which they incur. The typical example could be the *Tractatus Florianus* (edited by L.M. de Rijk).[10] Insofar as it is in this species of treatises that the '*distinctiones*' seem to play a most relevant role, although these do not seem to be their organising criterion, this species could be named '*Sophistaria sive Distinctiones*'.[11]

I have had the chance to examine seventeen treatises including logical analyses of the syncategorem '*an*', two dating from around the end of the 12th century, fourteen 13th-century ones, and one from the late 14th century. (I have not found analyses of this syncategorem in later works, and know of no reasons for this apparent lack of interest from then onwards; one might say that this syncategorem was a main point of interest to logicians for only one hundred years.) Some of these treatises I know only indirectly, since they have not been published and I have not been able to study the manuscripts at first hand; others I know only incompletely, since there is not a complete extant manuscript; others, finally, I know only imperfectly owing to difficulties I encountered in reading them. Nevertheless, the information at my disposal seems sufficient to attempt a classification of the treatises. The two 12th-century treatises are the *Ars Burana* (of which there is only one extant manuscript, published by L.M. de Rijk)[12] and the *Syncategoremata Monacensia* (partially

9 Sten Ebbesen, Mary Sirridge and Paul Streveler, 'The Pupils of the Master of Abstractions: *Abstractiones Digbeianae, Regiae & Venetae*', *Cahiers de l'Institut du Moyen Âge Grec et Latin* 74 (2003), 89-150: 142-3.

10 De Rijk, *Some Earlier Parisian Tracts*, 49-145.

11 On treatises of this genre, see De Rijk, *Some Earlier Parisian Tracts*.

12 L.M. de Rijk, *Logica Modernorum*, vol. II, part two (Assen, 1977), 175-213.

published by H.A.G. Braakhuis).[13] The former can be considered one of a kind, since its angle is radically different from those of later works; the latter, in spite of its title, seems rather to belong in the genre of '*Abstractiones*'.

Among the fifteen 13th- and 14th-century treatises I have examined, ten seem to be of the type I have characterised as theoretical, and five practical. Of the ten theoretical ones, three are '*Syncategoremata*': besides the work of Iohannes Pagus mentioned above as its paradigm, the *Syncategoremata* of Peter of Spain (edited by L.M. de Rijk)[14] and, in spite of its title, the *Sophistaria* of Matthew of Orléans (edited by J. Spruyt),[15] which is unusual in several ways. Four are '*Abstractiones*': besides the mentioned works of Richard Rufus and Herveus Raucus, and in spite of their titles, there are also William Sherwood's *Syncategoremata* (edited by J.R. O'Donnell)[16] and the *De puritate artis logicae* of Walter Burley,[17] in its *longior* and *brevior* versions (edited by P. Boehner). Lastly, three seem to conflate characteristics of either genre and for this reason can be considered to be of a mixed nature; these deal with questions related to the nature and meaning of the syncategorem '*an*', as well as to the formulation of logical rules governing its use, and they are the *Syncategoremata* written by Robert Bacon, Nicholas of Paris, and Henry of Ghent (all edited, completely or partially, by Braakhuis).[18] Regarding the five treatises belonging to the genre of '*Sophismata*', the *Sophismata determinata a maioribus magistris Parisius* (which, being unpublished, I know through fragments sent to me by S. Ebbesen) seems to bear some resemblance to the *Anonymus Catacheus*, whereas the *Sophismata logicalia* of MS Toledo 94-26 (also unpublished) may be related to the *Tractatus Florianus*.

The diverse treatises within the genre of '*Syncategoremata*', concerned with questions related to the nature and meaning of syncategorems rather than with the formulation of rules, differ in the degree of attention they pay to the analysis of sophisms: none in the work of Pagus, complementary and placed at the end of this chapter in the work of Peter of Spain, and more central in the work of Matthew of Orléans. Similarly the works in the genre '*Abstractiones*', which are primarily concerned with the fomulation of logical

13 Braakhuis, *De 13de eeuwse traktaten*, 95-104.

14 Peter of Spain, *Syncategoreumata*, ed. L.M. de Rijk, trans. J. Spruyt (Leiden-New York-Cologne, 1992).

15 Matthew of Orléans, *Sophistaria*, ed. J. Spruyt (Leiden-Boston-Cologne, 2001).

16 J. Reginald O'Donnell, 'The Syncategoremata of William of Sherwood', *Mediaeval Studies* 3 (1941), 46-93.

17 Walter Burley, *De puritate Artis Logicae*, ed. P. Boehner (Louvain-Paderborn, 1955).

18 Braakhuis, *De 13de eeuwse traktaten*, I: 105-67; II: 340-73.

rules illustrated with sophisms, differ in the degree of attention that they pay to questions related to meaning (none in the work of Herveus Raucus, almost none in that of Richard Rufus, also very little in those of William Sherwood and Walter Burley) or in the number of sophisms they examine (many in the first three, but none in the work of Burley). In view of the authors of treatises of either kind, one is inclined to attach the genre '*Syncategoremata*' to the Parisian milieu and the genre '*Abstractiones*' to Oxford, although Robert Bacon and Herveus Raucus raise an important problem in this regard.[19] Also, treatises within the genre '*Abstractiones*' suggest the existence of a tradition concerned with both theory and practice (rules and sophisms), whereas those in the genre '*Syncategoremata*' indicate a separation of the two and the use of '*Sophismata*' as a complement, which would also link this genre to Paris—on the other hand, the specific features of the genre '*Abstractiones*', linked to the Oxonian tradition, could be seen as a forerunner of the later treatises *De consequentiis*.[20]

Other meaningful differences could be pointed out that help to distinguish treatises of different genres: for example, the impact of the grammatical tradition and, as a consequence, the fact that attention is paid to a wider variety of forms of sentences (in which the syncategorem '*an*' plays several different roles) in the genre of '*Syncategoremata*', whereas those in the genres '*Abstractiones*' and '*Sophismata*' seem to focus on a single form of proposition (with the sentence governed by '*an*' being subordinated to a form of the verb '*scire*'). The adherence to a particular family of rules or to a particular type of sophism is also relevant. There are also differences between treatises in terminology (regarding the formulation of rules) or in strategy (regarding the way sophisms are analysed). Although these do not allow us to speak of direct influences or dependence between treatises (since there are probably other treatises, unknown or lost, that played an important role in the historical development of these theories), they do allow us to discuss the affinities among them. In this regard, it will be convenient to examine in greater detail the doctrines contained in these treatises.

I shall first deal with what could be called the pre-history of the logical analysis of the syncategorem '*an*', as exemplified in the *Ars Burana* and the

19 On the Oxonian and Parisian logical traditions, see Sten Ebbesen, 'OXYNAT: A Theory about the Origins of British Logic', in *The Rise of British Logic*, ed. Lewry, 1-17; Alain de Libera, 'The Oxford and Paris Traditions on Logic', in *The Cambridge History of Later Medieval Philosophy*, ed. Kretzmann-Kenny-Pinborg, 174-87.

20 See Niels J. Green-Pedersen, 'Early British Treatises on Consequences', in *The Rise of British Logic*, ed. Lewry, 285-307: 290.

Syncategoremata Monacensia, as well as Robert Bacon's *Syncategoremata* (seemingly the oldest of the 13th-century works I have had access to), already containing all the characteristic elements of the logical analysis of this syncategorem, which were to reappear in expanded or abbreviated form in later treatises. Then, I shall examine the treatment of one of the three most relevant sophisms connected with this syncategorem, namely '*Tu scis an de mentiente sit falsum Sortem esse illum*'.[21]

2 From the *Ars Burana* to Robert Bacon's *Syncategoremata*

The oldest logical analyses of the syncategorem '*an*' that I know of are in the *Ars Burana* and the *Syncategoremata Monacensia*, dating from the late 12th century. The analyses in this works, which complement one another, indicate that their origins lie in questions related to the distinction between the '*disciplinalis*' and '*dialectica*' '*quaestiones*' (or '*interrogationes*') (which can be traced back to Aristotle's *Topics* through Boethius' *De topicis differentiis*), and also in matters related to the '*significatum orationum*', that is to say, to the nature of the '*dicta*' and the '*appellatio dicti*', which had a central position in the debates among 12th-century schools of logic.

2.1 *The* Ars Burana

A contraposition is introduced in the *Ars Burana*, based on the contrast between enuntiative and interrogative sentences: that between '*enuntiabile*' and '*interrogabile*', which are the '*dicta*' signified in either type of sentence. Such '*dicta*', which are 'signified' by these types of sentences, can also be 'designated' with other types of expressions, called '*appellationes dictorum*'. The infinitive clauses could be taken as the paradigmatic form used to 'refer' to '*enuntiabilia*', which are 'signified' by means of enuntiative sentences; likewise, subjunctive clauses are taken as the paradigmatic form used to 'refer' to '*interrogabilia*', which are 'signified' by means of interrogative sentences. As to dialectic interrogations (concerning composition or division, and eliciting a simple 'yes' or 'no' answer), the *Ars Burana* restricts the use of the interrogative particle '*-ne*' to interrogative sentences ('*estne Sortes homo?*'), giving the particle '*an*' the function of expressing the '*appellatio dicti*' ('*an Sortes sit*

21 Note of the Editors: The unabridged version of this paper also contained a section on the nature and meaning of the syncategorem '*an*', one on the logical value of its location within the proposition, and another one on the logical rules that encapsulated the conventions relative to its meaning.

homo'). Thus, the expression '*an Sortes sit homo*' is regarded as the '*appellatio*' of the '*interrogabile*' that is signified by means of the interrogative sentence '*estne Sortes homo?*'. Therefore the particle '*an*' is not considered to be, strictly speaking, an interrogative particle, but a particle to construct the name of an '*interrogabile*'—the interrogative particle proper is '*-ne*', used to express interrogative sentences.

Any interrogative sentence asks for an answer, which needs to be an enuntiative sentence. This introduces the issue of the relationship between '*interrogabilia*' (signified by interrogative sentences) and '*enuntiabilia*' (signified by the enuntiative sentences that are the answers to the former). Leaving aside the consideration of truth, interrogative sentences may in principle have several answers. These can be expressed by means of several indicative sentences signifying several '*dicta*', which are in turn designated by means of several '*appellationes*'. In the *Ars Burana*, the analysis of this relationship between an interrogative sentence and its many possible answers leads us to regard the '*interrogabile*' as what is common to all the possible '*enuntiabilia*'-answers (and, in the case of the dialectic '*interrogabile*', as what is common to its two possible and contradictory answers). This also leads to a consideration of '*enuntiabilia*'-answers as '*dicta*' signified by the interrogative sentence. Hence the fact that unlike the infinitive clause, which designates an '*enuntiabile*' and is therefore regarded as a proper noun, the subjunctive clause, designating an '*interrogabile*' as well as the many possible '*enuntiabilia*' that are its possible answers, was regarded as a common noun. In the case of dialectic interrogations, the subjunctive clause '*an Sortes sit homo*' becomes the common noun of the '*enuntiabilia*' signified by means of the enuntiative sentences '*Sortes est homo*' and '*Sortes non est homo*', the two possible answers to the interrogative '*estne Sortes homo?*' (which '*enuntiabilia*' are designated by means of the infinitive clauses '*Sortem esse hominem*' and '*Sortem non esse hominem*'). Hence the '*appellatio*' '*an Sortes sit homo*' could suppose for either contradictory '*dicta*'. Although it is not stated explicitly in the *Ars Burana*, the '*appellatio*' '*an Sortes sit homo*' was taken as equivalent to the '*appellatio*' '*Sortem esse hominem vel Sortem non esse hominem*'.

Unfortunately, the only extant manuscript of the *Ars Burana* is abruptly interrupted in the course of the analyses of the syncategorem '*an*'. The analyses explained before are completed in the fragment with a study of the verbs with respect to which that '*appellatio*' can suppose (it is said that any verb may work this way, although true statements only result when the verb used signifies acts of understanding such as '*scire*', '*enuntiare*', etc.), and also with the formulation of a single rule: '*si unum contradictoriorum scitur sine an, reliquum scitur cum an'*. The latter can be taken as the basic rule for this syncategorem; although it is not formulated in later texts, it is used in grounding more complex rules.

2.2 *The* Syncategoremata Monacensia

The analyses in the *Syncategoremata Monacensia* seem to be developments of those found in the *Ars Burana*, although some basic aspects of the latter seem to have been forgotten or left aside. The *Syncategoremata Monacensia* uses the same twofold consideration of the '*appellatio*' '*an Sortes currat*', which can be seen either as related to the '*interrogabile*' or as related to the '*enuntiabilia*'-answers, but seems to have forgotten the distinction between the '*appellatio*' designating the '*interrogabile*' and the interrogative sentence signifying it, which is to say that it ignores the difference between sentence and noun, as well as the difference in function between the syncategorems '*-ne*' (expressing an '*interrogabile*') and '*an*' (used to construct the noun in order to refer to it). This loss is made manifest in the dropping of the use of the subjunctive. The construction of the syncategorem '*an*' with a verb in the indicative, expressing the interrogative sentence itself, is accepted (taking the place of the syncategorem '*-ne*'), and it is understood that the '*interrogabile*' that is common to all the '*enuntiabilia*'-answers is what is expressed (rather than designated) by means of the '*an*' sentence. Only when '*an*'-clauses are subordinated to verbs meaning operations of understanding can this suppose for the two contradictory '*enuntiabilia*' that are the answer to that '*interrogabile*'.

This change in the point of view of the analysis of the syncategorem '*an*' gave rise to the distinction between two uses of the particle '*an*': '*interrogative*' ('*an Sortes currit*') and '*infinite*' ('*ego scio an Sortes currit*'), the latter being at the centre of the analyses found in the *Syncategoremata Monacensia*, which formulates in an explicit way the equivalence of the '*appellatio*' '*an Sortes currit*' and the disjunction of its two possible answers, '*Sortes currere vel non currere*'.

In the *Syncategoremata Monacensia* the logical analysis of the syncategorem '*an*' is completed following two lines. First, by studying the problems related to the '*suppositio*' of the common '*appellatio*', which may '*immobilitari*' depending on its position within the sentence. Second, by formulating a series of rules for determining the meaning of the sentences that include this syncategorem, depending on whether it appears once or twice, and on either position: "'*An*' *bis posita, disiungit* ⟨*inter*⟩ *proposita. Semel posita, si praeponatur signo, disiungit inter* ⟨*contradictorie*⟩ *opposita; si postponatur signo universali, disiungit inter contraria; si proponatur signo particulari, disiungit inter subcontraria*." The attention paid to the different values of the syncategorem '*an*' depending on its position and on its single or double use is probably the cause of the disappearance of the nominal value of the '*appellatio*' '*an Sortes currat*'.

2.3 *Robert Bacon's* Syncategoremata

The insights on the syncategorem 'an' found in the *Ars Burana* and in the *Syncategoremata Monacensia* were further developed in 13th-century treatises of different genres. The oldest one that I have been able to peruse is Robert Bacon's *Syncategoremata*, although its contents reveal that it was preceded by a rich debate on the nature of this syncategorem. This work explicitly shows the influence of the grammatical tradition, which is made evident by the conflict between the works of Donatus (who deals with the particle '*an*' as a disjunctive conjunction) and Priscian (who deals with it as one of the dubitative or interrogative conjunctions).

Robert Bacon's *Syncategoremata* treatise is a further step in the process of transformation of the angle from which the meaning of the syncategorem '*an*' is approached. Bacon seems to base his analysis on the equivalence of the '*appellatio*' '*an Sortes currat*' and the disjunction of its possible answers, '*Sortem currere vel non currere*'. Then he focuses on the authorities of Donatus and Priscian, which he attempts to harmonise, rewording from a new outlook the issues on the '*quaestio dialectica*'. The '*interrogabilia*' (considered as what is common to the '*enuntiabilia*'-answers) disappear; they are replaced by the disjunction of the '*enuntiabilia*'-answers, now considered as '*dubitabilia*'. That is, an '*interrogabile*' is understood as a doubt concerning which of its two possible answers is the true one; this is the object of the question, the answer to which needs to be one of the parts of the disjunction of the contradictory '*enuntiabilia*' in which the '*interrogabile*' has been resolved. This change in outlook was formulated in a principle that was to preside over all the later analyses of the syncategorem '*an*': '*dubitato uno contradictorie oppositorum dubitatur et reliquum*'.

Bacon finds in this analysis a way round the conflicting authorities of Donatus and Priscian. The syncategorem '*an*' is, according to Priscian, principally a dubitative conjunction, since it is the expression of a '*dubitabile*'. However, since the doubt is what lies at the root of the question, which needs to be answered with one of the members of a disjunction, it is also, secondarily, an interrogative and disjunctive conjunction, as Donatus noted. Bacon seems not to understand these three functions (dubitative, interrogative, and disjunctive) as functions that the syncategorem '*an*' serves simultaneously, however; rather he sees them as functions that it may serve in different types of sentences. It may have a dubitative value in sentences such as '*eloquar an sileam*', an example taken from Priscian and ultimately from Virgil, which supports it with unquestionable authority. It may also have an interrogative value in sentences like '*an Sortes currat*', in which the particle '*an*' seems to take on the functions that the *Ars Burana* assigned to the particle '*-ne*'. Finally, it may also have a disjunctive value in sentences such as '*tu scis an Sortes currat*', which were to become the paradigmatic example of the use of '*an*', and the exclusive object of the 'logical rules'. The last two types seem to reflect the distinction between the '*interrogative*' and '*infinite*' uses found in the *Syncategoremata Monacensia*.

The dubitative meaning given to the particle '*an*' seems to introduce the Augustinian topic of the '*affectus animi*' into Bacon's work. The particle '*an*' is regarded as '*nota*' of an '*affectus animi*' resulting from the judgment of the '*virtus speculativa*' when moved by the '*virtus deliberativa*'. In the 'irreality' of what is expressed in a doubt, Bacon finds justification for the reason why the particle '*an*' takes a verb in the subjunctive (in accordance to the *Ars Burana*, and contradicting the *Syncategoremata Monacensia*). Similarly, in the expression of an '*affectus animi*' he finds justification for the fact that sentences with '*an*' take a verb signifying an act of the '*virtus speculativa*' (therefore, somewhat disagreeing with the *Ars Burana*).

The attribution of these three different functions to the syncategorem '*an*' raises several questions, which Bacon tackles succinctly, but which were to be taken up in the tradition that followed. First, it raises the question as to the possible 'equivocity' of this syncategorem (having several meanings according to its several uses), which Bacon solves by affirming that these '*plures acceptiones*', although diverse, are nevertheless '*fundatas super unam radicem*'. Second, he has to confront the problem of the apparent incompatibility of some of these functions and the requisite that the sentences take a verb meaning an act of the '*virtus speculativa*', such as '*scire*'—for if it is affirmed that one knows, it seems that there is no room left for doubt or interrogation. This Bacon solves simply by stating that this dubitative character does not preclude constructions with such verbs.

Third, the disjunctive value of the syncategorem '*an*' raises a question as to the differences between the syncategorems '*an*' and '*vel*', the paradigmatic disjunctive syncategorem. The disjunctive sentence '*Sortes currit vel non currit*' (the gist of the '*appellatio*' '*an Sortes currat*') is a necessary sentence, which makes the sentence '*tu scis Sortem currere vel non currere*' trivially true. In contrast, the sentence '*tu scis an Sortes currat*' is not necessarily true. What is the cause of the difference between the disjunctive conjunctions '*an*' and '*vel*', which explains the difference between the two types of sentences? Here Bacon confronts another tradition (which I know only through works postdating Bacon's *Syncategoremata*), which explains that difference by means of the notion of '*electio*'. According to this, '*an*' would mean a disjunction '*cum electione*', whereas '*vel*' would mean a disjunction '*sine electione*'; that is, '*an*' would entail the fact that one knows determinately which part of the disjunction is true (one can 'elect' the true part), whereas '*vel*' would only suggest that one of the two parts is known to be true (indeterminately; one cannot choose which).

Bacon rejects this analysis by virtue of two arguments, which are apparently conclusive, but which I have not found explicitly reproduced in any later text. On the one hand, he argues that the meaning of '*an*' needs to be uniform throughout its diverse uses, and that if it means a disjunction '*cum electione*', it should have the same meaning whenever it should mean a disjunction. However, it does not mean '*cum electione*' in the sentence '*tu dubitas an Sortes currat*', in which '*an*' expresses a disjunction, since the verb '*dubitare*' excludes '*electio*'. On the other hand, Bacon maintains that the '*electio*' is not a part of the meaning of '*an*', but rather that it arises '*ex accidente*' when '*an*' is constructed with verbs such as '*scire*' or others of the same nature. This equals accepting, at least for those particular verbs, the thesis of the opposite tradition, which Bacon has previously rejected because of the incompatibility of '*electio*' with the '*dubitatio*' that he assigned to '*an*' as its principal meaning. Bacon prefers to approach the difference between '*vel*' and '*an*' (in their disjunctive use) in a different way, and points out five differences: '*vel*' '*disiungit duo in essendo*', '*sine dubitatione*', '*posita in sermone*', '*inter terminos vel inter orationes*', and '*interponitur eis que disiungit*', whereas '*an*' '*disiungit duo in speculando*', '*cum dubitatione*', '*unum positum, alterum subintellectum*', always '*inter orationes*' and always '*anteponitur*' the given sentence.

Last, in regard to the meaning of the syncategorem '*an*', Bacon attends to the analysis of some syntactic characteristics deriving from the dubitative meaning, which he characterised as their principal meaning. Bacon, against the *Syncategoremata Monacensia*, considers the indicative construction of '*an*' to be '*incongrua*' and uses the analogy of the syncategorems '*an*' and '*si*' (which are sometimes interchangeable) to explain why '*an*' takes a verb in the subjunctive: the syncategorems '*an*' and '*si*' signify a doubt, and therefore '*trahunt orationem ad imperfectionem*' (which is why it takes a verb in the subjunctive); to this extent, Bacon argues, they need to be anteposed to the whole clause. This is probably why Bacon omits any consideration of the role of the position of the particle '*an*', which was one of the central points of the *Syncategoremata Monacensia*. On the other hand, in spite of having also given it a disjunctive meaning, Bacon maintains that the particle '*an*' does not express a nexus between two sentences, but a relation between the '*enuntiabile*' and the act of the '*virtus speculativa*' from which the doubting '*affectus animi*' arises. This seems to hinder the analysis of the duplicate use of '*an*', since sentences such as '*tu scis an Sortes currat an Plato disputet*' would seem to contain a simple juxtaposition of two '*dubitabilia*', each of which would admit two possible answers. However, Bacon upholds in this regard a thesis that will be the usual one concerning the interpretation of this type of sentence, as a doubt regarding the truth of either sentence, rather than the truth or falsity of either part of the pairs of contradictory propositions.

In Robert Bacon's *Syncategoremata*, the analyses of the syncategorem '*an*' are complemented by formulating a series of rules and examining a series of sophisms (apparently contradicting the value of those rules). It will suffice by now to point out, first, that some rules of inference (developing the rule found in the *Ars Burana*) are formulated, in addition to the rules that determine the meaning of the particle '*an*'—found in the *Syncategoremata Monacensia*, although those in the *Syncategoremata* are restricted to its simple or duplicate use, for any consideration of the possible value of its position has been omitted. This is also accompanied by some rules of 'bad consequence', which are used to examine the repercussions of the use of the particle '*an*' on some argumentative commonplaces, such as those related to the '*superior*' and the '*inferior*', or to several 'forms of opposition'. Second, the examination of sophisms is entirely subordinated to the justification of these rules, and Bacon's work pays attention to all the most characteristic sophisms, except those related to the possible value of the position of the syncategorem '*an*'.

Thus, Robert Bacon's work *Syncategoremata* contains all the elements that were to characterise the treatment of the syncategorem '*an*' in the diverse genres of treatises: a discussion of the meaning and nature of the particle '*an*' (a characteristic of the '*Syncategoremata*'); also, a formulation of rules determining the meaning of '*an*' and regulating the inferences with propositions involving its use (a characteristic of the '*Abstractiones*'); and finally an analysis of sophisms, common to all the genres. Although there is no complete extant manuscript of Bacon's *Syncategoremata*, and even if I have been able to peruse the Oxford manuscript (Digby 204) only, which is the more incomplete of the extant two, it seems that what is missing in this work only concerns the '*distinctiones*' by which some sophisms (connected to the value of the position of the particle '*an*') are resolved, which seems to be a characteristic of the '*Sophistaria sive Distinctiones*'.

This does not allow one to conclude that Bacon's *Syncategoremata* had a central role in the later development of the logical analyses of the particle '*an*' across the genres of treatises; rather, just that, by the first half of the 13th century, when the treatise was composed, the logical analyses of the syncategorem '*an*' had reached a high degree of development in treatises that are not known to us or have been lost. This determined the analyses of '*an*' in all subsequent genres of treatises. On the contrary, the lack of later follow-ups of some of the matters discussed in Bacon's *Syncategoremata* suggests that this work was not widely read, and that the principal sources known to later authors are to be found in other parallel works.

3 *'Tu scis an de mentiente sit falsum Sortem esse illum'*

Three sophisms, formulated in slightly differing variants, were taken as the 'topical sophisms' in connection to the syncategorem '*an*'. Their most usual formulations are

i) '*Tu scis an omnis homo sit Sortes an differat a Sorte*', illustrating two rules ('*non valet ab an semel posita ad an bis positam*', and '*non valet ab an praeposita signo universali ad an postpositam signo eidem*'), and also problems concerning the value of the position of the particle '*an*' in the 'canonical forms',[22] and concerning the '*resolutio*' of this kind of proposition in the light of the '*suppositio*' of their subject;
ii) '*Tu scis an de mentiente sit falsum Sortem esse illum*', illustrating another two rules ('*non valet ab inferiori ad superius, nec econverso*' and '*non valet ab opposito ad oppositum*'), as well as other problems, for example the problem of the conversion of the '*dictum*', or the problem raised by contradictory '*dicta*';
iii) '*Sortes scit an Plato sciat an Sortes sciat an Plato sciat aliquid de eo*', illustrating problems that are not tackled in any of the treatises from a theoretical point of view.

In fact, only the first of these sophisms is, strictly speaking, related to the specific problems raised in the logical analysis of the syncategorem '*an*'. The other two bring issues about the truth conditions of the '*dicta*', or about the '*appellatio dicti*', into the field of this peculiar type of proposition; these interesting issues had been dealt with in 12th-century treatises of logic but apparently

22 Note of the Editors: These canonical forms were established in one of the sections not included in this abbreviated version: they are propositions in which the particle '*an*' appears twice (for example, '*Tu scis an Sortes currat an Sortes non currat*'). The author considered such a 'canonical' expression (an explicit disjunction subordinated to the verb '*scire*') to be the most adequate in order to examine the issues raised by medieval logicians with regard to propositions containing the particle '*an*'.

were left aside in the following century, which makes these two sophisms seem like fossils here.

The analysis of these sophisms would seem to fit comfortably in treatises of the genre of '*Abstractiones*', as it illustrates rules of bad consequence; however, their great interest allowed them to generate a genre of their own: '*Sophismata*'. And, owing to the fact that these sophisms touch on issues related to the interpretation of the meaning of the particle '*an*', they were also incorporated into treatises of the genre of '*Syncategoremata*'.

In what follows I will examine the second sophism, '*Tu scis an de mentiente sit falsum Sortem esse illum*', which can be regarded as a 'topical formulation' of a type of sophism that is found in different wordings in different treatises: '*currente*' (Bacon) or '*sano*' (Nicholas of Paris) instead of '*mentiente*' (found in all the other treatises), or '*ipsum*' instead of '*illum*' (which variation may be due to changes in manuscripts, rather than to discrepancies between the works of different authors). The works of Herveus Raucus and Nicholas of Paris also tackle the sophism '*tu scis an A esse impossibile sit impossibile de impossibili*', which raises exactly the same problems concerning the impossibility of a '*dictum*' as the former does concerning falsity, and which can therefore be regarded as a variant of the same sophism.

Rather than raising any problem as to the syncategorem '*an*', this sophism actually introduces questions regarding the truth conditions of the '*dicta*', which were brought up when 12th-century logical schools debated over the being of the '*significatum orationum*'. They bring to the chapter devoted to the syncategorem '*an*' issues on the truth or falsity of the '*dicta*', considered '*simpliciter*' or '*de aliquo*' (a distinction that is found in the *Ars Meliduna* and other 12th-century treatises).[23] As to the analysis of this sophism, here the doctrine stands out according to which the '*dicta*' are true or false '*de aliquo*' only in regard to the subject of the very '*dictum*': they are neither true nor false in regard to anything else; that is, the '*dictum*' '*Sortem esse mentientem*' is true or false only '*de Socrate*' (depending on whether Socrates lies or not), but it is neither true nor false '*de Platone*' or of anything other than Socrates. If it is not true or false as to a given subject, neither is it '*enuntiabile*' as to the same subject, since only what can be true or false of a subject can be '*enuntiabile*' with regard to it. These theories seem to derive from those dealing with the being of '*dicta*' seen as 'entities': the 'being' of '*dicta*' cannot be separated from

---

23 For example, in the *Tractatus Anagnini* or in the *Tractatus de univocatione monacensis*. See De Rijk, *Logica Modernorum*.

the 'being' of the subject they are about. However, I have not found any explicit mention of this issue in any of the 12th- and 13th-century treatises that I have been able to study.

As to the analysis of the syncategorem '*an*', it should be pointed out that 'true' and 'false', considered as '*de aliquo*', are not necessarily 'immediate opposites'. Rather, they admit a middle term: neither true nor false. Therefore, 'not being true' ('of something') does not equal 'being false' (of the same), and vice versa with 'not being false' and 'being true'; similarly, a '*dictum*' by itself is not '*enuntiabile*' with regard to any given thing. Thus, even if the terms 'true' and 'false' behave as contradictory when '*dicta*' are taken '*simpliciter*' (since they are immediate contraries), they behave as contraries proper when the '*dicta*' are considered as '*de aliquo*'. Given the fact that contraries and contradictories behave in different ways with regard to the syncategorem '*an*', what is true or false '*de aliquo*' ('true' and 'false' being contrary, but seeming to be contradictory) proves to be very appropriate stuff for the construction of sophisms.

This difficulty as to the 'strictly contrary character' of the 'true' and 'false' predicates regarding the '*dicta*' taken as '*de aliquo*' is complemented with another two problems concerning 'conversion' and 'contradictoriness'. Since '*dicta*' can only be '*enuntiabile*' and true or false with regard to their subject, but the conversion exchanges the functions of subject and predicate, the converted '*dicta*' are neither '*enuntiabile*' nor true or false, regarding the same as the original '*dicta*', in spite of their being seemingly equivalent. In like manner, the contradictory '*dicta*' do not abide by the law of contradictories when seen as '*de aliquo*', although they share the same subjects and predicates, since they are not true or false regarding what is not their common subject. The fact that one of them is not true does not allow one to conclude that the other must be.

Therefore, taking the proposition '*tu scis an de mentiente sit falsum Sortem esse illum*', the following four sophistical inferences can be construed:

i) '*tu scis an de mentiente sit falsum Sortem esse illum; ergo tu scis an de mentiente sit verum Sortem esse illum*', breaking the rule '*non valet ab opposito ad oppositum*';
ii) '*tu scis an de mentiente sit falsum Sortem esse illum; ergo tu scis an de mentiente sit enuntiabile Sortem esse illum*', breaking the rule '*non valet ab inferiori ad superius*';
iii) '*tu scis an de mentiente sit falsum Sortem esse illum; ergo tu scis an de mentiente sit falsum illum esse Sortem*', breaking a rule specific to Sherwood, who formulated it bearing this in mind ('*non tenet cum hac dictione 'an' si permutetur relativum a praedicato in subiectum*'); and

iv) '*tu scis an de mentiente sit falsum Sortem esse illum; ergo tu scis an de mentiente sit falsum Sortem non esse illum*', about which no specific rule has been formulated.

The different treatises study this sophism from the point of view of one or more of these sophistical inferences. The most complete analysis is in the *Anonymus Catacheus*, the only one in which attention is paid to all four arguments. But all treatises with the exception of the *Sophistaria* of Matthew of Orléans offer very similar analyses (differing only in the layout of the arguments or the case, and as to which is the 'sophistic inference' i-iv that they study); on the contrary, Matthew's analysis is utterly heterodox. The common doctrine maintains that, as regards the given case, the sophism is true (it is not the proposition, but the inference in which it intervenes, that is sophistic in character). But the solution upheld by Matthew of Orléans is indeed what seems to be sophistical.

The Oxford manuscript of Robert Bacon's *Syncategoremata* stops abruptly at the beginning of the analysis of this sophism; for this reason, one may only say that the version analysed has the variant '*currente*', that the sophism is related to the rule '*non valet ab opposito ad oppositum*', and that the case used is the following: Socrates or Plato run (knowledge '*in universali*'), but it is not known which one of them runs (doubt '*in particulari*'). Herveus Raucus uses the usual form in the formulation and a similar case (with '*mentiente*'), and examines it in connection to argument i), as was to become usual: either Socrates or Plato lies; if Socrates lies, the '*dictum*' '*Sortem esse ipsum*' 'is true' '*de mentiente-Sorte*' and therefore 'is not false' '*de mentiente-Sorte*'; if Plato lies, that '*dictum*' 'is neither true nor false' '*de mentiente-Platone*' and therefore 'is not false' '*de mentiente-Platone*'. Therefore it 'is not false' '*de mentiente*' in either case, and you know that it is not false. Therefore '*tu scis an de mentiente sit falsum Sortem esse illum*', because you know it 'is not false'. But, to know that it 'is not false' does not equal saying that it should be true: if Socrates lies, the '*dictum*' '*Sortem esse ipsum*' is true '*de mentiente-Sorte*'; but if it is Plato who lies, that '*dictum*' is neither true nor false '*de mentiente-Platone*'; its truth value is different in either case, so it is not possible to know if it is true or false until we find out who lies. The consequent of inference i) is therefore false, incurring a '*fallacia consequentis*'.

Richard Rufus looks into the sophism in its common shape, using the same case, in connection to arguments i) and iii), and following a train of thought that is absolutely identical to Herveus'. It will suffice to say that the converted '*dictum*', '*ipsum esse Sortem*', is '*enuntiabile*' of whoever lies, be it Socrates or Plato, since the relative becomes the subject. If Socrates lies, that '*dictum*' is true '*de mentiente-Sorte*', but if Plato lies, it is false '*de mentiente-Platone*';

therefore, we cannot know whether it is true or false unless we know who lies. Therefore, it incurs a '*fallacia consequentis*'.

Rufus' analysis bears a distinctive feature (reproduced literally in the *Abstractiones Venetae*); I do not know whether it is due to corruption in the manuscript or originates from a consideration of the '*dictum*' from a peculiar point of view: it seems as if the '*dictum-enuntiabile*' could be regarded from the angle of the infinitive clause in the sophism, or from the angle of the given case (as seems to be the case in Rufus), but the analysis remains the same anyway. Richard also points out explicitly what this consideration of the '*dictum*' '*de aliquo*' entails with respect to 'conversion': the 'converse', which are '*simpliciter*' equivalent, are not equivalent '*de aliquo*'.

William Sherwood went one step further examining the sophism with regard to the first three arguments. His point remained otherwise the same as in the works discussed above; his only innovation is the following step: if it is true '*de mentiente-Sorte*', it is '*enuntiabile*' '*de mentiente-Sorte*'; but if it is neither true nor false '*de mentiente-Platone*', it is not '*enuntiabile*' '*de mentiente-Platone*'. Therefore '*enuntiabile*', seen as '*superior*', behaves in this regard exactly as '*verum*' seen as 'contrary'. The only characteristic change in Sherwood's analysis is his using the wording '*de mentiente non est falsum*' (which seems to have been used by Bacon as well) instead of '*non est falsum de mentiente*', used by Herveus and Richard. Sherwood maintains that all three cases incur a '*fallacia*' or '*paralogismus consequentis*'.

Peter of Spain looks into the sophism only with regard to argument iii), that is, as connected to an argument that is foreign to the rules formulated in the treatises of the genre '*Abstractiones*'. As Richard, he points to the loss of the equivalence of converse in their consideration '*de aliquo*'. But Peter of Spain introduces a new wording in his analysis of the sophism ('*non de mentiente est falsum*') and maintains that the argumentation '*peccat secundum sophisma accidentis*'. Matthew of Orléans deserves to be mentioned separately. As to the *Tractatus Florianus*, the sophism is only studied with regard to argument i); the wording used is '*de mentiente non esse falsum*' (as in Sherwood) and he considers that it '*peccat secundum consequens*', but he follows along the usual lines of analysis.

Nicholas of Paris, on the contrary, departs from the usual formulation: he uses '*sano*' instead of '*mentiente*', and as Herveus and the *Tractatus Florianus*, he looks into the sophism with regard to argument i) only, examined side by side with the rule '*non valet ab opposito ad oppositum*', but also using the wording '*non de sano est falsum*', as Peter of Spain. The substitution of '*mentiente*' for '*sano*' seems not to be without relevance: it leads Nicholas to mix the opposition '*verum/falsum*', typical of this sophism, with the opposition '*sanus/*

eger'. This obscures noticeably the sense of the problem, which is analysed according to the usual lines of argument. I do not know how Henry of Ghent analyses this sophism.

Of all treatises, the *Anonymus Catacheus* contains the most complete analysis of this sophism, as has been pointed out above. This analysis tackles the four arguments formulated above, in the same order. The angle of the analysis is the same as has been discussed for previous authors; however, some traits set it apart from all other treatises. First, it differs in the very formulation of the example case itself: instead of being a case in which it is known that either Socrates or Plato—we do not know who—lies, it has Plato and Socrates saying '*astra esse paria*' and '*astra esse imparia*', respectively. That is, it has two opposite propositions whose truth or falsity is not known; it is known, however, that one must be true and the other must be false. Either Plato or Socrates lies, but we do not know who; hence the use of '*mentiente*' in an example that is not related to '*insolubilia*'. Those '*dubitabilia*', which were linked to the analyses of the syncategorem '*an*' from the *Ars Burana* onwards, are useful to understand better why this sophism was formulated as it was. The same case formulation can be found in the *Sophismata determinata a maioribus magistris Parisius*, and everything leads one to think that this comes from a pre-existing tradition rather than being an innovation introduced by this treatise. This work uses alternately the wordings '*non est de mentiente falsum*' (different from the ones found in other treatises) and '*de mentiente non est falsum*' (found in Sherwood).

What is most interesting is, perhaps, the reappearance of the idea of '*problema*' ('*quaestio*') and of interrogative sentences with '*-ne*' as expressions of the '*interrogabile*' that is designated by means of the '*an*'-clause: '*quicumque scit determinare hoc problema: estne de mentiente falsum Sortem esse illum?, scit an de mentiente sit falsum Sortem esse illum*', which was not in such an explicit form in any of the other treatises studied. This seems to indicate that a tradition, later lost or forgotten, mediated between the *Ars Burana* and the *Anonymus Catacheus*; this tradition continued to pay attention to issues that can be found in the *Ars Burana* and that were not in any other treatise afterwards.

The analysis of the sophism is complemented with doctrinal explanations (dealt with instrumentally, without discussion) and contains more in-depth insights into issues such as the '*suppositio*' of '*mentiente*', the antecedent of the relative pronoun '*illum*', the 'canonical form' explaining the meaning of the sophism, the dubitative value of the syncategorem '*an*', the seemingly contradictory 'immediate opposites', the lack of equivalence of the '*dicta*' converted in their consideration '*de aliquo*', etc.

With regard to argument iv), dealt with in this treatise only, the problem raised by the negative '*dictum*' '*Sortem non esse illum*' lies in the fact that its behaviour as to falsity is the same as that of its opposite with regard to truth. If Socrates lies, '*Sortem non esse illum*' is false '*de mentiente-Sorte*', but if it is Plato who lies, it is neither true nor false '*de mentiente-Platone*', so until one finds out who lies one cannot know whether that '*dictum*' is false or not. In the same way that the '*dicta*' converted in their consideration '*de aliquo*' ceased to be regarded as equivalent, now the '*dicta*' cease to be regarded as contradictory, since in their consideration '*de aliquo*' it is not necessary that one be true and the other false. The first two arguments, as well as the fourth, are faulty '*secundum consequens*'; the third is '*secundum accidens*', according to Peter of Spain.

So far, all the authors propose the same analysis of the sophism '*tu scis an de mentiente sit falsum Sortem esse illum*', which was formulated in the same way in all treatises except Robert Bacon's. All these accept the proposition as true without needing to introduce any distinction. They differ in three ways: first, in regard to the 'sophistic argument', which they use to examine that sophism; the argument can be one or another, or several at the same time. Second, in the way they present their analysis: this can be more or less curt, and different wordings may be used. Third, from the point of view of the contents, the only difference concerns the fact that the arguments may be seen as incurring one fallacy or another. Matthew of Orléans is unique in diverging from this doctrine, as he maintains that the sophism is not true, but false, on account of, in my opinion, sophistic reasons.

Matthew studies the sophism in its usual layout, using the common case, and according to sophistic argument i). He also follows the usual analysis, and admits that argument i) is sophistic, that its conclusion is false, not following from the premise, that it '*peccat secundum consequens*', and all this for the same reasons as adduced by the common doctrine. That is to say, he admits all that can be regarded as the negative part of the doctrine, proving the falsity of the consequent. He also admits the doctrine regarding the conditions of truth for the '*dicta*' considered as '*de aliquo*'. But Matthew maintains that the argument by which the common doctrine proves the truth of the sophism (that is, the case analysis) is itself sophistic.

Apparently Matthew reaches this conclusion from the following two tenets. In the case proposed, it is not known if the one who lies is Socrates or Plato; therefore, '*Sortem esse mentientem*' and '*Platonem esse mentientem*' (as well as their respective converses and contradictories) are '*dubitabilia*' and therefore cannot be the object of '*scientia*'—the principle '*quod dubitatur de aliquo, non scitur de eodem*' operates here. The problem of the seeming incompatibility of the dubitative meaning of the syncategorem '*an*' and its construction with the verb '*scire*' (raised by Bacon and also found in later authors) seems somehow to re-emerge here. And, if these '*dicta*' are '*dubitabilia*', one cannot know whether they are true or false ('*quod non scitur de aliquo, non scitur esse verum vel falsum de eo*'). Matthew seems not to have noticed that '*conversas*' and '*contradictorias*', in their consideration '*de aliquo*', do not behave in the same way as in their consideration '*simpliciter*'. He also maintains that since the relative '*illum*' in '*Sortem esse illum*' refers to '*mentiens*', the '*dictum*' '*Sortem esse illum*' is equivalent to the '*dictum*' '*Sortem esse mentientem*', which, by virtue of the analysis above, we know to be '*dubitabile*' (and, therefore, any '*scientia*' is precluded, either with respect to the '*dictum*' or with respect to its being true or false).

Matthew uses these considerations to construct several arguments against the supposed and seeming truth of the sophism; among them

v) '*de mentiente dubitatur utrum sit verum Sortem esse illum; ergo de mentiente dubitatur utrum sit falsum Sortem esse illum; ergo est falsa hec propositio: tu scis an de mentiente sit falsum Sortem esse illum*', which Matthew justifies using the principle '*eadem est acceptio oppositorum*'. When constructing this argument, Matthew seems to have completely forgotten the consequences of considering the truth and falsity '*de aliquo*', in spite of having dealt with them in theoretical terms.

vi) '*tu scis an de mentiente sit falsum Sortem esse illum* (*mentientem*); *ergo tu scis an hec* (*propositio*) *sit falsa: Sortes est mentiens*'. Matthew regards the conclusion of this argument as equivalent to the proposition '*tu scis an hec propositio sit falsa: mentiens est Sortes*' and maintains that both are false. For this reason he considers the antecedent (the sophism) to be false as well—this is a fallacious argument, since the converse in their consideration '*de aliquo*' are not equivalent, as we have seen.

vii) '*tu scis de mentiente an sit falsum Sortem esse illum; ergo tu scis an Sortes sit mentiens*'. Matthew does not back the correctness of this consequence, which is also a fallacious argument.

In addition, Matthew construed other 'positive' arguments (built on the notion of '*electio*', on the disjunctive meaning of '*an*', and on the meaning of '*an*' in its duplicate use), complicating the argument considerably, but, in my opinion, they do not add anything worthy of our attention.

What is interesting here, rather than the 'positive' arguments backing the falsity of this sophism, is Matthew's argument against the 'case analysis' by which the common doctrine proves its truth. He maintains that 'case analysis' allows one to conclude that, if Socrates lies, '*tu scis de Sorte non esse falsum mentientem esse illum*'. An attribution '*rei subiectae*' operates in this clause; however, if one should use this proposition to conclude '*ergo tu scis de mentiente non esse falsum Sortem esse illum*', one would be making an attribution '*accidenti*', and therefore incurring a *fallacia accidentis*. Matthew was puzzled on noticing that Peter of Spain found a *fallacia accidentis* in argument iii) above, and here he looked for something similar to the problem of '*Coriscum venientem*'.

The change in the subject of the '*dictum*' ('*mentientem*' instead of '*Sortem*') evidences the fact that Matthew missed the sense of the argument. If Socrates should lie, one might as well conclude that '*tu scis de Sorte esse verum mentientem esse illum*', but the conclusion '*ergo tu scis de mentiente esse verum Sortem esse illum*' would not follow from here in the common doctrine. Matthew seems to have forgotten that every question entails knowledge '*in universali*', from which one may draw conclusions; that is, it is possible to draw conclusions '*de mentiente*' '*in universali*', in spite of not knowing '*in particulari*' if it is Plato or Socrates who is lying. However, Matthew seems to have noticed something in this regard, and closes his analysis stating:

> *Intelligendum tamen est quod cum ⟨in⟩ ipsa sit duplex compositio, una principalis, altera accidentalis (que attenditur ex attributione huius quod dico mentiens ad subiectum), dico ergo quod quantum ad principalem compositionem non est ibi falsitas, sed quantum ad compositionem que est ex attributione illius accidentis ad subiectum.*

The problem lies in that the sophism does not raise any question as to whether it is Socrates or Plato who is lying ('*compositio accidentalis*'), but it does as to whether the '*dictum*' '*Sortem esse illum*' is false or not, for which purpose it is sufficient to refer to the '*compositio principalis*'. Matthew seems to admit the common solution to the sophism, but to have also introduced a new problem that is in no way related to the sophism, and which disoriented him completely.

Besides the logical problem introduced by his analysis of the sophism, Matthew of Orléans' *Sophistaria* also raises a historical problem, since that solution is not presented as original and personal, but rather as the opinion of others, '*sicut quidam dicunt*'. But did any author really uphold that doctrine before him, or is it the case that Matthew misinterpreted the doctrine of, say, Peter of Spain, not having been able to distinguish between problems related to truth, conversion, or contradiction?

4 By Way of Conclusion

I think that the preceding pages shed some light on the logical significance of some of the discussions prompted by the logical analysis of the syncategorem '*an*', and also on their origin in the 12th century and their transformation in the 13th century. It is not possible to draw definitive conclusions, since other treatises still not examined or unknown might force us to introduce some corrections, and attention to other syncategorems might force us to adopt some different perspective. But I think that some relations and some characteristics have been clearly established.

On the other hand, it has been shown that some of the authors did in fact understand the issues they examined, and they faced the 'theoretical problems' brought on: they gave to these problems different solutions, which we can consider more or less satisfactory from the theoretical point of view, but which determine different 'schools'. Yet some other authors seem to have understood neither the issues raised nor the solutions proposed by the preceding authors. This poses a serious problem for the historian of ideas: even if the texts, taken as historical objects, are similar in many respects, they are not comparable if taken as theoretical objects. The problem is that they are there, they might have had a considerable influence, and without them the others might be inexplicable. Doing the history of ideas is not an easy task.[24]

24 I wish to thank Sten Ebbesen (who brought to my attention some of the texts that I discuss here) and Mary Sirridge (who kindly allowed me to use a draft of her edition of Richard Rufus' *Abstractiones*), the late Francesco Del Punta (who helped me to read through obscure passages in some of the manuscripts I study), Ana Moure (who helped me with some philological problems), H.A.G. Braakhuis (who provided me with a copy of his important work *De 13de eeuwse tractaten over syncategorematische termen*, which inspired this piece of research), Joke Spruyt (who gave me a copy of her edition of the *Sophistaria* of Matthew of Orléans), and Vincent Debiais in Paris and Pablo Perez d'Ors at Oxford (who sent me photocopies of the manuscripts of some unpublished treatises); their assistance helped to curb the incompleteness and mistakes of this work.

The Collection of Grammatical Sophismata in MS London, BL, Burney 330. An Exploratory Study

C.H. Kneepkens

Folios 10-16 of manuscript London, British Library, Burney 330 contain an anonymous collection of 38 grammatical sophisms all based on grammatically or semantically problematic biblical, liturgical or religious propositions. The collection is mentioned by Rosier and Roy in their article on grammar and liturgy in 13th-century sophisms; it was referred to by Irène Rosier in her study on 13th-century grammatical sophisms and listed in the catalogue of 13th-century sophismata by Ebbesen and Goubier, who dubbed it the *Sophismata grammaticalia Burneiana* (henceforth SGB).[1]

A detailed examination of the contents of this collection, paying particular attention to the way in which supposition terminology was adduced to prove the grammatical and semantic congruity, completeness or truth of the problematic propositions, will enhance our understanding of the religious language and the role of grammar and logic in the early 13th-century theological curriculum. As a first step on this exploration, it is important to take note of some general information regarding the manuscript and its contents.

* Thanks are due to Dr. Robert Olsen (Groningen) for help with the English translation of this article.

1 Irène Rosier and Bruno Roy, 'Grammaire et Liturgie dans les "Sophismes" du XIIIe Siècle', *Vivarium* 28 (1990), 118-35: 128, n. 31; Irène Rosier, 'Les sophismes grammaticaux aux XIIIe siècle', *Medioevo* 17 (1991), 175-230: 180 and 211-30; Sten Ebbesen and Frédéric Goubier, *A Catalogue of 13th-Century Sophismata*, 2 vols (Paris, 2010). Earlier references to this collection are found in G.L. Bursill-Hall, *A Census of Medieval Latin Grammatical Manuscripts* (Stuttgart-Bad Cannstatt, 1981), 115, no. 149.95 and C.H. Kneepkens, *Het Iudicium Constructionis. Het leerstuk van de constructio in de 2de helft van de 12de eeuw*, vol. 1 (Nijmegen, 1987), 639. The Burney 330 collection is also listed among the primary sources of the introduction to and edition of Robertus Anglicus' *Sophistria*: *La* Sophistria *de Robertus Anglicus*, ed. A. Grondeux and I. Rosier-Catach (Paris, 2006), 391.

 | DOI 10.1163/9789004324275_009

1 Manuscript Burney 330 and Its Contents

Josiah Forshall described the manuscript in the *Catalogue of the Burney Manuscripts in the British Museum* published in 1840.[2] It is a small parchment codex (*in octavo*) of fifteen folia, probably dating from the 13th century (*fortassis XIII*). According to the catalogue, ff. 1v-9r contain a treatise on hymnologic metrics,[3] and ff. 9v-15r a collection of grammatical questions about several propositions from Holy Scripture.[4]

The codex is interleaved with unnumbered paper sheets. The parchment leaves have two paginations and two foliations, all of them in Arabic numerals. The oldest pagination starts with page number 381 on the right top corner on the recto of the first parchment leaf, which is blank, continues on the alternating top right and left corners of respectively odd and even numbered pages, and ends with page number 410 on the verso of the last parchment folio, which otherwise contains only the Arabic numeral 54. Two foliations are found at the top right corners. One of them, beginning with number 1 and ending with 15, is placed on the recto of the first parchment leaf and ends on the recto of the last parchment leaf, all numbers having been crossed out. The other foliation starts on the last paper sheet before the first parchment leaf with number 1 and ends with 16 on the recto of the last parchment leaf. Finally, a pagination beginning with page number 1 and ending with page number 29, which is older than the two foliations but more recent than the pagination in the top margin, is found at alternating left and right bottom corners, starting on the recto of the first parchment leaf and ending on the recto of the last parchment leaf. The oldest pagination (pp. 381-410) shows that this manuscript was part of a much larger manuscript, in all probability before it entered Burney's library.

Folios 2v to 8v (pp. 382-94), line 29, are written *à longues lignes*: about 43 lines per page appear in a clear, bold book hand from the late 13th century. Folios 8v (from line 31 on) to 10r (p. 397) occur in a similar but different hand,

2 [Josiah Forshall], *Catalogue of Manuscripts in The British Museum*. New Series, Vol. I. Part II. *The Burney Manuscripts* ([London,] 1840), 90a: "Codex membranaceus, in 8vo., ff. 15, sec. fortassis XIII."

3 Forshall, *Catalogue*, 90a: "1. De metris Hymnorum liber. fol. 1. b.
Tit. 'Liber de metris himpnorum'.
Incip. 'De metris hymnorum locuturi, quia nonnulli rithmo sine metro scribi videntur, primo videamus, quid sit rithmus'."

4 Forshall, *Catalogue*, 90a: "2. Quaestiones grammaticales de variis locis Sacrarum Scripturarum. fol. 9. b.
Incip. 'Ex tribu Ruben xii. milia signati. Quaeritur de hac praepositione, ex, quid significet'."

while folios 10v to 16r (pp. 398-409) have also been written *à longues lignes*, with about 46 to 50 lines per page containing text in a different, clear but less bold book hand.

A closer inspection reveals that the text preserved on ff. 2v-10r (pp. 381-97) and called a "Liber de metris Hymnorum" in the 1840 catalogue actually comprises three separate treatises. The first, a treatise on hymnological metrics,[5] is announced by the words "Incipit Liber de metris himpnorum" in the upper margin of f. 2v and starts on the same folio-side:

> *Inc.*: De metris hymnorum locuturi quia nonnulli rithmo sine metro scribi uidentur. primo uideamus quid sit[6] rithmus. et in quo differat a metro. Deinde quid metrum. et que genera metrorum; ut ad ea de quibus intendimus. perueniamus.

The last hymn discussed is *Ave maris stella*:[7] "Quem himpnum ideo in fine ponimus" (f. 8v [p. 394], lin. 20). The treatise ends on f. 8v (p. 394):

> *Expl.*: Et nos hic finem operi nostro imponimus. petentes lectorem ut sicubi forte erraui. ipse benigne corrigat. et ueniam det. Nichil enim perfectum in humanis inuentionibus.
>
> Corde natus ex parentis ante mundi exordium. alpha et o. cognominatus. ipse fons et clausula. omnium que sunt fuerunt queque post futura sunt seculorum seculis.[8]

A metrical commentary on Boethius' *De consolatione philosophiae* commonly ascribed to Servatus Lupus is found at f. 8v (p. 394) line 31 to f. 10r (p. 397) line 5:[9]

> *Inc.*: Quinque libros philosophice consolationis insignis auctor Boetius xxvii uarietatibus respersit carminum. ut opus hiis gracius fieret...

5 I have not been able to identify the author of this treatise or to find another copy of it.

6 *add. MSc inter lin.*

7 For this hymn, see Joseph Szövérffy, *Die Annalen der lateinischen Hymnendichtung. Ein Handbuch*, I. *Die lateinischen Hymnen bis zum Ende des 11. Jahrhunderts* (Berlin, 1964), 219-20.

8 Prudentius, hymn. *Corde natus ex parentis*; cf. Szövérffy, *Die Annalen der lateinischen Hymnendichtung*, 85-7.

9 The text has been edited by Rudolf Peiper in the introduction to his edition of Boethius' *De consolatione Philosophiae* (Leipzig, 1871), xxiiii-xxviiii.

It ends on f. 10r (p. 397), line 3:

> *Expl.*: Eiusque permixtum est. Quam uariis terras animalia permeant figuris.[10]

A slight paraphrasis of the remark by Froumund of Tegernsee (*fl.* first quarter s. XI) from the beginning of the Lupus text follows the last words of the metrical commentary on f. 10r (p. 397), lines 3-6:

> Obserua uarium quicumque legeris finalem sillabam in omnibus metris indifferenter accipi. Dimetrum uero uel tetrametrum in metris iambicis. trochaicis et in anapesticis per duplices pedes[11] in reliquis per simplices computari.[12]

The third text consists of the section on metrical feet from Isidore's *Etymologiae*, book I, the author's name appropriately noted in the margin, sc. 'Hisidorus'.[13]

A collection of 38 grammatical sophisms then starts on f. 10v (p. 398) without any mention of title, reference to author, introduction or introductory tag:

> *Inc.*: Ex tribu ruben xii^{cim} milia signati.[14] Queritur de hac prepositione …

Unlike the three preceding treatises, this collection does not have any marginalia. The text ends on fol. 16r (p. 409) without any explicit or colophon, the drawn frame in the bottom margin containing only the name 'constantinople':

---

10 Boethius, *Philosophiae consolatio*, V, *metr.* V, 1, ed. L. Bieler (Turnhout, 1957), 100,52: "Quam uariis terras animalia permeant figuris!"

11 Added by another hand *inter lineas*.

12 For Froumund's text, see Georg Schepss, *Handschriftliche Studien zu Boethius De consolatione Philosophiae* (Würzburg, 1881), 39-40: "Incipiunt genera metrorum in librum Boetii quae domnus Lupus ut facilius studiosus lector accipere potuisset in lucem produxit. Observa autem quisquis legeris finalem syllabam in omnibus metris indifferenter accipi, dimetrum vero vel trimetrum vel tetrametrum in metris iambicis trochaicis et anapesticis per duplices, in reliquis per simplices computari."

13 Isidorus, *Etymologiae sive origines*, I, 17, 1-20, ed. W.M. Lindsay (Oxford, 1911 [reprint 1971]). The text of the Burney MS starts as follows: "Pedes sunt qui certis temporibus sillabarum insistunt. nec a legitimo spatio umquam recedunt" and ends with "Vnde non oportet has sillabas in carmine quolibet excedere. ut cartaginensium (!). ierosolimitanorum. constantinopolitanorum." A summary of Isidore's discussion of the origin of the names of the various metra (*Etym.* I, 39, 5-9) is found in the bottom margin of f. 10r (p. 397).

14 Apoc. 7.5.

Des.: et propria nomina dant intelligere locum in (!) discretione et appellatiua sine discretione.

2 The Collection of Grammatical Sophisms

As stated above,[15] all 38 sophisms start with a sophismatic proposition or phrase taken from the Bible, liturgy or other religious texts. Below is a list of these propositions along with their sources (if known), the number that the proposition is given in the Ebbesen-Goubier Catalogue (henceforth EGC), and references to other collections in which, according to EGC, the relevant proposition also occurs:[16]

01 EX TRIBU RUBEN XII^cim MILIA SIGNATI [f. 10v; p. 398]
Apoc. 7.5 EGC 219.1
*02 VOS ESTIS MUNDI, SED NON OMNES
Io. 13.10 EGC 1325.2 [1325.1: Paris, BnF lat. 15037, f. 164va; 1325.3: Paris, BnF lat. 3454, f. 47vb]
03 MANUS MEE QUE UOS FECERUNT CLAUIS CONFIXE SUNT[17]
CAO[18] 2589 EGC 355.1
*04 SERMONEM QUEM AUDISTIS NON EST MEUS
Io. 14.24 EGC 840.2 [840.1: Paris, BnF lat. 15037, f. 165va; 840.3: Cambridge, St. John's D.25, f. 110va-b; 840.4: Robertus Anglicus no 17a[19]]
05 EGO SUM UITIS UERA [f. 11r; p. 399]
Io. 15.1 EGC 197.1
06 VIS BAPTIZARI? VOLO
Rituale Romanum: Ad Sabb. sanctum; not in EGC

---

15 See above, pp. 294-5.

16 An asterisk in front of the serial number indicates that the proposition in question occurs more than once in EGC.

17 This sentence also occurs, in a metrically adapted form, in Alexander de Villa Dei's *Doctrinale*, l. 1473, ed. D. Reichling (Berlin, 1893; anast. reprint New York, 1974), 93: "sunt Domini, quae nos fecere, manus crucifixae."

18 CAO 2589 means the number of the antiphon in which this line occurs, according to the antiphons inventory by René-Jean Hesbert, *Corpus Antiphonalium Officii*, vol. III: *Invitatoria et Antiphonae* (Rome, 1968); in this case, it is the Antiphon "Ego sum alpha et omega," on 195.

19 Grondeux and Rosier-Catach, eds., *Sophistria*, 347.

07 DEUS CREAUIT OMNIA EX NICHILO
Nicolaus Paris.[20] EGC 166.1

*08 FACTUM EST UESPERE ET MANE DIES UNUS
Gn. 1.5 EGC 222.1[21] [221.1: Paris, BnF lat. 15037, f. 164ra]

*09 VIRGA TUA ET BACULUS TUUS IPSA ME CONSOLATA SUNT
Ps. 22.4 EGC 1322.1 [1322.2: Paris, BnF lat. 3454, f. 48ra; 1322.3: Robertus Anglicus no 22[22]]

10 REGES TERRE CONUENERUNT IN UNUM [f. 11v; p. 400]
Ps. 47.5 EGC 829.1

11 CUM GUSTASSET ARCHITRICLINUS AQUAM UINUM FACTUM[23]
Cf. Io. 2.9; *Missale Romanum*: 2nd Sunday after Epiphany—Communion EGC 142.1

12 SEMEN QUOD CECIDIT IN TERRAM BONAM. HII SUNT QUI UERBUM DEI AUDIUNT
Cf. Antiph. *Semen quod*[24] (cf. Lc. 8.8+21) EGC 835.1

13 LABIA DOLOSA IN CORDE ET CORDE LOCUTI
Ps. 11.3 EGC 331.1

14 MEDIA UITA IN MORTE SUMUS [f. 12r; p. 401]
CAO 3732[25] EGC 363.1

*15 DOMINUS REGNABIT IN ETERNUM ET ULTRA
Ex. 15.18 EGC 183.2 [183.1: Paris, BnF lat. 15037, f. 164rb-va]

*16 GENERATIO ET GENERATIO LAUDABIT OPERA TUA ET POTENTIAM TUAM PRONUNTIABUNT
Ps. 144.4 EGC 227.2 [227.1: Paris, BnF lat. 15037, f. 165va]

---

20 The same proposition was used by Nicholas of Paris in his Commentary on Aristotle's *Perihermeneias*; cf. C.H. Kneepkens, 'Significatio generalis and significatio specialis: Notes on Nicholas of Paris' Contribution to Early Thirteenth-Century Linguistic Thought', in *Medieval Analyses in Language and Cognition*, ed. S. Ebbesen and R. Friedman (Copenhagen, 1999), 17-43: 36, n. 51.

21 EGC erroneously reads 'quintus' instead of 'unus'. Consequently, EGC's numbers 221 and 222 ought to be combined, since they refer to the same leading proposition. For the correct text, see also Rosier, 'Les sophismes grammaticaux au XIIIe siècle', 222, no 57.

22 Grondeux and Rosier-Catach, eds., *Sophistria*, 376-8.

23 factam *Joh. ed. Vulgata, Missale Rom.* & *EGC* factum *MS Burn.*, which appears to be the problematised reading. Not in Rosier, 'Les sophismes grammaticaux au XIIIe siècle'.

24 Not in CAO; see *Heures à l'usage de la chapelle et paroisse du Roy, contenant Les Prieres qui s'y disent le Matin, le Soir, & au Salut... selon les usages de Rome & de Paris*, Paris (J.-F. Collombat) 1750, 262-3: "Le dimanche de la Sexagesime... [263] selon Paris. A Magnificat. Ant. Semen quod in spinas cecidit.... suffocantur: semen quod cecidit in bonam terram, hi sunt qui in corde bono & optimo audientes verbum retinent."

25 For the abbreviation CAO, see above, n. 18.

17 VENIET FORTIOR ME POST ME CUIUS NON SUM DIGNUS SOLUERE CORRIGIAM CALCIAMENTORUM EIUS
Mc. 1.7 (cf. Lc. 3.16) EGC 1303.1
*18 IN PACE IN IDIPSUM DORMIAM ET REQUIESCAM [f. 12v; p. 402]
Ps. 4.9 EGC 299.2 [299.1: Paris, BnF lat. 15037, f. 164va; 299.3: Robertus Anglicus no 26[26]; 299.4: Rog. Bacon, *SG*, ed. Steele, p. 185]
*19 DOMINUS UOBISCUM
Ru. 2.4 & Latin Catholic liturgy EGC184.1 [184.2: Rog. Bacon, *SG*, ed. Steele, p. 180-81]
*20 ITE, MISSA EST
Missale Romanum EGC 326.1 [326.2: Rog. Bacon, *SG*, ed. Steele p. 183-84][27]
*21 SEQUENTIA EWANGELII SECUNDUM IOHANNEM [f. 13r; p. 403]
Missale Romanum EGC 837.1[28]
22 MULIER QUE DAMPNAUIT, SALUAUIT[29]
EGC 368.1
23 QUI SUPER TE PEDIBUS AMBULAUIT[30]
Sabbat. sanct. Benedictio fontis EGC 764.1
*24 IUBILATE DEO OMNIS TERRA [f. 13v; p. 404]
Ps. 65.1 EGC 329.2 [329.1: Paris, BnF lat. 15037, f. 165ra]
25 ECCE LIGNUM CRUCIS IN QUO etc.
CAO 2522 EGC 191.1
26 DEPOST FETANTES ACCEPIT EUM [f. 14r; p. 405]
Ps. 77.70 EGC 148.1
27 VOCAUIT DEUS CUNCTA ANIMANCIA etc. UT UIDERET QUID UOCARET EA
cf. Gn. 2.19-20 EGC 1324.1
28 BENEDICITE AQUE QUE SUPER CELOS SUNT etc.
Dn. 3.60 EGC 111.1
29 SIT QUOD FEMINA DICAT: LETATUS SUM IN HIIS etc. [f. 14v; p. 406]
Ps. 121.1 EGC 332.1

---

26 Grondeux and Rosier-Catach, eds., *Sophistria*, 382-6.

27 See also EGC 327.1.

28 See also EGC 838.1 (*Sequentia sancti evangelii*; Paris, BnF lat. 15037) and 839.1 (*Sequentia sancti evangelii secundum Lucam*; Paris, BnF lat. 3572).

29 For this proposition and its early history in medieval linguistic discussions, see C.H. Kneepkens, 'Mulier Quae Damnavit, Salvavit. A Note on the Early Development of the Relatio simplex', *Vivarium* 14 (1976), 1-25. The earliest known occurrence is found in Abelard's writings, *Glossae super Peri hermeneias*, VI, 33, ed. K. Jacobi and C. Strub (Turnhout, 2010), 195 and 326-7.

30 For this proposition, see also Kneepkens, 'Mulier Quae Damnavit, Salvavit'.

30 TU AUTEM, DOMINE, MISERERE NOSTRI. DEO GRATIAS [f. 15r; p. 407]
Officium divinum[31] not in EGC
31 FACIES AQUILE DESUPER IPSORUM QUATUOR
Ez. 1.10 EGC 220.1
*32 BONUM ESSET EI SI NATUS NON FUISSET[32] [f. 15v; p. 408]
Mt. 26.24 EGC 116.1[33]
33 AUDITA EST UOX MILIA MILIUM DICENTIUM etc.
CAO 2440[34] EGC 105.1
34 MAIOR HORUM EST CARITAS
I Cor. 13.13 EGC 351.1
35 INICIUM SAPIENCIE TIMOR DOMINI
Sir. 1.16 EGC 305.1
36 VNAM PETII A DOMINO HANC REQUIRAM
Ps. 26.4 EGC 1267.1
37 ANTEQUAM HABRAHAM FIERET EGO SUM [f. 16r; p. 409]
Io. 8.58 EGC 97.1
*38 VESPERE AUTEM SABBATI QUE LUCESCIT IN PRIMA SABBATI
Mt. 28.1 EGC 1316.2 [1316.1: Paris, BnF lat. 15037, f. 164ra-b; 1316.3: Rog. Bacon, *SG*, ed. Steele, p. 189-90].

It is still not possible to attribute the collection as a whole or any of the sophisms to a known master or author, nor is there any explicit indication of the exact place or region of origin. On the other hand, the use of some sample sentences in Old French suggests that the composition occurred in France or England, since Anglo-Norman French was the prestige language in English society far into the 14th century.[35] In the discussion of the problem caused by the possible constructional relationship between the noun modifier 'fortior' and the relative 'cuius' in the biblical quotation "Veniet forcior me post me cuius non sum dignus etc." (Sophism 17), the common usage of a nominalised

31 It is an often used supplication prayer at the end of a lecture or sermon of the Divine Office.

32 The first line of this entry is also found immediately following the text of entry 29 at the end of f. 14v (p. 406): "Bonum esset ei si natus non fuisset. Queritur utrum hec dictio Bonum teneatur adiectiue uel substantiue," which is similar to the first line of entry 32, in which one finds, however, 'tenetur' instead of 'teneatur.'

33 See also EGC 115.1 Ms Paris, BnF lat. 15037, f. 165rb.

34 Hesbert, CAO 2440 (see above, n. 18): "Dum committeret bellum draco."

35 Cf. Nicholas Orme, *English Schools in the Middle Ages* (London, 1973), 72-5.

masculine or feminine adjective in vernacular, i.e., *Gallice,* is cited to support the suggested solution:

> [SGB, p. 401][36] Nos dicimus quod hec diccio 'forcior' est adiectiuum significacione, sed non uoce. Mediante tamen articulo in se incluso sic habet exponi [p. 402] 'ueniet forcior etc.': Gallice 'li plus fort de mei vendra'.

In Sophism 36, a discussion about the same linguistic phenomenon leads again to an appeal to vernacular usage:

> [SGB, p. 408] Nos dicimus quod mediante causa potest diccio sustantiuari in feminino genere et in masculino. Dicimus etiam quod hec propria 'albus currit', et hec diccio 'albus' sustantiuatur in masculino genere mediante articulo in se incluso, unde is est sensus 'li blund curt'.

In Sophism 19, the Old French translation is provided for the Latin 'Dominus vobiscum':

> [SGB, p. 402] Et dicimus quod hec diccio 'Dominus' supponit pro pace que est Dominus, ut potest intelligi in Gallico idiomate 'La pais deu seit entre uos'.

Reference to Paris as the native town or place of habitation in a sample sentence may suggest that this city was the location from which this sophism originated. Sophism 26 starts with Psalm 77.70 "Depost fetantes etc.," which was a famous sample sentence used in 12th- and 13th-century grammar to illustrate the accumulation of prepositions and its consequences for prepositional structure. Since the Latin preposition 'de' may have several consignifications, including an indication of geographic origin, the respondent argues that the proposition 'iste est de Parisius' is true, if the person in question was born in Paris. However, this proposition may also indicate the place where somebody mainly resides. The proposition 'iste est de Parisius' is therefore also true if the person has been living in Paris for many years. Furthermore, the preposition 'de' may also be followed by a geographic determination larger than a city or village. The various supra-local connotations of the preposition 'de' consequently led the author to distinguish between three grades of confused geographic

36 Henceforth, I only use the old pagination, which is most prominently and less ambiguously present in the MS.

localisation: wide, wider and widest! The example of the "wide determination" is "de Anglia"; of the "wider determination": "de ultra mare"; and finally "de loco" or "de patria," which, incidentally, is considered incorrect:

> [SGB, p. 405] *Solutio*. Hec prepositio 'de' <habet> plures consignificationes. Quandoque est consignificatiuum nationis uel patrie, ut cum dicitur 'iste est de Parisius'. Est enim locucio uera, si ibi natus fuerit. Quandoque consignificatiuum consuetudinis respectu loci uel degentie, ut in predicto exemplo. Et secundum hoc exigitur non quod ibi natus sit, sed quod ibi maneat ex consuetudine.
>
> Sed siue in prima siue in secunda acceptione, semper exigitur quod diccio sequens exprimat locum determinate, ut in predicto exemplo, uel indeterminate, et hoc tripliciter. Est enim determinatio loci magna, maior, maxima. Magna hic 'iste est de Anglia', maior: 'iste est de ultra mare', maxima: 'iste est de loco uel de patria'. Talem autem non recipimus, sed refutamus.

3 The Genre of Grammatical Sophisms and the Burney 330 Collection

The SGB consists of sophisms[37] of various length, although none of them is very long. It lacks a well-defined structure and omits any doctrinal introduction, concluding section or even opening or end tag.[38] The catalogue description of the manuscript labels the sophisms as 'quaestiones grammaticales', but the adequacy of this label for the contents of this collection remains questionable.

An analysis of the form and content of the so-called *quaestiones* shows that almost all of them meet the requirements of the 'sophism' formulated by Ebbesen and Goubier in the introduction to their Sophismata catalogue.[39] All the entries in the Burney 330 collection start with a sophismatic proposition or clause that is, in some way, a syntactic or semantic anomaly, and not a question

37 I use the term 'sophism' for a text headed by a problematic or sophismatic proposition, and containing a disputation consisting of problematisation and problem solution; cf. Ebbesen-Goubier, 'Introduction', *A Catalogue of 13th-Century Sophismata*, 9-10.

38 For structural criteria to describe the several collections of sophisms, see Rosier, 'Les sophismes grammaticaux aux XIIIe siècle', 177-8.

39 Ebbesen-Goubier, *A Catalogue of 13th-Century Sophismata*, 9-10.

about a puzzling grammatical phenomenon such as those encountered in the three *Quaestiones grammaticales* collections of Oxford MS CCC250,[40] the collection of grammatical sophisms and *quaestiones* that follows John de Wolve's grammatical *quaestiones* and *sophismata* in MS Paris, BnF lat. 15037[41] or the *Sophismata Anonymi Avenionensis*, edited by A. Grondeux.[42] Generally, the semantic or syntactic anomaly or incongruity of the sophismatic proposition is mentioned and problematised by one or more questions, almost always followed by sections 'in opposition' arguing that the proposition in question is false or grammatically incongruous, or incomplete and, therefore, false. The respondent sections offer a solution by proving that the proposition in question is grammatically well formed and/or complete, and therefore true, while refuting the arguments and conclusions in opposition.

To label this structure a grammatical sophism will require us to define the term and to distinguish it from a sophism in general. Grondeux and Rosier-Catach begin examining this issue in the introduction to their edition of Robertus Anglicus' *Sophistria*, drawing attention to Robert Kilwardby's remark that the mutual relationship between grammatical well-formedness (*congruitas*) and grammatico-semantic completeness (*perfectio*), or rather the priority given to this relationship, is often a key-notion of grammatical sophisms. Moreover, they refer to a similar discussion of *congruitas, perfectio* and figurative speech in the introductory sections of Roger Bacon's *Summa gramaticea*.[43] They also point out that sophisms mainly dealing with utterances that are incongruous with common syntactic rules or common semantic-syntactic rules of interpretation were, in the Middle Ages, labeled grammatical

40 Edited by C.H. Kneepkens, 'The Quaestiones grammaticales of the MS Oxford, Corpus Christi College 250', *Vivarium* 21 (1983), 1-34; 23 (1985), 98-123, and 27 (1989), 103-24.

41 Christine Brousseau-Beuermann, 'Les *Quaestiones* de Johannes de Wolve et les *Sophismata artis grammaticae* du MS Paris, Bibl. nat. lat. 15037', in *Gilbert de Poitiers et ses contemporains. Aux origines de la Logica modernorum*, ed. J. Jolivet and A. de Libera (Naples, 1987), 91-105: 101 [Ms Paris, BnF, lat. 15037, f. 164ra]: "De sophismatibus artis gramatice dicturi hoc ordine tenebamus: primo de quibusdam dictaminibus teologie quantum ad gramaticam" [minor corrections are mine].

42 Anne Grondeux, 'Sophismata Anonymi Avenionensis (ms. Clervaux, Abbaye Saint-Maurice 12)', *Cahiers de l'Institut du Moyen-Âge grec et latin* 73 (2002), 41-59.

43 Robert Kilwardby, *Super Priscianum minorem* (apud Grondeux and Rosier-Catach, eds., *Sophistria*, 25, n. 3): "Et quia iam dictum est de congruitate et perfectione orationis gramatice, consequenter queritur utra istarum conditionum precedit aliam. Hoc enim sepe tangitur in introductione sophismatum gramaticorum."

sophisms.[44] An analysis of the SGB shows that the doctrine of grammatical well-formedness and completeness is prominently present in the majority of the sophisms of this collection. Although all the problematic propositions stem from religious works, the focus is not on theological doctrine but grammatical issues, in particular syntax and the *confinium* between syntax and semantics in theological and religious utterances. These discussions were obviously intended as tools for teaching the practical application of key syntactic and grammatico-semantic notions in theological, liturgical and religious utterances in order to deepen a student's insight in this intricate matter.

The question concerning the possible function of these grammatical sophisms was first broached by Rosier and Roy, who interestingly suggest that such collections of grammatical sophisms might be the result of classroom debates.[45] The faith-based origin of all the lead sentences in the SGB implies that, to the medieval mind, they are always true despite their possible formal or superficial incongruity or incompleteness. The preconceived if not explicit instruction thus given to the respondent was to prove the correctness and, consequently, the truth of these problematic sentences when challenged by the opponent, as this truth was sanctioned by authority. Grammatical education, elementary lessons in debating and theological exegesis apparently went hand in hand!

4 The Analytical Toolkit of the Burney 330 Sophisms

A more detailed examination of two analysis tools that are applied in several Burney 330 sophisms may shed more light on the function of this collection in the education of late 12th- or early 13th-century budding intellectuals: (1) the distinction between three layers of grammatico-semantic perfection or completeness and (2) the grammatical and semantic supposition doctrines.

---

44 Grondeux and Rosier-Catach, eds., *Sophistria*, 25-6 and 50-72. For a thorough and profound discussion of the medieval theories and discussions of figurative speech and performative speech acts, see Irène Rosier, *La parole comme acte. Sur la grammaire et la sémantique au XIIIe siècle* (Paris, 1994), and Irène Rosier-Catach, *La parole efficace. Signe, rituel, sacré* (Paris, 2004).

45 Rosier and Roy, 'Grammaire et Liturgie dans les "Sophismes" du XIIIe Siècle', 120: "Les recueils de sophismes dont nous parlons ici sont probablement le résultat de disputes *in scholis*, orchestrées par le maître, en relation avec son activité essentielle de lecture des textes au programme."

a *The Distinction of the Layers of Completeness*

As noted above, almost all the problematic sentences or clauses presented in the SGB suffer from one or more syntactic and/or semantic deficiencies.[46] Several sophisms refer to three levels of syntactic-semantic completeness in order to solve the problems caused by these deficiencies and, accordingly, conserve the truth of the problematic proposition concerned. The distinction of the three layers is presented in full in Sophism 10 (p. 400) headed by the problematic sentence "Reges terre convenerunt in unum" (Psalm 47.5). This distinction is invoked to illustrate the manner in which the problem caused by the uncertainty of the grammatico-semantic status of 'unum' might be solved. If 'unum' is a noun modifier, it would be possible to indicate the noun modified by 'unum'. If 'unum' is a nominalised adjective, the resolution in 'una res' ought to be possible. Since the substitution of 'unam rem' for 'unum' makes the proposition false, this alternative cannot, however, be the case:

> [SGB, p. 400] Queritur ergo de hac dictione 'unum', utrum tenetur adiectiue an substantiue. Si adiectiue, ergo innitur alicui substantiuo ibi posito, quia perfecta est locucio. Si substantiue, ergo subpositiue; ergo supponit, queritur pro quo. Non est assignare.
>
> Item. Hec dictio 'unum' est dictio substantiuata; ergo habet resolui in hoc nomen generale 'res' et suum adiectiuum, ut sit sensus: Conuenerunt in unam rem. Sed hoc falsum.
>
> Item. Quam circumstanciam notat [notet *MS*] hec prepositio 'in'? Quia si localem, oportet quod aliqua dictio sequens designet locum; quod est falsum.

The respondent explicitly claims that the notion of completeness applies to three different levels of completeness of a sentence or utterance (*locutio*): 1) *perfectio expressionis sensus*: the level of the actual structure as spoken or written down, which can be identified as the presented surface structure of the sentence or the factual way in which the intended meaning has been expressed by means of the specific proposition or clause; 2) *perfectio constructionis*: the level of the correctly construed sentence, which may deviate from the structure of the expressed sentence and can be identified as the shallow or constructional structure; 3) *perfectio sensus* or *intellectus*: the level of the semantic content of the sentence in combination with the intended message

46 Cf. above, pp. 304-5. An exception is Sophism 6, "Vis baptizari? Volo," in which the incongruity between the intended and the factual participants of the communication triangle is at stake. The solution is sought by the respondent in the 'usus ecclesiasticus'.

of the sentence, which constitutes the meaning intended by the speaker or author:

> [SGB, p. 400] *Solutio.* Nos dicimus quod perfecta est locucio. Et notandum quod triplex est perfectio. Est perfectio sensus siue intellectus; est et constructionis; et est expressionis sensus. Duas primas perfectiones habet hec locucio, terciam non habet. Exigit enim aliquid ibi positum ad eius perfectionem quantum ad sensus expressionem, ut patebit inferius.

This implies that, in the case of this problematic sentence (Psalm 47.5), the respondent has to solve the conflict that apparently exists between the *perfectio sensus* and the *perfectio constructionis*, on the one hand, and the observed imperfection on the level of the expressed sentence, on the other.[47]

Use of the distinction between the perfection of the expressed sentence and the perfection of its meaning is also clearly shown by the solution to Sophism 4 (pp. 398-9), headed by the famous problematic sentence, "Sermonem quem audistis non est meus" (John 14.24). The problematic character of this proposition is indicated by the question: "Queritur utrum hec dictio 'sermonem' teneatur accusatiue uel nominatiue." The opponent argues that, if 'sermonem' is taken as a nominative term, there is no need to assume any figurative construction, as the statement is then unproblematic. If 'sermonem' is taken, however, as an accusative form, the construction cannot be explained as an example of antiptosis (*casus pro casu*), since this figure may not be invoked as an excuse (*excusare*) to use the accusative instead of the nominative case to indicate the subject of a finite verb:

---

47 The solution adduced by the respondent first repairs the surface imperfection: "Et hec dictio 'unum' tenetur adiectiue et non curat societatem substantiui, quia respicit consignificationem uerbi precedentis pro recompensatione substantiui, scilicet collectionem. Item. Hec prepositio 'in' consignificat localem circumstanciam et recompensatur terminus designans locum per principalem significationem uerbi precedentis, quia omnis uentio est a loco et ad locum. Debet ergo sic exprimi locucio: Reges terre ueniendo simul in locum collecti sunt." Finally, he adds a remark about the double meaning of the verb 'convenire' and the related difference in constructional behaviour: "Et notandum quod hoc uerbum 'conuenerunt' duas habet acceptiones. In una equipollet huic 'simul uenerunt'. Et secundum hoc exigit accusatiuum casum mediante prepositione. In alia acceptione equipollet huic uerbo 'consenserunt'. Et secundum hoc exigit ablatiuum casum mediante prepositione. Vnde is est sensus: Isti conuenerunt in hoc, idest consenserunt." The quotations in the main text and this footnote offer the complete text of Sophism 10.

> [SGB, p. 398] Si accusatiue, sed respicit hoc uerbum 'est' et magna repugnancia est inter accusatiuum et terciam personam uerbi; et nulla figura potest excusare talem repugnanciam; ergo incongrua est locucio.
>
> Si dicatur quod teneatur nominatiue, uel est nominatiuus uel accusatiuus. Si accusatiuus, ut prius. Si nominatiuus, sed nulla est improprietas inter nominatiuum et terciam personam uerbi; ergo non est ibi figura. Forte dicetur quod sit ibi antitosis, scilicet casus pro casu. Sed inter accusatiuum et terciam personam uerbi nullus est omnino respectus, et deinde ut prius.

In response to this objection, the respondent initially proposes to label this sentence a figurative structure in which antiptosis occurs, viz. the accusative 'sermonem' is used instead of the nominative 'sermo'. He then rejects this proposal and offers another solution, which he clearly prefers. He notes a discrepancy between the expressed or surface structure, in which the accusative 'sermonem' is in topic or front position, and the correctly construed structure of the sentence, in which the accusative 'sermonem' is enclosed in a relative clause. The author of the sophism explains the front position of 'sermonem' by pointing out that, although the possessive pronoun 'meus' may not be entirely correctly used in this sentence without a nominal subject as its reference, it may be rendered intelligible by placing the accusative 'sermonem' in front position. For a good understanding of this sophismatic sentence (the *perfectio sensus* or *intellectus*), the accusative 'sermonem' should be situated in the relative clause immediately after the relative 'quem' and a nominative case 'sermo' should be understood as occurring immediately following 'meus'. By carrying out such a transformation, the *perfectio expressionis* is made congruent with the *perfectio sensus*:[48]

> *Solutio*. Potest dici quod hec dictio 'sermonem' est nominatiui casus et tantum nominatiui. Vnde inter hanc dictionem 'sermonem' et terciam personam uerbi nulla est improprietas nec etiam aliqua figura. Sed ex hoc quod accusatiuus transumitur pro nominatiuo, prouenit improprietas et illa excusatur per figuram.
>
> Vel aliter et melius: Nos dicimus quod hec dictio 'sermonem' in nullo respicit terciam personam, sed determinat transitionem huius uerbi 'audistis'. Et hec dictio 'quem' adiungitur ei quasi adiectiuum substantiuo. [p. 399] Et licet hec dictio 'sermonem' precedit quantum ad superficiem, sequitur tamen ad sensum. Et hec dictio 'meus' est quoddam [quondam

48 One also meets the explicit application of this distinction in Sophisms 13, 14, 16, 24 and 31.

> MS] adiectiuum non curans societatem substantiui, sed trahit recompensationem substantiui de hac dictione 'sermonem'. Vnde is est sensus: Non est meus, scilicet sermo, quem sermonem audistis. Nec tamen dicimus quod ecliptica sit locucio, immo apponitur hec dictio 'sermo' ad euidenciam intellectus.[49]

Of course, the tension or even conflict between the expressed utterance and the intended meaning, and the manner of reconciling these two levels, constitute issues that determine the limits of linguistic acceptability and have been subject to discussion throughout the history of grammar and exegesis. For scholars in the Middle Ages, the third book of Donatus' *Ars maior*, Augustine's *De doctrina christiana*, and Priscian's, Cassiodorus' and Isidore's chapters on figurative speech were important textbooks on this topic, to mention only some of their most important sources from Late Antiquity.[50] In the early 13th century, this tension even led to the development of the intentionalist approach to language and grammar, as Irène Rosier-Catach has convincingly shown.[51]

Although the three-pronged distinction between the levels of linguistic perfection mentioned and applied in the GSB sophisms is related to the intentionalist theory, it has a far more primitive character than the sophisticated doctrine of the double *intellectus*[52] found in 13th-century university and intentionalist grammar (e.g., Kilwardby, Jordanus, master Arnoldus),[53] Robertus Anglicus'

49 The quotations in the main text offer the complete text of Sophism 4.

50 For the history of the rhetorical figures of speech and their role in exegesis in the early Middle Ages, see Anne Grondeux, *À l'école de Cassiodore. Les figures «extravagantes» dans la tradition occidentale* (Turnhout, 2013).

51 From Irène Rosier-Catach's several studies on this topic, I only mention her comprehensive *La parole comme acte*.

52 For the doctrine of the double *intellectus* in 13th-century grammar, see C.H. Kneepkens, 'Roger Bacon's Theory of the Double *Intellectus*: A Note on the Development of the Theory of *Congruitas* and *Perfectio* in the First Half of the Thirteenth Century', in *The Rise of British Logic*, ed. P. Osmund Lewry (Toronto, 1985), 115-42; for an in-depth study of the doctrine of the double *intellectus* and its relation to the intentionalist approach to grammar, see Rosier, *La parole comme acte*.

53 For 13th-century university grammar, see Irène Rosier-Catach, 'La tradition de la grammaire universitaire médiévale', in *Manuscripts and Tradition of Grammatical Texts from Antiquity to the Renaissance*, ed. M. De Nonno, P. De Paolis, and L. Holtz (Cassino, 2000), 449-98; for Kilwardby on figurative speech, see also Mary Sirridge, 'Robert Kilwardby: Figurative Constructions and the Limits of Grammar', in *De ortu grammaticae: Studies in Medieval Grammar and Linguistic Theory in Memory of Jan Pinborg*, ed. G.L. Bursill-Hall, S. Ebbesen, and K. Koerner (Amsterdam-Philadelphia, 1990), 321-37 and C.H. Kneepkens,

Sophistria and Roger Bacon's *Summa gramatica*.[54] Despite the reduced complexity, this distinction is, in the majority of the SGB sophisms, the cornerstone argument for the semantic completeness of the particular problematic proposition and its acceptance as a true statement. The direct source, however, of the approach implemented by SGB to reconcile the expressed and intended meaning of texts should not be sought in early 13th-century university grammar, but, to my mind, in the theological grammar that reached maturity in the last decades of the 12th century and that focused on the grammatical underpinning of deviant theological and religious speech. The roots of this development and its culmination in Peter the Chanter's *De tropis loquendi*[55] and William de Montibus' *Tropi*[56] have been studied by Franco Giusberti, Gillian Evans and Luisa Valente.[57]

In his introduction to *De tropis loquendi*, Peter the Chanter insists that, in considering the truth of texts, reference needs to be made to the truthfulness of authors. The first step to be taken by the Christian soul is to understand that the texts by learned authors, who have after all written their works under the guidance of God's hand, must always be considered sound. As a consequence, any apparent surface inconsistencies or contradictions are not inconsistent or contradictory at an underlying level. The methods recommended by Peter to

'Robert Kilwardby on Grammar', in *A Companion to the Philosophy of Robert Kilwardby*, ed. H. Lagerlund and P. Thom (Leiden-Boston, 2013), 17-64.

54 See also above, p. 305; for Roger Bacon's linguistic theories, see Irène Rosier-Catach, 'Roger Bacon and Grammar', in *Roger Bacon and the Sciences: Commemorative Essays*, ed. J. Hackett (Leiden, 1997), 67-102.

55 For Peter the Chanter, see the impressive study by John W. Baldwin, *Masters, Princes, and Merchants: The Social Views of Peter the Chanter and his Circle*, 2 vols. (Princeton, NJ, 1970), and Monique Boutry, *Introduction* to her edition *Petri Cantoris Parisiensis Verbum Adbreviatum. Textus conflatus* (Turnhout, 2004), vii-xii.

56 For William de Montibus, see Joseph W. Goering, *William de Montibus (c. 1140-1213). The Schools and the Literature of Pastoral Care* (Toronto, 1992), and Richard Sharpe, *A Handlist of the Latin Writers of Great Britain and Ireland before 1540* (Turnhout, 1997), 793-4.

57 Franco Giusberti, *Materials for a Study on Twelfth Century Scholasticism* (Naples, 1982); Gillian R. Evans, 'A Work of 'Terminist Theology'? Peter the Chanter's *De Tropis Loquendi* and Some *Fallacie*', *Vivarium* 20 (1982), 40-58 and eadem, *The Language and Logic of the Bible: The Earlier Middle Ages* (Cambridge, 1984 [paperback ed. 1991]), and Luisa Valente, *Phantasia contrarietatis. Contraddizioni scritturali, discorso teologico e arti del linguaggione nel* De tropis loquendi *di Pietro Cantore († 1197)* (Florence, 1997); see also eadem, 'Fallacie et théologie pendant la seconde moitié du XIIe siècle', in *Medieval Analyses in Language and Cognition*, ed. Ebbesen-Friedman, 207-36. For the theoretical-linguistic background of these more practice orientated grammars, see Luisa Valente, *Logique et théologie. Les écoles parisiennes entre 1150 et 1220* (Paris, 2008).

resolve apparent but not actual difficulties at the surface level include figures of construction and speech, as well as the explication of sophistic reasoning.[58] In fact, these are the underlying approach and methods that we encounter in the SGB.

b *The Doctrine of Syntactic and Semantic Supposition*

An examination of the use of supposition terminology shows that both fields of application, namely grammatical-syntactic supposition of the subject term (*supponere verbo*)[59] and logical-semantic supposition of substantively used terms (*supponere pro*),[60] are frequently present in SGB. The use of grammatical-syntactic supposition terminology does not significantly deviate from the way in which it occurs in grammatical and logical textbooks, as illustrated in Sophism 8 "Factum est uespere et mane dies unus" (Genesis 1.5), where subject-predicate gender agreement appears to be ignored:

> [SGB, p. 399] Queritur quid supponit huic uerbo 'est'. Si iste terminus 'dies unus', fieri non potest propter adiectiuum ei copulatum in neutro genere. Si iste terminus 'uespere et mane', hoc fieri non potest, cum sit terminus pluralis.
>
> *Solutio*. Ad hoc dicimus quod iste terminus 'factum est' est circumlocucio tercie persone uerbi passiui, scilicet fit. Et iste terminus 'dies unus' supponit ei.

The situation concerning logical-semantic supposition is quite different. There are indications that the author(s) of the sophisms was acquainted with the notions of personal and simplex supposition, as well as the difference between supposition and appellation. However, there are no explicit uses of the terms 'suppositio personalis, simplex, materialis' etc., despite this terminology being

58 Peter the Chanter, *De tropis*, partial ed. Giusberti, *Materials for a Study on Twelfth Century Scholasticism*, 106-8: "Primus modus soluendi sufficit simplici et christianae animae, quae doctores scribentes digito Dei in diuersis agnoscit habere sanum intellectum... Considerata igitur ueritate scriptorum quae pendet de ueritate auctoris, erit manifestum plura apparentia contraria non esse contraria. Non contentus autem hoc modo soluendi, secundum attemptet, compertoque tropo uel schemate loquendi, uel genere sophismatis, contrarietatem de facili soluere poterit..."

59 For a summary of the origins of grammatical supposition, see Karin Margareta Fredborg, 'Speculative Grammar', in *A History of Twelfth-Century Western Philosophy*, ed. P. Dronke (Cambridge, 1988) 177-95: 186-94.

60 For the medieval history of logical supposition, see L.M. de Rijk, *Logica modernorum*, vol. II, 1: *The Origin and Early Development of the Theory of Supposition* (Assen, 1967).

relatively common coin in textbooks on logic and collections of logical sophisms. The primary focus in the 38 sophisms is, however, placed on the phenomenon labeled in logical textbooks as figurative, metaphorical or improper supposition. This practice involves an equivocal use of language based on metaphorical speech. The discussion of the famous liturgical proposition "Manus mee que uos fecerunt clauis confixe sunt" (Sophism 3: taken from the Antiphon *Ego sum alpha et omega*) clearly presents two conflicting supposition domains: supposition *ex institutione* of Christ's carnal hands (the traditional personal supposition) and supposition *ex transsumptione* of God's hands standing for Divine Potency (metaphorical or improper supposition, in this case metonymical supposition). It is evident that the author was fully aware of the different domains of semantic supposition. The relative noun 'qu(a)e', the subject term of the relative clause denoting God's hands, refers to Christ's carnal hands, and, hence, results in a *relatio simplex*:[61]

> [SGB, p. 398] Hec dictio 'manus' hic posita supponit pro manibus carnalibus confixis, sed etiam ad eam fit relatio; ergo pro manibus carnalibus, et illis mediante relatione attribuitur fecisse uos; ergo falsa est locutio, quia manus carnales non uos fecerunt. Forte dicetur quod hec dictio 'que' refert simpliciter; ergo refert pro alia uel aliis manibus quam fit suppositio per hanc dictionem 'manus'; ergo Deus adminus habuit tres uel quatuor manus.
>
> Item. Manus mee confixe clauis sunt et manus mee fecerunt uos; ergo manus mee confixe sunt clauis et ille uel alie uos fecerunt; sed non ille; ergo alie; ergo Deus adminus habuit quatuor manus.
>
> *Solutio*. Hec dictio 'manus' unam habet suppositionem ex institucione, scilicet pro manibus carnalibus, aliam habet ex transumptione pro diuina potencia. Et notandum quod siue teneatur singulariter siue pluraliter, semper unum supponit, scilicet diuinam potenciam.
>
> Et concedimus quod hec dictio 'que' refert simpliciter pro diuina potencia, non tamen pro alia uel pro aliis manibus, quia hec dictio 'alia' adiuncta huic dictioni 'manus' semper sumitur pro manibus carnalibus.
>
> Item. Non ualet: Manus mee confixe sunt clauis et manus mee fecerunt uos; ergo manus mee confixe sunt clauis et ille uel alie fecerunt uos, ratione iam dicta.[62]

61 For the phenomenon of the *relatio simplex*, see above, n. 29.

62 The quotations in the main text offer the complete text of Sophism 3.

Notions of syntactic and metaphorical-semantic supposition are intermingled in the opposition section of Sophism 12, "Semen quod cecidit in terram bonam. Hii sunt qui uerbum Dei audiunt" (Antiph. *Semen quod* & Luke 8.8+21). Three arguments are advanced against accepting these two propositions as grammatically complete or perfect. The first one concerns the demonstrative function of the pronoun 'hii' and the relative function of the noun 'qui'.[63] In the second objection, the opponent inquires about the verb for which the noun 'semen' is the subject: "Cui uerbo fiat suppositio per hanc dictionem 'semen'?" The construction (*suppositio fit verbo*) that he uses derives from the intransitive construction 'supponere verbo', which belongs to grammatical-syntactic supposition terminology. In the third opposing argument, questions are asked about the antecedent of the relative noun 'quod':

> [SGB, p. 400] Queritur quid demonstretur per hanc dictionem 'hii' et pro quibus fiat relatio per hanc dictionem 'qui'. Item. Cui uerbo fiat suppositio per hanc dictionem 'semen'. Ad quid fit relatio per hanc dictionem 'quod', cum dicitur 'quod cecidit etc.'

The respondent proposes two solutions. In the first one, the problematic propositions are considered to be imperfect on the level of expression and should be rephrased by "Hii qui libenter uerbum Dei audiunt, [sunt, idest] designantur per semen quod cecidit etc." According to the respondent, this explanation requires a hidden preposition 'per', as well as a hidden accusative case for the noun 'semen' and the interpolation of 'esse' for 'significari' or 'designari':

> *Solucio.* Ad hoc duppliciter potest responderi. Dicimus enim quod hec dictio 'hii' et hec dictio 'qui' mutuo se respiciunt. Vnde sic ordinanda est locucio: Hii qui libenter uerbum Dei audiunt, sunt, idest designantur per semen quod cecidit etc. Et secundum hoc hec dictio 'semen' subintelligitur accusatiui casus mediante prepositione.
>
> Et notandum quod sicut uerbum dicendi quandoque sumitur pro uerbo essendi, ut cum dicitur 'equi dicuntur', idest sunt, eodem modo uerbum essendi quandoque ponitur pro uerbo dicendi, ut cum dicitur 'Petrus [peius *MS*] erit', idest dicetur. Ita in hac locucione uerbum essendi ponitur pro uerbo significandi, ut patet per expositionem superius dictam.

---

63 Medieval grammar considers the relative word 'qui, quae, quod' to be a noun instead of a pronoun.

The other solution proposed by the respondent is to consider 'semen' to be in the nominative case, which co-determines the inherence range of the verb 'sunt', i.e., the range of extra-linguistic entities to which the verb 'sunt' applies in this sentence. He claims that 'semen' supposits—here we are confronted with the metaphorical-semantic domain of supposition theory—for the good people because of the restrictive qualification of the term 'semen' by the relative clause: "quod cecidit in terram bonam." The correctness of combining a singular subject term, i.e., 'semen', with a plural finite verb is defended by pointing to the circumstance that, in this sentence, the singular word 'semen' supposits for the same extralinguistic entities as the plural demonstrative pronoun 'hii'. Accordingly, the finite verb is allowed to derive its number from each of them:

> Vel potest dici quod hec dictio 'semen' sit nominatiui casus et condeterminat inherentialem respectum huius uerbi 'sunt'. Supponit enim hec dictio 'semen' pro bonis ratione huius determinationis 'quod cecidit in terram bonam' et pro bonis fit demonstratio per hanc diccionem 'hii'. Et pro eisdem fit relatio per hanc dictionem 'qui'. Vnde sic ordinanda est locucio: Semen quod cecidit etc., sunt hii qui audiunt etc.
>
> Et hec diccio 'semen' in singulari numero competenter supponit uerbo pluralis numeri, quia pro eodem fit suppositio per hanc diccionem 'semen' et per hanc diccionem 'hii'. Vnde potest sortiri numerum ab utroque. Vnde patet solutio huius locucionis 'mandata tua meditatio mea est'.[64] Cum enim fit pro eodem suppositio, uerbum notans idemptitatem sortitur numerum ab utroque. Ita et hic 'semini tuo qui est Xpistus'[65] quantum ad genus, et de similibus similiter.[66]

A similar, mixed application of the syntactic and semantic doctrines of supposition is found in the opposition and response sections of Sophism 16, headed by the problematic proposition "Generatio et generatio laudabit opera tua et potenciam tuam pronuntiabunt" (Psalm 144.4). The problems advanced by the opponent relate to (1) the—semantic—supposition of both the terms 'generatio', (2) the copulative function of the conjunction 'et', (3) the grammatical-syntactic supposition of a subject term in plural form to a finite verb in singular, and (4) the supposition of one and the same subject term to singular and plural finite verbs:

---

64 Ps. 118.143; cf. Grondeux and Rosier-Catach, eds., *Sophistria*, 212-13.

65 Cf. Gal. 3.16.

66 The quotations in the main text offer the complete text of Sophism 12.

> [SGB, p. 401] Queritur de suppositione istarum diccionum 'generatio et generatio'. Si enim fiat suppositio pro proprietate que est generatio, falsa est locucio, quia proprietas non laudat.
>
> Item. Pro quocumque fiat suppositio, uidetur quod falsa sit locucio, quia pro eodem fit suppositio per generationem primo positam et per generationem secundo positam. Et hec coniunctio 'et' habet copulare inter diuersa. Et ita incongrua est locucio.
>
> Item. Hec coniunctio 'et' semel posita facit terminum pluralem et supponit uerbo singularis numeri; ergo incongrue.
>
> Item. Eidem termino attribuitur hoc uerbum 'pronunciabunt', quod est plurale. Et ita simul et semel fit attributio per uerbum singulare et uerbum plurale; ergo male.
>
> Item. Queritur qua ratione fit attributio per uerbum singularis numeri eidem termino.

The respondent rejects the opinion held by "sunt qui" that the subject term 'generatio et generatio' ought to be considered a singular term, notwithstanding the fact that it is plural according to its expressed form. He himself defends the view that it is plural. In his opinion, this plural subject supposits (*supponit verbo*) correctly to the singular finite verb, since it does not supposit for itself but for its parts (*supponit pro*). This—semantic—supposition (*supponere pro*) means that the plural subject term signifies a whole by referring to its parts and, according to its singular reference function, supposits to the singular finite verb. We are, therefore, confronted with the *figura locutionis* of synecdoche (*pars pro toto* or *vice versa*).[67] Accordingly, the respondent speaks of a 'sine(c)doc(h)a suppositio'.[68] Incidentally, the synecdoche theory defended in this sophism is analogous to the common 13th-century view of synecdoche, which accepts synecdoche as an example of the rhetorical trope *figura locutionis* as well as a *figura constructionis*, similar to the case of what is called in more recent Latin grammars the "Greek accusative" or "accusative of restriction" (e.g., "Sortes est albus pedem").[69]

It is interesting to note how the syntactic and semantic supposition doctrines are interchangeably applied in one proposition by means of only one

---

67 For the notion of synecdoche in grammatical sophisms, see Grondeux and Rosier-Catach, eds., *Sophistria*, 79-81.

68 See below, pp. 318-19.

69 See for the two rivaling theories on synecdoche in thirteenth-century grammar, Sirridge, 'Robert Kilwardby: Figurative Constructions and the Limits of Grammar' and Grondeux and Rosier-Catach, eds., *Sophistria*, 80-1.

finite verb 'supponit', which has been used here in a more or less zeugmatic way. The plural term 'generatio et generatio' is the subject term of the finite verb 'laudabit' (*supponit huic uerbo*); the term 'generatio et generatio' does not supposit here for the whole that it indicates but for its parts (*supponit pro suis partibus*), and it therefore represents a metaphorical supposition, namely *suppositio synecdochica*. This allows the plural term to supposit to a singular verb:

> [SGB, p. 401] *Solutio*. Sunt qui dicunt quod iste terminus 'generatio et generatio' est terminus singularis numeri. Et hec dictio 'et' diuisiue tenetur. Et est sensus: Et generatio et generatio laudabit. Et est simile 'Cartago Mariusque tulit'.[70] Et dicunt quod hoc uerbum 'pronunciabunt' in plurali attribuit rem suam supposito per terminum presentem habito respectu ad formam et non habito respectu ad intellectum, scilicet prout diuisiue intelligitur illa coniunctio.
>
> Nos autem dicimus quod copulatiue tenetur illa coniunctio. Et facit terminum pluralem. Et supponit huic uerbo 'laudabit' singularis numeri, sed non pro se, sed pro suis partibus. Vnde sinedochica est suppositio. Et hoc uerbum 'pronunciabunt' attribuit pluraliter rem suam supposito [termino *MS*] pro se et non pro partibus. Et ita congrua est attributio. Et est simile 'Socrates est crispus, magnus'. Vnam attributionem respicit hec locucio pro parte quia pro capite, aliam pro toto.

The reason why this figurative construction was applied may be found in the intention of the author who wrote the problematic proposition. Since the Psalmist intended to praise and extol God, he proclaims that every separate generation must praise the Lord, and all the generations taken together have to do the same:

> [*SGB*, p. 401] Et notandum quod non sine ratione apponitur uerbum in singulari et in plurali numero, sed ad extollentiam diuinam, scilicet quod quelibet generatio per se debet laudare et quelibet generatio coniunctim. Et hec dictio 'generatio' primo et secundo supponit pro rebus generatis et pro diuersis.[71]

These examples of the ways in which supposition terminology is used in SGB show that its application of the doctrine of grammatical-syntactic supposition conformed to common use in grammatical and logical contexts, as the

70 Lucanus, *De bello civili*, II, 92.

71 The quotations in the main text offer the complete text of Sophism 16.

phrase 'supponere verbo' was used in the last quarter of the 12th century to indicate that the subject term is governed by the finite verb of the sentence. The application of logical-semantic supposition in SGB shows a substantially different picture. Commonly, personal supposition is defined as the acceptance of a common nominal term (*supponere pro*) for its subordinates, i.e., the particulars that regularly fall under the signification label of the common substantive noun at issue. As already stated above,[72] SGB scarcely uses the term 'supponere pro' to refer to traditional logical-semantic personal supposition. In fact, the main emphasis falls on the variant of personal supposition known in contemporaneous textbooks of logic as metaphorical or improper supposition. Metaphorical supposition pertains to the metaphorical use of terms and is the property of a substantive term denoting a thing or things thus metaphorically signified. Generally, logicians treat metaphorical supposition with some disdain. For example, John Buridan excludes this kind of supposition from consideration by logicians and relegates it to the domain of poetics.[73] However, an interesting section on improper supposition is found at the end of the chapter on supposition in the 13th-century logical textbook *Cum sit nostra*. Unfortunately, the text of this treatise has come down to us in several versions with additions, corrections and other textual interventions. Nevertheless, its tenor (*sensus*) is perfectly clear, despite the imperfections in its presentation.[74] After discussing *suppositio (personalis) confusa et distributiva*, the author of *Cum sit nostra* presents four deviating types of supposition: *geminata, antonomatica, metonomatica* and *sinodochica*. In the first section, he deals with both *geminata*: 'Socrates et Plato currunt' and *antonomatica*: 'Apostolus [i.e., Paulus] dicit hoc'. In the next section, he discusses the last two kinds of supposition. This is followed by a third section, in which he explains, using sample sentences, the difference between proper and improper supposition. The section concludes by remarking that these two suppositions belong to the domain of grammar. Taken at face value, this implies that the discussion of both proper and improper supposition belongs to grammar, an inference that is completely against the tenor of the chapter and the entire tradition of medieval logic! The solution to this problem must be that the discussion

---

72 See above, p. 312.

73 John Buridan, *Summulae: De suppositionibus*, 4.3.1, ed. R. van der Lecq (Nijmegen, 1998), 38,8-10: "Sed de huiusmodi suppositione [sc. impropria] non pertinet ad scientias speculativas, sed ad sermones poeticos. Ideo haec suppositio praetermittatur ad praesens."

74 For the complicated transmission history of the text of *Cum sit nostra*, see De Rijk, *Logica modernorum*, vol. II, 1: *The Origin and Early Development of the Theory of Supposition*, 432-8.

of proper and improper was moved to or inserted in the wrong place, viz., between the end of the section on the two metaphorical suppositions and the final concluding sentence of this section, for it is the *suppositio synecdochica* and the *suppositio metonymica* that are the figurative or metaphorical suppositions belonging to the grammarian's domain:

> [*Cum sit nostra*, pp. 447-8][75] Item. Suppositionum alia geminata, alia antonomatica, alia metonomatica, alia sinodochica. Suppositio geminata est quando geminatur substantia, ut '*Socrates et Plato currunt*'. Antonomatica est quando terminus communis supponit pro eo cui maxime convenit nomen, ut '*Apostolus dicit hoc*', intelligitur Paulus; similiter: '*Philosophus dicit hoc*', intelligitur Aristotiles.
>
> Item. Suppositionum alia sinodochica, alia metonomatica. Suppositio sinodochica est quando pars supponit pro toto, vel econverso, ut '*prora est in mari*'; et est anterior pars navis; et ita ponitur pars pro toto. Suppositio metonomatica est quando continens ponitur pro contento, ut '*bibe ciphum*', idest *quod continetur in cipho*.
>
> > Item. Suppositionum alia propria, alia inpropria. Suppositio propria est illa quando terminus supponit pro sua significatione propria, ut '*homo currit*'. Inpropria est illa quando terminus supponit inproprie, ut '*Anglia pugnat*', idest *gens Anglie*.
>
> Et iste due suppositiones pertinent ad gramaticam.

A similarly loose and confused application of supposition terminology analogous to its use in SGB is noted by Luisa Valente in her conclusion to her discussion of the supposition doctrine of Peter the Chanter in his *De tropis loquendi*.[76] Giusberti had previously pointed out that Peter the Chanter considered metaphorical speech and figurative constructions to be unavoidable and even necessary in Biblical and religious language. As Giusberti consequently emphasises, Peter realised that the traditional toolkits of grammar and logic, although necessary, were, therefore, not sufficient for deeper analysis and profound exegesis of religious texts.[77] His *De tropis loquendi* was intended as an additional and

---

75 Ed. in De Rijk, *Logica modernorum*, vol. II, 2: *Texts and indices*, 413-51. Valente, *Phantasia contrarietatis*, 183, refers to the same text.

76 Valente, *Phantasia contrarietatis*, 188.

77 Giusberti, *Materials for a Study on Twelfth Century Scholasticism*, 96-7: "This is a clear expression of Peter's awareness of the possibilities, the purpose and the limits of the use of the *artes liberales* in theology.... Occasionally one even gets the impression that Peter sees the problem of Biblical language as part of the larger problem of religious

useful instrument for dealing with the improprieties and anomalies of religious language and thus arriving at a better understanding of the texts in the Bible, liturgy and theology.

5 Final Remarks

The exclusive focus on deviant linguistic usage in religious texts is a remarkable feature of the SGB. Although not always the case, the emphasis is prevalently placed on figurative and metaphorical speech, giving greater prominence to discussions of improper, figurative or metaphorical supposition. As a result of this particular attention to the metaphorical qualities of religious texts, this sophism collection displays close doctrinal affinity to the contextual approach focusing on religious speech that was developed in textbooks of theological grammar in the last decades of the 12th century. In addition to the traditional analytical instruments of grammar and logic, rhetoric and, in particular, the doctrine of the rhetorical tropes[78] played a prominent role in this approach, by allowing apparent linguistic anomalies of religious speech to be explained within the framework of linguistic well-formedness and completeness, and solving the conflict between the intended meaning and the linguistic surface structure of a text.[79]

Giusberti, Evans, Valente and Goering[80] have shown that, from the last decades of the 12th century onwards, the traditional exegesis of Biblical, liturgical and religious texts was strengthened by the newly developed analytical and exegetical instrument of theological grammar. This discipline was given its shape in newly created textbooks that met the requirements of the educational developments in the late 12th and early 13th centuries. These textbooks, which are exemplified by Peter the Chanter's *De tropis loquendi* and William

language, which might also include theology: 'Item. cum Sacra Scriptura non habeat congruos sermones rebus caelestibus de quibus loquitur, necesse est eam improprietate multiplici uti.'"

78 For the history of the rhetorical figures of speech and their role in exegesis in the early Middle Ages, see Grondeux, *À l'école de Cassiodore*.

79 For the tension between language, the traditional liberal arts and Biblical texts in the late 12th century, see also Luisa Valente, 'Langage et théologie pendant la seconde moitié du XIIe siècle', in *Sprachtheorien in Spätantike und Mittelalter*, ed. S. Ebbesen (Tübingen, 1995), 33-54.

80 Giusberti, *Materials for a Study on Twelfth Century Scholasticism*; Evans, *The Language and Logic of the Bible*; Valente, 'Langage et théologie pendant la seconde moitié du XIIe siècle'; Valente, *Phantasia contrarietatis*; Goering, *William de Montibus*.

de Montibus' *Tropi*, were written as aids-to-study for the theological curriculum of late 12th- and early 13th-century schools. The authors were targeting the less advanced students in theology who had already completed basic training in grammar and logic.[81] The medieval educational system used the sophism as an exercise complementary to reinforcing mandatory readings and textbook-based learning. In her survey of the medieval genres of teaching texts, Olga Weijers points out that this practice started in classroom instruction in grammar and logic, where the sophisms were, initially, of a simple and uncomplicated structure.[82] Although they were called 'grammatical sophisms', the present analysis of some of the SGB items shows that this collection of grammatical sophisms does not belong to the strictly grammatical and logical part of the educational curriculum in the late 12th and early 13th centuries. They in all probability constituted an exercise tool that provided support for the textbook-based instruction in theological grammar and, consequently, for an overall sermocinal analysis of improper language usage in religious texts. Establishing the exact place and function in the medieval educational system will have to wait, however, until the cornerstone texts of theological grammar are available in critical editions and their position in the medieval school curriculum has been fully ascertained.

---

81 Cf. Evans, *The Language and Logic of the Bible*, 146-9 and Goering *William de Montibus*, 349-54.

82 Olga Weijers, *Le maniement du savoir. Pratiques intellectuelles à l'époque des premières universités (XIIIe-XIVe siècles)* (Turnhout, 1996), 95-6.

Obligations and Conditionals

Mikko Yrjönsuuri

The medieval obligations logic concerned the duties of a respondent in a disputation that starts with some special obligation given to the respondent. Most typically, this special obligation binds the respondent to grant to the opponent a specified false sentence whenever the opponent puts it forward. This species of obligation was called *positio* and the specified sentence was called the *positum*. As the special obligation did not completely relieve the respondent from the general prima facie duties of logical coherence and of truthfulness, rules were given concerning how the respondent ought to act in such a disputation. The basic aim of the rules was usually to guide the respondent so that he could avoid granting and denying the same sentence, which was in the circumstances understood as granting further falsities in addition to what was specified in the obligation itself.

In this paper I will consider, in addition to *positio*, another species of obligations, *rei veritas*. This species too concerns laying down a false sentence to be accepted in the disputation, but in a way different from how the *positum* is accepted. Also, I will relate the treatment of *casus* in sophism 47 of Richard Kilvington's *Sophismata* to these two species of obligations. My particular problem in this paper is to understand how the three techniques can be and were used in analysing inferential relations between sentences.

1 Consequences in *Obligationes parisienses*

The anonymous early 13th-century treatise *Obligationes parisienses* claims that the study of inferential relations is the purpose of obligational disputations. The introduction of this text describes how an obligational disputation is useful in the acquisition of "knowledge of consequences" (*scientia de consequentiis*). The author thinks that when a special obligation is given and accepted, the disputation does not concern what is true or believed as such, but only in relation to the given obligation. Thus, anything that follows from the given obligation needs to be taken into account. If the respondent is given the duty to grant a specified sentence, therefore, he must also grant anything that follows logically from it in order to avoid contradicting himself.[1]

1 An edition of the treatise is in L.M. de Rijk, 'Some Thirteenth Century Tracts on the Game of Obligation II', *Vivarium* 13 (1975), 22-54: 27.

 DOI 10.1163/9789004324275_010

In general, the idea is understandable. Without any special obligation, the respondent can remain coherent simply by following the truth and granting only what is true. But when a false sentence is given as the starting point, logical coherence can be achieved only by careful observance of the logical relations between the sentences put forward in the disputation. Turning this general idea into actual practice is, however, rather complex, as can be noticed through actually engaging in an obligational disputation. Rules for the respondent are indeed needed to make the task easier when the number of sentences to be evaluated increases and their inferential relations get more complex. Furthermore, as the author of *Obligationes parisienses* notes, one may need to recognize different kinds of inferential relations.

In an interesting passage, the introduction of *Obligationes parisienses* points out that one needs to be aware how contingent (*casualis*) sentences differ from those expressing necessary subject matter.[2] The examples introduced by the author are illuminating. First, consider the following two sentences:

1. Socrates is an animal.
2. Socrates is a man.

Here 2 follows from 1 through Socrates' essence: if he exists, he is necessarily a man, and if he is an animal, he does exist. However, the inference from 1 to 2 is not a natural consequence (*consequentia naturalis*) according to the terminology used by the author. He seems to mean that no matter how necessary the inferential relation is, it is not grounded in anything like the conceptual inclusion of the consequent in the antecedent, as the standard requirement for natural consequences was at the time often formulated. It is valid, however, since 1 cannot be true without 2 also being true. The accidental character of the consequence can, as the author points out, easily be seen by comparison to the following pair of sentences:

3. Socrates is coloured.
4. Socrates is white.

Here 4 does not follow from 3, since there is no such logical connection, nor does Socrates' essence imply anything about his particular colour.

---

2 "And thus this genus of disputation is more used in contingent matters, since in them a consequence is more manifest than in necessary matters": De Rijk, 'Some Thirteenth Century Tracts II', 27.

A similar situation concerning validity can be found in the following disputation example, which the author of *Obligationes parisienses* discusses.[3] The example illustrates how inferential reasoning processes take place in obligational disputations. The idea is not just to take two sentences and to consider whether there is an inferential relationship between them, but rather to develop a more complex inferential structure. The following table gives as an ordered sequence the *positum*, the propositions put forward by the opponent, and the respective answers of the respondent with their appropriate explanations.

D1

Pos: Antichrist exists.	Accepted as possible.
Pr1: Antichrist is coloured.	Granted as sequent.
Pr2: Antichrist is white.	Denied as false non-sequent.
Pr3: Antichrist is not of a middle colour.	Granted as true non-repugnant.
Pr4: Antichrist is black.	Granted as sequent.

The advice given by the author is that in each step the respondent should proceed so that he first notes the actual truth value of the sentence put forward. If the sentence is false, he should consider a conditional sentence where the antecedent is a conjunction consisting of the *positum* together with all the granted sentences and the opposites of the denied sentences, and the consequent is the evaluated sentence. The point in considering the conditional is in finding out whether its consequent is sequentially relevant, or 'follows' in the disputation. Thus, the author thinks that conditionals are taken to express consequences.

If the respondent follows this advice in disputation D1, in the first step he first notes that Pr1 is false. Since nothing else has yet been put forward, the conditional to be considered is simple:

Con1: Pos –> Pr1

As the author notes, this conditional is true (If Antichrist exists, Antichrist is coloured). Perhaps interestingly, the conditional can be compared to the pair of sentences 1 and 2 above, and thus the consequence expressed by this conditional would not be a natural one (*naturalis*). No doubts about its validity or

3 De Rijk, 'Some Thirteenth Century Tracts II', 29-30.

acceptability[4] are nevertheless mentioned in the *Obligationes parisienses* text, which merely points out that the conditional is true. Therefore, Pr1 is sequent and needs to be granted despite its falsity.

In the next step, Pr2 is evaluated in a similar manner. It is first noted that it is false. Then, the respondent should consider the specified conditional. Its antecedent is a conjunction of the *positum* and the first proposition Pr1, which has been granted.

Con2: Pos & Pr1 –> Pr2

Now, this conditional is false, since it does not follow from Antichrist existing and being coloured that he is white. The respondent should therefore note that the proposition Pr2 is false, and does not follow from earlier granted propositions. Thus, it should be denied.

Further, when the respondent has to evaluate a proposition that he notes to be true, it has to be checked whether it is repugnant. This means that in the case of Pr3 the respondent should consider the following conditional:

Con3: Pos & Pr1 & –Pr2 –> –Pr3

As the author notes, this conditional is false and the negation of Pr3 does not follow, which means that Pr3 itself is not to be evaluated as repugnant. As it is true, it is then granted.

The conditional becomes increasingly complex when the disputation continues. When evaluating Pr4, the respondent notes its falsity and checks whether it follows through considering the conditional:

Con4: Pos & Pr1 & –Pr2 & Pr3 –> Pr4

Since this conditional expresses a valid inferential relation and is thus true, Pr4 must be granted despite its falsity.

This detailed description of what the respondent of an obligational disputation actually does makes clear the role of conditionals in the evaluation of the

4 An interestingly different case is the species of obligations called *positio impossibilis*. There only natural or direct (*recta*) consequences are acceptable. See, e.g., L.M. de Rijk, 'Some Thirteenth Century Tracts on the Game of Obligation I', *Vivarium* 12 (1974), 94-103: 118-19; translation in Anonymous, 'The Emmeran Treatise on Impossible *Positio*', in *Medieval Formal Logic*, ed. M. Yrjönsuuri (Dordrecht-Boston-London, 2001), 217-23: 218-19.

propositions. It remains, however, an open question what kinds of conditionals are considered true in this context. As already noted, the author does not require that a conditional be true only if it expresses a natural (*naturalis*) consequence. It is also evident that the anonymous author does not have in mind what is nowadays called a material implication. For the truth of the kind of conditional that the author has in mind it is required that there be some kind of necessary relation between the antecedent and a consequent.

Any reader with a 20th-century education in philosophy must at this point keep in mind that in the early 13th century there were no unanimously accepted general criteria for the validity of an inference apart from the semantic criterion that the antecedent cannot be true without the consequent. In particular, logicians were not educated with a concept of formal validity based on the substitutability of the material parts of the relevant sentences in the sense in which we nowadays know such a concept. Something like it may have been applicable to syllogistic logic, but logicians were from the context of the treatises of syncategorematic terms well aware of the fact that there are non-syllogistic valid inferences. Indeed, the above-mentioned examples from the *Obligationes parisienses* are non-syllogistic.

It seems that the obligational context proved useful in helping to distinguish different types of inferential validity. The conditional Con1 is not related to a formally valid inference in the sense in which we nowadays speak of formal validity. It is valid because of the nature of Antichrist: his nature differs from, e.g., angelic nature, so that if he exists, he must exist as a material object that has a colour. Furthermore, the disputation also accepts that the conditionals can rely on a three-part division of colours into white, black and the middle. This division appears to work in the example as a logical fact, a fact on which logical inferences can be grounded. If this fact could not be taken into account, the conditional Con4 would fail to be true. It is, however, central to the argumentation and thus the anonymous author clearly thought it to be acceptable in this context. The inferential considerations behind the truth evaluations of all the conditionals are obviously non-syllogistic and reflect no apparent formality based on substitutivity.

Given the author's remark in the introduction that the inference from 1 to 2 is not a natural one, he seems to distinguish these inferences from direct conceptual containment. The inference from 2 to 1 would reflect the conceptual containment of 'animal' in 'man' that can be made explicit by the definition of man as a rational animal. The anonymous author could perhaps accept that as a 'natural' consequence. But the conditionals considered in D1 are not of this kind.

It is clear, on the other hand, that the anonymous author did not think that these conditionals would be counterfactual conditionals in the sense in which 20th-century logicians discussed counterfactuals. First, if we apply our contemporary classifications of conditionals, these are to be understood in the indicative mood. Furthermore, their truth seems to be taken to be logical. In order to see in what sense their truth is logical, however, we need to consider more complexities in the obligational structure, and in particular the species of obligations called '*rei veritas*'.

When distinguishing between the different kinds of obligations, the anonymous author points out that in the kind of obligation called '*rei veritas*' answers differ from those given in *positio*. That is, if the respondent is obligated to the sentence 'Antichrist exists' in the species *rei veritas*, he should answer with doubt to the sentence 'Antichrist is white'.[5] The author's point seems to be applicable to the respondent in the disputation example D1. He denies Pr2 in D1. If he is instead in a disputation proceeding with a *rei veritas*, he should answer with doubt at Pr2. That is, the disputation would proceed as follows:

D2

RV: Antichrist exists.	Accepted as possible.
Pr1: Antichrist is coloured.	Granted as sequent.
Pr2: Antichrist is white.	Doubted.

It seems that the author thought that in *rei veritas* the answers should be given on the basis of reasoning that has to some extent the same mode of thought that we find in the 20th-century understanding of counterfactual conditionals. If Antichrist existed, he would be of some colour, but the respondent does not know which. It is noteworthy that in D1 (based on a *positum*) the answers to Pr2 and Pr3 (which are judged non-sequent and non-repugnant) are given in accordance with their actual truth-value and not in relation to a situation where 'Antichrist exists' is true. Assigning a colour to Antichrist is false because actually Antichrist does not exist and thus has no colour either. But in D2, where the obligation is in the species *rei veritas*, answers reflect the situation where the given sentence is true: this appears to be reminiscent of counterfactual reasoning. Unfortunately *Obligationes parisienses* does not contain a proper discussion of *rei veritas*. From other treatises we do find somewhat more substantial discussions, which indeed point in the direction that it was understood as the kind of obligational disputation that leans on counterfactual

5 De Rijk, 'Some Thirteenth Century Tracts II', 28.

reasoning. The respondent is often required to answer as if he knew the *rei veritas* to be true.[6]

As a further complexity, *Obligationes parisienses* as well as other obligations treatises discuss disputation examples involving a double structure of both *rei veritas* and *positum*. First some contingent sentence is given as the *rei veritas* and then something else, often its opposite, is given as a *positum*. Consider the following disputation:[7]

D3

RV: Socrates is black.	Accepted as possible.
Pos: Socrates is white.	Accepted as possible.
Pr1: Socrates is white and you are not a bishop.	Denied as false non-sequent.
Pr2: Socrates is white.	Granted as sequent.
Pr3: You are a bishop.	Granted as sequent.

Here *rei veritas* is used to ascertain the falsity of the *positum*, and more exactly the falsity of the first conjunct of Pr1. If Socrates was white as the *positum* claims, the conjunction would be true (given that the respondent is a student in logic and not a bishop), but the possible truth of the *positum* is not at issue in the disputation. The role of the *positum* is not to serve as a basis of counterfactual reasoning, but as a false premise in logical reasoning. *Positum* is used in the inferential determination of correct answers, but the truth values considered in the answers are decided on the basis of the *rei veritas*. The disputation D3 is given by the author as an unproblematic illustration of his rule that on the basis of a false *positum* it is possible to prove any contingent proposition in the disputation. The rule as such also attests to the idea that *positum* is not developed counterfactually but as a starting point of logical inferences. Thus, the point is exactly that Pr3 is a false sentence completely unrelated both to the *rei veritas* and to the *positum* before the inferential structure is built. Still, it has to be granted in the disputation.

The double structure of the *rei veritas* and the *positum* seems to be in place in order to make explicit the separation of truth and logic in obligational disputations. While *rei veritas* provides the ground for truth-value evaluations, *positum* is used in logical inferences. This structure emphasizes the detachment

6 See Sara Uckelman, '*Sit verum obligationes* and Counterfactual Reasoning', *Vivarium* 53 (2015), 90-113.

7 De Rijk, 'Some Thirteenth Century Tracts II', 31.

of the *positum* from genuine truth-value considerations. The *positum* is not to be taken as true, but as a starting point of inferences in the disputation.

2 Obligations and the *Casus* in *Sophismata*

13th-century obligations treatises often use the word '*casus*' at the place where the author of *Obligationes parisienses* used in the above example the expression '*in veritate*' associated with the species of obligations called *rei veritas*. The term *casus* associates the technique with practices used in the context of what were then called sophisms (*sophismata*). In a sophism, there is a *casus* given, and on the basis of the *casus* arguments are constructed for and against some specific sentence called the sophism itself. As the 13th-century treatments of sophisms often use other technicalities of obligational disputations also, we may ask whether the *casus* in a sophism ought to be understood as a kind of obligation, and perhaps more exactly an obligation in the species *rei veritas*?

This would be a straightforward question to ask of any medieval logician who knew both genres. Unfortunately nothing seems to be said about the matter in the 13th-century texts known to modern scholars. But in the early 14th century Richard Kilvington seems to tackle the issue. In sophism 47 of his *Sophismata*,[8] he turns to a discussion of the rules of obligations, apparently because he thinks that in a sophism one should obey the rules of obligations. Kilvington's discussion has been considered by many scholars writing on obligations,[9] and I will not go into all of its details here. For our purposes the main point is that he seems to be claiming that the standard rules for *positio* will not work in the sophism that he is discussing. If they are obeyed, the sophism cannot be solved. Instead, he puts forward a revision of the rules. It seems that his thinking is similar to what 13th-century thinkers had in connection to *rei veritas*. It is noteworthy though that Kilvington clearly aims at

8 Edition in Richard Kilvington, *The Sophismata of Richard Kilvington*, ed. N. Kretzmann and B. Ensign Kretzmann (Oxford, 1990); translation in Richard Kilvington, *The Sophismata of Richard Kilvington. Introduction, Translation and Commentary*, N. Kretzmann and B. Ensign Kretzmann (Cambridge, 1990).

9 See esp. Angel d'Ors, '*Tu scis regem sedere* (Kilvington, S47[48])', *Anuario filosófico* 24 (1991), 49-74: 66-7; and Stephen Read, 'Richard Kilvington and the Theory of Obligations', in this volume.

devising suitable rules, while no 13th-century author is known to have even tried to give rules for answering in a *rei veritas* disputation. For example, the above-considered anonymous author of *Obligationes parisienses* simply refrains from giving any rules.

The core of the revision to the obligational rules Kilvington suggests is that the respondent ought to grant what would be true if the *positum* were true. As he recognizes, this principle requires that the respondent ought to grant anything that follows logically. In this respect, his rules are similar to what we find in the earlier authors. But there is more. He suggests that a sentence like Pr1 in D3 above is affected by the *positum* and ought not be denied but instead granted. Kilvington's point is that if you assume that Socrates is white, the conjunction 'Socrates is white and you are not a bishop' ought to be evaluated as consisting of a sentence assumed to be true and an independent truth. A conjunction of truths should then be evaluated as true and thus it ought to be granted in the disputation. This reasoning seems characteristically counterfactual in a sense related to the 20th-century discussion.

The actual sophism Kilvington discusses has the *casus* "if the king is seated, you know that the king is seated, and if the king is not seated, you know that he is not seated" (let us call this K). The *casus* thus tells that whether the king is seated or not, you will know it. As I read Kilvington's text, he is thinking that obligational rules ought to help in evaluating the *sophisma* sentence "You know that the king is seated." Let us therefore construct the sophism as an obligational disputation with the *casus* as a starting point.

As is clear to any logician, the *casus* implies nothing about whether the king is seated and thus does not decide which one of the contradictory pair you know, but it does imply that you know one of them. This logical structure can be used in an obligational disputation in many ways. Consider first the following example following the standard rules for *positio*:

D4

Pos: K	Accepted as possible.
Pr1: You know that the king is not seated.	Denied as false non-sequent.
Pr2: You know that the king is seated.	Granted as sequent.

Kilvington does not accept these answers. He takes it to be problematic that inverting the order of Pr1 and Pr2 for another disputation would yield the opposite answers. If Pr2 were put forward first, it would have to be denied, and after it Pr1 granted. According to the rules given by the author of *Obligationes parisienses* (and, e.g., Walter Burley) this would be correct and unproblematic.

But consider the following disputation in the species of *rei veritas* following the suggestion made by the author of *Obligationes parisienses* discussed above in connection to disputation D2:

D5

RV: K	Accepted as possible.
Pr1: You know that the king is not seated.	Doubted.
Pr2: You know that the king is seated.	Doubted.

The respondent has to answer with doubt because he cannot judge which one of the two he would know. This is the way Kilvington thinks that the sophism ought to be treated. It seems that he requires that in sophisms the *casus* should be treated in the way that 13th-century authors treated *rei veritas* and not in the way *positum* was treated. From this viewpoint he may be described as trying by his revision to give rules of *rei veritas*, which earlier authors had opted not to attempt.

We need to attend to one more sentence in Kilvington's discussion. He formulates a clear counterfactual conditional in order to prove his point:[10]

CF

For if you were in Rome and you were not a bishop, this would have to be denied: 'You are in Rome' and 'you are a bishop' are alike [in truth value].

The sentence comes in connection with an obligational disputation that could proceed as follows:

D6

Pos: You are in Rome.	Accepted as possible.
Pr1: You are a bishop.	Denied as false non-sequent.
Pr2: 'You are in Rome' and 'you are a bishop' are alike.	Denied as repugnant.

Kilvington's counterfactual conditional cited above (CF) is similar to the conditional suggested by the author of *Obligationes parisienses* as a help for the respondent in evaluating Pr2. It has otherwise the same antecedent, but formulated in the subjunctive mood, whereas the *Obligationes parisienses* recommends the indicative mood. In the consequent, there is a slight difference. In CF, Kilvington does not have Pr2 directly as the consequent, but jumps to

10 Kilvington, *Sophismata*, S47 (cc).

the practical conclusion concerning its evaluation. This difference I take to be insignificant here.

D6 follows the standard rules of obligations. However, the example that Kilvington actually discusses does not have Pr1 as a proposition explicitly put forward but jumps directly to what is Pr2 in the table. Without the respondent first denying that he is a bishop, according to the standard rules Pr2 would be evaluated as true and irrelevant, because it is actually true and its opposite does not follow from the *positum* alone (conditional Pos → –Pr2 is false). Kilvington wants, however, the respondent to consider the situation as it would obtain if the *positum* were true and to give his answers in accordance with that situation. He does not ask the respondent to evaluate conditionals of the type introduced by the author of *Obligationes parisienses*, but he wants the respondent to answer as he would if the situation were as described by the *positum* together with some actual facts, as here the fact that the respondent is not a bishop.

Kilvington does not have any rules concerning which facts can be taken into account. He seems to be rather safe in assuming that being in Rome would not make the respondent a bishop, or (following David Lewis' understanding of counterfactuals)[11] that the world where the respondent is still a young logic student despite going to Rome is more similar to the actual world than if he were in Rome as a bishop. However, as 20th-century logicians have noticed, introducing additional premises in counterfactual reasoning is not always as innocent as it is in this example. Kilvington does not have anything to say about this problem, or how the reasoning should proceed apart from the general idea that the respondent ought to think of what he would grant if he were in the situation.

This general idea does, however, provide Kilvington a solution to the sophism he is discussing. If the respondent considers what he would grant if he were in the situation described by the *casus*, he has to refrain from denying that he knows the king to be seated or that he knows that the king is not seated. However, neither of these follows from the *casus*, and thus there also is no reason to grant either one of them. If the *casus* were true, the respondent would know one of the alternatives to be true, but he does not actually know which one, and thus he has to doubt both in the actual disputation. As William Heytesbury was later to point out,[12] this has the unhappy consequence that

11 David Lewis, *Counterfactuals* (Oxford, 1973).

12 William of Heytesbury, "The Verbs 'Know' and 'Doubt'", trans. N. Kretzmann and E. Stump, in *The Cambridge Translations of Medieval Philosophical Texts*, Vol. 1: *Logic and Philosophy of Language* (Cambridge, 1988), 436-9.

the respondent must doubt whether he knows in a situation where knowing would seem to imply knowing that one knows. Kilvington's solution is thus not fully satisfactory.

Here our interest, however, is simply the distinction between the two approaches adopted by the author of *Obligationes parisienses* in his treatment of *positio* and by Kilvington in his *Sophismata*, sophism 47. The anonymous author invites the respondent to look at the actual sentences and the concepts used in them—and to ignore how the situation would be if the *positum* were true. Instead of this, Kilvington would have the respondent consider the situation and answer on that basis—without much recognition of the logical relations between sentences.

Conclusion

The central difference between the theories of obligations in *Obligationes parisienses* and Kilvington's *Sophismata*, sophism 47, is that Kilvington relies on counterfactual reasoning and has considerations based on the truth of counterfactual conditionals. The conditionals that *Obligationes parisienses* discusses are best described as expressing relations of logical validity. It is, however, noteworthy that *Obligationes parisienses* recognizes that the validity at issue need not be of the kind that he calls 'natural'.

Given that the obligational disputations considered also rely on principles of basic propositional logic, we must distinguish altogether four kinds of inferential relationships. First, inferential connections that we nowadays would not hesitate to call formally valid inferences in basic propositional logic. For example, from the denial of a part of a conjunction, the denial of the conjunction follows. Second, natural consequences (*consequentia naturalis*) where the inferential connection is based on the conceptual containment of the consequent in the antecedent. These a modern logician might call analytic, perhaps in distinction from being formally valid. For example, 'if Socrates is a man, he is an animal'. Third, consequences that do not fill either of these two strong criteria of validity but fill the modal criterion of it being impossible for the antecedent to be true without the consequent. For example, 'if Socrates is an animal, he is a man'. And fourth, the weaker inferential relationship that was in the 20th century labelled counterfactual reasoning. Here the modal criterion of validity is not filled, but still there is some warrant for moving from the antecedent to the consequent.

It seems thus that the anonymous author of *Obligationes parisienses* is right in connecting the art of obligations to the 'knowledge of consequences' (*scientia de consequentiis*). This art is indeed a useful tool in bringing forward considerations of various kinds of inferential relationships. Given that the 13th and early 14th centuries were a period in which logic saw much development, and given the conceptions of what it means for there to be an inferential connection between a set of premises and a conclusion, it seems not to be far-fetched to suppose that the technique of obligational disputations played an important role in these developments. Insofar as this is the case, it is very important to bear in mind that the discussion concerning obligations concentrated on intra-linguistic or syntactic relations between sentences. While medieval logicians did think that an inference is valid only if the premises cannot be true without the conclusions, authors writing on obligations were interested in inferential relations whose validity could be seen from conceptual or syntactic relations between sentences. This seems to suggest that most authors thought that obligational disputations in the standard species of *positio* ought not be understood from the viewpoint of model-theoretical interpretations of consequences. This is exactly where *rei veritas* differs from *positio*, and the reason why Kilvington wanted to revise the rules. What is more at stake in standard *positio* is the relation between proof-theoretically interpreted consequences and alethic modalities. The core philosophical question is, thus, to spell out how and when exactly a sentence is repugnant to another so that they cannot both be true.[13]

13 For further discussions of how validity was understood in late medieval logic, see, e.g., Catarina Dutilh-Novaes, 'Form and Matter in Later Latin Medieval Logic: The Cases of *suppositio* and *consequentia*', *Journal of the History of Philosophy* 50 (2012), 339-64; Calvin Normore, 'The Necessity in Deduction: Cartesian Inference and Its Medieval Background', *Synthese* 96 (1993), 437-54; Stephen Read, 'Inference', in *The Cambridge History of Medieval Philosophy*, ed. R. Pasnau (Cambridge, 2010), 173-85. For 20th-century theories, see, e.g., John Etchemendy, *The Concept of Logical Consequence* (Harvard, 1990).

Si tantum pater est non tantum pater est: An English Sophisma from the Late Thirteenth Century

Sten Ebbesen

Si tantum pater est, non tantum pater est was a very popular sophisma in the 13th century, witness the 27 entries for it in Ebbesen and Goubier's catalogue (2010), where it has the number 919. The standard proof and disproof are succinctly stated by Richard, the Master of Abstractions [919.27]:[1]

> 1. Probatio: Si tantum pater est, pater est; et si pater est, filius est; et si filius est, non tantum pater est; ergo a primo: si tantum pater est, non tantum pater est. (Proof: If there is only a father, there is a father; and if there is a father, there is a child; and if there is a child, there is not only a father; therefore, from the start: if there is only a father, there is not only a father.)
>
> 2. Contra: Oppositum sequitur ad suum oppositum, ergo etc. (Disproof: Here [i.e., in the conditional sophismatic proposition] one of two opposite propositions is claimed to follow from the other, [which is impossible], therefore [the sophismatic proposition is false].)

Several solutions were proposed, most of them claiming that *tantum pater est* is ambiguous because the exclusion operated by the *dictio exclusiva 'tantum'* may affect either of two aspects of the term (*pater*) on which it operates, e.g., *Potest fieri exclusio ratione formae substantialis vel ratione formae accidentalis*. But the sophisma was not just one of several designed to investigate how exclusive operators (*tantum, solus*) work; it was also a tool for investigating the logical behaviour of relative terms.[2] The two tasks were faced jointly in

1 Entries of the type [919.27] refer to the catalogue in vol. II of Sten Ebbesen and Frédéric Goubier, *A Catalogue of 13th-Century Sophismata*, 2 vols (Paris, 2010).

2 More about *tantum* sophismata in Sten Ebbesen, 'Tantum unum est. 13th-Century Sophismatic Discussions around the Parmenidean Thesis', *The Modern Schoolman* 72 (1995), 175-99, and Sten Ebbesen, 'The More the Less. Natural Philosophy and Sophismata in the Thirteenth century', in *La nouvelle physique du XIVe siècle*, ed. S. Caroti and P. Souffrin (Florence, 1997), 9-44:

 | DOI 10.1163/9789004324275_011

a question often asked in connection with the sophisma: "Can an exclusive operator added to one of a pair of correlatives exclude the other?" (*Utrum dictio exclusiva addita uni correlativorum excludat reliquum*). A debate about this question will be found in the text edited below.

Ms Worcester Cathedral Q.13 is a gold-mine for anyone with an interest in philosophy as it was studied in Oxford in the late 13th century. It is all in the hand of one John Aston, and in all probability produced during his Oxford days in the 1290s.[3] Most of the works he copied were by English masters (the earliest being a chapter of William of Sherwood's *Introduction to Logic*—1230s?), and this also applies to the 22 *Sophismata Wigornensia* (Ebbesen-Goubier 2010: 1.42), five of which carry attributions to named English masters, whereas the rest are anonymous.

The *Si tantum pater est*... edited below skips the *corpus sophismatis*. "The proof and the disproof are common knowledge," the author says (*0.1*), and then (*0.2*) proceeds to list five problems one might reasonably debate, items 4-5 revealing that the proof and disproof he considered common knowledge were, indeed, the ones found in Richard's *Abstractiones*. Then starts a discussion of the first problem, *Utrum dictio exclusiva addita etc.* After (*1*) *rationes principales* a respondent delivers (*2.1*) a solution, which is then (*2.2*) attacked by somebody else. The respondent counters the objections (*2.3*), only to have his counter-arguments attacked (*2.4*). So far, there is nothing that could not quite as well have come from a Parisian debate, but then the ping-pong between respondent and attacker(s) goes on for much longer than usual in Paris.[4] When it is over, the formula *Ad principale* (*3*) (an English trait) heralds the introduction of three new *rationes principales*, and this occasions a new, but shorter round of ping-pong, followed by yet another *Ad principale* (*4*) and a short round of ping-pong. Finally, a new response (*5*) is proposed to replace the one given by the respondent in (*2*). Then suddenly the *problema* stops. There is no magisterial determination, once again a trait that is shared by several English sophismata from the decades around 1300, but most unusual, if at all attested, in Parisian sophismata.

19-24 with edition of relevant texts on 33-44. Further texts in Sten Ebbesen, 'Sophismata and Physics Commentaries', *Cahiers de l'Institut du moyen-âge grec et latin* 64 (1994), 164-95.

3 For a description of the ms and its contents, see Rodney M. Thomson, *A Descriptive Catalogue of the Medieval Manuscripts in Worcester Cathedral Library* (Cambridge, 2001), 127-8.

4 Ways of structuring sophismata are discussed in Sten Ebbesen, 'How to Build Your Own Sophisma (Late 13th-Early 14th-Century Style)', in *Sophismata. Histoire d'une pratique philosophique*, ed. A. de Libera, L. Cesalli and F. Goubier (Paris, forthcoming).

Actually, in the Worcester manuscript the text breaks off already after *3.1.2*, but the same *problema* is found in another collection of English sophismata from the 13th century, *Sophismata Pragensia*,[5] which does contain the sections *3.1.3-5*. I see no reason to think that they are a secondary addition, and so I have included them in the edition. In the Prague version there is nothing after section *5*. The Worcester version continues with a discussion of whether *tantum* can operate on the subject as well as on the predicate of a proposition.[6] Although the formulation is slightly different, the point debated is the one raised as the third of the five *problemata* in *0.2*, so the text probably reflects the same oral event, but the structure of this putative *Problema 3* is much less complex than that of *Problema 1*. A question is raised (*0*), a *No*-answer is given (*1*), a counter-argument is introduced (*2*), and then the ping pong continues until move (*5*), after which nothing follows, neither a determination of problem 3 nor a discussion of the last two of the five original problems.

If the text preserved is all there ever was, and if it reasonably faithfully mirrors an oral event, we are thus presented with three types of abbreviation of the full format for a gala performance of a sophismatic disputation:

A. Not all of the problems initially proposed were actually debated.
B. The first problem was the only one to receive the full treatment with (a) *rationes principales*, (b) a respondent's preliminary determination, and (c) a ping-pong debate, subsequent problems getting shorter shrift.
C. There was no magisterial determination.

A and *B* seem to have been common procedures both in Oxford and in Paris, presumably aimed at keeping the duration of a disputation within reasonable limits. But to all appearances, the possibility of dropping the magisterial determination (*C*) was an Oxford peculiarity.

Differences in disputation formats did not prevent Oxford and Paris scholars from borrowing from each other. An anonymous Parisian *Si tantum pater est, non tantum pater est* [919.6], No XVIII in what I have dubbed *Sophismata Florentino-Brugensia*,[7] appears to have cribbed arguments *1-5* (and possibly a

5 For *Sophismata Pragensia*, see Ebbesen-Goubier, *A Catalogue*, 1.39.

6 More about this problem in Sten Ebbesen, '*Modi significandi* in Logic and Grammar', in *Modern Views of Medieval Logic*, ed. C. Kann, B. Loewe, C. Rode and S.L. Uckelman (Leuven, forthcoming).

7 About this composite collection, see Ebbesen-Goubier *A Catalogue*, 1.32. Further information in Sten Ebbesen, 'Boethius de Dacia et al. The Sophismata in mss Bruges SB 509 and Florence Med.-Laur. S. Croce 12 sin., 3', in *Sophisms in Medieval Logic and Grammar. Acts of*

lost *6*) from the Worcester sophisma's *Problema 3*. To make them fit into the mould of a standard Parisian *quaestio* the author of the derivative version supplied an initial argument *Quod sic* and used *1* as the matching (*i*) *Quod non*. He then produced a determination of his own, but again used the English material for the *Ad rationes* section, which contains three items:

a. *Ad Quod non* (*i*)
b. *Ad Quod non* (*ii*)
c. *Ad Quod non* (*iii*)

For item *a* the Parisian author simply used argument *2*, the Worcester text's answer to *1* = *i*. He had not, however, inserted arguments *3* and *5* as further *rationes principales quod non*. He now, apparently, regretted his omission, and so in *b* introduced *3* disguised as a recapitulation of the non-existant *Quod non* (*ii*), and *4* as its refutation. Similarly in *c* argument *5* appears as a recapitulation of a non-existant *Quod non* (*iii*) and is followed by a refutation, which may be the Parisian master's own invention, but could also be an original argument *6* that did not make it into John Aston's manuscript.

The following table clearly demonstrates the virtual identity of the two texts in the relevant passages:

Sophismata Florentino-Brugensia XVIII	**Sophismata Wigorniensia 17**
(*i*) Nulla dictio ponit suum significatum circa aliquid circa quod non ponit suum modum significandi; sed adverbium non potest ponere suum modum significandi circa subiectum cum sit proprie adiectivum verbi, et ita non potest ponere suum significatum circa subiectum; et ita videtur quod non potest esse determinatio illius. [...]	*1*. Et quod non probatio, quia nulla dictio ponit suum significatum circa aliquid circa quod non ponat suum modum significandi; sed adverbium non potest ponere suum modum significandi circa subiectum, cum sit proprie adiectivum verbi, et ita non potest ponere suum significatum circa subiectum. Et ita non potest esse illius determinatio.

the 9th European Symposium for Medieval Logic and Semantics, ed. S. Read (Dordrecht, 1993), 45-63, where the relationship of sophisma XVIII to the Worcester sophisma is discussed on pp. 52-3.

Sophismata Florentino-Brugensia XVIII

Ad (i)

Cum dicitur quod dictio non ponit suum significatum circa aliquid nisi circa quod suum modum significandi, dicamus quod verum est quod nulla dictio ponit suum significatum circa aliquid circa quod non ponit suum modum significandi aliquem, sed non oportet quod iste modus significandi sit generalis. Unde dico quod 'tantum' ponit aliquem modum significandi circa subiectum quia significat per modum specificantis, sed tamen non cum illo ordinatur gratia modi significandi generalis unde adverbium est, immo solum per ipsum est determinatio verbi.

Ad (ii) Et quod ulterius arguitur[8] quod quicquid repugnat generali repugnat speciali, unde quod repugnat animali repugnat homini,

dicendum quod verum est. Sed cum dicitur quod repugnat modo significandi generali ipsius adverbii quod subiectum determinet, dicendum quod verum est per se, repugnat enim ei per se quod ipsum subiectum determinet, sed non repugnat ei quod per accidens determinet gratia alicuius modi significandi specialis concomitantis[9] modum istum significandi generalem ipsius adverbii.

Sophismata Wigorniensia 17

2.

Dico quod verum est quod nulla dictio ponit suum significatum circa quod non ponit suum modum significandi aliquem, sed non oportet quod ille modus significandi sit generalis. Unde dico quod 'tantum' ponit aliquem modum significandi circa subiectum, quia significat per modum specificantis; sed tamen cum illo non ordinatur gratia modi significandi generalis unde adverbium est, immo per illum solum verbum determinatur.

3. Contra.

Quicquid repugnat generali repugnat speciali, unde quicquid repugnat animali et homini.

4.

Dicendum quod verum est. Et cum dicitur quod modo significandi generali ipsius adverbii repugnat quod subiectum determinet, dicendum quod verum est per se, repugnat enim per se quod ipsum determinet; sed non illi repugnat quod per accidens ipsum determinet, id est gratia alicuius modi significandi specialis concomitantis modum istum generalem, sicut non repugnat adverbio quod construatur cum dativo per accidens,

8 arguitur] repugnat **B**.

9 concomitantis **W** *secutus scripsi*] communicantis **B**.

Sophismata Florentino-Brugensia XVIII

Unde non dicitur modus significandi per modum acquisitionis in adverbio specialis propter hoc quod iste modus significandi inducat modum significandi generalem ipsius adverbii, immo quod illum concomitetur sicut et multos modos significandi aliarum partium orationis, sed dicitur modus significandi specialis quia non omnibus adverbiis competit.

Ad (*iii*) Et quod ulterius arguitur: "Ad hoc quod duae dictiones ordinentur inter se non sufficit quod sit proportio quantum ad aliquos modos significandi, sed requiritur quod non sit ⟨im⟩proportio quantum ad alios. Verbi gratia, quamvis 'homo' et 'currunt' conveniunt in aliquibus modis significandi, quia tamen improportionantur quantum ad alios modos significandi, ⟨ideo est incongrua haec 'homo currunt'. Et sic in proposito videtur,⟩ quod quamvis 'homo' vel 'tantum pater' proportionantur quantum ad aliquos modos significandi, quia cum unum significat per modum specificantis, alterum vero per modum specificabilis, tamen ibi est improportio quantum ad modos significandi generales. Ideo videtur esse incongrua."

Sophismata Wigorniensia 17

non unde adverbium est sed gratia modi significandi per modum acquisitionis modum significandi adverbii concomitantis;

unde non dicitur modus significandi per modum acquisitionis in adverbio specialis propter hoc quod ille modus significandi indu⟨ca⟩t modum significandi adverbii unde adverbium est, immo illum concomitatur sicut et multos alios modos significandi aliarum partium orationis, sed dicitur modus specialis quia omnibus adverbiis non competit.

5. Contra.

Ad hoc quod duae ⟨dictiones⟩ ordinentur inter se non sufficit quod sit proportio quantum ad aliquos modos significandi, sed requiritur quod non sit improportio quantum ad aliquos modos significandi. Verbi gratia, quamvis 'homo' et 'currunt' conveniunt quantum ad aliquos modos significandi, quia tamen improportionantur quantum ad alios modos, ideo est incongrua haec 'homo currunt'. Et sic in proposito videtur, quia quamvis 'homo' vel 'tantum pater' proportionantur quantum ad aliquos modos significandi, quia tamen unum significat per modum specificantis, alterum vero per modum specificabilis, quia tamen ibi est improportio quantum ad modos significandi generales, ideo videtur esse incongrua.

Sophismata Florentino-Brugensia XVIII	Sophismata Wigorniensia 17
– Dicendum quod non valet, quia ad talem constructionem modi significandi generales non requiruntur; unde sicut congrue dicitur 'video homines', et 'video hominem' ita bene dicitur, quia modus significandi qui est numerus nihil facit ad talem constructionem, ita 'tantum' ordinari potest cum subiecto gratia modi significandi specialis, quia modi significandi generales nihil faciunt ad talem constructionem, immo accidunt tali[10] ordinationi.	

In principle, the continental version could be the source of the insular one, but the assumption of the opposite has the great advantage of explaining in a simple way why the Worcester text has a structure that is perfectly normal for an Oxonian sophisma, whereas there are irregularities in the structure of the Parisian text.

Text

Manuscripts

W = Worcester, Cathedral Library, Q.13, ff. 53rA-53vB. English, 1290s.
P = Praha, Knihovna Metropolitní Kapituly, M.83, ff. 23rA-24vA. English (?), late 13th c.
B = Brugge, Stedelijke Openbare Bibliotheek, 509, ff. 104rA-104rB. French (?), early 14th c.

In the text shared by *W* and *P*, there are numerous small stylistic differences. Thus *W* tends to use first-person active forms when introducing an argument (*dico*), whereas *P* prefers the impersonal passive (*dicitur*). There is one significant shared error: *pro veritate* for *pro qualitate* in 2.5.1. John Aston first wrote *pro veritate*, but then must have realized that the text was corrupt, and tried to emend it, but applied the wrong remedy, changing the two words into *secundum veritatem*. In 2.2.2 both manuscripts have the incorrect reference

10 accidunt] accidit **B**.

7° Metaphysicae instead of *4°*, but in this case the corruption need not have occurred in the transmission of the sophisma; it could go back to the author's source. In *2.3.2* and *2.6.1* *homoeoteleuta* are responsible for the absence in *P* of text preserved in *W*. Thus *W* cannot be descended from *P*. The shared text offers no incontrovertible evidence that the opposite cannot be the case, but assuming a derivation of *P* from *W* would necessitate the gratuitous assumption that *P* does not owe *3.1.3sqq.* to the same source as the preceding text.

Where available, I have based the text on *W*. The apparatus is exhaustive as regards the readings of *W* and *P*. In problem 3, deviations of *B* from *W* are only recorded when not due to the adaptation of the text to a new format. For a comparison of the *W* and *B* versions, see the table above.

I have imposed my own orthography, punctuation and paragraphing on the text. All matter in italics has been added by me.

SI TANTUM PATER EST NON TANTUM PATER EST.

0.1 Corpus sophismatis

Probatio[11] et improbatio patent.

0.2 Problemata proposita

Circa istud sophisma plura possunt quaeri. Primum potest[12] esse ad evidentiam veritatis istius propositionis, utrum dictio exclusiva addita uni correlativorum excludat reliquum. Secundum de veritate propositionis in se. Tertium[13] erit de dictione exclusiva adverbiali, utrum possit ponere suum significatum[14] circa subiectum cum sit adiectivum ipsius verbi. Quarto potest quaeri de consequentiis positis in probatione sophismatis. Ultimo de improbatione, utrum iste modus improbandi fuerit bonus "Hic demonstratur oppositum sequi ad suum oppositum, ergo condicionalis falsa."

⟨*Problema 1. Utrum dictio exclusiva addita uni correlativorum excludat reliquum*⟩

De primo arguitur[15] sic:

1 Rationes principales

11 probatio—patent **W**] *om.* **P.**

12 potest—propositionis **W**] *om.* **P.**

13 tertium—ergo condicionalis falsa **W**] tertio de dictione exclusiva adverbiali utrum posset ponere suum significatum circa ipsum nomen cum sit adiectivum ipsius verbi **P.**

14 significatum] in *add. & del.* **W.**

15 arguitur sic **W**] *om.* **P.**

1.1 Et[16] ostendo quod dictio exclusiva addita uni correlativorum non excludat reliquum sic: Dictio exclusiva addita alicui termino non excludit illud quod sequitur ad ipsum; sed unum correlativorum[17] sequitur ad alterum; ergo[18] dictio exclusiva addita uni correlativorum non excludet reliquum. Maior patet, quoniam dictio exclusiva addita homini non excludit animal, cum ad ipsum sequatur. Minor patet per locum a relativis;[19] sequitur enim 'si pater est, filius est'.

1.2 Ad[20] oppositum arguo sic: Dictio exclusiva addita alicui excludit ab[21] eo illud quod est diversum in esse tantum[22] respectu inclusi, ut patet hic[23] 'tantum Socrates currit, non ergo Plato currit'; multo[24] ergo fortius dictio exclusiva addita[25] alicui excludet illud quod est diversum in esse et in[26] essentia ab eo; sed unum correlativorum est[27] diversum ab altero non solum in esse sed in essentia, esse[28] enim unius non est esse alterius nec essentia **/W 53rB/** unius essentia alterius. Ergo[29] dictio exclusiva addita uni correlativorum excludet reliquum.

2. Responsio cum disputatione

2.1 Responsio

2.1.1 Positio

Ad[30] hoc respondetur dicendo quod dictio exclusiva addita uni correlativorum excludit reliquum, et ratio huius est quia dictio exclusiva addita alicui excludit omne diversum ab eo de quo potest dici vere 'hoc non est hoc'; sed

---

16 et ostendo quod dictio—reliquum sic **W**] Quod dictio—reliquum probatio **P**.

17 correlativorum sequitur **W**] relativorum consequitur **P**.

18 ergo—reliquum **W**] ergo ipsum non excluditur **P**.

19 relativis **W**] relatione **P**. *De loco a relativis videatur, e.g., Anon., Abbreviatio Montana, in Logica Modernorum, ed. L.M. de Rijk (Assen, 1967) II.2, 73-107: 93*: "Regula est a relativis: 'si pater est, et filius est'. Unde locus? A relativis. Regula: posito uno relativorum, ponitur aliud."

20 ad—sic **W**] oppositum arguitur sic **P**.

21 ab eo—inesse **W**] omne diversum in esse ab eo **P**.

22 tantum—inclusi **W**] *om.* **P**.

23 hic **W**] *om.* **P**.

24 multo ergo **W**] ergo multo **P**.

25 addita—illud **W**] *om.* **P**.

26 in essentia ab eo **W**] essentia **P**.

27 est—solum **W**] non est solum diversum ab alio **P**.

28 esse enim—essentia alterius **W**] *om.* **P**.

29 ergo—reliquum **W**] ergo excludit reliquum **P**.

30 ad hoc respondetur dicendo **W**] dicitur ad problema **P**.

unum[31] correlativorum universaliter non est alterum, cum sint opposita. Ideo dictio exclusiva addita uni correlativorum excludit reliquum.

2.1.2 Solutio rationum principalium

2.1.2.1 Ad 1.2 Et concedatur ratio ad istam partem adducta.

2.1.2.2 Ad 1.1 Ad argumentum[32] in oppositum respondetur. Et[33] dicitur ad maiorem, quod dictio exclusiva addita alicui non excludit illud quod sequitur ad ipsum,—verum est si sequatur ad ipsum tamquam aliquid quod est de eius significato, et de tali ponitur exemplum. Nunc autem unum correlativorum non est de significato alterius, ideo[34] non procedit illa ratio.

2.2 Contra ista (*2.1*) arguitur sic:[35]

2.2.1 Et primo contra positionem et rationem positionis (*2.1.1*). Videtur enim[36] quod dictio exclusiva addita uni correlativorum[37] non excludat reliquum, non obstante quod unum non sit reliquum. Et hoc arguo[38] sic: Non minorem inseparabilitatem habet unum correlativorum ab[39] alio quam accidens et substantia; sed dictio exclusiva addita accidenti non excludit substantiam, et tamen accidens non est substantia /**P 23rB**/ nec econverso; ergo dictio[40] exclusiva addita uni correlativorum non excludit reliquum propter illam causam. Probatio assumpti est quoniam sequitur 'tantum albedo est, ergo accidens est, et si accidens est, ergo[41] substantia est, ergo a primo: si tantum albedo est, ergo[42] substantia est'.

2.2.2 Contra responsionem ad argumenta[43] (*2.1.2.2*) arguitur[44] sic, et videtur[45] quod unum correlativorum sit de significato et[46] de essentia alterius,

---

31 unum correlativorum universaliter **W**] universaliter unum correlativorum **P**.

32 argumentum **W**] rationem **P**.

33 et—verum est **W**] cum arguitur "Dictio exclusiva addita alicui etc.", dicitur quod ista maior est vera **P**.

34 ideo—ratio **W**] quare non procedit ratio **P**.

35 sic **W**] *om.* **P**.

36 enim **W**] *om.* **P**.

37 correlativorum **P**] *om.* **W**.

38 arguo **W**] arguitur **P**.

39 ab alio **W**] a reliquo **P**.

40 dictio—correlativorum **W**] *om.* **P**.

41 ergo **W**] *om.* **P**.

42 ergo **W**] *om.* **P**.

43 argumenta **W**] argumentum **P**, *fortasse recte*.

44 arguitur **P**] ag()ur **W**.

45 videtur **W**] probatur **P**.

46 et de essentia alterius **W**] alterius et de essentia **P**.

quoniam idem significatur per nomen definiti et per ipsam definitionem, ut[47] vult Aristoteles 7° Metaphysicae;[48] sed unum correlativorum cadit in definitione alterius, et illud quod ponitur[49] in definitione alicuius[50] est de[51] significato et de essentia eius, cum definitio dicat essentiam et quiditatem definiti; ergo unum correlativorum est de significato alterius; quare dictio[52] exclusiva addita uni non excludit reliquum.

2.3.1 Ad primum argumentum[53] (*2.2.1*) dico[54] quod sicut non sequitur 'tantum pater est, ergo filius est',[55] ita dico[56] quod non sequitur 'tantum albedo est, ergo substantia est'. Licet enim[57] absolute sequatur 'albedo est, ergo substantia est', tamen ad albedinem esse prout sequitur ad illud antecedens 'tantum albedo est' non sequitur subiectum esse, quia non ponebatur[58] nisi cum praecisione.

2.3.2 Ad aliud (*2.2.2*). Cum dicitur "Illud[59] quod cadit in definitione alicuius est[60] de significato et essentia definiti" verum[61] est—si sit definitio in prima veritate[62] definitionis; tamen[63] si sit definitio data per additamentum, non oportet; et definitio[64] relativi est per additamentum, unde[65] ponitur unum correlativorum in definitione alterius tamquam terminans[66] dependentiam alterius; et[67] sic unum correlativorum non est de significato alterius licet cadat in eius definitione, et propter hoc excluditur per dictionem exclusivam.

---

47 ut vult Aristoteles 7° **W**] per Aristotelem in 7° **P**.
48 *Immo in quarto. Cf.* Arist., *Metaph.* IV.7.1012a23-24.
49 ponitur **W**] cadit **P**.
50 alicuius **P**] alicuius *vel* alterius **W**.
51 de significato et de essentia eius **W**] de eius essentia **P**.
52 dictio—reliquum **W**] etc. **P**.
53 argumentum **W**] *om.* **P**.
54 dico **W**] dicitur **P**.
55 est **P**] *om.* **W**.
56 dico quod **W**] *om.* **P**.
57 enim **P**] *om.* **W**.
58 ponebatur **W**] ponitur **P**.
59 illud quod **P**] quod illud **W**.
60 est—definiti **W**] etc. **P**.
61 verum est **W**] dicitur quod verum est **P**.
62 veritate definitionis **W**] *inv.* **P**.
63 tamen **W**] sed **P**.
64 definitio relativi **W**] *inv.* **P**.
65 unde **P**] unum **W**.
66 terminans dependentiam] terminans respectum **P**: determinans dependentiam **W**.
67 et sic—alterius **W**] *om.* **P**. *Nota homoeoteleuton.*

2.4.1 Contra[68] primam responsionem (*2.3.1*) arguo sic, et ostendo quod sequitur 'tantum albedo est, ergo substantia est' quia sequitur 'tantum albedo est, ergo album est, et si album est, substantia est, ergo etc.' Probatio primae consequentiae est[69] quia oppositum consequentis non potest stare cum antecedente; sequitur enim 'si nullum album est, ergo nulla albedo est', et sic non tantum albedo est;[70] ergo prima consequentia fuit bona.

2.4.2 Contra aliud (*2.3.2*) ostendo[71] quod relativa faciunt unum significatum, quia quaecumque faciunt unum intellectum, et unum significatum; sed relativa faciunt[72] unum intellectum, nam impossibile est intelligere unum praeter reliquum; ergo unum est de significato alterius. Cuius[73] oppositum dicebatur.

2.5.1 Ad primum (*2.4.1*) dico[74] quod non sequitur 'tantum albedo est, ergo[75] album est'. Et[76] ad probationem "ex opposito consequentis etc." dico[77] quod non sequitur 'nullum album est, **/P 23vA/** ergo nulla albedo est' nisi sumendo albedinem pro[78] qualitate quae est in subiecto, et sic non fuit[79] consequens ad[80] istam 'tantum albedo est'.

2.5.2 Ad aliud (*2.4.2*) dico[81] quod non faciunt unum significatum. Et cum dicitur quod faciunt unum intellectum, dico[82] quod falsum est, quia licet non[83] possum intelligere patrem esse nisi intelligam filium esse, hoc tamen intelligere non est unum intelligere; sed [quia] intelligere patrem esse non **/W 53vA/** [non] est intelligere filium esse, licet intelligere patrem sit illud ad quod consequitur intelligere filium esse.

---

68 contra primam responsionem arguo sic et ostendo **W**] contra primum arguo sic et probatur **P**.

69 est quia **W**] *om.* **P**.

70 est **P**] *om.* **W**.

71 ostendo **W**] arguitur sic et probatur **P**.

72 faciunt unum intellectum **W**] sunt huiusmodi **P**.

73 cuius—dicebatur **W**] *om.* **P**.

74 dico **W**] dicitur **P**.

75 ergo] tantum *add.* **W**.

76 et **W**] *om.* **P**.

77 dico **W**] dicitur **P**.

78 pro qualitate quae est in subiecto *scripsi*] pro veritate quae est in subiecto **P**; quae est in subiecto pro veritate **W** *a.c.*: quae est in subiecto secundum veritatem **W** *p.c.*

79 fuit **W**] est **P**.

80 ad istam **W**] *om.* **P**.

81 dico **W**] dicitur **P**.

82 dico **W**] dicitur **P**.

83 non possum—consequitur intelligere filium esse **W**] intelligere filium esse sequitur ad intelligere patrem esse, non tamen intelligere filium esse est ingelligere patrem esse **P**.

2.6.1 Contra primum (*2.5.1*). Commentator super IX Metaphysicae[84] dicit quod qui ponit accidens esse separatum facit de accidente substantiam; sed qui ponit[85] albedinem esse sine substantia ponit[86] accidens esse separatum; ergo qui ponit albedinem esse sine substantia facit de albedine substantiam. Ergo[87] sequitur 'si tantum albedo est, substantia est' quod negabatur[88] prius.

2.6.2 Contra aliud (*2.5.2*). Aristoteles[89] vult quod impossibile est[90] intelligere lineam nisi[91] stantem super duo puncta; et tamen intelligere lineam est intelligere unum et non duo. Quare similiter in proposito intelligere aliquam formam relativam fundatam super[92] duos terminos, ut paternitatem supra patrem et filium, non est intelligere[93] duo sed unum.

2.7 Ad hoc (*2.6.2*) dicitur quod intelligere lineam stantem super[94] duo puncta non est unum intelligere sed duo.

2.8 Contra hoc (*2.7*) potest argui sic: Intelligere lineam stantem super duo puncta est intelligere lineam finitam, et hoc est unum intelligere; quare etc. Et potest ratio confirmari per Aristotelem in 4° Metaphysicae[95] dicentem quod qui[96] aliquid intelligit unum intelligit, et qui unum non[97] intelligit nihil intelligit.

3. Alterae rationes ad principale cum disputatione inde orta

3.1 Ad principale arguitur sic:

3.1.1 Dictio exclusiva addita toti non excludit partem. Et ratio huius est quia ad positionem totius sequitur positio partis; cum ergo ad positionem unius

---

84 *Locum non inveni. Cf.* Aegidius Aurelianensis, *Quaest.* GC *1.14, ed. Z. Kuksewicz (Amsterdam, 1993), 55*: "philosophi dicerent quod quicumque dicit posse accidens esse sine subiecto, ille facit de accidente substantiam."

85 ponit] *om.* **P** *a.c.*

86 ponit—sine substantia **W**] *om.* **P**. *Nota homoeoteleuton.*

87 ergo **W**] quare **P**.

88 negabatur **P**] negatur **W**.

89 Arist., *Metaph.* II.2.993b23-24. *Cf.* Petrus de Alvernia, *Quaest. Cael. 1.19, ed. G. Galle (Leuven, 2003), 108*: "sicut dicitur II Metaphysicae, quicumque imaginatur lineam imaginatur illam stantem super duo puncta".

90 est **W**] sit **P**.

91 nisi **W**] non **P**.

92 super **W**] supra **P**.

93 intelligere duo **W**] *inv.* **P**.

94 super **W**] supra **P**.

95 Arist., *Metaph.* IV.4.1006b10; *Les Auctoritates Aristotelis. Un florilège médiéval, ed. J. Hamesse (Louvain, 1974), 123,99.*

96 qui **W**] quis **P**.

97 non **W**] *om.* **P**.

correlativi sequitur positio alterius,[98] dictio exclusiva addita uni non potest[99] excludere reliquum.

3.1.2 Item, quod interimit consequens interimit antecedens; sed filius est consequens ad patrem; quod ergo interimit filium interimit[100] patrem. Sed si sequatur[101] 'tantum[102] pater, non ergo filius',[103] sequitur 'tantum pater, non ergo pater'. Ergo videtur[104] quod dictio exclusiva addita uni correlativorum non potest excludere reliquum.

3.1.3 Item[105] ad principale: Dictio exclusiva alicui termino /**P 23vB**/ addita excludit illud quod est diversum; ergo si non excludat illud quod est magis diversum, nec illud quod est minus; sed ⟨accidens⟩ magis est diversum a subiecto quam unum correlativorum ab altero; sed dictio exclusiva addita accidenti non excludit substantiam, quia illud magis[106] diversum est a subiecto quod negatur ab eo quam illud quod affirmatur; sed si sic dicatur 'tantum homo est', non igitur excluditur accidens,[107] et tamen vere negatur ab eo sic dicendo 'homo non est accidens'. Quod[108] accidens non excluditur probatio, quia si dicam sic 'homo est' non excluditur risibile, et tamen risibile est accidens respectu hominis. Ergo etc.

3.2 Dicitur (*ad 3.1.3*) quod dictio exclusiva etc. excludit illud quod est extrinsecum respectu subiecti, non tamen excludit illud quod est intrinsecum, et quia risibile est intrinsecum, ideo non potest excludi.

3.3.1 Contra (*3.2*). Quod aliquid intrinsecum excluditur probatio, quia dato quod non, opposita starent simul, quia si sic dicam 'tantum animal est homo' ibi excluditur caput animalis; et caput animalis est de intrinseco; ergo aliquid intrinsecum excluditur, quia caput animalis. Probatio, quia si non, ista starent simul 'tantum animal est homo' et 'non animal est homo'; sed ista 'tantum animal est homo' valet istam 'nihil aliud quam animal est homo', et sic ista stabunt simul 'nihil aliud quam animal est homo' et 'non animal est homo', et ista sunt opposita; ergo etc.

---

98 alterius] ergo *add.* **P**.
99 potest excludere **W**] excludit **P**.
100 interimit] et *add.* **P**.
101 sequatur **W**] sequitur **P**.
102 tantum pater non **W** *et* **P** *p.c.*] non tantum pater **P** *a.c.*
103 filius] ergo *add.* **P**.
104 videtur—reliquum **W**] dictio exclusiva etc. **P**.
105 item *et quae sequuntur usque ad finem Problematis 1 sola auctoritate codicis* **P** *nituntur.*
106 magis] maius **P**.
107 accidens] antecedens **P**.
108 quod] quia **P**.

3.3.2 Item. Ostenditur quod in antecedente non includuntur opposita, quia dictio exclusiva non excludit aliquid quod ponitur per praeiacentem; sed ista praeiacens 'pater est' ponit filium esse; ergo ista 'tantum pater est' non excludit filium esse.

3.4.1 Quod aliquid extrinsecum[109] excluditur probatio: ut vult Aristoteles in libro Physicorum,[110] cum dicit "sequitur 'tantum unum est, et illud unum est principium, ergo principiatum est'", et tamen principiatum est quoddam [prin] extrinsecum respectu principii; ergo etc.

3.4.2 Ad primum (*3.3.1*) dicitur quod caput animalis excluditur respectu praedicari, non tamen excluditur respectu esse, et de tali exclusione loquimur[111] in proposito.

4. Alia ratio ad principale cum disputatione inde orta

4.1 Item, ad principale arguitur sic: Dictio exclusiva addita alicui termino non excludit aliquod suppositum inclusum, sed accidit idem suppositum /**P 24rA**/ esse patrem et filium, et sic idem secundum suppositum pater et filius, ergo dictio exclusiva etc.

4.2 Contra 4.1 Dicitur quod quando pater et filius sunt in eodem supposito, iste filius non est correlativum patris; sed quando sunt distincti secundum suppositum, iste filius est correlativum patris.

4.3 Contra 4.2 Contra illud. Ponamus quod sint tres homines, sc. Socrates, et[112] Plato [et Cicero] et Vergilius, ita quod Socrates sit pater Platonis [vel Ciceroni⟨s⟩], et Plato Vergilii. Igitur tunc sic dicendo 'tantum pater est' non excluditur Plato, et tamen Plato est filius qui est correlativum patris, sc. Socratis, et hoc patet cum uterque sit pater.

5. Altera responsio

Aliter responsum fuit dicendo quod in isto antecedente[113] 'tantum pater est' intelliguntur opposita, quoniam dictio exclusiva addita termino respectivo deminuit ab eo, quia excludit omne diversum, et ita cum eius correlativum sit aliquo modo diversum tollit ipsum, et ita aliquid ad quod[114] habet respectum, ergo deminuit a ratione eius, et ideo non sequitur 'tantum pater est, ergo pater est', quia non est pater nisi secundum quid, sicut non sequitur 'homo mortuus, ergo homo'.

---

109 extrinsecum] intrinsecum **P**.

110 Arist., *Ph.* 1.2.185a4-5.

111 loquimur] *potius* loquitur—lo$^{(ur)}$ **P**.

112 et *scripsi*] *om.* **P** *a.c.*, vel *s.l.* **P** *p.c.*

113 antecedente] consequente **P**.

114 quod] hoc **P**.

⟨*Problema 2 deest*⟩

Problema *3*

0. Quaeritur utrum haec dictio 'tantum' possit esse determinatio subiecti vel praedicati indifferenter.

1.[115] Et quod non probatio, quia nulla dictio ponit suum significatum circa aliquid circa quod non ponat suum modum significandi; sed adverbium non potest ponere suum modum significandi circa subiectum, cum sit proprie adiectivum verbi, et ita non potest ponere suum significatum circa subiectum. Et ita non potest esse illius determinatio.

2. Dico quod verum est quod nulla dictio ponit suum significatum circa quod non ponit suum modum significandi aliquem, sed non oportet quod ille modus significandi sit generalis. Unde dico quod 'tantum' ponit aliquem modum significandi circa subiectum, quia significat per modum specificantis; sed tamen cum illo non ordinatur gratia modi significandi generalis unde adverbium est, immo per illum solum verbum determinatur.

3. Contra (*2*). Quicquid repugnat generali repugnat speciali, unde quicquid repugnat animali et homini.

4. Dicendum quod verum est. Et cum dicitur (*3*) quod modo significandi generali ipsius adverbii repugnat quod subiectum determinet, dicendum quod verum est per se, repugnat enim per se quod ipsum determinet; sed non illi repugnat quod per accidens ipsum determinet, id est gratia alicuius modi significandi specialis concomitantis modum istum generalem, sicut non repugnat adverbio quod construatur cum dativo per accidens, non unde adverbium est sed gratia modi significandi per modum acquisitionis modum [[ad]] significandi adverbii concomitantis; unde non dicitur modus significandi per modum acquisitionis in adverbio specialis propter hoc quod ille modus significandi inducat[116] modum significandi adverbii unde adverbium est, immo illum concomitatur sicut et multos alios modos significandi **/W 53vB/** aliarum partium orationis, sed dicitur modus specialis quia omnibus adverbiis non competit.

5. Contra (*4*). Ad hoc quod duae ⟨dictiones⟩[117] ordinentur inter se non sufficit quod sit proportio quantum ad aliquos modos significandi, sed requiritur quod non sit improportio quantum ad alios[118] modos significandi. Verbi gratia, quamvis 'homo' et 'currunt' conveniunt quantum ad aliquos modos significandi,

---

115 *Hinc textus codicibus* **W** *et* **B** *nititur.*

116 inducat **B**] induat **W**.

117 dictiones *ex* **B** *addidi.*

118 alios *cum* **B** *scripsi*] aliquos **W**.

quia tamen improportionantur quantum ad alios modos, ideo est incongrua haec 'homo currunt'. Et sic in proposito videtur, quia quamvis ['homo' vel][119] 'tantum pater' proportionantur quantum ad aliquos modos significandi, quia [tamen][120] unum significat per modum specificantis, alterum vero per modum specificabilis, quia tamen ibi est improportio quantum ad modos significandi generales, ideo videtur esse incongrua.

⟨*** *Reliqua, si qua fuerunt, desunt*⟩

---

119 homo vel] *secludi iussit censor anonymus ab ephemeride cui nomen Vivarium adhibitus, cui gratias ago.*

120 tamen **W**] cum **B**.

Ex impossibili quodlibet sequitur (Angel d'Ors)

Calvin G. Normore

In a remarkable series of articles over a period of twenty years Angel d'Ors explored and subjected to a critical examination some of the most fundamental features of medieval—and indeed of any—logic. In what follows I will concentrate on just one of these papers, '*Ex impossibili quodlibet sequitur* (Jean Buridan)'.[1]

Professor d'Ors' work in medieval logic informed and was informed by a number of central convictions about logic itself. One of these was that logic was an essentially incomplete subject. As he put it:

> In my opinion it is not possible, within logic, to establish an effective criterion which would permit the determination of the soundness or unsoundness of a consequence (and, deriving from this, the truth or falsehood of the corresponding conditional proposition), for the adequate response to such a question can be no other than all of logic in its entirety, that is to say, the set of all its particular doctrines. But logic is not a finite discipline capable of being completed.[2]

The picture of logic as essentially incomplete is both medieval and modern. In the wake of Gödel's incompleteness theorem we are now used to the thought that for any finite set of axioms or rules there are truths of arithmetic (and so one presumes necessary truths) which cannot be proved using them, and while one occasionally finds among medieval logicians the thought that some particular logical system (usually syllogistic) exhausts the 'good' inferences, it is far from the common view—as the number of treatises devoted to non-syllogistic inferences of various kinds testifies.

A second central conviction informing Professor d'Ors work was that, while there is an intimate connection between the truth of certain conditionals and the validity of related arguments, a connection intimate enough perhaps to support a deduction theorem, nonetheless conditionals and relations of consequence are beasts of very different kinds, the former being propositions which

1 Angel d'Ors, '*Ex impossibili quodlibet sequitur* (Jean Buridan)', in *Argumentationstheorie: Scholastische Forschungen zu den logischen und semantischen Regeln korrecten Folgerns*, ed. K. Jacobi (Leiden, 1993), 195-212.

2 D'Ors, '*Ex impossibili quodlibet sequitur* (Jean Buridan)', 196 (and for the quotation just below).

 | DOI 10.1163/9789004324275_012

have truth values and the latter relations among propositions and not propositions themselves. Again this conviction of Professor d'Ors captures an insight, though, as we shall see, within medieval logic the picture is complicated.

A third conviction guiding Professor d'Ors, one connected with but distinct from his conviction of the essential incompleteness of logic and the impossibility of an effective criterion of sound consequence, was that there is no *proprium* which characterized all and only good inferences and hence that no complete definition of good inference, not even one which would not provide an effective criterion, could, even in principle, be had. He writes:

> In my opinion, a 'proprium' of sound consequence does not exist; there is no sign which can serve to manifest the soundness of a sound consequence; there are at best 'necessary accidents', properties which apply to all sound consequences but not only to them. These properties, therefore, cannot serve as a criterion for the soundness of consequence, but at best, negatively, as a criterion of unsoundness.

Such 'necessary accidents' may be, for example, that 'it is not the case that the antecedent is true and the consequent false', or that 'it is impossible for the antecedent to be true and the consequent false'; these 'necessary accidents', with as many qualifications as deemed appropriate, can to a greater or lesser extent come close to the sought, non-existent 'proprium'. The consideration of one or another of these 'necessary accidents' as 'proprium' of sound consequence constitutes, in my opinion, a serious logical error, and is one of the roots of the disorientation suffered by logical research since many centuries ago, without thereby wanting to deny the possible interest and usefulness of systems constructed from such a consideration.[3]

From his (quite correct as I think) view that any logical system would be incomplete, Professor d'Ors drew the conclusion that the very notion of good consequence was primitive and could only be identified with the (incompletable) set of acceptable rules of inference. This conclusion was supported by his conviction that, perhaps in fact and certainly according to many medieval logicians, modal notions such as necessity and impossibility were equivocal and gained such clarity as they had by their interaction with rules of inference, and hence could not be relied on for a univocal definition. Inspired by this picture, Professor d'Ors undertook a trenchant and insightful examination of a number of medieval attempts to analyze the notion of consequence and undertook too to show how certain developments in the medieval history of

---

3 D'Ors, '*Ex impossibili quodlibet sequitur* (Jean Buridan)', 196-7.

logic, certain forms of *Obligatio* for example, made sense in the light of debate over such analyses. This paper examines a small fragment of Professor d'Ors' programme and its relation to some aspects of Jean Buridan's account of the consequence relation.

One issue worth clarifying at the beginning is just what we mean in this context by consequence. Medieval theorists inherited the term *consequentia* from a variety of ancient sources including Boethius, Cicero and Aulus Gellius. It seems to have been used by these writers in ways which might reflect either Aristotle's term 'akolouthesis' or the closely related Stoic 'akoloutheia', both of which might be translated into English as 'following' and both of which have a use outside logical contexts.[4] Since Aristotle and the Stoics had very different accounts of inference and since both traditions had been modified and adapted throughout later Antiquity, medieval theorists thinking about and commenting on antique texts had many masters.

The contemporary (to us) notion of logical consequence is also indebted to many traditions. Again there is general agreement on some terminology—an argument is valid just in case its conclusion is a logical consequence of its premises—but exactly what validity and logical consequence involve is a hotly debated issue. There are at least two major families of approaches. One is proof-theoretic and takes the notion of validity to be very closely related to that of proof, where a proof is an ordered set of propositions each of which is either a premise or is obtained from earlier members of the set by the application of one of an accepted set of rules—usually rules which operate on what might be called the form of the propositions involved. Members of the family differ about which rules are acceptable but agree that an argument is valid if its conclusion is obtained from its premises by application of the accepted rules. The second family is model-theoretic where a model is a representation (usually a set-theoretic structure) of a situation. Again which models are acceptable varies among members of this family and again there is agreement that an argument is valid if there are no models representing the premises that do not also represent the conclusion. Since it is agreed that an argument is valid just in case its conclusion is a logical consequence of its premises, the different ways of understanding validity carry over into different understandings of consequence.

Contemporary logicians usually attempt, at least for logical systems weak enough, to finesse arguments about the relations between proof-theoretic and model-theoretic understandings of valid argument by developing for such

4 Cf. Taki Suto, *Boethius on Mind, Grammar and Logic: A Study of Boethius' Commentaries on Peri hermenias* (Leiden, 2011), 163-6.

logical systems both a formal semantics, i.e., a model theory, and a proof structure, i.e., a set of acceptable rules, and proving (in a sense familiar in mathematics) that the two validate the same valid arguments. Gödel's Incompleteness Theorem shows that this cannot be done for systems whose models include models of arithmetic, and so one has the choice of either regarding such systems as not really logics (and so regarding many intuitively acceptable inferences as non-logical), of taking the model theory as basic in characterizing a notion of valid argument (and so of consequence) which can be approximated but not completely characterized by any proof theory, or of taking the proof theory as basic and so insisting that many intuitively valid inferences are not valid after all.

Medieval logicians were not concerned with modeling arithmetic and they did not develop anything like model theory, but they were concerned to examine those arguments formulated in a somewhat regimented Latin that were intuitively compelling. It is plausible that any argument formulable in any formal system can be formulated in natural language (supplemented perhaps with new vocabulary but nothing else) so that the collection of 'valid' arguments (understood as those intuitively compelling arguments formulable in natural language) exceeds that which can be proved in any particular (non-trivial) set of axioms and rules.[5] Thus within medieval approaches to logic the search for a *proprium* of consequence might be understood either as the search for a semantic feature which characterized (what we might call) the relation between the premises and conclusions of exactly the intuitively valid arguments or as the search for syntactic properties which would characterize any acceptable system of rules of inference. What one might expect of medieval logicians who thought there was such a *proprium* would be either a proposal about such a semantic feature and the development of a system of rules in an attempt thus to characterize it, or the development of a set of rules and an effort to discover what semantic feature they captured. What complicates such a picture is that medieval logicians inherited from antiquity several different systems of rules, notably Aristotle's assertoric and modal syllogistic and various systems of Topical rules some of which, at least, came with claims that they characterized as logical consequence. Thus what one finds in medieval logic is a tension between efforts to show that all the intuitively compelling inferences can be accounted for in terms of those systems of rules and efforts to find a system of rules to characterize the inferences which have characteristics antecedently picked out as likely to be *propria* of consequence.

5 I say 'non-trivial' because one can, of course, just take each valid argument as itself primitive and each necessary truth as an axiom.

These efforts are complicated by what seems to be a pervasive ambiguity of terms like 'ergo' and 'igitur' in Latin, 'therefore' in English, and similar particles in other European languages between a broadly truth-preserving and a broadly causal/explanatory sense.[6] Given this ambiguity it is not surprising that efforts to capture the sense of such particles have ridden off in all directions.

Given that each may be understood in very different ways, the question of the relation between *consequentia* and consequence is a complicated one. The actual trajectory of medieval logic seems to have been determined in some measure at least by the failure of Abelard's effort to reconcile central features of Aristotle's own logic (which had no discussion of sentential connectives) with intuitive principles governing conjunction, disjunction and negation. Abelard had proposed a system apparently inspired in part by Boethius' distinction between accidental and natural *consequentia*. Abelard proposed that an argument was valid if it met the condition Boethius had proposed for an accidental *consequentia*, i.e., it was impossible for the antecedent to be true and the consequent false, while the truth of a conditional required the quite tight semantic connection between the terms in the antecedent and those in the consequent of a natural *consequentia*—roughly that the sense of the consequent be contained in that of the antecedent. Alberic of Paris showed that Abelard's system for conditionals was incompatible with some very plausible rules for manipulating hypothetical sentences (notably that a conjunction implies each conjunct), and in the aftermath it seems that Adam of Balsham's proposal, that a conditional be taken to be true just in case the argument from its antecedent to its consequent was valid, won the day.[7] For the next two centuries it seems to have been the dominant conception of good inference, until in the second half of the fourteenth century there was a revival of the thought that good inference required a meaning connection between premises and conclusion of an argument and truth a similar relation between antecedent

---

6 This ambiguity was brought to my attention by André Gombay in the context of his work on Descartes' cogito. Cf. André Gombay, *Descartes* (Malden – Oxford – Carlton, 2007), especially 32-4. There are (at least) two ways of understanding the cogito. On one his thinking causes his existence; on the other it reveals it. Recall the joke about Descartes being asked if he would like coffee, replying 'I think not' and promptly vanishing!

7 This development was discovered by Christopher J. Martin, 'William's Machine', *The Journal of Philosophy* 83 (1986), 564-72. Adam of Balsham was an English philosopher working in Paris. His school was on or near the so-called 'Little Bridge' across the Seine and hence he is also referred to as Adam Parvipontanus and his followers as the Parvipontani. For a thorough (and excellent) discussion of the relation between conditionals and *consequentiae* in Buridan and some of his near-contemporaries, cf. Peter King, 'Consequence as Inference: Medieval Proof Theory 1300-1350', in *Medieval Formal Logic*, ed. M. Yrjönsuuri (Dordrecht, 2001), 117-45.

and consequent of a conditional, a thought which seems in many ways a return to that involved in Boethian natural *consequentia*.

A central issue here is what exactly is a *consequentia*? Boethius introduces the notion in his Second Commentary on the *Perihermenias* in the context of discussing conditional sentences, and it seems that the term remained closely connected with conditionals throughout the Middle Ages. This raises the question of the relation between *consequentia* and consequence since, as Professor d'Ors emphasized, while the truth of conditionals and the consequence relation are intimately connected, they are not the same thing and conflating them is a road to confusion. One significant difference is that conditionals can be either true or false, while there is no such thing as a consequence that does not obtain. If an argument is bad it is because its premises and conclusion are not related by the consequence relation, not because there is some other relation or family of relations by which they are related. This point gets real bite if we consider the situation at the beginning of the 14th century, where writers seem quite willing to speak of good and bad or valid and invalid *consequentiae*. For example, as Professor d'Ors points out, while Walter Burley is careful not to identify conditional and *consequentia*, he speaks of both good and bad *consequentiae* as if there were two relations, one obtaining when a *consequentia* is good and another when it is not.[8]

Conditional propositions have antecedents and consequents, identified by their syntactic role. It is because we can so identify them that it makes sense to talk of a conditional even where there is no consequence. As Professor d'Ors indicated, a striking fact about Buridan's account in his *Tractatus de Consequentiis* (TC) is that, unlike Burley (and unlike Ockham for that matter), he claims that *consequentiae* are just conditional propositions consisting of two propositions joined by the connectives 'si' or 'ergo' or something equivalent to them. He draws no distinction between the functions of these connectives. Buridan does, however, distinguish arguments from conditionals in general. When he turns to *argumenta* in the TC he claims that they are *consequentiae* differing from other conditional propositions in that their antecedents and consequents are asserted. In the *Summulae de Dialectica* (SDD) he presents his view somewhat differently, claiming that 'consequentia' is ambiguous and that the ambiguity is syntactically marked. He writes:

> The third section describes consequence, and from this description it is obvious that a consequence is a sort of hypothetical proposition. Next,

8 D'Ors, '*Ex impossibili quodlibet sequitur* (Walter Burley)', *Archives d'histoire doctrinale et littéraire du moyen âge* 57 (1990), 121-54.

> it notes that there are two kinds of consequence, the first of which is a conditional proposition that asserts neither the antecedent nor the consequent (e.g., 'if a donkey flies, then it has wings') but asserts only that the latter follows from the former. Such a consequence, therefore, is not an argument, for it does not conclude to anything. The other kind of consequence is an argument, given that the antecedent is known, or is known better than the consequent, and this asserts the antecedent, and from this it assertively infers the consequent. In a conditional we use the conjunction 'if', whereas in an argument we use the conjunction 'therefore'.[9]

Common between the two presentations is the claim that *consequentiae* are hypothetical sentences. Where they differ is about whether *argumenta* are themselves conditional sentences—at least in the same sense in which other *consequentiae* are.

In 'What the Tortoise Said to Achilles' Lewis Carroll points out that treating inferences as mere conditional sentences can at best lead to an infinite regress because in a conditional neither the antecedent nor the consequent is asserted.[10] Buridan seems sensitive to precisely this point. In the TC he attempts to deal with it while continuing to treat arguments as conditionals by adding the rider that the antecedents and consequents of *argumenta* are asserted. In the SDD he prefers to draw a distinction between conditionals, which are *consequentiae* whose antecedents and consequents are not asserted, and another species of hypothetical in which both are asserted. In both he is committed

9 Buridan, *SDD* 7.4.5, trans. Gyula Klima, *John Buridan's Summulae de Dialectica: An Annotated Translation, with a Philosophical Introduction* (New Haven, 2001), 575. (Translations from Buridan's *Summulae de Dialectica* are my (usually slight) modifications of Klima's.) "Tertia clausula describit consequentiam, ex cuius descriptione apparet quod consequentia est quaedam propositio hypothetica. Deinde notat duplicem esse consequentiam, scilicet unam quae est propositio condicionalis, et illa nec asserit antecedens nec asserit consequens (ut 'si asinus uolat, asinus habet alas'), sed solum asserit quod hoc sequitur ad illud. Et ideo talis consequentia non est argumentum; nihil enim concludit. Alia consequentia est argumentum si antecedens sit notum et notius consequente, quae asserit antecedens et ob hoc infert assertiue consequens. In condicionali autem utimur hac coniunctione 'si' et in argumento hac coniunctione 'ergo'." Quotations of the Latin text are from Hubert Hubien's (still!?) unpublished working edition, which can be found in a number of places on the internet, notably on Peter King's excellent website. Cf. http://individual.utoronto.ca/pking/resources/buridan/Summulae_de_dialectica.txt.

10 Lewis Carroll, 'What the Tortoise Said to Achilles', *Mind* 4 (1895), 278-80.

to the claim that an argument is a proposition rather than a sequence of propositions.[11]

For Buridan a *consequentia* asserts that a relation of consequence obtains. He is aware that one might insist that there is no *consequentia* if there is no consequence, but he regards it as *ad placitum* whether one speaks that way or instead claims that if there is no consequence there is a bad, false, or invalid *consequentia*. Buridan is, as Professor d'Ors highlighted, also committed to the claim that what makes a conditional true is just what makes a *consequentia* good. Buridan puts his own distinctive spin on this. Whereas Adam of Balsham and almost all of the tradition following him had claimed that what makes a conditional true and a *consequentia* good is that it is impossible for the antecedent to be true and the consequent false, Buridan proposes instead a criterion that runs not on truth but on what Hans Herzberger has called 'correspondence'.[12] He claims that in order for a proposition to be true it must be not only that things are as the proposition claims them to be (correspondence), but that the proposition itself exist (what Herzberger calls 'realizability') and that some further semantic conditions be satisfied. On his account the truth of a conditional and the goodness of a *consequentia* (or since it is a also a proposition, its truth) requires not that it be impossible for its antecedent to be true and its consequent false but that it be impossible that things be/have been/will be as the antecedent has it and not be as the consequent has it.[13]

---

11 I use 'proposition' to translate 'propositio'. Buridan maintains that propositions are particular non-repeatable collections of sounds, marks, or mental items. It is a striking feature of his semantics that two propositions looking exactly alike may have very different semantic properties. For example a proposition equiform to 'The sentence in the box is false' and located within a box is an instance of the Liar and false, while another equiform with it located outside the box will be true. There is, within Buridan's philosophy, a principled reason for identifying *consequentiae* with propositions. Buridan denies that there are relations and that there are semantic types. Hence if we are to answer the question what a *consequentia* is, that it is a proposition seems an attractive possibility. Why he does not identify an *argumentum* with one or more sentences taken together rather than with a single hypothetical sentence is not clear to me.

12 Cf. Hans G. Herzberger, 'Dimensions of Truth', *Journal of Philosophical Logic* 2 (1973), 535-56.

13 Although there is a tradition (the 'correspondence theory of truth') which has it that truth just is correspondence, Buridan argues that other conditions (some of them semantic) also have to be met for a sentence to be true. Cf. Stephen Read, 'The Liar Paradox from Thomas Bradwardine Back to John Buridan', *Vivarium* 40 (2002), 189-218, and Stephen Read, 'The Truth Schema and the Liar', in *Unity, Truth and the Liar: The Modern Relevance of Medieval Solutions to the Liar Paradox*, ed. S. Rahman, T. Tulenheimo and E. Genot

Since the only difference between the condition for the truth of a conditional, the condition for the goodness of a *consequentia* and the condition for the presence of a good argument is that in the last case the antecedent and consequent are asserted, it seems clear that Buridan intends the condition they have in common to characterize the consequence relation, i.e., that one proposition is a consequence of the other just in case it is impossible for things not to be as the one has it if they are as the other has it. How plausible is this characterization?

Like the original Parvipontanean criterion, this, of course, puts the notion of impossibility front and centre. One element in Professor d'Ors scepticism about there being a *proprium* of consequence was his conviction that medieval writers like Buridan did not have a univocal conception of modal notions like impossibility. Professor d'Ors writes:

> With respect to the first question, [of the meaning of 'impossible' in the definition of consequence] Buridan does not tell us anything explicitly, but it seems that from his 'Tractatus' a clear response can be inferred: in the definition of antecedent, the term 'impossible' appears in all its multiple meanings. This multiplicity is precisely that upon which the multiplicity of forms of antecedence, and derivatively of consequence, is founded and which Buridan and all the medieval tradition see to. Here the impossible is as much the impossible 'secundum quid' as the impossible 'simpliciter', as much that which is 'materially' impossible as that which is 'formally' impossible; and hence arises the division of consequence into sound 'ut nunc' ('secundum quid') and 'simpliciter', and into material and formal.[14]

He defends this assessment with the following text:

> Again there are also other formal consequences on account of the formal impossibility of the antecedent or the formal necessity of the consequent. For since from the impossible anything follows and the necessary follows from anything, if a proposition is impossible thanks to form, there

(New York, 2008), 3-18 and Terence Parsons, 'Comments on Stephen Read's "The Truth schema and the Liar"', ibid., 129-34, for some relevant discussion.

14 D'Ors, '*Ex impossibili quodlibet sequitur* (Jean Buridan)', 204-5.

> will be a formal consequence from it to anything, and, if it is necessary thanks to form, there will be a formal consequence from any other to it.[15]

Crucial here is whether we are to understand impossibility and necessity *gratia formae* as distinctive kinds of impossibility and necessity or understand them as impossibility and necessity understood generically but *shown* to be such by the form. Professor d'Ors understood them in the first way and saw them as part of a general picture in which modal notions are equivocal. I propose that we understand them in the second way and as part of a general picture in which Buridan has a single basic conception of modality and regards other uses of modals as restrictions on it.

At first glance Buridan might seem an unlikely author to hold that the basic modal notions are univocal, because in the *Tractatus de Demonstratione* in his SDD he distinguishes four different degrees of necessity. He writes:

> The first grade of necessity is that in which the sentence, its signification standing, can be falsified through no power nor related otherwise than as it signifies. Another grade is that which is impossible to be falsified or to be related otherwise through a natural power, although it may be possible supernaturally and miraculously, like 'the heaven is moved', 'the world is spherical', 'every place is full'. A third grade is supposing the *constantia* of the subject, like 'an eclipse of the moon is through the interposition of the earth between the sun and moon', 'Socrates is a human', 'Socrates is capable of laughter'. For these are called necessary because it is necessary whenever Socrates exists for him to be a human and capable of laughter and it is necessary whenever there is an eclipse of the moon for it to be through an interposition ... etc. Now there is a fourth grade according to restriction. For just as 'possible' is said sometimes widely in connection with every time, present, past and future, and sometimes restrictedly in connection with the present or future, granting that which is said in the

15 Jean Buridan, *Tractatus de Consequentiis*, ed. H. Hubien (Louvain, 1976), 20: "Item, sunt etiam aliae consequentiae formales propter formalem impossibilitatem antecedentis vel formalem necessitatem consequentis. Cum enim ex impossibili sequatur quodlibet et quod necessarium sequatur ad quodlibet, si propositio gratia formae sit impossibilis erit consequentia formalis de ea ad quamlibet et si sit gratia formae necessaria erit consequentia formalis de omni alia ad ipsam."

end of the first book of *De Caelo* that there is no ability (*virtus*) or power (*potestas*) with respect to the past . . .[16]

---

16 Buridan, *SDD* 8.6.3, trans. Klima, 733. Ed. Hubien: "Et adhuc possent poni alii gradus, ex eo quod oportet propositionem per se esse necessariam, quia sunt diuersi gradus necessitatis et, secundum hoc, etiam perseitatis. Est enim primus gradus necessitatis quia per nullam potentiam est possibile propositionem falsificari stante significatione, uel aliter habere quam significat. Alius gradus est quia impossibile est falsificari uel aliter habere per naturalem potentiam, licet sit possibile supernaturaliter et miraculose, ut 'caelum mouetur', 'mundus est sphaericus', 'omnis locus est plenus'. Tertius gradus est ex suppositione constantiae subiecti, ut 'eclipsis lunae est per interpositionem terrae inter solem et lunam', 'Socrates est homo', 'Socrates est risibilis'. Haec enim dicuntur necessariae sic quia necesse est quandocumque est Socrates ipsum esse hominem et risibilem, et necesse est quandocumque est eclipsis lunae ipsam esse per interpositionem . . . et caetera. Adhuc est quartus gradus, secundum restrictionem. Nam sicut 'possibile' dicitur aliquando ample, in ordine ad omne tempus praesens, praeteritum et futurum, et aliquando restricte, in ordine ad praesens uel futurum, iuxta illud quod dicitur in fine primi de Caelo quod non est uirtus siue potestas ad praeteritum, scilicet eius quod est factum secundum eius quod est factum esse uel futurum esse; quod enim fuit dicimus quod necesse est fuisse et impossibile est non fuisse. Ita et 'necesse' et 'impossibile' dicuntur secundum restrictionem uel ample. Ample igitur dicimus Aristotelem posse ambulare quia potest nunc aut potuit aut poterit ambulare; ideo sic dicimus istam possibilem 'Aristoteles ambulat', et istam 'Aristoteles ambulauit' et istam 'Aristoteles ambulabit', quia quaelibet talium potest nunc uel potuit prius aut poterit posterius esse uera, et nulla istarum est necessaria uel impossibilis; sed istae essent necessariae secundum Aristotelem 'homo est animal', 'deus est iustus'. Restricte autem dicimus Aristotelem non posse ambulare, quia nec potest ambulare nunc, nec poterit ambulare in futuro; et sic dicimus hanc impossibilem 'Aristoteles ambulat', uel 'Aristoteles ambulabit', et hanc dicimus necessariam 'Aristoteles ambulauit', et hanc etiam 'Aristoteles non ambulat', uel 'Aristoteles non ambulabit'. Quod autem sic ample sumant philosophi aliquando possibilitatem, impossibilitatem et necessitatem apparet per Aristotelem, primo Caeli, qui ponit quod generabile et corruptibile conuertuntur ad inuicem, et similiter ingenerabile et incorruptibile. Et hoc non est uerum secundum possibilitatem restrictam. Idem enim significat 'generabile' et 'possibile generari', et similiter 'corruptibile' et 'possibile corrumpi'; nunc igitur secundum restrictam possibilitatem ille equus qui generatus est non potest generari, et sic ipse non est generabilis, sed ingenerabilis, et tamen potest corrumpi, et sic est corruptibilis, et non incorruptibilis. Et sic non conuertuntur 'generabile' et 'corruptibile', cum ille equus sit corruptibilis et non generabilis, nec conuertuntur 'ingenerabile' et 'incorruptibile', cum ille equus sit ingenerabilis et non incorruptibilis. Oportebat igitur illas conuertibilitates intelligere secundum possibilitates ample sumptas. Sic igitur uno modo dicitur propositio necessaria simpliciter et per se simpliciter quia non potest nec potuit nec poterit falsificari. Dicitur autem alia necessaria secundum quid et per se secundum quid, et improprie, quia non potest esse falsa nec poterit, quamuis potuit esse uel fuit falsa. Necessitas autem simpliciter et perseitas simpliciter pertinent ad demonstrationes proprie dictas, et

Despite this apparent diversity, however, Buridan is clear that the first of these grades is the basic one. Simo Knuuttila has shown that remarks by Buridan in Book VII, question 3 of his commentary on the *Physics* depend upon taking the second grade of necessity as a restriction of the first.[17] The third grade in turn is most naturally taken as a restriction of the second but could be understood to be a restriction of each of the first two, a restriction to those cases for which issues of existential import do not arise.[18] As for the fourth sense, Buridan had raised the question of the relation between it and one or both of the first two in an earlier section of his *Summulae* and argued that it is a restricted sense used not in the demonstrative sciences but in narrative accounts.[19]

We can thus safely conclude, I think, that Buridan thinks the first 'grade' of necessity to be basic and thinks of the others as restrictions on it. This is also, I suggest, what he thinks about the impossibility 'as of now' (*ut nunc*) or 'as of then' (*ut tunc*) involved in the eponymous *consequentiae*. Impossibility *ut nunc*

---

non necessitas uel perseitas secundum quid. De necessitate enim uel possibilitate secundum quid propositio contingens et falsa uertitur in necessariam, et uera et contingens in impossibilem, ut haec, uel talis, fuit falsa 'Plato disputauit', quae modo est uera, et haec fuit uera 'Plato disputat', quae modo est impossibilis."

17 Simo Knuuttila, 'Necessities in Buridan's Natural Philosophy', in *The Metaphysics and Natural Philosophy of John Buridan*, ed. J.M.M.H. Thijssen and J. Zupko (Leiden, 2001), 65-76.

18 The issues here are akin to those involved in some understandings of the sophism 'Omnis homo de necessitate est animal'. Cf. Sten Ebbesen, 'By Necessity', in *Mind and Modality*, ed. V. Hirvonen, T.J. Halopainen and M. Tuominen (Leiden, 2006), 141-52.

19 Buridan, *SDD* 1.8.5, trans. Klima, 75-6: "We should note, however, lest someone should object, that 'possible' is sometimes taken broadly, namely, indifferently in relation to the past and the future, and so is 'necessary'; as when we say everything to be possible which either is, was, or will be, or even when it just does not imply a contradiction [to say] that it is, was or will be. In this sense we would concede 'Aristotle can be' [*Aristotiles potest esse*]', or 'Aristotle is able to run', and we would deny 'Aristotle necessarily does not run'. In another sense it is taken to be restricted to the future, so that nothing is said to be possible to be, unless it either will be or at least it does not imply a contradiction [when we say] that it is or will be, in the sense in which it is said, in Bk. 1. of *On the Heavens*, that there is no power [*potestas*] over the past. For in this sense we would say that a horse which perished cannot be, and that it cannot walk, and that it is necessary that it is not, and in this sense we would also say that the proposition 'Aristotle walks' is impossible, whereas it, or a proposition similar to it, was true, and we would also say that the proposition 'Aristotle does not walk' is necessary, even if at some time it was false. Whence in this sense what was once possible becomes impossible and what was contingent becomes necessary. But in the present context I speak about necessity and impossibility broadly, for this is how we speak in the demonstrative sciences, although we speak differently in narrative stories."

is just impossibility in the basic sense under the conditions in which the way things are now (or then) is held constant. Moreover, if Buridan has a distinct conception of modality *gratia formae* he never mentions it in his *ex professo* modal discussions and there would seem to be no obvious way to relate it to the other modal notions he does mention.[20]

Supposing then that we have a univocal sense of necessity (and impossibility), there is no bar from the side of the modal notions involved to characterizing consequence in modal terms. Thus we are back with Buridan's modified version of the Parvipontanean criterion as the foundation of his logic.

Much of Buridan's TC is an articulation of this criterion. A crucial step in this articulation is an elegant meta-argument that whatever will follow if we conjoin a necessary truth to the antecedent of a *consequentia* will follow from the antecedent alone. Buridan writes:

> Proof: because let A be a proposition from which together with many necessary ones adjoined to it the conclusion B follows; I say that B follows from A. Because if B follows from those necessary ones without A, then it is necessary, therefore it follows from anything. If indeed B does not follow from those necessary ones without A, then either A is impossible, and thus anything follows from it, or A is possible. Then either it is impossible for B not to obtain (*stare*), while A obtains, and then B follows from A, or it is possible for B not to obtain, while A obtains. If an opponent suppose this, then, since A cannot obtain without all the necessary ones obtaining at the same time, it follows that it is possible that, A obtaining together with all the necessary ones, B not obtain. Therefore B does not follow from A along with those necessities adjoined to it, which is contrary to what was posited.[21]

---

20 For further discussion of Buridan's modal theory cf. Calvin Normore, 'Buridanian Possibilities', in *Logic and Language in the Middle Ages*, ed. J.L. Fink, H. Hansen and A.M. Mora-Márquez (Leiden, 2012), 389-402.

21 Buridan, *TC*, ed. Hubien, 36: "Probatio. Quia sit A propositio ad quam cum multis necessariis sibi appositis sequitur conclusio B; dico quod ad A sequitur B. Quia si B sequatur ad illas necessarias sine A, tunc ipsa est necessaria, ideo sequitur ad quamlibet. Si uero B non sequatur ad illas necessarias sine A, tunc uel A est impossibilis, et sic ad eam sequitur quaelibet, uel A est possibilis. Et tunc uel impossibile est A stante non stare B, et sic adhuc ad A sequitur B, uel possibile est A stante non stare B. Et si hoc ponat aduersarius, tunc, quia non potest A stare quin simul stent omnes necessariae, sequitur quod possibile est A stante cum omnibus necessariis non stare B. Ergo B non sequitur ad A cum quibusdam necessariis sibi appositis, quod est contra positum." The translation is mine, but I have benefited from a draft translation by Stephen Read.

Buridan goes on in his next conclusion to show that anything follows from a contradiction. The argument he has in mind is that which Christopher Martin identified as William's Machine, was advanced by Alexander Neckham, is often referred to as the Principle of the Pseudo-Scotus and gained a new life in the 20th century as the 'Lewis Argument'. Buridan presents it using an example:

> Proof: I posit for the sake of example that this follows: every B is A and some B is not A, so a stick stands in the corner. Since it follows 'Every B is A and some B is not A' therefore every B is A, because from a conjunction there follows any of its conjuncts. Hence it follows 'Every B is A therefore every B is A or a stick stands in the corner', since anything implies itself in a disjunction with anything else. Then from this and the second part of the first antecedent I may argue thus: every B is A or a stick stands in the corner; and some B is not A; therefore a stick stands in the corner. This holds through the Topic *a divisione* because given two things posited under a disjunction, if either is rejected the other may be concluded. Therefore from the first to the last, from the first antecedent the stated conclusion follows, because whatever follows from the consequent follows from the antecedent.[22]

With this argument in hand Buridan goes on to argue that, if one accepts the formal proof that anything follows from a contradiction and accepts that adding a necessary proposition to the premises of an argument does not strengthen the argument, one is committed to the conclusion that anything follows from an impossibility. The proof is simple.

Consider the formal proof that q follows from p&-p. Suppose now that p is impossible. Then -p is necessary. Then -p adds no strength to the argument from p to q. Since we have already granted that q follows formally from p&-p, we must therefore grant that q follows from p alone. Since any argument from

---

22 Buridan, *TC*, ed. Hubien, 37: "Probatio. Pono, gratia exempli, quod sequatur omne B est A et quoddam B non est A; ergo baculus stat in angulo. Quia sequitur omne B est A et quoddam B non est A; ergo omne B est A, quia ad copulatiuam sequitur quaelibet eius pars. Deinde sequitur omne B est A; ergo omne B est A uel baculus stat in angulo, quia ad quamlibet sequitur ipsamet sub disiunctione ad quamlibet aliam. Tunc ex ista et secunda parte primi antecedentis arguam sic: omne B est A uel baculus stat in angulo; et quoddam B non est A; ergo baculus stat in angulo. Et iste syllogismus tenet per locum a diuisione, quia duobus positis sub disiunctione si alterum interimatur reliquum concludetur. Ergo, de primo ad ultimum, ex primo antecedente sequebatur dicta conclusio, quia quidquid sequitur ad consequens sequitur ad antecedens." Translation my own, though again I have benefitted from a draft translation by Stephen Read.

an impossible premise p to a conclusion q can thus be turned into a formal argument, the inference from an impossible premise has the same strength as that from a contradiction.

The strength of this meta-argument turns on the claim that neither adding nor subtracting a necessary sentence from a set of premises affects the validity of the argument. There will, of course, be an analogous claim that neither adding nor subtracting an impossibility from a disjunctive conclusion will affect the validity of the argument. How plausible is this and what does it indicate about the strength of the modality involved in the claim that if a *consequentia* is good (or true) it is impossible that things be as the antecedent has them and not be as the consequent does?

Professor d'Ors pointed out that Buridan's own proof for the principle that what follows from an antecedent with a necessary conjunct follows from the other conjuncts alone rests on the claims that anything follows from an impossibility and that the necessary follows from anything. Hence it cannot be used to ground those claims. Nonetheless the principle has independent plausibility and can be derived directly from the Parvipontanean criterion or Buridan's variant of it. Here is such a derivation.

Let N be a necessary truth. Let p be some other sentence. Since things are as N has it in every possible situation, they are as N&p has it in just those situations in which they are as p has it.

Suppose now that some sentence q does not follow from p but does follow from N&p. Then, since q does not follow from p, there is a situation s in which things are as p&-q has it. Since q does follow from N&p, there is no situation in which things are as N&p&-q has it. If things are as p&-q has it in s, they are as p has it in s and so they are as N&p has it in s. If they are as p&-q has it in s, they are as -q has it in s. Hence they are both as N&p has it in s and as -q has it in s and so they are as N&p&-q has it in s. Hence q does not follow from N&p after all. Hence it is contradictory to suppose that q follows from N&p but not from p alone.

What all this shows, I suggest, is that although Buridan draws a distinction between formal and material consequence and although he claims that no consequence is evident unless it can be shown to be equivalent to a formal consequence, since in fact, given the principle that adding or subtracting a necessary premise makes no difference to an argument, all good material *consequentiae* are equivalent to good formal *consequentiae*, Buridan has a univocal conception of good consequence and it is in terms of his modified form of the Parvipontanean criterion.

Could this be the *proprium* of consequence Professor d'Ors thought a will-o-the-wisp?

To be the *proprium* of consequence Buridan's condition must not validate any intuitively unacceptable *consequentiae* or claim as true any false conditionals. Here there are at least two issues. One is technical. Tarski argued, and no one has seen how to gainsay him, that no language can consistently express all of its own semantics. The Parvipontanean condition for consequence essentially involves the concept of truth, and, as both medieval and modern work on the Liar indicates, whether the truth-predicate has a definite and consistent extension is a question fraught with difficulty. If it does not, then it would seem the Parvipontanean proposal would not either, and so it could not be said to be a *proprium* in the sense Professor d'Ors had in mind. Buridan is fully aware of the difficulties of accounting for consequence in terms of truth and modifies the Parvipontanean condition for at least two different reasons. One is that, as someone who thinks propositional tokens to be the bearers of semantic properties, he insists that the truth of a propositional token requires its existence, while the satisfaction of the correspondence condition typically does not. This alone, he suggests, is enough to show that attempts to define consequence in terms of truth will go awry. For example he asks us to consider the *consequentia*

> Every proposition is affirmative, therefore no proposition is negative.[23]

Intuitively this is valid, yet in any situation in which the antecedent is true the consequent does not exist and so is not true, hence truth is not preserved—though correspondence is.

The other reason Buridan has for rejecting the Parvipontanean condition is that he thinks that in a number of cases involving propositional tokens containing terms standing for themselves (or sometimes for other propositional tokens), whether the token is true may give rise to paradox where whether things are as it signifies them to be does not. For example, on his view things are as the Liar proposition 'This proposition is false' signifies (that is, the proposition is false), but the proposition cannot be true, for if it were true it would be both true and false, which is a contradiction.

That the Parvipontanean condition fails to carve out consequence precisely seems plausible in the light of these considerations. What is less clear, however, is whether Buridan's own condition fares any better. Consider the *consequentia*

> God exists, therefore this *consequentia* is invalid.[24]

---

23 Buridan, *SDD* ch. 8, trans. Klima, 952.

24 "Deus est, igitur ista consequentia non valet, demonstrata eadem": Pseudo-Scotus, *In librum primum Priorum analyticorum Aristotelis questiones*, q. 10, in Johannis Duns Scoti

The antecedent is necessary, let us suppose, and things are in every case as it signifies them to be, so the *consequentia* is valid on Buridan's criterion just in case things are in every case as the consequent has them be, i.e., just in case the *consequentia* is invalid. Thus if the *consequentia* is valid, it is invalid. Suppose now that it is indeed invalid. Then, since things are in every case as the antecedent has it, there must be a case in which they are not as the consequent has it, i.e., there must be a case where the *consequentia* itself is valid. But if in one case, then in every case, so if the consequence is invalid, it is valid! We have then it would seem a paradox of correspondence. Indeed one might think that any notion powerful enough to supply a plausible criterion for consequence would be powerful enough to enable the language to express its own semantics and hence, as Professor d'Ors surmised, that no such notion and so no semantic criterion of consequence can be found.

Even were such a criterion possible, there is some reason to doubt that it would be Buridan's. First, as Professor d'Ors stressed, Buridan's criterion has as immediate consequences that anything follows from the impossible and the necessary follows from anything. The principle that anything follows from an impossibility does not appear in any ancient logic of which I am aware. Aristotle is committed to rejecting it, Michael Frede once suggested that the third Stoic indemonstrable was designed precisely to avoid the special case of it which would have anything follow from a contradiction, and Christopher Martin has argued that both Boethius and Philoponus would reason from impossible premises without supposing that just anything would be entailed by them.[25] It is not until the early 12th century, with the logical system of Adam of Balsham, that we find anyone explicitly endorsing the principle that just anything follows from what is impossible. Adam's school, the Parvipontani, apparently endorse the principle as a corollary of their account of good inference. As Buridan's discussion of the various 'grades' of modality makes clear, for him at least the notions of impossibility and necessity involved in such a claim are not formal notions, and there is no reason to think they are such that anyone but an omniscient God could tell in every case whether a claim is indeed impossible or necessary. Thus the Parvipontanean criterion of consequence and Buridan's modified version of it both allow that there may be consequences

Opera Omnia (Paris, 1891-95) 1: 103-8: 103. The example has been extensively discussed. Cf. Stephen Read, 'Self Reference and Validity Revisited', in *Medieval Formal Logic*, ed. M. Yrjönsuuri (Dordrecht-Boston-London, 2001), 183-96.

25 Cf. Michael Frede, *Die Stoische Logik* (Göttingen, 1974) and Christopher J. Martin, *Theories of Inference and Entailment in the Middle Ages*, PhD Dissertation, Princeton University, 1999.

which no finite mind ever will know to obtain and, since for Buridan an argument is a *consequentia* whose antecedent and consequent are asserted, good arguments which no proponent ever will know to be good (or bad). This is counter-intuitive enough to suggest to some that the Parvipontanean criterion and its Buridanian modification are both too generous.

There is another, though related, issue. Consider a dispute like that between the Greek and Latin churches over the *Filioque* doctrine. The Greek church claims it to be impossible that the Holy Spirit be spirated by both the Father and the Son, the Latin church it to be impossible that the Holy Spirit be spirated by the Father alone. Obviously it would be pointless for the theologians of one church to assume the impossibility of the others' position in attempting to persuade those of the other. What they will attempt to do is to argue using rules both accept from the others' premise to a conclusion both regard as impossible. Such argument will have to appeal to rules which do not rely on the Parvipontanean criterion or Buridan's modification of it. In short such argument will have to presuppose that some impossibilities are more impossible than others! This reaction seems already present in Buridan's own milieu. Christopher Martin has suggested that it is central to Scotus' use of the formal distinction. Something like it seems equally central to John Wyclif's logic. It is, of course, embedded also in the relevance logics of our own time. What this suggests to me is that, technical issues aside, the question whether there is a *proprium* of consequence cannot be answered until we are clearer about the notion of consequence we have in mind. Buridan, together with Ockham and, as far as I have been able to determine, the later 'nominalist' tradition more generally, think of consequence as a matter of relations among the ways things might be. Others, like Abelard or Scotus, think of consequence in more fine-grained ways. This is a dispute that transcends any plausible boundary of logic and suggests that the issue of the nature of consequence is one fundamental for philosophy as a whole. With this, I think, Professor d'Ors would have agreed!

Richard Billingham and the Oxford *Obligationes* Texts: Restrictions on *positio*

E. Jennifer Ashworth

The study of Oxford *Obligationes* texts in the 14th century owes much to the work of Angel d'Ors.[1] Fittingly, it is also a subject linked with Spain through the work attributed to Juan de Pastrana, the publication of the Oxford *Sophistrie* in 1503, and the presence of texts by Richard Billingham and others in Spanish libraries.[2] In this paper, I intend to focus on one aspect of a group of texts associated with the University of Oxford, namely the restrictions placed on the very first rule of the type of obligations called *positio*, and their relation to the sophismata introduced to illustrate the very difficulties that these restrictions were intended to counter. One of my intentions here is to show what was said in a series of rather modest texts that must have been used in actual teaching. First, however, it is necessary to say something about the *Obligationes* treatises themselves and what they were about.

1 About the Texts: Introductory Remarks

I shall start with a few introductory remarks about the English texts on which I base my discussion, and the general nature of *obligationes*. Texts on *obligationes* probably have their origin in the early 13th century, but the theory is found in its fully developed form in the *De obligationibus* of Walter Burley, written in 1302.[3] The other major English figure of the early 14th century was Roger

1 See especially Angel d'Ors, 'Sobre las *Obligationes* de Richard Lavenham', *Archives d'histoire doctrinale et littéraire du moyen âge* 58 (1991), 253-78; Angel d'Ors, '*Sortes non currit vel Sortes movetur* (Roger Swyneshed, *Obligationes*, § 137-138)', *Archives d'histoire doctrinale et littéraire du moyen âge* 60 (1993), 165-72; Angel d'Ors and Manuel García-Clavel, 'Sobre las *Obligationes* de Robert Fland. *Antiqua et nova responsio*', *Revista de Filosofía* 7 (1994), 51-8. For some discussion, see E.J. Ashworth, 'Autour des *Obligationes* de Roger Swyneshed: la *nova responsio*', *Les études philosophiques* 3 (1996), 341-60.

2 See below for details.

3 Romuald Green, *The Logical Treatise "De Obligationibus": An Introduction with Critical Texts of William of Sherwood and Walter Burley*, Ph.D. dissertation, University of Louvain, 1963.

 | DOI 10.1163/9789004324275_013

Swyneshed, whose *Obligationes* was probably written beween 1330 and 1335.[4] His doctrines were somewhat different from those of Burley, and were echoed in the later texts of Robert Fland[5] and Richard Lavenham.[6] Another important figure was Ralph Strode (d. 1387), who is known to have been a fellow of Merton College, Oxford in 1359 and 1360. However, in this paper I will be focusing on the work by Richard Billingham, who was a fellow of Merton College in 1344 and regent master of arts in 1349. His *Obligationes*, with the incipit "*Obligatio est quaedam ars*," appears in a number of manuscripts, some with small variations, and some with more elaborate variations.[7] The manuscripts I have used are the following:[8]

1. Cambridge, Corpus Christi College, MS 244/245, ff. 13v-18v.
2. Cambridge, Corpus Christi College, MS 378, ff. 48r-57r.
3. Oxford, Bodleian Library, MS lat. misc. e 79, ff. 18ra-24ra.
4. Padova, Biblioteca Antoniana, MS 407, ff. 34vb-36ra. This text contains only rules, and none of the sophismata.
5. Roma, Biblioteca Angelica, MS 1053, ff. 36v-39v. This text is closely related but not identical to the others.
6. Roma, Biblioteca Casanatense MS 5445, ff. 119v-130v, incomplete. This text may be ascribed to Billingham.[9]

---

4 Paul Vincent Spade, 'Roger Swyneshed's *Obligationes*: Edition and Comments', *Archives d'histoire doctrinale et littéraire du moyen âge* 44 (1977), 243-85.

5 Paul Vincent Spade, 'Robert Fland's *Obligationes*: An Edition', *Mediaeval Studies* 42 (1980), 41-60.

6 Paul Vincent Spade, 'Richard Lavenham's *Obligationes*. (Edition and Comments by Paul Vincent Spade)', *Rivista Critica di Storia della Filosofia* 33 (1978), 225-42.

7 For some discussion, based on fewer manuscripts, see E.J. Ashworth, 'English *Obligationes* Texts after Roger Swyneshed: The Tracts beginning *Obligatio est quaedam ars*', in *The Rise of British Logic*, ed. P.O. Lewry (Toronto, 1985), 309-33. For more details of texts and studies, see E.J. Ashworth, '*Obligationes* Treatises: A Catalogue of Manuscripts, Editions and Studies', *Bulletin de philosophie médiévale* 36 (1994), 118-47.

8 Manuscripts that I have not studied are Barcelona, Archivo de la Corona de Aragón, MS Ripoll 166, ff. 49r-54r and ff. 55r-59r; Padova, Biblioteca Universitaria MS 1123, ff. 3vb-5va; Sevilla, Biblioteca Capitular y Colombina, MS 5-1-12, ff. 23v-33v (I owe this reference to Angel d'Ors); Toledo, Biblioteca del Cabildo, MSS 94-27 f. 63r (opening lines only) and 94-28 ff. 164r-168v; Worcester, Cathedral Library F 118, ff. 8vb-10ra.

9 L.M. de Rijk, 'Richard Billingham's Works on Logic', *Vivarium* 14 (1976), 121-38: 132 notes that the *Obligationes* are preceded by the colophon: "Expliciunt supposiciones et consequencie barlingam. Incipiunt obligaciones."

7. Salamanca, Biblioteca de la Universidad, MS 1735, ff. 89r-95v. This *Obligationes* text is clearly ascribed to Billingham.[10]
8. Salamanca, Biblioteca de la Universidad, MS 1882, ff. 34r-v and 29r-33v. This incomplete text, closely related but not identical to the other Oxford texts, is ascribed to Juan de Pastrana.[11]
9. Città del Vaticano, Biblioteca Apostolica Vaticana, MS Urb. lat. 1419, ff. 62v-66v.
10. Città del Vaticano, Biblioteca Apostolica Vaticana, MS Vat. lat. 3065, ff. 95vb-98vb.
11. Città del Vaticano, Biblioteca Apostolica Vaticana, MS Vat. lat. 4269, ff. 192v-196r.

I shall also use one early printed text, to be referred to as LSO: *Libellus Sophistarum ad usum Oxoniensium* (London, 1510). The *Obligationes* text found on sign. C 5r-sign. D 1v is a version of the Billingham text. Various editions exist, one of which was printed in Spain.[12]

Another related printed text, published in 1483, to be referred to as the 1483 *Logica*, contains material from the Oxford *Obligationes*, combined with material taken from Paul of Venice's *Logica parva*.[13]

---

10 I have used the transcription by Angel d'Ors and José Miguel Gambra, 'Salamanca, Univ. 1735 (II)', *Cuadernos del instituto de historia de la lógica*, serie A, n. 2, Madrid: 1994, supplemented by my own earlier transcription.

11 I have used the transcription kindly provided to me by Angel d'Ors. I have not seen the manuscript. For more on Juan de Pastrana and his *Logica*, see Angel d'Ors, 'Logic in Salamanca in the Fifteenth Century. The *Tractatus Suppositionum Terminorum* by Master Franquera', *Vivarium* 51 (2013), 427-63: 430-2.

12 *Summa utilissima dialetice oxoniensis: que communiter sophisteria dicitur anglie* [Seville, 1503]. Angel d'Ors kindly provided me with a photocopy of this work. For details of other editions of the Oxford *Libelli Sophistarum* as well as the related Cambridge *Libelli Sophistarum*, see E.J. Ashworth, 'The "Libelli Sophistarum" and the Use of Medieval Logic Texts at Oxford and Cambridge in the Early Sixteenth Century', *Vivarium* 17 (1979), 134-58. For a French edition, probably produced for the English market, see E.J. Ashworth, 'A Note on an Early Printed Logic Text in Edinburgh University Library', *The Innes Review* 30 (1979), 77-9.

13 *Logica* [Oxford, Theodoric Rood, ca. 1483]. A transcription of the section on *obligationes* (sign. O 5v-sign. R 6r) is found in F. Pironet, *Guillaume Heytesbury: Sophismata Asinina* (Paris, 1994), 582-609. She calls the work 'Logica Mertonensis', presumably because one of the two surviving copies is found in the library of Merton College, Oxford. For an analysis of the contents, see E.J. Ashworth, 'A Note on Paul of Venice and the Oxford *Logica* of 1483', *Medioevo* 4 (1978), 93-9.

2 What Are *Obligationes*?

The immediate purpose of these texts was to describe a certain kind of disputation. I say 'the immediate purpose' because over the years there have been a number of disputes about their ultimate purpose,[14] and the most recent theory, put forward by Catarina Dutilh Novaes, is that they are concerned with rational dialogical practices, a guide for the rational disputant on how to preserve consistency in an actual debate.[15] This view ties in very nicely with the remark occasionally found in texts that the purpose is to train students to answer logically,[16] and also with the fact that no actual records of an obligational debate seem to have been made.

The general structure of an obligational disputation was always the same. There were two players, the opponent, whose function was to propose a series of propositions, and the respondent, whose function was to reply in each case either "I grant it" (*concedo*) or "I deny it" (*nego*) or "I doubt it" (*dubito*), that is, "I am not in a position either to grant or to deny it." Occasionally one finds a fourth legitimate response, namely "I distinguish it" (*distinguo*), that is, "I would like to make a distinction between different senses of the proposition in question," but this response is rarely found.[17] There were various types of disputation, including *depositio* in which the respondent had to deny the opponent's initial proposition, *impositio* in which the initial proposition stipulated a new signification for a word or phrase, and *dubie positio* in which the respondent had to doubt the initial proposition. Billingham (MS 7) included a section on *impositio*, as did MSS 3, 6, and 8 (Juan de Pastrana), but the other texts associated with Billingham only discussed *positio* and *depositio*.

In standard accounts of *positio*, the opponent begins by putting forward a proposition, the *positum*, that the respondent has to evaluate for logical or metaphysical possibility. If, and only if, the proposition is possible, the

14 For discussion, see Catarina Dutilh Novaes, *Formalizing Medieval Logical Theories:* Suppositio, Consequentiae *and* Obligationes (Dordrecht, 2007), 147-54.

15 Catarina Dutilh Novaes, 'Medieval *Obligationes* as a Theory of Discursive Commitment Management', *Vivarium* 49 (2011), 240-57.

16 See, e.g., Paul of Venice, *Logica Magna. Part II. Fascicule 8.* [*Tractatus de Obligationibus*], ed. and trans. E.J. Ashworth (Oxford, 1988), 32. Note 3 on p. 33 contains further references.

17 See William of Ockham, *Summa Logicae*, ed. P. Boehner, G. Gál, and S. Brown (St. Bonaventure, NY, 1974), 736; E.J. Ashworth, 'The "Obligationes" of John Tarteys: Edition and Introduction', *Documenti e Studi sulla tradizione filosofica medievale* 3 (1992), 653-703: 677-8; and *Obiectiones casuum* in *Libellus Sophistarum ad usum Cantabrigiensium* ([London]: Richard Pynson, 1497), sign. F iii r.

respondent must admit it.[18] The pragmatic considerations here are obvious: if the proposition is logically or metaphysically impossible (such as "God does not exist"), then anything follows, so that the disputation will be pointless. On the other hand, if the proposition is necessary, then only necessary propositions will follow, so that the disputation will be unduly constrained. The exclusion of necessary propositions was usually implicit rather than explicit,[19] but Swyneshed and Lavenham excluded them explicitly.[20] Brinkley excluded them on the grounds that only propositions that could rationally be doubted should be put forward,[21] and Strode (2. 20) referred to the custom of positing only false contingent propositions.[22] Once the *positum* has been admitted by the response "I admit it" (*admitto*), the game can begin. The opponent proposes the *positum*, and the respondent has to grant it, or so it seems.[23] Subsequently the opponent puts forward a series of propositions, each of which the respondent has to evaluate. If a proposition follows from the set composed of the propositions already granted and the negations of those already denied, it must be granted; if it is inconsistent with the set composed of the propositions already granted and the negations of those already denied, it must be denied; and if neither of these situations applies, then the proposition is dubbed 'irrelevant' (*impertinens*) and the reply must be based on what the respondent knows about the truth value of the proposition in question. The game ends if the opponent manages to lure the respondent into accepting a contradiction, either by granting and denying the same proposition, or by granting (or denying) a proposition whose negation (or affirmation) would follow from the set composed of the propositions already granted and the negations of those already denied. Obviously, the respondent's task is to avoid these traps, so if the respondent is very adept, the game will only end when the opponent

18 Certain kinds of pragmatic inconsistency could lead to the refusal to admit a possible proposition: see E.J. Ashworth, 'Inconsistency and Paradox in Medieval Disputations: A Development of Some Hints in Ockham', *Franciscan Studies* 44 (1984) [Printed 1988], 129-39. See also Paul of Venice, *Logica Magna*, 84 and note 12, 85-7.

19 A possible proposition can be either necessary or contingent: see e.g. Ockham, *Summa Logicae*, ed. Boehner-Gál-Brown, 330.

20 Swyneshed, ed. Spade, 253, §18 and 254, §20; Lavenham, ed. Spade, 228, §5.

21 *Richard Brinkley's Obligationes. A Late Fourteenth Century Treatise on the Logic of Disputation*, ed. P.V. Spade, and G.A. Wilson (Münster, 1995), 16, §22.

22 Section and paragraph references are to my as-yet unpublished edition of Strode's *Obligationes*, based on fourteen manuscripts.

23 For possible exceptions, see below. See also Paul of Venice, *Logica Magna*, ed. Ashworth, 84 and note 12, 85-7.

says "Time over!" (*cedat tempus*),[24] or when he is silent for a significant period of time,[25] or when the participants turn to other topics, or even start trading insults.[26]

In what follows I shall ignore the problems that arise as the disputation progresses, particularly in relation to the question of how irrelevant propositions are to be defined and handled, for this paper is concerned only with the steps of admitting and proposing the initial *positum*.

3 Restrictions on the *Positum*

I shall start with the main rule for *positio* as we find it in MS 5, f. 36v.[27] It has six clauses:

> This is the first rule: (1) you should grant every *positum* that has been admitted when it is proposed, provided that (2) it is put forward according to the form of the *positum* (3) during the time of the obligational disputation (4) and is known to be such by you, and (5) it is not inconsistent with the *positum*, and (6) wherever there is no *obligatio* relevant to it. (*Prima regula est ista: omne tibi positum et a te admissum sub forma positi propositum* [corr. ex 'positum'] *durante tempore obligationis et a te scitum fore tale non repugnans posito et ubicumque non est obligatio ad hoc pertinens est a te concedendum.*)

24 Ockham, *Summa Logicae*, ed. Boehner-Gál-Brown, 736, explains the phrase by adding: "Hoc est, cesset tempus obligationis."

25 Tarteys, ed. Ashworth, 673: "... quando opponens notabiliter diu tacet."

26 Paul of Venice, *Logica Magna*, ed. Ashworth, 20-2 has a full discussion of possible outcomes, but most people confined themselves to "Cedat tempus."

27 Other versions of the rule are found in MS 1, f. 14r; MS 2, f. 48r; MS 3, f. 18 ra; MS 4, f. 34vb; MS 6. f. 119v; MS 7, f. 89v, p. 33; MS 9, 62v; MS 10, ff. 95vb-96ra; MS 11, f. 192v; LSO, sig. C 5r; 1483, sig. O 6r, p. 582. See also Paul of Venice, *Logica Magna*, ed. Ashworth, 52. MS 8, p. 1 sketches part of the rule, but lacks any clear statement of the rules for *positio* as such. Billingham in MS 7 has: "Omne tibi positum, sub forma positi propositum, scitum a te esse positum, non repugnans posito, et a te admissum durante tempore obligationis est a te concedendum." D'Ors put "non repugnans posito, et a te admissum" within square brackets, but they are essential components of the rule. MS 4 states the rule like this: "Unde prima regula sit ista: omne tibi positum, sub forma positi propositum in tempore obligationis, scitum a me fore ita, non repugnans posito nec positioni, est a te concedendum."

Preliminary: the Step of Admission

The rule as found here does not make the conditions for admission explicit, but it was assumed that only propositions that were possible could be admitted. Thus MS 3 has as its second rule "Every possible proposition that is not inconsistent is admissible" (*omne possibile non repugnans est admittibile*),[28] and Tarteys has as his first rule "Nothing that is per se impossible is admissible" (*Nullum per se impossibile est admittibile*).[29] MS 4, after stating the rule, adds:[30] "For instance, I posit 'You are running' to you. This should be admitted, because it is possible. Whenever it is proposed during the time of the *obligatio*, it should be granted as if it were true" (*Ut, pono tibi istam "tu curris." Ista est admittenda, quia possibilis. Quandocumque proponitur durante tempore obligationis, est concedendum tamquam verum*).

MSS 3, 9 and 10 added the word '*bene*' to '*admissum*', thus stressing that the rule only applies to *posita* that have been correctly admitted.[31] Four later authors, Tarteys, Peter of Mantua, Paul of Pergula, and the author of a commentary on the *Obligationes* of Marsilius of Inghen made an interesting use of the presence or absence of '*bene*' in their discussion of the sophisma "P is posited and admitted" when P was an impossible proposition, such as "Man is an ass" (*homo est asinus*).[32] If the *positum* was "P is posited to you and correctly admitted by you" (*P est tibi positum et a te bene admissum*) it had to be rejected, because it was impossible, but if '*bene*' was omitted, the sophisma could proceed, and one could discuss whether "P should be granted" (*P est concedendum*) can be legitimately inferred from the *positum*.[33]

However, we should note that other authors of *Obligationes* texts were more inclined than the Oxford *Obligationes* to place their restrictions on *admissio*

28 MS 3, f. 18ra. Strode, 2.13, has a fuller formulation which seems to envisage a disputation with more than one *positum*: "omne possibile scitum esse possibile non repugnans alicui posito vel admisso cum ponitur est a te admittendum, et solum tale cum ponitur."

29 Tarteys, ed. Ashworth, 672. See also Paul of Venice, *Logica Magna*, ed. Ashworth, 50.

30 MS 4, f. 34vb.

31 MS 3, f. 18ra; MS 9, f. 62v; MS 10, f. 96ra. See also Tarteys, ed. Ashworth, 673.

32 Paul of Pergula, *Logica and Tractatus de sensu composito et diviso*, ed. Sister Mary Anthony Brown (St. Bonaventure, NY-Louvain-Paderborn, 1961), 118-19; Riccardo Strobino, *Concedere, Negare, Dubitare. Peter of Mantua's Treatise on Obligations*, Ph.D dissertation, Scuola Normale Superiore, Pisa, 2009, 97; Tarteys, ed. Ashworth, 689-90; Città del Vaticano, Biblioteca Apostolica Vaticana, MS Pal. lat. 995, f. 188ra-b.

33 For a discussion of this and related sophismata, see E.J. Ashworth, '"Tu curris" (vel "homo est asinus") est tibi positum: l'histoire d'un sophisme dans les traités sur les *Obligationes*', in *Sophismata: l'histoire d'une pratique philosophique*, ed. A. de Libera, L. Cesalli, F. Goubier and L. Gazziero (Paris, forthcoming).

itself. While logical and metaphysical inconsistency is clearly barred by everyone, there are at least three problematic kinds of pragmatic inconsistency that could be dealt with in different ways:[34] (1) the *positum* can be inconsistent with the opponent's act of positing, as with "Nothing is posited to you" (*Nihil est tibi positum*)"; (2) it can be inconsistent with the respondent's act of admitting, as with "You do not exist" (*Tu non es*); and (3) it can involve some kind of self-reference, perhaps through its syntactic properties, as with "You are running and no conjunction is posited to you" (*Tu curris et nulla copulativa est tibi posita*). There were four possible responses to the first two cases (the third will be discussed below):

(1) In his *Perutilis Logica*, Albert of Saxony simply refused to admit any *positum* that was inconsistent with the *obligatio*, the *admissio*, or the two taken together (as with "You are not under an obligation" (*Tu non es obligatus*).[35]
(2) Swyneshed admitted these cases, but said that any *positum*, such as "Nothing is posited to you" (*Nihil est tibi positum*), that was inconsistent with the *positio* should be treated as irrelevant.[36] He then explained that "Nothing is posited to you" should be doubted.[37]
(3) Strode held that one can simply admit such propositions, grant them, and either grant whatever follows from them or deny whatever is inconsistent with them.[38]
(4) The Oxford *Obligationes* were content to go ahead with the admission of pragmatically inconsistent *posita*, but preferred to place their restrictions on the *propositum*, the putting forward of the *positum* that had been admitted. This involved them in a discussion of some of the very sophismata that Albert of Saxony had prevented from arising.

We now turn to the discussion of the separate clauses.

Clause one: "You should grant every *positum* that has been admitted when it is proposed, provided that:"

34 See Ashworth, 'English *Obligationes* Texts', 314-15 and Ashworth, 'Inconsistency and Paradox', 133.

35 Albertus de Saxonia, *Perutilis Logica* (Venice, 1522: reprint Hildesheim-New York, 1974), f. 49rb; Albert von Sachsen, *Logik*, ed. and trans. H. Berger (Hamburg, 2010), 1242-6.

36 Swyneshed, ed. Spade, 265, §62, §64.

37 Swyneshed, ed. Spade, 271, §92.

38 Strode, 2. 28-32. See also Paul of Venice, *Logica Magna*, ed. Ashworth, 84-6 and note 12, 85-7.

Being proposed is the first step after the admission, but the *positum* can also be proposed at a later stage. This possibility features in the discussion of the next clause.

Clause two: "It is put forward according to the form of the *positum*."

This is a standard restriction of the rule in *Obligationes* texts, though it is omitted by MS 8. The restriction could be applied to synonyms, such as 'Marcus' and 'Tullius', both said of Cicero,[39] but in the Oxford *Obligationes* it is applied to pronouns and pronominal adjectives. It was illustrated by means of two related sophismata.[40]

Clause two: first sophisma
MS 3 contains an inserted discussion of the first rule in which the issue is examined by means of this case:[41]

(1) "The other of these is true" (*Reliquum istorum est verum*), pointing to the contradictories "The king is sitting down" (*rex sedet*) and "No king is sitting down" (*nullus rex sedet*). Admitted and granted because it is the *positum*.
(2) "One of these is true" (*Alterum istorum est verum*). Granted as following.
(3) "The other of these is true" (*Reliquum istorum est verum*).

Problem: If this is denied, it looks as if the *positum* is denied. If it is granted, "Each of these is true" (*Utrumque istorum est verum*) will follow, and that implies that you have implicitly accepted two contradictories.

Solution: In its second appearance, "The other of these is true" is not proposed in the same form. In the *positum*, 'the other' is taken indefinitely, but in the new *propositum* 'the other' is taken relatively.[42]

---

39 See Burley, ed. Green, 3.06.

40 To make sense of these in English, I have had to translate the Latin slightly differently in each.

41 MS 3, f. 18va-b.

42 See Paul of Venice, *Logica Magna*, ed. Ashworth, 52-4 for this sophisma and further references, including to Burley. See also *Martinus Anglicus: De obligationibus, Über die Verpflichtungen*, ed. and trans. F. Schupp (Hamburg, 1993), 6-8, §9.

Clause two: second sophisma

A somewhat similar sophisma is used in three of the other Oxford texts and in the 1483 *Logica*.[43]

(1) "The other of these is running," pointing to you and me (*Alter*[44] *istorum currit, demonstrando te et me*). Granted because it is the *positum*.
(2) "One of these is not running" (*Aliquis istorum non currit*). Granted because it is true and irrelevant.
(3) "One of these is running" (*Unus istorum currit*). Granted because it follows from the *positum*.
(4) "The other of these is running" (*Alter*[45] *istorum currit*). Granted because it is the *positum*.
(5) "Each of these is running" (*Uterque istorum currit*).

Problem: This has been denied by step 2, so it ought not to be granted. But if it is denied, then the legitimate inference of (5) from (3) and the *positum* has been rejected.

Solution: Accept steps 2 and 3 and deny "*Alter istorum currit*" in step (4) because it was proposed under another form than it was posited. '*Alter*' is first non-relational, but in (4) it becomes relational.[46] Alternatively, LSO added, without any explanation, one might deny the argument that (5) follows from (3) and the *positum*.

What is particularly interesting about the application of the restriction in these sophismata is that it shows the part that could be played by changing contexts in a disputation. The spoken sounds are the same, but their signification has been altered by the way the dialogue has developed.[47]

Clause three: "It is put forward during the time of the obligational disputation."

The point here is that outside the time of the obligational disputation, which begins with the step of admission and ends with "*cedat tempus*," or one of the

43 MS 2, f. 51r; MS 9, f. 63v-64r; LSO, sign. C 6r; 1483, sign. P 5r, 589-90.

44 LSO has 'Aliquis'.

45 MS 9 has 'Aliquis'. Pironet's transcription of 1483, *Sophismata Asinina*, 589, adds an extraneous 'non' before 'Alter'.

46 MS 2, LSO, and the 1483 *Logica* do not add this explanation of why the form is different.

47 For more about the issue of context sensitivity, see Riccardo Strobino, 'Contexts of Utterance and Evaluation in Peter of Mantua's *Obligationes*', *Vivarium* 49 (2011), 275-99, especially 278.

variants on that, one is supposed to abide by truth. This does not happen within an obligational disputation, because the point is to see what follows from a *positum* that is normally false together with whatever else the opponent might care to propose. The clause could be taken as too obvious to mention, though most sources from Burley on do include it. It is present in all our MSS, along with LSO and the 1483 *Logica*. One of the interesting features of the clause is that it allows for two kinds of meta-dialogue.[48] For instance, within the disputation the opponent may put forward the inference "You have granted P, therefore you have replied badly," and this will have to be treated quite differently than it would be treated in the period after the disputation when the student's performance is discussed with candour and honesty.[49]

Clause four: "It is known to be such by the respondent."[50]

MSS 8 and 9 omit clause four, as do Swyneshed, Lavenham, and Tarteys. The other texts, as well as LSO and the 1483 *Logica*, include it, as do Fland, Brinkley, Martinus Anglicus, Strode, and Paul of Venice.[51] In his suppositions Swyneshed does include 'known by someone' (*scitum ab aliquo*) in his remarks about irrelevant propositions. That is, along with other restrictions, one should grant those known to be true, deny those known to be false, and doubt those known to be uncertain.[52] However, this addition is not significant, since it is difficult to see what other instruction could be given for the response to irrelevant propositions, and we already know that *posita* are to be treated in terms of their possibility rather than their truth.

In his discussion, Paul of Venice limits 'known to be such' to knowing that P is the *positum*. He uses the example of someone to whom: "This is true: 'You are

48 For some problems of meta-dialogue, see d'Ors and García-Clavel, 'Sobre las *Obligationes* de Robert Fland', 54-5.

49 See Strode, 2.23: "Secunda conclusio: quod non est inconveniens respondentem concedere quandoque se male respondere, vel negare se bene respondere." In 2.25 he adds: "Unde maximum inconveniens est extra tempus obligationis concedere quod infra male respondisti, cum sit extra tempus rei veritas fatenda ..."

50 For discussion of this epistemic clause, see Catarina Dutilh Novaes, 'Ralph Strode's *obligationes*: The Return of Consistency and the Epistemic Turn', *Vivarium* 44 (2006), 338-74, especially 358-62. See also Dutilh Novaes, *Formalizing Medieval Logical Theories*, 186-214, especially 202-5.

51 Fland, ed. Spade, 43 §1; Brinkley, ed. Spade-Wilson, 40 §106; *Martinus Anglicus*, ed. Schupp, 4 §7; Strode, 2.14; Paul of Venice, *Logica Magna*, ed. Ashworth, 52.

52 Swyneshed, ed. Spade, 255 §25, 256 §29, 256 §30. See also Burley, ed. Green, 3 §14, for a similar requirement for irrelevant propositions.

in Rome' " has been posited, but who thinks that the *positum* was "You are in Rome." The respondent ought then not to grant "This is true: 'You are in Rome'."[53] This seems rather unhelpful as guidance for useful dialogue, especially as no further indication is given of how the unfortunate respondent can deal with his mistake. More importantly, it seems an example of the problem raised by Dutilh Novaes, namely that of a conflict between seeing the rules as normative and seeing them as descriptive.[54] She writes: "Hence, if Respondent's logical knowledge is deficient, given the epistemic clause, he is properly speaking not responding badly [...]. So the epistemic clauses, albeit realistic, jeopardize the normative character of *obligationes*." She adds that "one way to make sense of the obligational rules thus formulated is to view them as descriptive rules [...]. But the purpose of obligational treatises is presumably that of spelling out rules of how to respond correctly (how to win the game) and not that of serving as a description of how such disputations actually take place."

Later, in his tract on *obligationes*, Paul of Venice took up the discussion of the sophismata used by Ralph Strode to illustrate the clause.[55] These included "Let the case or the proposition that I am thinking about be posited" (*ponatur iste casus vel ista propositio quam cogito*), and "I posit one or other of 'The king is sitting down' and 'No king is sitting down', which you know to be contradictories that mutually contradict each other" (*Pono tibi alterum istorum "rex sedet" et "nullus rex sedet", que scias esse contradictoria inter se contradicentia*). These sophismata are genuine examples of *posita* that do not meet the requirement that the *positum* be known as such. This ties in well with Dutilh Novaes' suggestion that another way to interpret such clauses is to view them as related to the explicit formulation of the propositions being put forward—as opposed to their 'mental' formation.[56] However, the Oxford *Obligationes* do not contain any sophismata of this sort, though epistemic issues feature in the Oxford collection of sophismata known as *Obiectiones obligationum secundum usum Oxonie*, as well as in *Obiectiones casuum*, the similar Cambridge collection. For instance, if the *positum* "You know every truth" (*omne verum sciatur a te*) is granted, and then both "The king is sitting down" and "No king is sitting

53 Paul of Venice, *Logica Magna*, ed. Ashworth, 54.

54 Dutilh Novaes, 'Ralph Strode's *obligationes*', 361. See also Dutilh Novaes, *Formalizing Medieval Logical Theories*, 204-5.

55 Strode, 5.1-14. and 5.38-49. For Paul of Venice's interpretation of Strode's sophismata, see *Logica Magna*, ed. Ashworth, 122-37.

56 Dutilh Novaes, 'Ralph Strode's *obligationes*', 361; Dutilh Novaes, *Formalizing Medieval Logical Theories*, 205.

down," which you know to be contradictories, are proposed, will it follow that the same proposition is both known to you and doubted by you?[57]

Clause 5: "It is not inconsistent with the *positum*."

This clause is somewhat difficult to construe, and two versions are found in the Oxford texts, though there seems to be no reason to believe that the difference is merely a matter of a copyist's error. The clause as quoted here is found in MSS 5, 6 and 7, and is cited by both Fland[58] and the *Obligationes* found in the Cambridge *Libellus Sophistarum*.[59] The alternative version, "It is not inconsistent with the *positio*," is found in MSS 1, 2, the 1483 *Logica*, and LSO, as well as in Swyneshed, Lavenham, and Martinus Anglicus.[60] Both versions are combined in MS 4, which has "It is not inconsistent with either the *positum* or the *positio*" (*non repugnans posito neque positioni*), and in the Cambridge *Obiectiones casuum* various formulations appear in the discussion of "Nothing is posited to you" (*nihil sit vobis positum*).[61] MSS 3, 8, 9, 10 and 11 do not have any version of clause five in their statements of the rule, but in MSS 3 and 11 inconsistency with either the *positum* or the *positio* is introduced at a later stage (see below).[62]

The version reading "It is not inconsistent with the *positio*" is the easiest to make sense of, provided that we take '*positio*' in a broad sense. Thus LSO explains that any *positio* implies the existence of the one who posits, the one to whom the case is posited, and the *positum* itself,[63] and so a *positum*

57 *Obiectiones obligationum secundum usum Oxonie*, Oxford, New College MS E 289 (ff. 21r-23v), f. 21r; *Obiectiones casuum*, sign. F 2r.

58 Fland, ed. Spade, 47, §23. His discussion is in the context of the *nova responsio* of Swyneshed and why a *positum* such as "Nulla obligatio tibi fit" can be denied 'quando repugnat posito'.

59 *Obligationes* in *Libellus Sophistarum ad usum Cantabrigiensium*, sign. C 4r-C 6r. The rule (on sign. C 4r) has "non repugnans posito eiusdem positionis," but the manuscript version, Cambridge, Gonville and Caius College, MS 182/215, 42, has only "non repugnans posito."

60 Swyneshed, ed. Spade, 265 §62; Lavenham, ed. Spade, 228-9, §6; *Martinus Anglicus*, ed. Schupp, 4, §7.

61 In the first of the three versions of the rule in *Obiectiones casuum*, sign. F 1r, we read "non repugnans posito durante tempore eiusdem positionis," which suggests that the phrase "durante tempore" had been omitted in the *Obligationes* found in the same volume (see note 59). The second version reads "non repugnans positioni" and the third version reads "non repugnans posito."

62 MS 3, f. 19ra-b and f. 20va; MS 11, f. 193r.

63 LSO, sign. C 5v.

inconsistent with a *positio* is a *positum* that negates the existence of any one of those three. It was this version of the clause that was explicitly rejected by Brinkley, who wrote that one should not add the phrase "and not inconsistent with the *positio*" (*nec repugnans positioni*).[64] Strode also indicated his disagreement with the clause when he wrote: "The third thesis is that when a possible *positum* is inconsistent with a *positio*, it should be admitted, and when it is proposed, it should be granted, but the *positio* should be denied when it is proposed" (*Tertia conclusio: quod cum positum possibile repugnat positioni, debet etiam admitti, et cum proponitur concedi, sed positio proposita debet negari*).[65] In his subsequent discussion, he gave several reasons why this was the course to follow, thus indicating his disagreement with at least some of his Oxford contemporaries.

A little more light can be shed on both versions of clause five by a consideration of three sophismata. First let us consider the sophisma "You do not exist" (*tu non es*), found in all the manuscripts except for MS 4, which has no sophismata, and MS 10,[66] and which is also found in LSO and the 1483 *Logica*.[67] MSS 1, 6, 8, 9, and the 1483 *Logica* made no appeal to clause five, but were content to grant the *positum* and to deny any subsequent proposition inconsistent with it, namely any proposition that entailed your existence, such as "You are a man" (*tu es homo*). Indeed, MSS 6 and 7 appealed to clause two when they remarked that it would be wrong to deny the *positum* when it was proposed, because it had the accepted form. Four manuscripts offer the reader the same solution along with an alternative. MS 2 wrote that the *positum* could be denied on the grounds that the rule should be understood as applying where there was no contrary *obligatio* (*regula habet intelligi ubi non sit obligatio in contra*), that is, there was an appeal to clause six (see below). MS 5 said it could be denied because it was inconsistent with the *admissio*, and MS 11, whose version of the rule did not include clause five, wrote that one could say that the rule could be understood as applying to a *positum* that was not inconsistent with the *positum* (*regula contingit intelligi sic, de posito non repugnante positi* [*sic*]). This point was elaborated on in MS 3, whose rule also lacked the clause, which said that one could admit the *positum* and then deny it because it was

64 Brinkley, ed. Spade-Wilson, 15 §13.

65 Strode, 2.28.

66 MS 10, f. 96rb, has what might be a brief garbled version, with "Tu non es homo" as the *positum* and "Tu non es" as a subsequent *propositum*.

67 MS 1, f. 14v; MS 2, f. 49r-v; MS 3, f. 19ra-b; MS 5, f. 37r; MS 6, ff. 121v-122r; MS 7, f. 90v, p. 35; MS 8, p. 2; MS 9, f. 63r-v; MS 11, f. 193r; LSO, sign. C 5v; the 1483 *Logica*, sign. P 2v, p. 586. See also Paul of Venice, *Logica Magna*, ed. Ashworth, 170, and note 28, 71-3.

inconsistent with the *positum*, and that if further appeal was made to the rule for granting *posita*, one should say that the rule is to be understood as referring to a *positum* not inconsistent with the *positio*.[68] MS 3 also added the further possibility of granting an affirmative proposition, presumably one that was inconsistent with the *positum*, such as 'You are a man', and then denying that one had granted it. LSO gave no alternatives, but simply said that one should admit the *positum* and then deny it because the rule should be understood as applying to the case where the *positum* was not inconsistent with the *positio* (*regula habet intelligi ubi positum non repugnat positioni*).

In MS 7 Billingham, who had the first version of clause five in his statement of the rule, and did not use it in his discussion of the main sophisma, "You do not exist," turned to the second version of clause five in his subsequent discussion.[69] He considered a case in which the opponent posits "This proposition is posited to you, 'You do not exist' " (*ponatur quod ista propositio sit tibi posita: 'tu non es'*). This can be correctly (*bene*) admitted and then denied because the rule is understood as applying to a *positio* that is not inconsistent (*regula habet intelligi de positione non repugnanti*). Alternatively, he added, when it is posited one can deny it on the grounds that the proposition itself is impossible, since it contains the two contradictories "You exist" and "You do not exist."

One might think that discussions of a second sophisma, "No proposition is posited to you" (*Nulla propositio est tibi posita*), as found in all the MSS except MSS 1 and 4, as well as in LSO and the 1483 *Logica*,[70] might also have made use of clause five. However, all these sources were content to grant the *positum* when proposed and then to deny "Some proposition is posited to you." MS 6 remarked that there was another solution, but that it was no good (*nihil valet*). This other solution is presumably that mentioned by Swyneshed in relation to '*repugnat positioni*',[71] by Fland in relation to '*repugnat posito*',[72] and by the Cambridge *Obiectiones casuum* in relation to both clauses, namely that the

68 MS 3, f. 19ra-b: "Huic dicitur admittendo positum et quando proponitur, negatur quia repugnat posito, et quando ulterius allegatur regula, respondendum est quod regula habet intelligi de posito non repugnanti positioni. Vel aliter potest respondere [corr. ex respondes], scilicet concedere omnes propositiones negativas et negare affirmativas. Vel si concedit aliquam affirmativam, debet concedere quod concedit illam."

69 MS 7, f. 90v, p. 35. In 'English *Obligationes* texts', 316, and Paul of Venice, *Logica Magna*, n. 28 on p. 171, I wrongly interpreted these remarks as applying to "Tu non es."

70 MS 2, f. 49v; MS 3, f. 19rb; MS 5, ff. 36v-37r; MS 6, f. 122r; MS 7, ff. 90v-91r, pp. 35-6; MS 8, p. 2; MS 9, f. 63v; MS 10, f. 96rb; MS 11, f. 193r; LSO, sign. C 5v; the 1483 *Logica*, sign. P 2v, p. 586. See also Paul of Venice, ed. Ashworth, 170 and note 27, 171.

71 Swyneshed, ed. Spade, 271, §§91-2.

72 Fland, ed. Spade, 47, §§23-4, using a similar sophisma ("Nulla obligatio tibi fit").

positum should be denied.[73] Their use of both clauses is clarified by Fland's remark that the *positum* was inconsistent with the *positum* when it entailed the opposite of the *positio*.[74]

The third sophisma to be considered is "You are running and no conjunction is posited to you" (*Tu curris et nulla copulativa est tibi posita*), which in most sources has the added clause "and this remains posited to you, and nothing else [is posited]" (*et maneat ista tibi posita, et nulla alia*).[75] This sophisma is found in nearly all the Oxford *obligationes* texts in relation to a rule for conjunctions.[76] The standard form of this rule is: "Note that every conjunction from which the opposite of the *positum*[77] follows should be denied" (*Et nota quod omnis copulativa ex qua sequitur oppositum positi est neganda*), and one answer to the posited sophisma was: "One replies by admitting the *positum*, and when it is proposed it is denied, because the *positum* is inconsistent with the *positio*" (*Huic dicatur admittendo positum, et quando proponitur negetur, quia positum repugnat positioni*).[78] However, there were some variants of the rule. MS 6, without giving the sophisma, simply says that a conjunction from which the opposite of the *positum* follows should not be admitted, and MS 8 (Juan de Pastrana) says that a conjunction should only be admitted if its principal parts are compossible, and that given the phrase '*nulla alia*', the parts of the sophisma are not compossible, so it cannot be admitted. There were also some variant solutions of the sophisma. Only MS 3, LSO and the 1483 *Logica* have the phrase '*repugnat positioni*', while MSS 2, 7 and 10 simply appeal to inconsistency,[79] and MS 5 focuses on the denial of the proposition "You are not under an obligation" (*tu non es obligatus*) on the grounds that it does not follow

73 *Obiectiones casuum*, sign. F 1r: "... illa est regula: omne mihi positum et a me admissum sub forma positi propositum, et non repugnans posito durante tempore eiusdem positionis est concedendum. Sed in casu posito, ⟨positum⟩ est repugnans positioni, et ideo non compellet concedere positum."

74 Fland, ed. Spade, 47 §24: "Et sciendum quod positum repugnat posito quando ex posito sequitur oppositum positionis."

75 MSS 7 and 8 omit "et nulla alia" while MS 3, MS 5, and the 1483 *Logica* omit the entire clause. MS 1, MS 4, and MS 6 lack the sophisma.

76 MS 2, f. 52v-53r; MS 3, f. 20va; MS 5, f. 38r; MS 7, f. 92v, p. 39; MS 8, p.6; MS 9, f. 64v; MS 10, f. 97rb; MS 11, f. 194r, LSO, sign. C 7r; the 1483 *Logica*, sign. Q 1r, pp. 592-3. MS 1 and MS 4 have neither rule nor sophisma; MS 6, f. 126v has a version of the rule without the sophisma.

77 MS 3 has "positionis."

78 LSO, sign. C 7r.

79 MS 10, f. 97rb writes "Huic dicitur negando positum quia categoricae repugnant," which suggests an alternative reading for 'copulativae' in MS 7, f. 92v. D'Ors (transcription, p. 39)

from the second clause of the *positum*, given that something else might have been posited.[80] To the argument that it does follow, because only that conjunction was posited to you, the author replied that that could be denied because in positing a conjunction each principal part is also posited. MSS 9 and 11 do not give a clear solution.

On the whole, the various discussions of the three sophismata suggest that little distinction, if any, was made between a *positum*'s inconsistency with a *positum* and with a *positio*.[81] A *positum* is inconsistent with that very *positum* when it denies the existence of one of the three elements involved in its positing or *positio*, that is, the existence of the opponent or his action of positing, the respondent or his actions, and the *positum* itself, just as it is inconsistent with its *positio* for the very same reason. One might also suggest that a rational interpretation of the first version of clause five would read it as "It is not inconsistent with [some other] *positum*." This is not borne out by my investigation of the sophismata in the Oxford *Obligationes*, but I suspect this is what Strode meant when he wrote (2.13) that "every possible proposition known to be possible [and] not inconsistent with any *positum* or *admissum* should be admitted by you when it is posited" (*omne possibile scitum esse possibile non repugnans alicui posito vel admisso cum ponitur est a te admittendum*).[82]

Clause six: "Wherever there is no *obligatio* relevant to it."

This final clause found in MS 5 is not found in any of the other manuscripts, though it is found in Swyneshed, Lavenham, the Oxford *Obiectiones obligationum* and the Cambridge *Obiectiones casuum*, with the explanation that the application of the clause is triggered by the presence of such words as 'positum' in the *positum*.[83] The two latter sources relate the clause to the sophisma " 'Man

has "Huic dicitur negando positum, quia ⟨partes⟩ copulativae repugnant etc." which also makes good sense.

80 For a similar discussion and further references, see Paul of Venice, *Logica Magna*, ed. Ashworth, 328-30 and 329, note 5.

81 These remarks go some way to settle the problems raised by d'Ors and García-Clavel, 'Sobre las *Obligationes* de Robert Fland', 70-1.

82 I now accept comments about my earlier interpretation made by Dutilh-Novaes, 'Ralph Strode's *obligationes*', 367; Dutilh Novaes, *Formalizing Medieval Logical Theories*, 209.

83 Swyneshed, ed. Spade, 265, §62: "Omne positum sine obligatione ad hoc pertinente non repugnans positioni in tempore positionis est a te concedendum." In §63 he explains that "positum sine obligatione ad hoc pertinente est tale quod fatendum est fore positum ubi non obligatur quod illud sit positum ..." Lavenham, ed. Spade, 228-9, §6: "Omne positum

is an ass' is posited to you" (*'Homo est asinus' est tibi positum*),[84] and they use it to avoid a type of obligational inconsistency, that which is brought about by the passage from one level of dialogue to another. Thus they allow one to grant " 'Man is an ass' is the *positum*," but then to deny both "Man is an ass" and the proposition "One should grant 'Man is an ass' " on the grounds that although "Man is an ass" is a (or the) *positum*, it is not a *positum 'sine obligatione ad hoc pertinente'* and so it is not a *positum* to which the rule "every *positum* should be granted" applies.

Clause six may be related to an addendum to the rules found in MS 7: "And all these rules should be understood as applying where there is no *obligatio* to the contrary (and there is an *obligatio* to the contrary when there is an *obligatio* against one of the aforesaid rules)" (*Et omnes istae regulae habent intelligi si non sit obligatio in contrarium (et tunc fit vel est obligatio in contrarium quando fit obligatio contra aliquam regulam praedictam)*).[85] This restriction also appears in MSS 6 and 9, without the bracketed clause, and in MS 2 it is attached to the rule that contradictories should not be granted, again without the bracketed clause.[86] This addendum could apply to the case in which " 'Man is an ass' is the *positum*" is posited, but it could also apply to the case of a disputation with a second *positum*.

---

et admissum quando non est pertinentia obligationis vel repugnantia positionis est concedendum." In §7 he explains "Pertinentia obligationis est quando obligatur quod aliqua propositio sit posita vel admissa vel obligata." *Obiectiones obligationum*, f. 21r "... omne mihi positum sub forma propositi propositum et sine obligatione ad hoc pertinenti non repugnans positi [*sic*] est a me concedendum. Sed in casu isto "homo est asinus" non est mihi positum sine obligatione ad hoc pertinenti, quia est tibi posita sub obligatione, scilicet cum ista particula 'est tibi positum'." *Obiectiones casuum*, sign. F 6r "... ista propositio 'homo est asinus', quamvis debet concedi quod sit posita et admissa, est tamen positum cum obligatione ad hoc pertinente, et ideo non oportet concedi per regulam." Angel d'Ors has argued that the restriction is completely redundant: d'Ors, 'Sobre las *Obligationes* de Richard Lavenham', 270.

84 For full discussion, see Ashworth, '"Tu curris" (vel "homo est asinus")'.

85 MS 7 f. 90r, p. 34.

86 MS 6, f. 121r; MS 9, f. 63r; MS 2, f. 49r. See above for the use made in an alternative solution to the sophisma "Tu non es" in MS 2, f. 49v.

Conclusion

One of the things shown by this study is that the series of manuscripts that offer versions of Billingham's *Obligationes* are very much working documents, whose variations seem to reflect the differing approaches of those who actually used the work. In this they are very different from the manuscripts of Strode's *Obligationes,* to choose but one possible example, for although there are variations among these manuscripts, they tend to reflect a slightly different choice of vocabulary or small expansions or contractions of Strode's original text rather than anything more significant.

Richard Kilvington and the Theory of Obligations

Stephen Read

We owe an immense debt to Angel d'Ors for his extensive and persistent research into identifying the real author of the famous *Tractatus*, for centuries (as he showed) wrongly attributed to Pope John XXI. I recall with pleasure the occasion in 1997 on which some of us visited the burial place of the true Peter of Spain, Lizarra (Estella), where the mayor dedicated a street (a very short street, but a whole street, nonetheless) to one of the foremost logicians of the Middle Ages. As Mark Twain might have said, scholars, that is, one scholar in particular, Angel, has shown that the logical works of Peter of Spain were not written by him but by another man, a Basque, with the same name.

Angel d'Ors also made significant contributions to our understanding and interpretation of medieval logic, in particular, to the debate over the validity of the spread law, *ex impossibili quodlibet*, and to the correct account of the development of the theory of obligations. The current paper tackles these two issues and benefits considerably from d'Ors' incisive reflections.

The distinctive contribution of medieval logic in the Latin West began in the 12th century in response to the rediscovery of the bulk of Aristotle's logical writings, hitherto known there largely through the rather elementary and simplistic writings of Boethius. Most stimulating seems to have been the circulation of Aristotle's treatise *De sophisticis elenchis*, and Book VIII of the *Topics*. The latter contains his discussion of disputation, arguably the inspiration for that most original and initially puzzling genre of medieval logical treatises, those on obligations. Supposition theory, appellation and insolubles all puzzled early scholars of medieval logic in the 19th and 20th centuries, but none so much as these disputations and dialogues between opponent and respondent with their positing, accepting, granting, denying, doubting and *casus* in the treatises on obligations.

One of the most original, exciting, and, as d'Ors showed, misleading proposals for the interpretation of the game of obligations was that put forward by Norman Kretzmann and developed by Paul Spade, that it should be understood as a logic of counterfactuals. Kretzmann and Spade seized on some remarks in Richard Kilvington's *Sophismata* to support their claim. As the title shows, Kilvington's *Sophismata* is not a treatise on obligations, but a collection of 48 sophisms, 44 being about logical problems in physics, the final four raising logical puzzles in the theory of knowledge. Richard Kilvington, along with Thomas Bradwardine, was one of the initiators of a movement which came in

 | DOI 10.1163/9789004324275_014

retrospect to be called the "Oxford Calculators." Its members signalled the first real advance over Aristotle in the theory of dynamics, to some extent anticipating the epoch-making insights of the 17th century. The connection with obligations is that in Kilvington's treatise, as in Bradwardine's *Insolubilia*, which preceded it by only a few years, we find a constant use of the terminology of logical obligations.[1] That the usage was so endemic and, as d'Ors argues,[2] found its way into inappropriate contexts supports the thesis that obligations were extensively used as logical exercises for pedagogical purposes.

But Kretzmann and Spade fasten on Kilvington's remarks on obligations in his treatment of Sophism 47 to argue for a different rationale for obligations, namely, "that the aim of obligational disputation was the same as the aim of counterfactual reasoning generally: to investigate conditions in a world that is different from the actual world in one respect (or in a few respects) but *otherwise as much like the actual world as possible*."[3] The sophism focuses on the proposition 'You know that the king is seated', attempts, as is common practice in sophismatic treatises, to argue both for and against the sophismatic sentence, and finally proposes a solution to dispel the apparent contradiction. The arguments, and the solution, however, employ the obligational language of granting, denying and doubting. There are several species of obligations, the primary one being *positio*. In every obligation, as already noted, there are two agents, the opponent and the respondent. The opponent starts by outlining a *casus*, or hypothesis, a background situation against which the obligation will take place, and in possible *positio*, puts forward a proposition, the *positum*, normally false both in the *casus* and in fact (if not, the *positio* will be less interesting and perhaps less challenging). The respondent should accept the *positum* if it nonetheless could be true in the *casus*, after which the opponent presents a succession of propositions (*proposita*), to each of which the respondent must reply either by granting it, or by denying it, or by doubting it, according to strict rules. These rules vary between different authors. The set of rules to which Kilvington takes exception seem to be those found in one of the most detailed of the obligational treatises which have survived, that due to Walter Burley, composed some twenty years before Kilvington was writing,

1 See, e.g., Mikko Yrjönsuuri (ed.), *Obligationes: 14th Century Logic of Disputational Duties* (Helsinki, 1994), 108.

2 Angel d'Ors, '*Tu scis regem sedere* (Kilvington, S47[48])', *Anuario filosófico* 24 (1991), 49-74: 66-7.

3 Norman and Barbara E. Kretzmann, *The Sophismata of Richard Kilvington: Introduction, Translation and Commentary* (Cambridge, 1990), 344. (All citations in English from Kilvington are from this translation.)

also in Oxford, and indeed just across the street from Kilvington's college of Oriel, at Merton College. According to Burley, one must first decide whether a particular *propositum* is relevant (*pertinens*) or not, that is, whether it either follows from, or is inconsistent with, the collection of propositions consisting of the *positum* together with any propositions previously granted and the contradictories of any previously denied. If it follows from them, it is said to be *pertinens sequens*, and should be granted, if inconsistent with them, it is said to be *pertinens repugnans*, and should be denied. Otherwise, it is irrelevant (*impertinens*), and should be granted if true according to the *casus*, denied if false according to the *casus*, and should be doubted if the *casus* leaves it indeterminate. A common example of the last sort, left indeterminate by the *casus*, is whether the king is seated or not. It is striking that Sophism 47 posits at the outset that you know whether the king is seated or not. But it does not specify which.

What results is a sequence of responses, granting, denying and doubting the *proposita*, and thereby a collection of propositions, those granted and the contradictories of those denied. The subtlety and complexity of the result stems from the fact that there are two separate criteria for inclusion in the set, one depending on the logical relation to previous responses, the other on what was laid down in the *casus*. Nonetheless, it is arguable that the respondent has a winning strategy: provided the *positum* is consistent with the *casus* (and if not, the respondent should not have accepted it), care by the respondent can ensure that the resulting set will also be consistent.[4] Thus if the respondent contradicts himself, that is, both grants and denies the same proposition, or grants something contradictory, he really has made an error, and he is rightly said by Burley's rules to have erred and to lose the game. The obligation ends either when this happens, or after a pre-agreed time, after which the respondent's performance is discussed and evaluated.

Sophism 47 starts with a *casus*, in this case, that if the king is seated, you know he is, and if he is not seated, you know that too. Then two examples of obligational dialogue are given—for the first, see Figure 1.

As Stump observes,[5] the obligation has a somewhat unusual form, since it is really a sophism rather than an obligation, in that there does not seem to be a *positum*, or perhaps the *positum* is arbitrary, as we will see shortly. Step 1 is

4 See, e.g., Catarina Dutilh Novaes, *Formalizing Medieval Logical Theories: suppositio, consequentiae and obligationes* (Dordrecht, 2007), 161.

5 Eleonore Stump, 'Obligations: From the Beginning to the Early Fourteenth Century', in *Cambridge History of Later Medieval Philosophy*, ed. N. Kretzmann, A. Kenny, and J. Pinborg (Cambridge, 1982), 315-34: 329. Cf. d'Ors, '*Tu scis regem sedere*', 59 n. 26.

0.	[arbitrary]	Accepted (the positum)
1.	Either the king is seated or he is not	Granted (law of excluded middle)
2.	You know that the king is seated or you know that the king is not seated	Granted (follows from 1. by the casus)
3.	You do not know that the king is not seated	Granted (irrelevant and true)
4.	You know that the king is seated	Granted (follows from 2. and 3.)

FIGURE 1 *Proof of the Sophism*

implicit, being a law of logic, and the actual reasoning starts at line 2, which follows logically from the *casus*. Line 3 is granted since what we noted is standard doctrine: that you do not know whether the king is seated or not, is not affected by the *casus*. The sophism (that is, the sophistic proposition) consequently follows by the rule nowadays known as Disjunctive Syllogism or as Modus Tollendo Ponens:

> The sophisma is proved in the following way. You know that the king is seated or you know that the king is not seated, but you do not know that the king is not seated; therefore, you know that the king is seated. The major is evident by the hypothesis, and the minor is evident because it is a true nonincompatible. That is evident, for these are not incompatible: 'If the king is seated, you know that the king is seated; and if the king is not seated, you know that the king is not seated' and 'You do not know that the king is not seated'.[6]

However, Kilvington proceeds to give a very similar obligation which disproves the sophism. See Figure 2.

Actually, this is not a disproof of the sophismatic proposition, so much as a proof of something incompatible with and contrary to it. As we said, you do not know that the king is seated nor do you know that the king is not seated, so both are false. But we can prove, it seems on the basis of the *casus*, both that

6 Trans. Kretzmann, 164; Richard Kilvington, *The Sophismata of Richard Kilvington*, ed. N. Kretzmann and B.E. Kretzmann (Oxford, 1990), 126: "Tunc probatur sophisma sic. Tu scis regem sedere vel tu scis regem non sedere, sed tu non scis regem non sedere; igitur tu scis regem sedere. Maior patet per casum, et minor patet quia est vera non repugnans. Quod patet, nam ista non repugnant: 'Si rex sedet, tu scis regem sedere; et si rex non sedet, tu scis regem non sedere' et 'Tu non scis regem non sedere'." (All citations in Latin from Kilvington are from this edition.)

0.	[arbitrary]	Accepted (the *positum*)
1.	Either the king is seated or he is not	Granted (law of excluded middle)
2.	You know that the king is seated or you know that the king is not seated	Granted (follows from 1. by the *casus*)
3′.	You do not know that the king is seated	Granted (irrelevant and true)
4′.	You know that the king is not seated	Granted (follows from 2. and 3′.)

FIGURE 2 *Disproof of the Sophism*

you know he is and that you know he is not. The problem is not that we have proved something false, but that we have proved two things which are incompatible. Which is right?—neither, as Kilvington will say (p. 132): you do not know either of them, so you should express doubt both about his being seated and about his not being seated.

What is notable about the whole sophism is that, as d'Ors noted,[7] what Kilvington observes is that the rules of obligation are not really appropriate to his task, which is to explore the counterfactual consequences of the *casus*, and that Kretzmann and Spade went astray in reading Kilvington's comments as revealing the purpose of obligations, possibly after Kilvington's revision, to be the articulation of counterfactual reasoning:

> [Kilvington] has assigned [the Art of Obligations] a distinct purpose and, in doing so, has changed the nature of it. It is for this reason, in my opinion, that it would be more correct to talk about not simply a reform of the Art of Obligations but the founding of a new Art, which could stand alongside it or perhaps replace it.[8]

Kilvington is not proposing to revise the rules of obligations. He is pointing out that we need to deal with irrelevant propositions differently from the way the obligational rules dictate—indeed, effectively, to treat those propositions as relevant after all. Rather than infer, as Kretzmann did in the passage cited above, "that the aim of obligational disputation was the same as the aim of counterfactual reasoning generally," we should infer from Kilvington's rejection

7 D'Ors, '*Tu scis regem sedere*', 72.

8 D'Ors, '*Tu scis regem sedere*', 72: "… le ha asignado un fin distinto, y, con ello, ha cambiado su naturaleza. Por esta razón, en mi opinión, habría que hablar, más que de una reforma del Arte de las Obligaciones, de la constitución de un nuevo Arte, que pudo convivir con aquel, o tal vez reemplazarle."

of the obligational rules as unfit for counterfactual reasoning that this was not their aim at all.

We will come to Kilvington's revision shortly. First, we should consider further the fact that the obligational reasoning given by Kilvington in the proof and disproof of the sophism seems to lack a *positum*. We should not think, as it seems some have done,[9] that the *positum* and *casus* are identical, or that *casus* and *positum* can play the same role. Better to think of the *positum* as arbitrary.

Another possibility, which d'Ors moots, is that Kilvington is here thinking in terms not of *positio* but of the species of obligation called *sit verum* (or *rei veritas*). Sara Uckelman makes a strong case that, at least in some obligations treatises, *sit verum* does model counterfactual reasoning.[10] In an early 13th-century treatise, *Obligationes Parisienses*,[11] irrelevant propositions in *sit verum* are evaluated as if what was supposed to be true were indeed true. Then Kilvington's hypothesis (that if the king is seated, you know that the king is seated, and if the king is not seated, you know that the king is not seated) would not be the *casus*, but the object of *sit verum*. This would connect closely with the fact that, in obligations treatises contemporary with Kilvington, *sit verum* is often described as specifying what the respondent knows, does not know or doubts.[12] However, the fact that Kilvington refers (as we will see shortly) to the "common doctrine" for irrelevant propositions as contrasting with such a rule indicates that he is not in fact thinking in these terms.

For it becomes clear as Kilvington's discussion of the sophism proceeds that his real target is a form of reasoning found in one of Burley's rules. Burley writes:

---

9 Stump, 'Obligations', 329; Kretzmann, *The Sophismata of Richard Kilvington: Introduction, Translation and Commentary*, 330. Cf. d'Ors, '*Tu scis regem sedere*', 65 n. 35.

10 D'Ors, '*Tu scis regem sedere*', 72; Sara L. Uckelman, '*Sit verum obligationes* and Counterfactual Reasoning', *Vivarium* 53 (2015), 90-113.

11 See L.M. de Rijk, 'Some Thirteenth Century Tracts on the Game of Obligation II', *Vivarium* 13 (1975), 22-54.

12 See, e.g., William of Ockham, *Summa Logicae* (*Opera Philosophica* I), ed. P. Boehner, G. Gál, and S. Brown (St. Bonaventure, NY, 1974), III-3, ch. 45; Walter Burley: "It is usually said that *sit verum* creates an obligation on a state of mind, and since states of mind are of three kinds, namely, the state of knowledge, of doubt and of ignorance, this obligation is of three kinds, either through a verb of knowing, or through a verb of doubting, or through a verb if ignorance. For example, 'Let it be true that you know you are running', or 'Let it be true that you doubt you are running'." See Romuald Green, *An Introduction to the Logical Treatise De Obligationibus, With Critical Texts of William of Sherwood [?] and Walter Burley*, Ph.D. dissertation (Katholieke Universiteit Leuven, 1963), vol. 2, 94-5.

> When a false contingent proposition is granted, one can prove any false proposition compatible with it.[13]

He gives two ways to construct an obligation to this end. The first is given in Figure 3. Kilvington complains:

0.	You are in Rome	Accepted (the unstated *casus* confirms that you are not in Rome)
1.	You are not in Rome or you are a bishop	Granted (irrelevant, but true because you are not in Rome)
2.	You are a bishop	Granted (follows from 0. and 1.)

FIGURE 3 *Proof of Burley's Rule*

> Thus I say—as regards a familiar example so that it may be understood more easily—that when 'You are in Rome' has been posited, it is not the case that anything false that is compossible with it can be proved, such as 'You are a bishop', and the like.[14]

Kilvington then proceeds to take Burley's second proof apart, which differs from the first in replacing the *propositum* at line 1 with " 'You are in Rome' and 'You are a bishop' are alike" (in truth-value, or perhaps modal status[15]). But as d'Ors emphasizes,[16] the reasoning in Kilvington's sophism is modelled on Burley's first proof.

If we replace the particular propositions in Burley's first proof with schematic variables, we can see that what we have here is an instance of a famous proof of *ex falso quodlibet*. For as Burley says, given any false (contingent)

13 Walter Burley, 'Obligations (Selections)', in N. Kretzmann and E. Stump, *Cambridge Translations of Medieval Philosophical Texts* vol. 1: *Logic and the Philosophy of Language* (Cambridge, 1988), 369-412, §3.61, 391: "Alia regula est ista: posito falso de contingenti, contingit probare quodlibet falsum sibi compossibile." Green, *An Introduction to the Logical Treatise De Obligationibus*, vol. 2, 57.

14 Trans. Kretzmann, 127; ed. Kretzmann, 130: "Unde dico—in communi exemplo, ut facilius intelligatur—quod posita ista 'Tu es Romae', non contingit probare aliquod falsum sibi compossibile, ut istam: 'Tu es episcopus', et similia."

15 See Kretzmann, *The Sophismata of Richard Kilvington: Introduction, Translation and Commentary*, 336.

16 D'Ors, '*Tu scis regem sedere*', 63.

proposition, we can prove any other (false) proposition—indeed, given any false proposition (or any pair of contradictory propositions—or indeed, any impossible proposition), we can prove any other proposition whatever. The proof was famously used by Lewis and Langford to rebut objections to strict negative paradox:[17]

> The one serious doubt [...] concerning the adequacy of Strict Implication to the problems of deduction in general arises from the fact that strict implication has its [own] paradoxes [...] 'If *p* is impossible, then *p* strictly implies any proposition *q*'; and [...] 'If *q* is necessary, then any proposition *p* strictly implies *q*'.

Their response to the first "paradox" is to deduce *q* from '*p* and not-*p*', arguing that any impossible proposition is equivalent to some such conjunction: assume '*p* and not-*p*' is true; then *p* is true, so '*p* or *q*' is true; and 'not-*p*' is also true; so *q* is true. That is, if *p* is false, then assuming *p*, we have '*p* or *q*' from the assumption, and 'not-*p*' by hypothesis, so *q*, by Disjunctive Syllogism.

Aristotle is often understood as claiming in *Prior Analytics* II.15 that only falsehoods can follow from contradictory, or even contrary, premises, at least syllogistically. Whether or not this is the right interpretation of that chapter, the above argument, and the claim that anything follows from contradictory or impossible premises, seems to have been an innovation made in the 12th century.[18] It is the basis of Burley's rule: suppose (the *casus*) that *p* is false. Posit *p*, then propose 'not-*p* or *q*'—granted (irrelevant and true). Then propose *q*—granted as *pertinens sequens*, following from *p* and 'not-*p* or *q*'. Thus *ad impossibile* (*p* and not-*p*) *sequitur quodlibet* (*q*).

Like Lewis and Langford, d'Ors thinks that negative strict paradox is a putative counterexample to the claim that an argument is valid if and only if it is impossible that things are as the premises signify and not as the conclusion signifies[19]—the account adopted by Buridan,[20] at least given Buridan's *caveat* that 'as ... signifies' must not be taken literally but must be spelled out in terms

17 C.I. Lewis and C.H. Langford, *Symbolic Logic* (New York, 1932), 248, response on 250.

18 See Christopher Martin, 'William's Machine', *Journal of Philosophy* 83 (1986), 564-72.

19 Angel d'Ors, '*Ex impossibili quodlibet sequitur* (John Buridan)', in *Argumentationstheorie. Scholastische Forschungen zu den logischen und semantischen Regeln korrekten Folgerns*, ed. K. Jacobi (Leiden, 1993), 195-212: 211.

20 *Iohannis Bvridani: Tractatvs de Conseqventiis* I, c. 3, ed. H. Hubien (Louvain, 1976).

of supposition.[21] But d'Ors finds the above argument, rehearsed by Buridan in conclusion 7 of Book I of his *Treatise on Consequences*, less convincing. Indeed, d'Ors claims that the argument is circular.[22] The problematic step is the claim that any impossibility is equivalent to, or at least entails, an explicit contradiction. Buridan gives the argument in conclusion 6: suppose p is impossible. Then p and 'not-p' entail the explicit contradiction 'p and not-p'. But if p is impossible, 'not-p' is necessary. If we can show that necessary truths can be suppressed, that is, that q follows from some premises X if q follows from X and r, whenever r is necessary, then it will follow that 'p and not-p' follows from p alone. But the proof of Suppression depends on *ex impossibili quodlibet* (and its converse, *necessarium sequitur a quolibet*): for either q follows from r alone, in which case q is necessary (since r is) and so q follows from anything (including X); or not, in which case either X is impossible, in which case anything follows from it (including q); or finally, X is possible, in which case either it is impossible to have X without q, in which case q follows from X, or not. But this last case, that it is possible for X to stand together with the necessary truth r without q, is ruled out by hypothesis. The argument is blatantly circular, and so the famous "Lewis proof" does not show that anything follows from an impossibility, and so does not defend the claim that a valid argument is one in which it is impossible for things to be as the premises signify without their also being as the conclusion signifies.

Lewis and Langford would be unmoved by this argument, for like many modern logicians, they identify necessary truths with tautologies and impossibility with the denial of tautology.[23] But Buridan, like other medieval logicians, did not have such a restricted conception of logic. For them, not all valid arguments were formally valid, and they included materially valid arguments as worthy of the logician's notice. Buridan's definition of validity in terms of preservation of how things signify (things are as the conclusion signifies whenever they are as the premises signify—with the *caveat* already mentioned) includes not only the formally valid ("holding in all terms" as he puts it: i.e., preserved under uniform substitution) but also the materially valid, that is, analytic and enthymematic consequence.[24] To support *ex impossibili* and *ex falso* inference in these cases, the Lewis argument is of no avail, as d'Ors observed.

21 See *Iohannis Bvridani: Tractatvs de Conseqventiis* I, c. 9, ed. Hubien; and Buridan, *Summulae de Practica Sophismatum* II, conc. 14, ed. F. Pironet (Turnhout, 2004).

22 D'Ors, '*Ex impossibili quodlibet sequitur* (John Buridan)', 210.

23 Lewis and Langford, *Symbolic Logic*, 248-9.

24 *Iohannis Bvridani: Tractatvs de Conseqventiis* I, c. 4, ed. Hubien.

But d'Ors takes further objection to the Lewis argument. I have explained elsewhere how the final step of Disjunctive Syllogism is valid (relevantly) in rule form but not in thesis form (as it is in classical and intuitionistic logic).[25] D'Ors finds this distinction in Domingo de Soto's *Summulae*;[26] he agrees that if both *p* and 'not-*p* or *q*' are asserted absolutely, that is, categorically, then *q* can be inferred and asserted categorically too; but if *p* and 'not-*p* or *q*' are asserted only on assumption (as they are if each is inferred from one conjunct of '*p* and not-*p*', dialetheism aside), then to infer *q* is no more valid than to infer, say, *q* from *p* by uniform substitution if *p* was only assumed, not proved (categorically). That is exactly the diagnosis and rebuttal of Lewis' argument found in relevance logic.[27]

In point of fact, one does not need to appeal to Lewis' (and Langford's) argument, even if it were legitimate to do so (as d'Ors has disproved), to support the inference of an arbitrary proposition from an impossibility. For example, Burley appeals to the topic 'from the less':[28]

> Anything follows from the impossible and the necessary from anything [...] For in both cases it is argued affirmatively through the topic 'from the less'. For it is less apparent that [...] 'A man is an ass' is true than that 'Socrates runs' is true. And if what is less apparent exists, what is more apparent will exist. Therefore, if a man is an ass, 'Socrates runs' follows. This holds through the topic 'from the less'.[29]

Burley observes, however, that this argument might not allow one to infer anything whatever from the impossible: "for from the less impossible the more impossible does not follow."[30] Thus he restricts himself to the claim that from

25 Stephen Read, 'Formal and Material Consequence, Disjunctive Syllogism and Gamma', in *Argumentationstheorie*, ed. Jacobi, 233-59: 253.

26 D'Ors, 'Las *Summulae* de Domingo de Soto: Los limites de la regla «Tollendo ponens»', *Anuario Filosofico* 16 (1983), 209-17.

27 See, e.g., Read, 'Formal and Material Consequence', 235-7.

28 Walter Burley, *On the Purity of the Art of Logic*, trans. P.V. Spade (Yale, 2000), 61-2.

29 Walter Burley, *De Puritate Artis Logicae*, ed. P. Boehner (St Bonaventure, NY, 1955), *Tractatus Brevior*, 248: "... ex impossibili sequitur quodlibet et necessarium sequitur ad quodlibet [...] nam utrobique arguitur per locum a minore affirmative. Nam minus videtur, quod [...] haec sit vera: 'Homo est asinus', quam quod illa sit vera: 'Sortes currit', et si illud, quod minus videtur, sit, et illud, quod magis videtur, erit'; igitur: Si homo est asinus, sequitur: Sortes currit, et hoc per locum a minore."

30 Walter Burley, *De Puritate Artis Logicae*, ed. Boehner, *Tractatus Brevior*, 248: "... quia ex minus impossibili non sequitur magis impossibile."

the impossible anything less impossible, in particular, anything contingent, follows.

Let us come back to Kilvington's 47th sophism and his objection to Burley's obligational rule *ex falso*: "when a false contingent proposition has been granted, one can prove any false proposition compatible with it." What Kilvington wants to propose is that there are cases, such as the sophism here, which should rather be doubted. To this end, he makes a salutary observation. It is clear that one often grants a false proposition in an obligational disputation—indeed, the subtlety of the game usually depends on the falsehood of the *positum*, at least according to the *casus*. Thus granting is different from truth and should not be confused with it. No more should denial be confused with falsehood: once again, one may be obliged to deny something one knows full well to be true. What Kilvington observes, and is much harder to grasp, is that doubting is different from being in doubt, that one may be obliged to express doubt about a *propositum* about which one is not in doubt at all. This is hard to see, since the obligational rules seem to require one to express doubt only about irrelevant propositions about which one does not know whether they are true or false—that are not specified by the *casus*, and those seem to be precisely the *proposita* about which one is in doubt. But this is to overlook the central point of Kilvington's sophism, observed by d'Ors, which is to reject Burley's rules for replying to irrelevant *proposita* as inappropriate for discussing counterfactuals: not by proposing a different theory of obligations, but by setting aside those rules and proposing that one must express doubt about a *propositum* which Burley's rules would force one to grant.

The crucial passage is this:

> In reply to the argument it must be granted that you know that the king is seated or you know that the king is not seated. But the assumed minor premise—viz., 'You do not know that the king is not seated'—must be doubted. For if the king is seated, you do not know that the king is not seated—by the hypothesis—and the antecedent must be doubted; therefore, the consequent must be doubted.[31]

If we granted the minor premise ('You do not know that the king is not seated'), the sophism ('You know the king is seated') would follow by Disjunctive

31 Trans. Kretzmann, 132; ed. Kretzmann, 135: "Ad argumentum concedendum est quod tu scis regem sedere vel tu scis regem non sedere. Sed minor coassumpta est dubitanda—scilicet, haec: 'Tu non scis regem non sedere'. Quia si rex sedet, tu non scis regem non sedere—per casum—et antecedens est dubitandum; igitur consequens est dubitandum."

Syllogism. But that is absurd, for we would then have shown that the king is seated simply from the *casus* (which does not specify whether the king is seated or not) and an instance of the law of excluded middle ('Either the king is seated or the king is not seated'), which is simply a law of logic and again does not specify which disjunct obtains. On the other hand, if we denied the minor premise, it would follow that you do know that the king is not seated, again determining whether he is seated. The only possibility is to express doubt about the *propositum*, even though you do know that you don't know that the king is not seated. Burley's rule for irrelevant truths (cited at line 3 of the proof of the sophism) must be rejected.

This rejection and revision is found a little earlier in Kilvington's discussion in the passage on which Kretzmann and Spade alight. Kilvington writes:

> And when it is argued, 'This is true and irrelevant; therefore, this must be granted', I reply that if one is speaking of what is irrelevant as that expression is commonly taken—for a proposition that neither follows from nor is incompatible with what has been posited or granted, and so on—this follows:[32] 'This proposition is true and irrelevant; therefore it must be granted'. But if the term 'irrelevant' is taken for a proposition that is true now and that would not be true in virtue of its being in fact as is signified by the positum, then I say that the proposition '[You are not in Rome or you are a bishop]' is relevant[33] to the positum—i.e., 'You are in Rome'. For if you were in Rome and you were not a bishop, this would have to be denied: '[You are not in Rome or you are a bishop]'.[34]

32 The Kretzmanns' translation here reads "this does not follow." But the standard rule for true irrelevant propositions is that they must be granted.

33 The Kretzmanns have "irrelevant" here. My emendation is supported by three manuscripts and again, I believe, makes better sense. Perhaps the confusion here between *pertinens* and *impertinens* explains why many commentators are unsure whether Kilvington is giving a different criterion for being relevant or a different rule for how to respond to irrelevant propositions. See, e.g., Eleonore Stump, 'Roger Swyneshed's Theory of Obligations', *Medioevo* 7 (1981), 135-74, reprinted in her *Dialectic and Its Place in the Development of Medieval Logic* (Cornell, 1989), 228-9; Yrjönsuuri, *Obligationes*, 121-2.

34 Trans. Kretzmann, 131; ed. Kretzmann, 134: "Et quando arguitur 'Ista est vera et impertinens; igitur ista est concedenda', ad illud dico quod loquendo de impertinenti ut communiter sumitur—pro propositione non sequenti vel repugnanti posito vel concesso, et ita de aliis—[non] sequitur 'Haec propositio est vera et impertinens; igitur est concedenda'. Si tamen accipiatur iste terminus 'impertinens' pro propositione quae nunc est vera et quae non foret vera ex hoc quod ita foret ex parte rei sicut significatur per positum, tunc dico quod ista propositio '[Tu non es Romae vel tu es episcopus]' est [im]pertinens huic

That is, the major premise is relevant to the *positum*, since its truth-value is affected by whether the *positum* is true, and would be false if the *positum* were true, i.e., if you were in Rome. Given that you are in Rome but not a bishop, it is false and should be denied.

Kilvington accordingly rejects the common way of treating irrelevant *proposita*: they should not be granted if they are true and denied if they are false, but should be granted if they would be true if the *positum* were true and likewise denied if they would be false. Thus the *positum* is relevant to their evaluation. Consequently, Sophism 47 should be doubted. For given the *casus*, that if the king is seated you know it and if he is not you know that too, and given that you do not know whether the king is seated (as is common in obligations), you do not know whether you know that the king is seated:

> But it must be doubted whether the king is seated or is not seated, and it must be doubted whether you know that the king is seated [...] And yet, although the proposition must be doubted by you, it must not be granted that the proposition 'The king is seated' is in doubt for you.[35]

To sum up: early training in the logical art of obligations led to the terminology and practice of granting, denying and doubting becoming endemic in logical treatises. But Kilvington realised that the way irrelevant propositions are treated in obligations can lead to unwarranted inconsistencies when employed outside their natural home. This becomes dramatically clear once the classic argument for *ex impossibili quodlibet*, discovered in the 12th century and made famous by Lewis and Langford in the 20th century, was used by Burley to establish an *ex falso* rule in obligations: admitting any false *positum* commits the respondent to granting any other falsehood compatible with it. However, rather than proposing simply to revise the rule for irrelevant propositions, Kilvington is best understood, as argued by Angel d'Ors, as proposing to set aside the common practice of obligations and to realise that in reason-

---

posito, quod est 'Tu es Romae'. Quia si tu esses Romae et non esses episcopus, haec foret neganda: '[Tu non es Romae vel tu es episcopus]'." As well as substituting Burley's first example for his second (which Kilvington cites here), I have also emended the Latin text following the apparatus given by the Kretzmanns, as in the English translation in the text.

35 Trans. Kretzmann, 131; ed. Kretzmann, 135: "Sed dubitandum est utrum rex sedet vel non sedet, et ideo dubitandum est an tu scis regem sedere [...]. Et tamen, licet ista propositio sit dubitanda a te, non tamen est concedendum quod ista proposito 'Rex sedet' est tibi dubia."

ing about counterfactual situations one cannot separate relevant propositions from irrelevant ones in the usual way. For seemingly 'irrelevant' propositions would take a different truth-value if things were as signified by the *positum*. Consequently, far from obligations having the aim of modelling counterfactual reasoning, as suggested by Kretzmann and Spade, they are inconsistent with that aim and unsuitable for its prosecution.

The Signification of the Copula in Fernando de Enzinas' *Syncategoremata*

Paloma Pérez-Ilzarbe

1 Fernando de Enzinas and His *Tractatus de compositione propositionis mentalis*

Fernando de Enzinas († 1523) was one of the brilliant Spanish logicians who studied and taught at the University of Paris when the Nominalist development of terminism was flourishing at the begining of the 16th century.[1] He lectured as a master of arts at the colleges of Sainte-Barbe and Beauvais, but shortly before his death he moved to Alcalá to teach *summulae*. He became very popular in Spanish universities, and his works were enthusiastically studied in Alcalá and Salamanca.[2]

This research is based on the *Tractatus de compositione propositionis mentalis*, of which Angel d'Ors had prepared a transcription.[3] Angel was able to identify four editions of this text, two of 1526 and two of 1528. An edition of 1521 is also cited by scholars, which some library catalogues list with the title *Tractatus de actibus sincathegoreumaticis siue de compositione propositionis mentalis*. I reproduce below Angel's notes about the editions he had located:

> a) Petrus Gromors and Iohannes Parvus, Paris, 1526. One copy located at the Monastery of Santa María de la Vid (Burgos):

1 E.J. Ashworth, *Language and Logic in the Post-Medieval Period* (Dordrecht, 1974); Alexander Broadie, *The Circle of John Mair. Logic and Logicians in Pre-Reformation Scotland* (Oxford, 1985).

2 Vicente Muñoz Delgado, 'La lógica en la Universidad de Alcalá durante la primera mitad del siglo XVI', *Salmanticensis* 15 (1968), 161-218: 177-84; 'Fernando de Enzinas (†1523) eminente lógico vallisoletano', in *Homenaje a Alfonso Candau* (Valladolid, 1988), 271-87.

3 Muñoz Delgado offers a description of the contents in 'La lógica en la Universidad de Alcalá'. Ashworth and Perler have also paid attention to this text, emphasising its interest and originality. See, for example, E.J. Ashworth, 'Mental Language and the Unity of Propositions: A Semantic Problem Discussed by Early Sixteenth Century Logicians', *Franciscan Studies* 41 (1981), 61-96; Dominik Perler, 'Diskussionen über mentale Sprache im 16. Jahrhundert', in *'Res et verba' in der Renaissance*, ed. E. Kessler and I. Maclean (Wiesbaden, 2002), 29-51.

 | DOI 10.1163/9789004324275_015

Ai(r): Ferdinandi de Enzinas / Tractatus de compositione propositionis mentalis, actu-/-um sincathegoreumaticorum naturam manifestans, et / ad noticias introductorius, a magistro Roberto Uvan-/-cop scoto recognitus, atque in suam integritatem restitu-/-tus, [P. Gromors emblem] Venundantur Parrisiis apud Petrum / Gromorsum et Ioannem Parvum.

Explicit: xxx(vb): Explicit liber de compositione propositionis mentalis, sive de actibus sincathegoreuma-/-ticis Ferdinandi de enzinas, vallis oletanei, Parri-/-siis anno domini M.D.XXVI.

b) Tractatus de compositione mentalis ... et ad noticias introductorias a Roberto V.... Ferdinandi de Enzinas, Venundantur Parrisiis, apud Petrum Gaudoul, 1526. One copy located at the Cathedral of Oviedo.

c) Tractatus de compositione propositionis mentalis actuum syncategorematicorum naturam manifestans et ad notitias introductorias a magistro Roberto Uvancop noviter recognitus atque in suam integritatem restitutus, Paris, Pedro Gaudoul, 1528 (30 fols. in 4º) (Tractatus de verbo mentis et Syncategorematicis?)

d) Antonius du Ry, Lyon, 1528. Copies located in Granada and León:

Title page: Ferdinandi de Enzi-/-nas Tractatus de compositione propositionis men-/-talis: actuum sincathegoreumaticorum naturam / manifestans: et ad notitias introductorius: a magistro / Roberto Uvancop scoto noviter recognitus: atque / in suam integritatem restitutus. / 1528.

Colophon: Explicit liber de compositione propositionis men-/-talis: sive de actibus sincathegoreumaticis Fer-/-dinandi de enzinas: vallis oletanei: Lugduni / impressus per Antonium du Ry / anno domini.M.D.xxviii. / Penultima die men-/-sis Maii.

The *Tractatus de compositione propositionis mentalis* is intended to be a discussion about syncategorematic mental acts, although this is preceded by the study of the related question as to whether or not a mental proposition is composed of parts (hence the title of the treatise).[4] After Ockham, the issue of

4 This question was widely discussed in the post-medieval period. See Ashworth, *Language and Logic in the Post-Medieval Period*, 51-2, and 'Mental Language and the Unity of Propositions';

the existence and nature of mental syncategorems was a big one,[5] and this is echoed in Enzinas' pages. In his investigation into the nature and signification of mental syncategorems, he touches on a number of important logical themes. Among many other points, Enzinas produces a brief but interesting discussion on the signification of the copula, or rather, of the copulae: 'est' and 'fuit' (ff. 11va-12rb of the Lyon edition).[6]

Concerning syncategorems in general, Enzinas holds the common opinion, according to which syncategorematic terms signify no thing or things (*aliquid vel aliqua*), although they signify in some way (*aliqualiter*).[7] The analysis of the signification of the copula, although intended to substantiate this thesis, does much more than merely present another example of a syncategorem and its signifying *aliqualiter*. The most interesting aspect of these few paragraphs is that they raise important questions about the complex relations between propositions and time, which are crucial to understand the nature and logical properties of propositions. This is an interesting development of terminist logic: although the effect of tense in the supposition of terms is widely studied, the signification of time by the copula is usually taken for granted, so Enzinas' study of this topic represents an enrichment of the theory of the properties of terms. This development is closely linked to the interest in mental language and mental syncategorems.

Enzinas' results can be summarised in the following three theses: a) the copula has its own syncategorematic signification, independent of the signification of subject and predicate; b) the copula has a twofold signification: first it signifies in a 'unitive way', but *in addition* it imports time; c) what distinguishes

---

Gabriel Nuchelmans, *Late-Scholastic and Humanist Theories of the Proposition* (Amsterdam-Oxford-New York, 1980), 94-102.

5 Aurélien Robert, 'Les Deux Langages de la Pensée: A Propos de Quelques Réflexions Médiévales', in *Le Langage mental du Moyen Âge à l'Âge classique*, ed. J. Biard (Louvain-Paris, 2009), 145-68: 157-61; Gino Roncaglia, 'Mesino de Codronchi's Discussion on *Syncategoremata* and Mental Language in his *Quaestiones* on *De interpretatione*', in *Aristotle's Peri hermeneias in the Latin Middle Ages. Essays on the Commentary Tradition*, ed. H.A.G. Braakhuis and C.H. Kneepkens (Groningen-Haren, 2003), 149-63.

6 A digital copy of the book is available at the Biblioteca Virtual Miguel de Cervantes.

7 See Nuchelmans, *Late-Scholastic and Humanist Theories of the Proposition*, 28-31; E.J. Ashworth, 'The Structure of Mental Language: Some Problems Discussed by Early Sixteenth Century Logicians', *Vivarium* 20 (1982), 59-83. For an overview of the distinction *categorema/syncategorema* and the semantics of syncategorems, see the entry 'Syncategoremata' by Gyula Klima in *Encyclopedia of Language and Linguistics, Second Edition*, ed. K. Brown (Oxford, 2006) 12: 353-6. For in-depth studies, issue 25/2 (2003) of *Histoire Épistémologie Langage*, edited by Irène Rosier-Catach, is entirely devoted to syncategorems.

one copula from the other ('est', 'fuit') is also syncategorematic in character (it is also an *aliqualiter*).

As we shall see, these theses are linked to Enzinas' views about mental language: a) the mental copula is an act of combining subject and predicate; b) the mental copula is, by its nature, intrinsically tensed; c) the different copulae are different kinds of mental acts that are characterised by different modes of signifying.

2 Mental Propositions and Their Parts: The Syncategorematic Signification of the Copula

In the pages I am focusing on, Enzinas makes several steps in order to determine more and more accurately the signification of the copula. In the first stage, the signification of the copula is merely separated from the signification of the categorematic terms to which it is attached. This first approach to the copula is just intended to combat the opinion that the significations of subject and predicate are somehow absorbed by the syncategorematic signification of the copula that joins them.[8]

This discussion about signification is placed at the level of mental language: Enzinas explores the intellective acts that are involved in the signification of mental propositions.[9] He examines an argument for the thesis that the copula 'est', as well as signifying *aliqualiter*, also signifies the things signified by the categorematic terms that accompany it.[10] He reproduces an argument that takes as an example a proposition with 'est' used predicatively (*de tertio adiacente*) and apparently manages to prove that in 'homo est asinus' the copula 'est' signifies men and donkeys.

The argument is derived (explicitly) from a relational conception of the signification of propositions and (implicitly) from the notion of *significare* as

8 This is, for example, Hieronymus Pardo's opinion. See Nuchelmans, *Late-Scholastic and Humanist Theories of the Proposition*, 37-8.

9 See Enzinas' intellectual context on this issue in Ashworth, 'Mental Language and the Unity of Propositions' and 'The Structure of Mental Language'; Claude Panaccio, *Le discours intérieur. De Platon à Guillaume d'Ockham* (Paris, 1991), 291-301.

10 Fernando de Enzinas, *Tractatus de compositione propositionis mentalis* (Lyon, 1578), f. 11va: "Aliquod sincathegoreuma significat aliquid; et non est maior ratio de uno quam de alio; ergo quodlibet. Antecedens probatur: hec copula 'est' quando est de tertio adiacente significat quicquid importatur per extrema; ergo etc."

representing to a cognitive power (in this case, to the intellect).[11] On the one hand, the signification of the propositional copula in 'homo est asinus' is explicated in a relational way: the copula 'est' unitively signifies men with respect to donkeys.[12] On the other, a leap is made from the linguistic to the intellectual level: from 'significare compositive' to 'intelligere'.[13] The relational signification implies a relational understanding, and therefore the requirements for the intellect to have this kind of 'with respect to …' understanding are examined: for the intellect to understand some things as unitively related to some others it is necessary that the intellect understand not only the 'respect to', but also the related things. This is why in the case proposed it would be required that men and donkeys be signified by the propositional copula.[14] This is, of course, connected to a certain position about the structure of the proposition: a mental proposition is considered to be a non-composite mental act.[15]

---

11 See E.J. Ashworth, 'Jacobus Naveros (fl. ca. 1533) on the Question: Do Spoken Words Signifiy Concepts or Things?', in *Logos and Pragma*, ed. L.M. de Rijk and H.A.G. Braakhuis (Nijmegen, 1987), 189-214; Paul J.J.M. Bakker, 'Syncatégorèmes, concepts, équivocité. Deux questions anonymes, conservées dans le ms. Paris, B.N., lat. 16.401, liées à la sémantique de Pierre d'Ailly (c. 1350-1420)', *Vivarium* 34 (1996), 76-131; Joël Biard, 'Pierre d'Ailly: Langage, Concept, Représentation', in *Le Langage mental du Moyen Âge à l'Âge classique*, ed. Biard, 169-83; Stephan Meier-Oeser, 'Medieval Semiotics', *The Stanford Encyclopedia of Philosophy* (Summer 2011 Edition), E.N. Zalta (ed.), URL = <http://plato.stanford.edu/archives/sum2011/entries/semiotics-medieval/>.

12 Enzinas, *Tractatus*, f. 11va: "Probatur antecedens: capta hac propositione: 'homo est asinus', illa copula 'est' significat compositive vel unitive homines respectu asinorum."

13 Biard places in Peter of Ailly the point of departure of a tendency to assimilate language and knowledge via the notion of representation: Biard, 'Pierre d'Ailly: langage, concept, représentation'.

14 Enzinas, *Tractatus*, f. 11va: "Sed impossibile est intellectum intelligere homines respectu asinorum quin etiam intelligat homines et asinos; ergo illa copula 'est' significat homines et asinos."

15 Enzinas has in mind the theory of mental propositions of Hieronymus Pardo, with whom Enzinas shows his disagreement throughout the *Tractatus*, especially in the first pages, where he refutes his main theses. On Pardo's theory, see Paloma Pérez-Ilzarbe, 'Jerónimo Pardo on the Unity of Mental Propositions', in *Le Langage mental du Moyen Âge à l'Âge classique*, ed. Biard, 185-204, as well as Ashworth, 'Mental Language and the Unity of Propositions' and 'The Structure of Mental Language'; Nuchelmans, *Late-Scholastic and Humanist Theories of the Proposition*. Friedman traces back this 'one act' theory to Durand of St. Pourçain: Russell L. Friedman, 'Mental Propositions before Mental Language', in *Le Langage mental du Moyen Âge à l'Âge classique*, ed. Biard, 95-115.

In response to this argument, Enzinas deploys his conception of mental propositions as composed of several intellective acts.[16] He agrees with the objector in attributing that kind of relational signification to propositions, and hence he admits that when the copula connects subject and predicate in the proposition 'homo est asinus' the intellect understands men and donkeys in a new, relational, way.[17] But he disagrees with respect to the elements that are involved in this relational understanding.

Enzinas, who takes the mental proposition to be composed of parts, assigns to each of the intellective acts a distinctive element of the propositional signification. So, instead of assigning to the copula the signification of both the things related (for example, men and donkey) and of the way of being related (for example, *unitive*), Enzinas separately assigns to the categorematic intellective acts the signification of the things related and to the syncategorematic intellective act the signification of the way of being related.[18] He concludes thus that the copula signifies no thing, but it just signifies in a way. As usual, Aristotle's authority is invoked to confirm this (*Peri hermeneias*, 16b24-25).[19] But in addition, Enzinas highlights the syncategorematic signification of the copula by telling us that it is incorrect to interpret Aristotle as saying that the copula signifies a composition:[20] it rather signifies in a 'suitable for uniting' way (*unitive seu compositive*).[21]

16 On the history of this 'compositional' theory of mental propositions, see Alfonso Maierù, 'Mental Language and Italian Scholasticism in the Fourteenth and Fifteenth Centuries', in *John Buridan and Beyond. Topics in the Language Sciences*, ed. R.L. Friedman and S. Ebbesen (Copenhagen, 2004), 33-67; Stephan Meier-Oeser, 'Mental Language and Mental Representation in Late Scholastic Logic', ibid., 237-65; Friedman, 'Mental Propositions before Mental Language'.

17 Enzinas, *Tractatus*, f. 11va: "Ad hanc replicam respondeo quod intellectus, adveniente hac copula 'est', intelligit unitive homines in ordine ad asinos qualiter antea non intelligebat..."

18 Enzinas, *Tractatus*, f. 11va: "... sed hoc non est per copulam, sed intelligit solum homines et asinos per notitias quas habet hominum et asinorum, et intelligit unitive per copulam."

19 Enzinas, *Tractatus*, f. 11va: "Et hoc est quod Aristoteles voluit quando dixit: ly 'est', si purum dixeris, nihil significat, sed significat quandam compositionem quam sine extremis non est intelligere; id est, ly 'est' solitarie positum nihil significat, sed significat quandam compositionem, id est, compositiv[o]⟨e⟩ in ordine ad aliqua que sine extremis non potest intelligi."

20 This issue can be traced back to a dispute between Chatton and Wodeham, in the first half of the 14th century: see Gino Roncaglia, *Palestra Rationis: Discussioni su natura della copula e modalità nella filosofia 'Scolastica' tedesca del XVII secolo* (Florence, 1996), 106.

21 Enzinas, *Tractatus*, f. 11va: "Ex quo patet hanc propositionem: ly 'est' significat compositionem seu unionem esse de rigore falsam, nisi capiatur loco huius: ly 'est' significat unitive seu compositive."

So far, Enzinas has settled a first position on the signification of the copula, by stressing its syncategorematic character and understanding this character in accordance with the standard opinion of the terminist tradition. But a mere distinction from the categorematic signification of the extremes does not suffice to fully characterise the signification of the copula. Terminist logic has inherited (via the *logica antiquorum*) the Aristotelian conception of the basic elements that constitute a proposition: noun and verb. The copula, which inside the terminist tradition is classed as a syncategorem, in Aristotelian terms can be also classed as a verb, which forces us to further qualify the signification of the copula.

3 The Copula as a Verb: Does the Copula Signify Time?

Enzinas examines the first implications of the verbal character of the copula by considering a second objection against the common opinion about syncategorems: if, according to Aristotle, a verb is that which consignifies time, it seems to follow that the copula 'est' in 'homo est asinus' in fact signifies something, namely, the present time.[22]

From this point on, Enzinas inquires more thoroughly into the signification of the copula, with the aim of clarifying whether and in what sense it can be said that the different forms of the copula signify time (*qualiter copulae significent tempus*). His analyses are progressively deeper: he starts by considering the copula as a verb, and he combines the Aristotelian idea of 'consignificare tempus' with the terminist idea of a 'respect to time' in the signification of the copula; second, he analyses the structure of mental propositions, trying to identify the element in a mental proposition that could effect the signification of time; finally, he engages in an onto-semantic investigation of the relation proposition-time, which will result in the finding of a specific signification for each of the copulae.

Concerning the copula as a verb, Enzinas explains the traditional answer given by the defenders of the common opinion about syncategorems: they translate the Aristotelian idea of 'consignificare tempus' into the terminist language about the syncategorematic signification of the copula. To say that the copula consignifies a time is just to say that the copula makes its syncategorematic union *with respect to* the present, the past, or the future.

---

22 Enzinas, *Tractatus*, f. 11vb: "Sed contra hoc arguitur: Ly 'est' in propositione assumpta significat tempus; ergo significat aliquid. Antecedens probatur per Aristotelem dicentem 'verbum est quod consignificat tempus' etc."

For the orthodox defenders of the common opinion, time is not an *aliquid* that is signified by the copula, but it is something *with respect to which* the signification of the copula is exerted (*significare... ad aliquam differentiam temporis*). If, for example, in an affirmative proposition, the copula is denoting that the predicate applies to the subject, the consignification of time just adds that this is denoted *with respect to* the present, the past, or the future.[23]

At this level of analysis (a merely linguistic explication of the phrase 'consignificare tempus'), time would seem to be something external to the signification of the copula. But again signification requires an analysis of the mental language, where a deeper sense of 'consignificare tempus' appears. Enzinas does not stop at the formula 'significat unitive in ordine ad aliquam differentiam temporis', but he tries to discover what exactly this *respect to time* amounts to. He engages in a semantic-epistemic inquiry, asking what happens on the side of the intellect when the copula exerts its syncategorematic function with respect to time.

He inspects an opinion that states that if we admit that the copula 'est' makes the syncategorematic union with respect to one or other difference of time, then we have to admit that the intellect somehow understands (*intelligit*) the present, the past, or the future. For example, in the case of the proposition 'homo est asinus', for the present-tensed copula 'est' to signify with respect to the present, the intellect must understand the present time.[24]

The proof of this statement is similar to the argument examined previously intended to prove that the copula signifies the things signified by the categorematic terms: it goes from *significare* to *intelligere*. Enzinas had replied to that argument by showing that the mental proposition contains other parts, different from the copula, which are apt to signify these things. To this argument Enzinas replies by investigating whether or not there are other parts in the mental proposition that could be apt for signifying the present time.

---

23 Enzinas, *Tractatus*, f. 11vb: "Ad hanc replicam respondent omnes communes: ly 'est' non significat tempus; et dicunt quod consignificare tempus nihil aliud est quam significare unitive ad aliquam differentiam temporis, id est, denotare predicatum competere subiecto pro aliqua differentia temporis (nec hinc sequitur verbum significare tempus)."

24 Enzinas, *Tractatus*, f. 11vb: "Contra hoc arguitur: Ly 'est' significat tempus; ergo etc. Probatur: bene sequitur: ly 'est' significat unitive in ordine ad aliquam differentiam temporis in hac propositione: 'homo est asinus', ergo intellectus intelligit aliquam differentiam temporis..."

4 The Elements of a Mental Proposition: Which of the Parts Can Signify Time?

According to the standard opinion about the composition of a mental proposition, there are three parts (though only two cognitions) implied in the mental proposition 'homo est asinus': a cognition (*notitia*) of men that corresponds to the subject 'homo', a cognition of donkeys that corresponds to the predicate 'asinus', and a syncategorematic act (an intellective *actus* that is not a cognition) that makes the predicative union.[25]

But the focus on time forces the logician to revise this straightforward structure. There are two ways of complicating the picture: a) one can make the signification of the copula more complex, b) or one can make the structure of the mental proposition more complex.

a) A complex signification for the copula. According to the more traditional approach, it seems obvious that none of the cognitions can make the intellect understand the present time. This seems to imply that the remaining intellective act, the one corresponding to the copula 'est', is that by which the intellect understands the present, and as a consequence, that the 'est' in some sense signifies the present.[26] In sum, the mental copula 'est', on the one hand, makes the predicative union, but, on the other, this syncategorematic act somehow signifies the present. This traditional way thus proposes a double signification for the copula, in virtue of which the copula would not be a pure syncategorem. This is the opinon on which the mentioned argument is based.

b) A more complex structure for mental propositions. Some defenders of the common opinion about syncategorems, unwilling to admit this double signification for the copula, maintained a curious thesis about the mental proposition to which the vocal proposition is subordinated. They propose four basic parts for the mental proposition. The elements of the corresponding mental proposition are not only the cognition corresponding to the subject, the cognition corresponding to the predicate, and the syncategorematic act corresponding to the copula, but a fourth element is added that makes the link to the

25 Nuchelmans, *Late-Scholastic and Humanist Theories of the Proposition*, 36-7. On the 14th-century discussion whether mental syncategorems are 'concepts' or 'acts', see, for example, Roncaglia, 'Mesino de Codronchi's Discussion on *Syncategoremata* and Mental Language'; Bakker, 'Syncatégorèmes, concepts, équivocité'.

26 Enzinas, *Tractatus*, f. 11vb: "... sed non intelligit aliquam differentiam temporis per ly 'homo', nec per notitiam asinorum; ergo intelligit per illum actum 'est'; quare sequitur quod ly 'est' significat tempus."

adequate difference of time: for example, '*in tempore presenti* homo *est* asinus'.[27] The twofold signification that the first opinion associated with the copula is in this second opinion split into two elements: the mental copula takes only the *significare unitive*, and the connotation of time is made by a different mental act. The mental proposition would contain then, besides the categorematic cognitions corresponding to subject and predicate, an atemporal syncategorematic cognition that makes the predicative union (the mental copula 'est') and a temporal modifier that indicates the difference of time with respect to which the predicative union is effected (the 'in tempore presenti' modifier).

This way of analysing mental propositions saves the purely syncategorematic character of the copula, but it has consequences concerning its signification. On the one hand, an atemporal mental copula would after all fail to meet the Aristotelian definition of a verb as something that consignifies time.[28] On the other, a serious problem is that an atemporal copula would lack a specific signification and would fail to be distinguished from other syncategorematic unitive acts (for example, a conjunction).[29]

Enzinas is not willing to pay such a price, so he prefers to keep the three-part analysis of mental propositions, and thus he has to admit that the copula 'est' in a sense signifies the present time.[30] But he warns the reader that this does not convert the copula into a categorematic term. Although the copula signifies something (it signifies time), it also signifies *aliqualiter* (it signifies in a unitive way). The copula has therefore a mixed signification, partly syncategorematic and partly categorematic (*unitive significare* + *importare tempus*). The order of the elements in this twofold signification is important: first the copula has a syncategorematic signification, and second it also brings in time.[31] This is the reason why Enzinas can say that the copula, unlike connotative terms, does not have a principal significate (*principale significatum*) to which

27 Enzinas, *Tractatus*, f. 11vb: "Propter hoc nonnulli dixerunt hanc propositionem: 'homo est asinus', subordinari huic: 'in tempori presenti homo est asinus'."

28 Enzinas, *Tractatus*, f. 11vb: "Sed hoc a multis est impugnatum, tum quia illa copula 'est' non consignificaret in propositione illa mentali 'homo in tempore presenti est asinus' tempus aliquo modo (quod tamen oportet ex diffinitione verbi)."

29 Enzinas, *Tractatus*, f. 11vb: "Tum etiam quia significatio de ly 'est' non differret a significatione illius coniunctionis etc."

30 Enzinas, *Tractatus*, f. 11vb: "Quare respondeo absolute ly 'est' significare tempus propter rationem tactam."

31 Enzinas, *Tractatus*, f. 11vb: "Nec propterea sequitur ly 'est' esse purum cathegoreuma, quia etiam aliqualiter significat (videlicet unitive). Unde significatio totalis de ly 'est' non est nisi significare unitive in ordine ad subiectum et predicatum, et ultra suum aliqualiter sive unitive significare importare tempus."

the consignification of time is added: the principal signification is syncategorematic and hence there is no significate on this side.[32] This simply means that 'consignificare' is here taken in an improper sense.

So far only the present-tensed copula 'est' has been mentioned, and its signification has been explained in a general way, making only reference to some (unspecified) 'difference of time'. To obtain a deeper understanding of the signification of the copula Enzinas has to go into the signification of the different copulae: 'est' and 'fuit'.[33]

5 'Est' versus 'Fuit': Which Time Is Signified by Each of the Copulae?

In principle, it seems natural to answer that the present-tensed copula signifies the present and the past-tensed copula signifies the past. But this simple answer becomes puzzling when one realises, first, that time passes (the present becomes past, and the future becomes present, and then also past), and second, that propositions are themselves temporal entities (in the sense that they are formed at a time and they can have a duration), so not only their own existence but also their having a signification occurs at a time, and thus they are affected by the passage of time. In this context it makes sense to ask 'which present' is signified by the present-tensed copula of a given proposition.

An extra complication might arise from the twofold way of considering time, either as an extended duration (*tempus*) or as a point-like instant (*instans*). Enzinas remains neutral in principle about whether the time signified by the copula is a span of time or an instant, but in general he chooses to speak about instants for the sake of simplicity. In any case, his approach to the signification of time is extensional, in the sense that he is considering a set of instants/spans that might be signified, and he asks which particular instants/spans in this set are in fact signified by each of the copulae.

32 Enzinas, *Tractatus*, ff. 11vb-12ra: "Et si arguas contra hoc: Sequitur quod est connotativus, postquam ultra suam principalem significationem importat seu dat intelligere aliquid, ad hoc nego consequentiam, quia ad aliquid esse terminum connotativum requiritur, ultra principale significatum (id est, materiale), aliquid aliud vel aliqualiter det intelligere; modo ly 'est' non habet principale significatum. Sed questio est de nomine utrum ly 'est' sit connotativum necne, sed postquam non est terminus cathegoreumaticus dicendum est quod nec est connotativus nec absolutus."

33 Enzinas does not mention in this context the future-tensed copula 'erit'. I am inclined to think that his analysis cannot be transposed to the third difference of time: given the extensionalist character of Enzinas' semantics, the metaphysical asymmetry between past and future might be an obstacle to such a transposition.

5.1 *The Copula 'Est' Signifies This Present Instant*

In his analysis of this question, Enzinas first presents a dilemma between two possibilities: either the copula signifies only the present instant or it signifies any instant.[34] He starts by considering the seemingly natural view that the present-tensed copula 'est' signifies only the present instant. The adoption of a tensed perspective in the analysis of propositions has significant effects at the level of truth values. Enzinas explores the implications that this option could have in this respect.

When the duration of propositions is taken into account, we can ask about the instant at which a proposition is true: the whole set of instants at which the proposition exists can be taken as points of reference. The standard answer is that a proposition is only true for the instant that is imported by the copula 'est'. But, according to this first opinion on the signification of the copula, the instant imported by the copula 'est' is just *hoc presens*. This implies that when this instant passes by, the proposition cannot be true anymore.

Enzinas does not make explicit the kind of truth conditions that are being used in the objections he reports, but we can suppose that some kind of 'significatur qualiter est' is being put into play. Of course, this simple formula gets complicated when time is taken into account.

The first complication arises when time is taken into account as part of the signification of propositions: an explication of the truth conditions of the proposition must then include the instant that is signified by the copula. For example, the proposition 'Deus est' is taken to signify 'Deus *in hoc instanti* est'.[35] Therefore, for the proposition 'Deus est' to be true it will be required that God exist *at this instant*.

But the second complication arises when the proposition is considered as a temporal entity, and the passage of time is taken into account. Let us assume, for example, that the proposition 'Deus est' is formed at instant A, but then a second instant B arrives (that is, instant A becomes past and instant B is now present) and the proposition keeps existing at B. We can now ask about the truth value of the proposition not only at A but also at B. Therefore, in order to determine the truth value both at A and at B, we will have to take into account the signification of the proposition both at A and at B.

The opinion reported by Enzinas takes for granted that the time signified by the present-tensed copula is the time that is present *when the proposition*

34 Enzinas, *Tractatus*, f. 12ra: "Sed contra hoc arguitur: Si hec copula 'est' importaret tempus vel instans, vel solum hoc presens significat vel quodlibet."

35 In some of Enzinas' examples the 'est' occurs as second adjacent: this does not make any significant difference to his arguments.

is formed: to signify 'Deus *in hoc instanti* est' would then be to signify 'Deus *in A instanti* est'. If the time signified by the copula is the time that is present when the proposition is formed, when a new instant B arrives, the proposition (formed at A) will still signify 'Deus *in A instanti* est'. But if the signification does not change with the passage of time, then the proposition 'Deus est' would be false at B, since the truth condition that was the case at A is not the case at B anymore.

This consequence is not a mere curiosity about the fact that the truth value of a proposition changes with time. It is of great importance for Enzinas, since this means that no proposition can be necessary (in the sense of true at any time), not even 'Deus est'.[36] If the copula 'est' only signifies the present instant, the truth value could never remain the same through the passage of time.[37]

5.2 *The Copula 'Est' Signifies Any Instant Which Happens to Be Present*

A possible way to defend the prima facie natural position that the present-tensed copula signifies the present, without encountering this undesired outcome, is to avoid the mismatch between the time signified by the proposition (instant A) and the posterior time at which its truth value is considered (instant B). At this point Enzinas reports an intermediate opinion that still maintains that the copula signifies the present but abandons the assumption that the time signified by the present-tensed copula is the time that is present *when the proposition is formed*: instead, the natural thing for the copula is to effect the syncategorematic union with respect to the instant that is present *whenever the copula exists*. The duration of the proposition has then an immediate effect on the signification of the copula: according to this opinion, when the proposition exists at instant A, the copula signifies this single instant A, but when the proposition exists at instant B, the signification of the copula is somehow extended, so that it *also* signifies instant B.[38] The copula comes thus to progressively signify the whole set of instants that happen to be present during the existence of the proposition.

---

36 Enzinas, *Tractatus*, f. 12ra: "Si primum, sequitur quod nulla propositio est necessaria, nam si aliqua esset, maxime esset hec: 'Deus est'; sed hec non potest esse vera nisi per instans hoc presens quod illa copula 'est' importat, cum post hoc instans seu tempus illa erit falsa, quia sensus eius erit: 'Deus in hoc instanti est' [anima]; ergo propositum."

37 This is, by the way, a different question from the problem, also discussed by Enzinas' contemporaries, whether a mental proposition *can* change its truth value over time. See Nuchelmans, *Late-Scholastic and Humanist Theories of the Proposition*, 128-38.

38 Enzinas, *Tractatus*, f. 12ra: "Si forte dixeris quod natura illius copule 'est' est talis quod unit pro quolibet instanti in quo ipsa est, ita quod quando ipsa est in instanti ⟨'a'⟩ significat 'a' instans et quando in 'b' significat etiam 'b'…"

This intermediate solution may allow us to solve the problem about the change of truth value, but it generates some other strange consequences concerning the signification of the copula: on the one hand, a problem concerns the duration that this solution introduces into the signification of the copula; on the other, a difficulty remains that is common to any opinion that restricts the signification of the copula 'est' to the present time or instant.

First, this way of determining the signification of the copula forces one to take the copula of a given proposition in an equivocal way.[39] When the span during which the proposition exists is taken into account, this duration is transferred to the signification of the copula, so that at instant B the 'est' makes its syncategorematic union for an extended time (*tempus*), not for a single instant. This means that the 'est' has to be taken first (at A) as making its union for the present instant and then (at B) as making its union for the present time (the duration of the proposition), simply by the fact that the passage of time extends the set of instants that happen to be present *during* the existence of the proposition.

Second, from the idea that the copula 'est' signifies the present, it follows that different tokens of the present-tense copula 'est' existing at different moments of time (one in the past and the other in the future) would not be synonymous: they would not signify the same time, since the former would in fact signify only instants that now are past (the instants that were present when it existed) and the latter only instants that now are future (the instants that will be present when it will exist).[40]

It seems, then, that the consideration of an 'extended' present is not a satisfactory amendment of the opinion that the copula signifies the present. Enzinas then explores the other extreme, the opinion that the copula 'est' signifies any time.

5.3 *The Copula 'Est' Signifies Any Instant*

But now problems seem to arise concerning both signification and truth values. First, the undesired consequence concerning signification would be that (given that we apply the same analysis to the past-tensed copula 'fuit') the present-tensed copula 'est' and the past-tensed copula 'fuit' would be synonymous,

---

39 Enzinas, *Tractatus*, f. 12ra: "... contra hoc arguo: Sequitur quod illa copula capitur equivoce (cum per solam mutationem temporis acquirat ⟨novam⟩ significationem)."

40 Enzinas, *Tractatus*, f. 12ra: "Preterea sequitur quod copula que ante hoc fuit et copula que erit, quamvis utraque sit de presenti, non erunt synonime, quia una solum instantia preterita importat (postquam in illis fuit) et alter instantia solum futura (quia non fuit in preteritis)."

since they would both signify any time: *quodlibet temporis*, that is, any element in the set of instants/spans of time, extensionally considered.[41] Second, the undesired consequence concerning truth values is that the truth condition that makes the past-tensed proposition 'Adam fuit' true (the fact that Adam existed at a past time) would also serve to make the present-tensed proposition 'Adam est' true (since that Adam existed at a past time is also signified by it): if we take the whole set of instants to be signified by the copula (this instant, and this instant, and this instant, and so on, from past to present), we find some instants in the past at which Adam's existence is a fact, which will be enough to make the proposition true.[42]

Up to this point, three possibilities have been explored: the copula signifies the single instant which is present when the proposition is formed, the copula signifies the set of instants which are present during the existence of the proposition, the copula signifies the set of all instants. As we have seen, each of these possibilities raises its own difficulties, and now Enzinas has to choose the best option.

The problem with necessary propositions seems to be the most serious: the first option is discarded without any further comment. Concerning the second option, the problem of equivocation is also serious: Enzinas finds it unacceptable that the mental copula can make its union both for an instant and for a duration. Equivocation must not be allowed at the level of mental language: the idea that the copula makes its union for any instant at which it exists (that is, having its consignification of time progressively extended from the first instant to the whole time that is present during the existence of the proposition) must therefore be mistaken.[43]

Enzinas then introduces a qualification in the idea that the copula makes the predicative union for any instant at which it exists: this is only true if we are talking about an actual union (*unione actuali*). But we can also have in mind a potential union (*unione potentiali*), and in this case we can say that the copula makes its union for any instant whatever. At the level of actual signification, we can say that the present-tensed copula signifies only present instants (that

41 Enzinas, *Tractatus*, f. 12ra: "Si dicas nunc secundum (videlicet quod copula de presenti quodlibet temporis importat), contra hoc arguitur: Sequitur etiam quod copula de preterito omne tempus importat, et si[t]⟨c⟩ copula de preterito et presenti erunt synonime."

42 Enzinas, *Tractatus*, f. 12ra: "Preterea sequitur quod hec concederetur: 'Adam est', cum ly 'est' tempus preteritum importat (et non propter aliud conceditur hec: 'Adam[us] fuit')."

43 Enzinas, *Tractatus*, f. 12ra: "Ad hanc replicam respondeo quod hec copula 'est' in mente, si uniat pro instanti, non potest unire pro tempore; et tunc, quando queris utrum ne importet hoc instans presens vel quodlibet, respondeo quod quodlibet."

is, the instants that happen to be present when the proposition exists) and the past-tensed copula signifies only past instants (the instants that happen to be past when the proposition exists). But at the level of potential signification, we must say that both copulae signify the whole set of instants that constitute the complete extension of time.[44]

Enzinas mentions an analogous division of supposition into two species, actual and potential.[45] This makes it clear that it is the actual union that matters when truth and falsity are involved (in the same way as it is the actual supposition that determines the truth value of the proposition). The reader must infer that this solves the problem concerning 'Adam est' and 'Adam fuit': it is the actual union that counts in order to determine the truth value of propositions. Thus, the truth condition of 'Adam est' is not fulfilled even if we admit that the 'est' signifies every point of time.

Only the (serious) difficulty about the synonymy of the different copulae remains to be solved. Enzinas has to find a specific signification for each copula, compatible with the opinion that both ('est', 'fuit') signify any time.

6 Any Copula Signifies Any Instant: Are 'Est' and 'Fuit' Synonymous?

Enzinas firmly states that although both the present-tensed copula and the past-tensed copula import any instant, their signification is not the same. A specific *modus* of signifying any instant belongs to each of them: the present-tensed copula 'est' signifies any instant *per modum presentialitatis*, whereas the past-tensed copula 'fuit' signifies any instant *per modum preteritionis*.[46] That is, there is not a particular set of points of time signified by each copula (present

---

44 Enzinas, *Tractatus*, f. 12ra: "Et pro improbationis declaratione notandum est quod copula de presenti unit solum pro instanti in quo ipsa est unione actuali, sed pro quolibet unit unione potentiali (sicut ly 'homo' supponit tantum pro homine actu existente in hac: 'homo est animal', sed suppositione potentiali pro quolibet homine qui possibiliter supponit); et ly 'fuit' omne instans preteritum actualiter importat et pro quolibet tali unit, sed unione potentiali pro quolibet unit."

45 Although the terminology 'actual supposition'/'potential supposition' is used at the time of Enzinas (see Ashworth, *Language and Logic in the Post-Medieval Period*, 78), the sense intended here is more close, in my opinion, to the classical division between *suppositio naturalis* and *accidentalis*.

46 Enzinas, *Tractatus*, f. 12ra-b: "Et sic tam copula presentis quam preteriti importat omne instans, sed in hoc differt [quod] una ab alia ⟨quia⟩ hec per modum preteritionis significat, hoc est, connotat quodlibet instans per modum preteritionis, et illa connotat quodlibet instans per modum presentialitatis (capio ly 'connotare' improprie)."

instants/past instants), but the signification of 'est' and 'fuit' is specified by their particular way of signifying any time (by way of presentness/by way of pastness).

Recall that Enzinas is talking about the potential signification of the copula. The present-tensed copula 'est' *can* make its union for any instant of time (and the past-tensed copula 'fuit' *can* make its union for the same set of instants), and thus both signify the whole set of instants, but the present-tensed copula signifies these instants in a way that the past-tensed copula does not. The signification of the copulae is therefore not completely determined unless one makes reference to this way of signifying. 'Consignificare tempus' involves more elements than it appeared to at first sight.

As far as the specific signification of each copula is concerned, the correct question is not, therefore, *which* time is signified by each copula, but *how* time is signified by each copula. What distinguishes 'est' from 'fuit' is not the particular set of instants that are (potentially) signified, but the way the whole set is signified. This means that there are two *aliqualiter* involved in the signification of the copula: as an element of the principal signification, there is the way in which the copula relates subject and predicate; and as an element of the added signification, there is the way in which each copula consignifies time.

Here is the originality of Enzinas' solution, in comparison, for example, with John Dorp's, who also discusses this problem: Dorp simply turns to the distinction signification/acception,[47] whose analogy in Enzinas (actual/potential signification) is intended to solve a very different problem. Enzinas clearly separates the question about truth values from the question about signification. He has found that the signification of the copula is doubly syncategorematic, so a complete determination of the signification of 'est' must include these two *aliqualiter*.

The fragment that I am considering ends with a paragraph that uses the modistic terminology of 'modi significandi accidentales' in order to stress the essential character of this second *aliqualiter* that Enzinas has found in the signification of the copula. If the signifying by way of presentness or by way of pastness were accidental to the copulae (just like cases, for example, are accidental to a noun), the vocal or written 'est' would be subordinated to the same mental copula as the vocal or written 'fuit'. But this is impossible, because there are two different ways of *dare intelligere* involved.[48]

47 See Nuchelmans, *Late-Scholastic and Humanist Theories of the Proposition*, 131.

48 Enzinas, *Tractatus*, f. 12rb: "Et ex hoc patet copulas illas non esse synonimas de significatione essentiali (ut quidam dicit), quia non significant eodem modo (postquam aliqualiter una dat intelligere ultra suum principale aliqualiter significare qualiter alia non dat

7 Conclusion: The Signification of the Copula in Enzinas' *Syncategorems*

In this brief but insightful fragment, we have seen Enzinas reaching a detailed determination of the signification of the copula, from a statement of its principal syncategorematic signification to a clarification of its consignification of time. This second aspect involved several steps: first, the admission of a categorematic component in the signification of the copula (the copula signifies time); second, the stance taken with respect to the question as to which time is signified (the copula signifies any time); and third, the original proposal of a further syncategorematic signification included in the consignification of time (the whole set of times is differently signified by one copula and the other).

In my opinion, Enzinas' interest in the question as to *how* the different copulae signify time is an indication that an extensionalist approach to signification falls short of the needs of a comprehensive semantic theory. When tensed propositions come to complicate the picture, something intensional fights to make a space for itself. Enzinas feels that consignifying the present time is something more than pointing to this or that instant that at some point or other happens to be present. Unfortunately, in these pages he does not develop his proposal, so we are left wondering what exactly this *connotare per modum presentialitatis* might have been.

---

intelligere); si enim solum differrent penes modum significandi accidentalem, viderentur eidem subordinari (quod est impossibile). Et pro hec patet ad formam argument[um]⟨i⟩."

Bibliography

1 Sources (Printed)

Abelardus, see Peter Abelard.

Albertus Magnus [Albert the Great], *Liber I Elenchorum* (Venice, 1632).

Albertus de Saxonia, *Perutilis Logica* (Venice, 1522; reprint Hildesheim-New York, 1974); edited with German transl. in Berger (2010).

Alexander, *In Aristotelis Analyticorum Priorum Librum I Commentarium*, ed. Wallies (Berlin, 1883).

Alexander, *In Aristotelis Metaphysica Commentaria*, ed. Hayduck (Berlin, 1891).

Alexander, *In Aristotelis Topicorum Libros Octo Commentaria*, ed. Wallies (Berlin, 1891).

Ammonius, *In Aristotelis Categorias Commentarius*, ed. Busse (Berlin, 1895).

Ammonius, *De Interpretatione Commentarius*, ed. Busse (Berlin, 1897).

Anselm of Canterbury, *De Grammatico*, in *S. Anselmi Cantuariensis Archiepiscopi Opera Omnia* 1, ed. Schmitt (Stuttgart-Bad Cannstatt, 1968), 145-68.

Apuleius, *Peri hermeneias* (*Opera* III), ed. Thomas (Stuttgart, 1970).

Aristotle, *Aristoteles Latinus. De interpretatione vel Periermenias. Translatio Boethii*, ed. Minio-Paluello (Bruges-Paris, 1965).

Aristotle, *Categories*: English transl. in Edghill (1928) and in Ackrill (1963); French transl. in Bodéüs (2002) and in Ildefonse & Lallot (2002).

Aristotle, *Metaphysics*: English transl. in Ross (1966).

Aristotle, *Peri Hermeneias*: English transl. in Ackrill (1963).

Aristotle, *Prior Analytics*: English transl. in Smith (1989).

Aristotle, *Sophistical Refutations*: French transl. in Dorion (1995).

Aristotle, *Topics*: English transl. in Pickard-Cambridge (1991); French transl. in Brunschwig (1967-2007).

Arnauld, A. and P. Nicole, *La Logique*, ed. P. Clair and F. Girbal (Paris, 1970).

Ars Burana, in de Rijk (1967) II-2, 175-213.

Ars Emmerana, in de Rijk (1967) II-2, 143-174.

Avicenna, *Al-Burhān*, ed. Affifi (Cairo, 1956).

Avicenna, *Al-Maqūlāt*, ed. Anawati, El-Ehwani, El-Khodeiri, and Zayed (Cairo, 1959).

Boethius, *Commentarii in Librum Aristotelis Peri ermeneias*, prima editio, ed. Meiser (Leipzig, 1877).

Boethius, *Commentarii in Librum Aristotelis Peri ermeneias*, secunda editio, ed. Meiser (Leipzig, 1880).

Boethius, *In Categorias Aristotelis Commentaria*, in *Patrologia Latina* 64 (Paris, 1891), 159-294.

Boethius, *De syllogismo categorico*, in *Patrologia Latina* 64 (Paris, 1891), 793-832.

Boethius, *Philosophiae consolatio*, ed. Bieler (Turnhout, 1957).

Dialectica Monacensis, in de Rijk (1967) II-2, 453-638.

Dominicus Soto, *Summulae* (Salamanca, 1554; reprint Hildesheim, 1980).

Dominicus Soto, *In Porphyrii Isagogen, Aristotelis Categorias, librosque de Demonstratione Commentaria* (Venice, 1587; reprint Frankfurt, 1967).

Fallacie Parvipontane, in de Rijk (1962), 551-609.

Fernando de Enzinas, *Tractatus de compositione propositionis mentalis* (Lyon, 1578).

Hamilton, W., *Lectures on Logic* (Boston, 1858).

Henry of Ghent, *Syncategoremata*, in Braakhuis (1979).

Herveus Raucus, *Abstractiones*, in de Libera (1986).

Introductiones Montanae minores, in de Rijk (1967) II-2, 7-71.

Iohannes Pagus, *Syncategoremata*, partially edited in Braakhuis (1979), 184-246.

John Buridan, *Iohannis Bvridani Tractatvs de Conseqventiis*, ed. Hubien (Louvain, 1976).

John Buridan, *Summulae: De suppositionibus*, ed. van der Lecq (Nijmegen, 1998); English transl. in Klima (2001).

John Buridan, *Summulae: De Practica Sophismatum*, ed. Pironet (Turnhout, 2004); English transl. in Klima (2001).

John Tarteys, *Obligationes*, in Ashworth (1992).

Libellus Sophistarum ad usum Cantabrigiensium ([London], 1497).

Libellus Sophistarum ad usum Oxoniensium (London, 1510).

Logica (Oxford, ca. 1483); transcription of the section on *obligationes* in Pironet (1994), 582-609.

Logica 'Cum sit nostra', in de Rijk (1967) II-2, 413-51.

Martinus Anglicus, *De obligationibus. Über die Verpflichtungen*, ed. and trans. Schupp (Hamburg, 1993).

Matthew of Orléans, *Sophistaria*, ed. Spruyt (Leiden-Boston-Cologne, 2001).

Michael of Ephesus, see Pseudo-Alexander.

De Morgan, A., *Formal Logic* (London, 1926).

Nicholas of Paris, *Syncategoremata*, in Braakhuis (1979).

Obligationes parisienses, in de Rijk (1975).

Paul of Pergula, *Logica and Tractatus de sensu composito et diviso*, ed. Brown (St. Bonaventure-Louvain-Paderborn, 1961).

Paul of Venice, *Tractatus de Obligationibus*, in *Logica Magna*. Part II. Fascicule 8, ed. and trans. Ashworth (Oxford, 1988).

Peter Abelard, *Super Periermeneias*, in *Logica 'Ingredientibus'* III, ed. Baeumker (Münster, 1933).

Peter Abelard, *Dialectica*, ed. de Rijk (Assen, 1970).

Peter Abelard, *De intellectibus*, ed. Morin (Paris, 1994).

Peter Abelard, *Glossae super Peri hermeneias*, ed. Jacobi and Strub (Turnhout, 2010).

Peter of Spain, *Tractatus Called Afterwards Summule logicales*, ed. de Rijk (Assen, 1972).
Peter of Spain, *Syncategoreumata*, ed. de Rijk, trans. Spruyt (Leiden-New York-Cologne, 1992).
Peter Tartaretus, *In Universam Philosophiam Opera Omnia* (Venice, 1621).
Peter the Chanter, *De tropis*, partial ed. in Giusberti (1982), 106-8.
Philoponus, *In Aristotelis Categorias Commentarium*, ed. Busse (Berlin, 1898).
Philoponus, *In Aristotelis Analytica Priora Commentarius*, ed. Wallies (Berlin, 1905).
Porphyrius, *In Aristotelis Categorias Commentarium*, ed. Busse (Berlin, 1887).
Porphyrius, *Isagoge*, trilingual edition in Norro and Rovira (2003).
Pseudo-Alexander, *In Aristotelis Sophisticos Elenchos*, ed. Wallies (Berlin, 1898).
Pseudo-Scotus, *In librum primum Priorum analyticorum Aristotelis questiones*, in Johannis Duns Scoti *Opera Omnia* II, ed. Vivés (Paris, 1891), 81-197.
Priscianus, *Institutiones grammaticae*, ed. Hertz, 2 vol. (Leipzig, 1855-1888; reprint Hildesheim-New York, 1981).
Recorde, R., *The Whetstones of Witte* (London, 1557).
Richard Brinkley, *Richard Brinkley's Obligationes. A Late Fourteenth Century Treatise on the Logic of Disputation*, ed. Spade and Wilson (Münster, 1995).
Richard Kilvington, *The Sophismata of Richard Kilvington*, ed. Kretzmann and Kretzmann (Oxford, 1990); English translation in Kretzmann and Kretzmann (1990).
Richard Lavenham, *Obligationes*, in Spade (1978).
Robert Bacon, *Syncategoremata*, in Braakhuis (1979).
Robert Fland, *Obligationes*, in Spade (1980).
Robertus Anglicus, *Sophistria*, in Grondeux and Rosier-Catach (2006).
Roger Swyneshed, *Obligationes*, in Spade (1977).
Simplicius, *In Aristotelis Categorias Commentarium*, ed. Kalbfleisch (Berlin, 1907); English transl. in Chase (2003).
Sophismata Anonymi Avenionensis, in Grondeux (2002).
Summa Sophismatum Disputabilium sive Abstractiones Venetae, in Ebbesen et al. (2003).
Summa Sophisticorum Elenchorum, in de Rijk (1962), 257-458.
Syncategoremata Monacensia, partially edited in Braakhuis (1979), 95-104.
Thomae de Vio Caietani, *In Praedicabilia Porphirij, Praedicamenta, Postpraedicamenta & libros Posteriorum Analyticorum Aristotelis Commentaria* (Paris, 1572).
Tractatus Florianus, in de Rijk (1988), 49-145.
Walter Burley, *Expositio super Artem Veterem Porphyrii et Aristotelis* (Venice, ca. 1476/78).
Walter Burley, *De Puritate Artis Logicae*, ed. Boehner (St. Bonaventure-Louvain-Paderborn, 1955); English transl. in Spade (2000).
Walter Burley, *Obligationes*, English transl. of some selections in Kretzmann and Stump (1988), 369-412.
Whately, R., *Elements of Logic* (London, 1826).

William of Ockham, *Summa Logicae* (Opera Philosophica I), ed. Boehner, Gál and Brown (St. Bonaventure, NY, 1974).
William of Ockham, *Expositio super libros Elenchorum* (Opera Philosophica III), ed. Del Punta (St. Bonaventure, NY, 1979).
William of Sherwood, *Introductiones in Logicam*, ed. and transl. Brands and Strub (Hamburg, 1995); English transl. in Kretzmann (1966).
William of Sherwood, *Syncategoremata*, in O'Donnell (1941).

2 Secondary Literature

Ackrill, J.L., *Aristotle's Categories and De Interpretatione* (Oxford, 1963).
Adams, M. McCord, 'Re-reading *De Grammatico*, or Anselm's Introduction to Aristotle's *Categories*', *Documenti e studi sulla tradizione filosofica medievale* 11 (2000), 83-112.
Amerini, F., 'Tommaso d'Aquino, il desiderium e la logica', in *Il desiderio nel Medioevo. Atti del convegno Il desiderio nel pensiero medievale*, ed. A. Palazzo (Rome, 2014), 207-22.
Angelelli, I., *Studies on Gottlob Frege and Traditional Philosophy* (Dordrecht, 1967).
Anonymous, *Heures à l'usage de la chapelle et paroisse du Roy, contenant Les Prieres qui s'y disent le Matin, le Soir, & au Salut... selon les usages de Rome & de Paris* (Paris, 1750).
Ashworth, E.J., *Language and Logic in the Post-Medieval Period* (Dordrecht, 1974).
Ashworth, E.J., 'A Note on Paul of Venice and the Oxford *Logica* of 1483', *Medioevo* 4 (1978), 93-9.
Ashworth, E.J., 'A Note on an Early Printed Logic Text in Edinburgh University Library', *The Innes Review* 30 (1979), 77-9.
Ashworth, E.J., 'The "Libelli Sophistarum" and the Use of Medieval Logic Texts at Oxford and Cambridge in the Early Sixteenth Century', *Vivarium* 17 (1979), 134-58.
Ashworth, E.J., 'Mental Language and the Unity of Propositions: A Semantic Problem Discussed by Early Sixteenth Century Logicians', *Franciscan Studies* 41 (1981), 61-96.
Ashworth, E.J., 'The Structure of Mental Language: Some Problems Discussed by Early Sixteenth Century Logicians', *Vivarium* 20 (1982), 59-83.
Ashworth, E.J., 'Inconsistency and Paradox in Medieval Disputations: A Development of Some Hints in Ockham', *Franciscan Studies* 44 (1984) [Printed 1988], 129-39.
Ashworth, E.J., 'English *Obligationes* Texts after Roger Swyneshed: The Tracts beginning *Obligatio est quaedam ars*', in *The Rise of British Logic*, ed. P.O. Lewry (Toronto, 1985), 309-33.
Ashworth, E.J., 'Jacobus Naveros (fl. ca. 1533) on the Question: Do Spoken Words Signifiy Concepts or Things?', in *Logos and Pragma*, ed. L.M. de Rijk and H.A.G. Braakhuis (Nijmegen, 1987), 189-214.

Ashworth, E.J., 'The "Obligationes" of John Tarteys: Edition and Introduction', *Documenti e Studi sulla tradizione filosofica medievale* 3 (1992), 653-703.

Ashworth, E.J., '*Obligationes* Treatises: A Catalogue of Manuscripts, Editions and Studies', *Bulletin de philosophie médiévale* 36 (1994), 118-47.

Ashworth, E.J., 'Autour des *Obligationes* de Roger Swyneshed: la *nova responsio*', *Les études philosophiques* 3 (1996), 341-60.

Ashworth, E.J., '"*Tu curris*" (*vel "homo est asinus"*) *est tibi positum*: l'histoire d'un sophisme dans les traités sur les *Obligationes*', in *Sophismata: l'histoire d'une pratique philosophique*, ed. A. de Libera, L. Cesalli, F. Goubier and L. Gazziero (Paris, forthcoming).

Bäck, A., 'Philoponus on the Fallacy of Accident', *Ancient Philosophy* 7 (1987), 131-46.

Bäck, A., *On Reduplication* (Leiden, 1996).

Bäck, A., *Aristotle's Theory of Predication* (Leiden, 2000).

Bakker, P.J.J.M., 'Syncatégorèmes, concepts, équivocité. Deux questions anonymes, conservées dans le ms. Paris, B.N., lat. 16.401, liées à la sémantique de Pierre d'Ailly (c. 1350-1420)', *Vivarium* 34 (1996), 76-131.

Baldwin, J.W., *Masters, Princes, and Merchants: The Social Views of Peter the Chanter and his Circle*, 2 vols. (Princeton, NJ, 1970).

Barnes, J., *Truth etc.* (Oxford, 2007).

Berger, H. (ed.), *Albert von Sachsen, Logik* (Hamburg, 2010).

Biard, J., 'Pierre d'Ailly: Langage, Concept, Représentation', in *Le langage mental du Moyen Âge à l'Âge Classique*, ed. J. Biard (Louvain-Paris, 2009), 169-83.

Bidez, J., 'Boèce et Porphyre', *Comptes rendus des séances de l'Académie des Inscriptions et Belles-Lettres* 66 (1922), 346-50.

Bodéüs, R., *Aristote. Catégories* (Paris, 2002).

Bonevac, D., *The Art and Science of Logic* (Mountain View, CA, 1990).

Bonitz, H., *Index Aristotelicus* (Graz, 1955).

Bos, E.P., 'La théorie de la signification de la "vox significativa ad placitum" dans les *Introductiones Montanae Maiores*', in *Gilbert de Poitiers et ses contemporains*, ed. J. Jolivet and A. de Libera (Naples, 1987), 73-90.

Boschung, P., *From a Topical Point of View: Dialectic in Anselm of Canterbury's* De Grammatico (Leiden, 2006).

Boutry, M., *Introduction to her edition Petri Cantoris Parisiensis Verbum Adbreviatum. Textus conflatus* (Turnhout, 2004).

Boyer, C., *A History of Mathematics*, Second Edition (Hoboken, NJ, 1991).

Braakhuis, H.A.G., *De 13de eeuwse traktaten over syncathegorematische termen. Inleidende studie en uitgave van Nicolaas van Parijs'* Sincategoreumata (Meppel, 1979).

Braakhuis, H.A.G., 'English Tracts on Syncategorematic Terms from Robert Bacon to Walter Burley', in *English Logic and Semantics from the End of the Twelfth Century to the Time of Ockham and Burleigh*, ed. H.A.G. Braakhuis, C.H. Kneepkens, and L.M. de Rijk (Nijmegen, 1981), 131-65.

Brentano, F., *Von der mannigfachen Bedeutung des Seienden nach Aristoteles* (Freiberg, 1862; repr. Hildesheim, 1960); trans. R. George, as *On The Several Senses of Being in Aristotle* (Berkeley, 1975).

Broadie, A., *The Circle of John Mair. Logic and Logicians in Pre-Reformation Scotland* (Oxford, 1985).

Brousseau-Beuermann, C., 'Les *Quaestiones* de Johannes de Wolve et les *Sophismata artis grammaticae* du MS Paris, Bibl. nat. lat. 15037', in *Gilbert de Poitiers et ses contemporains. Aux origines de la Logica modernorum*, ed. J. Jolivet and A. de Libera (Naples, 1987), 91-105.

Brunschwig, J., *Aristote. Topiques*, 2 vols. (Paris 1967-2007).

Bueno, A.A., 'Aristotle, the Fallacy of Accident and the Nature of Predication', *Journal of the History of Philosophy* 26 (1988), 5-24.

Bursill-Hall, G.L., *A Census of Medieval Latin Grammatical Manuscripts* (Stuttgart-Bad Cannstatt, 1981).

Calboli, G., 'Les modes chez Priscien (GL 3, 235.16-267.5)', in *Priscien. Transmission et refondation de la grammaire de l'Antiquité aux Modernes*, ed. M. Baratin, B. Colombat, and L. Holtz (Turnhout, 2009), 315-29.

Cameron, M., 'What's in a Name? Students of William Champeaux on the *vox significativa*', *Bochumer Philosophisches Jahrbuch für Antike und Mittelalter* 9 (2004), 93-114.

Carroll, L., 'What the Tortoise Said to Achilles', *Mind* 4 (1895), 278-80.

Chase, M., ed. and trans., *Simplicius: On Aristotle's Categories 1-4* (London, 2003).

Copi I. and C. Cohen, *Introduction to Logic*, Ninth Edition (New York, 1994).

Dahl, N., 'Two Kinds of Essence in Aristotle', *Philosophical Review* 106 (1997), 233-65.

Dorion, L.A., *Aristote. Les refutations sophistiques* (Paris, 1995).

Duerlinger, J., 'Predication and Inherence in Aristotle's Categories', *Phronesis* 15 (1970), 175-203.

Dutilh Novaes, C., 'Ralph Strode's *obligationes*: The Return of Consistency and the Epistemic Turn', *Vivarium* 44 (2006), 338-74.

Dutilh Novaes, C., *Formalizing Medieval Logical Theories: Suppositio, Consequentiae and Obligationes* (Dordrecht, 2007).

Dutilh Novaes, C., 'Medieval *Obligationes* as a Theory of Discursive Commitment Management', *Vivarium* 49 (2011), 240-57.

Dutilh Novaes, C., 'Form and Matter in Later Latin Medieval Logic: The Cases of *suppositio* and *consequentia*', *Journal of the History of Philosophy* 50 (2012), 339-64.

Ebbesen, S., *Commentators and Commentaries on Aristotle's* Sophistici Elenchi, 3 vols. (Leiden, 1981).

Ebbesen, S., 'OXYNAT: A Theory about the Origins of British Logic', in *The Rise of British Logic*, ed. P.O. Lewry (Toronto, 1985), 1-17.

Ebbesen, S., 'Boethius de Dacia et al. The *Sophismata* in mss Bruges SB 509 and Florence Med.-Laur. S. Croce 12 sin., 3', in *Sophisms in Medieval Logic and Grammar. Acts of the 9th European Symposium for Medieval Logic and Semantics*, ed. S. Read (Dordrecht, 1993), 45-63.

Ebbesen, S., '*Sophismata* and Physics Commentaries', *Cahiers de l'Institut du Moyen-Âge Grec et Latin* 64 (1994), 164-95.

Ebbesen, S., '*Tantum unum est.* 13th-Century Sophismatic Discussions around the Parmenidean Thesis', *The Modern Schoolman* 72 (1995), 175-99.

Ebbesen, S., 'The More the Less. Natural Philosophy and *Sophismata* in the Thirteenth century', in *La nouvelle physique du XIV*[e] *siècle*, ed. S. Caroti and P. Souffrin (Florence, 1997), 9-44.

Ebbesen, S., 'Language, Medieval Theories of', in *Routledge Encyclopedia of Philosophy*, version 1.0 (London-New York, 1998), 157.

Ebbesen, S., 'By Necessity', in *Mind and Modality*, ed. V. Hirvonen, T.J. Halopainen and M. Tuominen (Leiden, 2006), 141-52.

Ebbesen, S., 'The Traditions of Ancient Logic-cum-Grammar in the Middle Ages—What's the Problem?, *Vivarium* 45 (2007), 136-52.

Ebbesen, S., 'Concrete Accidental Terms: Late Thirteenth-Century Debates about Problems Relating to Such Terms as "album"', in *Topics in Latin Philosophy from the 12th-14th centuries. Collected Essays of S. Ebbesen* (Farnham, 2008) 109-51.

Ebbesen, S., 'The Present King of France Wears Hypothetical Shoes with Categorical Laces', in *Topics in Latin Philosophy from the 12th-14th Centuries. Collected Essays of Sten Ebbesen*. Volume 2 (Farnham, 2009), 15-30 (originally published in *Medioevo* in 1981).

Ebbesen, S., '*Modi significandi* in Logic and Grammar', in *Modern Views of Medieval Logic*, ed. C. Kann, B. Loewe, C. Rode and S.L. Uckelman (Leuven, forthcoming).

Ebbesen, S., 'How to Build Your Own Sophisma (Late 13th-Early 14th-Century Style)', in *Sophismata. Histoire d'une pratique philosophique*, ed. A. de Libera, L. Cesalli and F. Goubier (Paris, forthcoming).

Ebbesen, S. and F. Goubier, *A Catalogue of 13th-Century Sophismata*, 2 vols (Paris, 2010).

Ebbesen, S., M. Sirridge and P. Streveler, 'The Pupils of the Master of Abstractions: *Abstractiones Digbeianae, Regiae & Venetae*', *Cahiers de l'Institut du Moyen-Âge Grec et Latin* 74 (2003), 89-150.

Edghill, E.M., trans., *Categoriae*, in *The Works of Aristotle*, ed. W.D. Ross, vol. 1 (Oxford, 1928).

Etchemendy, J., *The Concept of Logical Consequence* (Harvard, 1990).

Evans, G.R., 'A Work of "Terminist Theology"? Peter the Chanter's *De Tropis Loquendi* and Some Fallacie', *Vivarium* 20 (1982), 40-58.

Evans, G.R., *The Language and Logic of the Bible: The Earlier Middle Ages* (Cambridge, 1984 [paperback ed. 1991]).

Finocchiaro, M., 'Fallacies and the Evaluation of Reasoning', in idem, *Arguments about Arguments* (Cambridge, 2005).

[Forshall, J.], *Catalogue of Manuscripts in The British Museum.* New Series, Vol. I. Part II. *The Burney Manuscripts* ([London,] 1840).

Fredborg, K.M., 'Speculative Grammar', in *A History of Twelfth-Century Western Philosophy*, ed. P. Dronke (Cambridge, 1988) 177-95.

Frede, M., *Die Stoische Logik* (Göttingen, 1974).

Frede, M., 'Categories in Aristotle', in *Essays in Ancient Philosophy* (Minneapolis, 1987).

Frede, M. and G. Patzig, *Aristoteles "Metaphysik Z"*, 2 vols. (Munich, 1988).

Friedman, R.L., 'Mental Propositions before Mental Language', in *Le langage mental du Moyen Âge à l'Âge Classique*, ed. J. Biard (Louvain-Paris, 2009), 95-115.

Galonnier, A., '(Au sujet) de Grammarien', in *Le Grammarien; De la vérité; la liberté du choix; la chute du diable: Anselme de Cantorbéry*, ed. A. Galonnier, M. Corbin and R. de Ravinel (Paris, 1986), 25-49.

Galonnier, A., 'Le De Grammatico et l'origine de la théorie des proprietés des termes', in *Gilbert de Poitiers et ses Contemporains: aux Origines de la Logica Modernorum*, ed. J. Jolivet and A. de Libera (Naples, 1987), 353-75.

Galonnier, A., 'Sur quelques aspects annonciateurs de la littérature sophismatique dans le *De grammatico*', in *Anselm: Aosta, Bec and Canterbury: Papers in Commemoration of the Nine-Hundredth Anniversary of Anselm's Enthronement as Archbishop, 25 September 1093*, ed. D.E. Luscombe and G. Evans (Sheffield, 1996), 209-28.

Gambra, J.M., 'Medieval Solutions to the Fallacy of Accident', in *Argumentationstheorie. Scholastische Forschungen zu den logischen und semantischen Regeln korrekten Folgerns*, ed. K. Jacobi (Leiden, 1993), 431-50.

Gambra, J.M., 'The Fallacy of the Accident in Peter of Spain Tractatus and in Other Thirteenth-Century Works', in *Medieval and Renaissance Logic in Spain*, ed. I. Angelelli and P. Pérez-Ilzarbe (Hildesheim, 2000), 21-60.

Gambra, J.M., 'La théorie aristoteliciènne de la différence dans les Topiques', *Philosophie Antique* 3 (2003), 21-56.

Garcea, A., 'Le passioni presso gli antichi: un percorso attraverso le *Tusculanae Disputationes* di Cicerone', in *Passioni, emozioni, affetti*, ed. C. Bazzanella and P. Kobau (Milan, 2002), 1-18.

García Norro J.J. and R. Rovira, *Porfirio. Isagoge* (Barcelona, 2003).

Gelber, H., 'The Fallacy of Accident and the *Dictum de omni*: Late Medieval Controversy over a Reciprocal Pair', *Vivarium* 25 (1987), 110-45.

Georges, T., 'Die Verwurzelung von Abelards Ethik im Denken Augustins', *Archa Verbi* 3 (2006), 9-30.

Gilson, É., *Héloïse et Abélard* (Paris, 1938; second edition, 1948).

Giusberti, F., *Materials for a Study on Twelfth Century Scholasticism* (Napoli, 1982).

Goering, J.W., *William de Montibus (c. 1140-1213). The Schools and the Literature of Pastoral Care* (Toronto, 1992).

Gombay, A., *Descartes* (Malden-Oxford-Carlton, 2007).

Grabmann, M., *Die Sophismataliteratur des 12. und 13. Jahrhunderts mit Textausgabe eines Sophisma des Boetius von Dacien* (Münster, 1940).

Green, R., *An Introduction to the Logical Treatise* De Obligationibus, *With Critical Texts of William of Sherwood [?] and Walter Burley*, PhD dissertation, Katholieke Universiteit Leuven, 1963 [revised version in manuscript form: *The Logical Treatise "De Obligationibus": An Introduction with Critical Texts of William of Sherwood and Walter Burley*].

Green-Pedersen, N.J., 'Early British Treatises on Consequences', in *The Rise of British Logic*, ed. P.O. Lewry (Toronto, 1985), 285-307.

Grondeux, A., 'Sophismata Anonymi Avenionensis', *Cahiers de l'Institut du Moyen-Âge Grec et Latin* 73 (2002), 41-59.

Grondeux, A., *À l'école de Cassiodore. Les figures "extravagantes" dans la tradition occidentale* (Turnhout, 2013).

Grondeux, A. and I. Rosier-Catach, *La Sophistria de Robertus Anglicus*. Étude et edition critique. Avec la collaboration de Ch. Brousseau-Beuerman et M. Sirridge (Paris, 2006).

Grondeux, A. and I. Rosier-Catach, 'Les *Glosulae super Priscianum* et leur tradition', in *Arts du langage et théologie aux confins des XIe et XIIe siècle*, ed. I. Rosier-Catach (Turnhout, 2011), 107-79.

Guilfoy, K., 'Peter Abelard's Two Theories of the Proposition', in *Medieval Theories on Assertive and Non-Assertive Language. Acts of the 14th European Symposium on Medieval Logic and Semantics*, ed. A. Maierù and L. Valente (Florence, 2004), 36-57.

Hamblin, C.L., *Fallacies* (London, 1970).

Hamesse, J. (ed.), *Les Auctoritates Aristotelis. Un florilège médiéval* (Louvain, 1974).

Henry, D.P., *The De Grammatico of St. Anselm: The Theory of Paronymy* (Notre Dame, 1964).

Herzberger, H.G., 'Dimensions of Truth', *Journal of Philosophical Logic* 2 (1973), 535-56.

Hesbert, R.-J., *Corpus Antiphonalium Officii*, vol. III: *Invitatoria et Antiphonae* (Rome, 1968).

Hitchcock, D., 'Fallacies and Formal Logic in Aristotle', *History and Philosophy of Logic* 21 (2000), 207-21.

Ildefonse, F. and J. Lallot, *Aristote. Catégories* (Paris, 2002).

Iwakuma, Y., '*Instantiae*: An Introduction to a Twelfth Century Technique of Argumentation', *Argumentation* 1 (1987), 437-53.

Iwakuma, Y., 'Alberic of Paris on Mont Ste Geneviève against Peter Abelard', in *Logic and Language in the Middle Ages*, ed. J.L. Fink, H. Hansen and A.M. Mora-Márquez (Leiden, 2012), 27-47.

Jacobi, K., 'Die Semantik sprachlicher Ausdrücke, Ausdrucksfolgen und Aussagen in Abailards Kommentar zu Peri Hermeneias', *Medioevo* 7 (1981), 41-89.

Jacobi, K., C. Strube and P. King, 'From *intellectus verus/falsus* to the *dictum propositionis*: The Semantics of Peter Abelard and his Circle', *Vivarium* 34 (1996), 15-40.

Kann, C., 'Assertive and non-Assertive Sentences. Classifications of the *oratio perfecta* in the Thirteenth Century', in *Medieval Theories on Assertive and Non-Assertive Language. Acts of the 14th European Symposium on Medieval Logic and Semantics*, ed. A. Maierù and L. Valente (Florence, 2004), 245-57.

King, P., '*Consequence* as Inference: Medieval Proof Theory 1300-1350', in *Medieval Formal Logic*, ed. M. Yrjönsuuri (Dordrecht-Boston-London, 2001), 117-45.

King, P., 'Anselm's Philosophy of Language', in *The Cambridge Companion to Anselm*, ed. B. Davies and B. Leftow (Cambridge, 2004), 84-110.

Klima, G., 'Socrates est species', in *Argumentationstheorie. Scholastische Forschungen zu den logischen und semantischen Regeln korrekten Folgerns*, ed. K. Jacobi (Leiden, 1993), 489-504.

Klima, G., 'The Semantic Principles Underlying Saint Thomas Aquinas's Metaphysics of Being', *Medieval Philosophy and Theology* 5 (1996), 87-141.

Klima G., *John Buridan's Summulae de Dialectica: An Annotated Translation, with a Philosophical Introduction* (New Haven, 2001).

Klima, G., 'Syncategoremata', in *Encyclopedia of Language and Linguistics*, Second Edition, ed. K. Brown (Oxford, 2006) 12: 353-6.

Kneepkens, C.H., '*Mulier Quae Damnavit, Salvavit.* A Note on the Early Development of the *Relatio simplex*', *Vivarium* 14 (1976), 1-25.

Kneepkens, C.H., 'The *Quaestiones grammaticales* of the MS Oxford, Corpus Christi College 250', *Vivarium* 21 (1983), 1-34.

Kneepkens, C.H., 'Roger Bacon's Theory of the Double Intellectus: A Note on the Development of the Theory of *Congruitas* and *Perfectio* in the First Half of the Thirteenth Century', in *The Rise of British Logic*, ed. P.O. Lewry (Toronto, 1985), 115-42.

Kneepkens, C.H., *Het Iudicium Constructionis. Het leerstuk van de constructio in de 2de helft van de 12de eeuw*, vol. 1 (Nijmegen, 1987).

Kneepkens, C.H., '*Significatio generalis* and *significatio specialis*: Notes on Nicholas of Paris' Contribution to Early Thirteenth-Century Linguistic Thought', in *Medieval Analyses in Language and Cognition*, ed. S. Ebbesen and R. Friedman (Copenhagen, 1999), 17-43.

Kneepkens, C.H., 'Robert Kilwardby on Grammar', in *A Companion to the Philosophy of Robert Kilwardby*, ed. H. Lagerlund and P. Thom (Leiden-Boston, 2013), 17-64.

Knuuttila, S., 'Necessities in Buridan's Natural Philosophy', in *The Metaphysics and Natural Philosophy of John Buridan*, ed. J.M.M.H. Thijssen and J. Zupko (Leiden, 2001), 65-76.

Knuuttila, S., *Emotions in Ancient and Medieval World* (Oxford, 2006).

Kretzmann, N., *Wiliam of Sherwood's Introduction to Logic* (Minneapolis, 1966).

Kretzmann, N., '*Syncategoremata, exponibilia, sophismata*', in *The Cambridge History of Later Medieval Philosophy*, ed. N. Kretzmann, A. Kenny, and J. Pinborg (Cambridge, 1982), 211-45.

Kretzmann, N. and B.E. Kretzmann, *The Sophismata of Richard Kilvington: Introduction, Translation and Commentary* (Cambridge, 1990).

Kretzmann N. and E. Stump, *The Cambridge Translations of Medieval Philosophical Texts*, Vol. 1: *Logic and Philosophy of Language* (Cambridge, 1988).

Kung, J., 'Aristotle on Thises, Suches, and the Third Man Argument', *Phronesis* 26 (1981), 207-47.

Lenz, M., 'Peculiar Perfection: Peter Abelard on Propositional Attitudes', *Journal of the History of Philosophy* 43 (2005), 377-86.

Lenz, M., 'Are Thoughts and Sentences Compositional? A Controversy between Abelard and a Pupil of Alberic on the Reconciliation of Ancient Theses on Mind and Language', *Vivarium* 45 (2007), 169-88.

Lewis, C.I. and C.H. Langford, *Symbolic Logic* (New York, 1932).

Lewis, D., *Counterfactuals* (Oxford, 1973).

Lewis, F.A., 'Accidental Sameness in Aristotle', *Philosophical Studies* 42 (1982), 1-36.

Lewis, F.A., *Substance and Predication in Aristotle* (Cambridge, 1991).

Lewis, F.A., 'Self-Knowledge in Aristotle', *Topoi* 15 (1996), 39-58.

Lewry, O., 'Boethian Logic in the Medieval West', in *Boethius: His Life, Thought, and Influence*, ed. M. Gibson (Oxford, 1981), 90-134.

de Libera, A., 'The Oxford and Paris Traditions on Logic', in *The Cambridge History of Later Medieval Philosophy*, ed. N. Kretzmann, A. Kenny, and J. Pinborg (Cambridge, 1982), 174-87.

de Libera, A., 'La littérature des abstractiones et la tradition logique d'Oxford', in *The Rise of British Logic*, ed. P.O. Lewry (Toronto, 1985), 63-114.

de Libera, A., 'La littérature des *Sophismata* dans la tradition terministe parisienne de la seconde moitié du XIIIe siècle', in *The Editing of Theological and Philosophical Texts from the Middle Ages*, ed. M. Asztalos (Stockholm, 1986), 213-44.

de Libera, A., 'Les Abstractiones d'Hervé le Sophiste (Hervaeus Sophista)', *Archives d'histoire doctrinale et littéraire du Moyen Âge* 52 (1986), 162-230.

Maierù, A., 'Mental Language and Italian Scholasticism in the Fourteenth and Fifteenth Centuries', in *John Buridan and Beyond. Topics in the Language Sciences*, ed. R.L. Friedman and S. Ebbesen (Copenhagen, 2004), 33-67.

Mansion, S., 'Notes sur la doctrine des catégories dans les Topiques', in *Aristotle on Dialectic: the Topics*, ed. G.E.L. Owen (Oxford, 1968), 189-201.

Marenbon, J., *The Philosophy of Peter Abelard* (Cambridge, 1997).

Marenbon, J., 'Abélard, le verbe 'être' et la prédication', in *Langage, sciences, philosophie au XIIe siècle*, ed. Biard (Paris, 1999), 199-216.

Marenbon,J., 'Some Semantic Problems in Anselm's *De grammatico*', in *Latin Culture in the Eleventh Century*, ed. M. Herren, C. McDonough and R. Arthur (Turnhout, 2002), 73-86.

Marenbon, J., '*Dicta*, Assertion and Speech Acts: Abelard and some Modern Interpreters', in *Medieval Theories on Assertive and Non-Assertive Language. Acts of the 14th European Symposium on Medieval Logic and Semantics*, ed. A. Maierù and L. Valente (Florence, 2004), 59-80.

Marenbon, J., 'Logic at the Turn of Twelfth Century: A Synthesis', in *Arts du langage et théologie aux confins des XIe et XIIe siècle*, ed. I. Rosier-Catach (Turnhout, 2011), 181-217.

Marmo, C., 'Una semantica del verbo nella grammatica e nella teologia tra XII e XIII secolo', in *Medieval Theories on Assertive and Non-Assertive Language. Acts of the 14th European Symposium on Medieval Logic and Semantics*, ed. A. Maierù and L. Valente (Florence, 2004), 185-206.

Martin, C.J., 'William's Machine', *The Journal of Philosophy* 83 (1986), 564-72.

Martin, C.J., *Theories of Inference and Entailment in the Middle Ages*, PhD Dissertation, Princeton University, 1999.

Martin, C.J., 'Abelard on Logic', in *The Cambridge Companion to Abelard*, ed. J.F. Brower and K. Guilfoy (Cambridge, 2004), 158-99.

Martin, C.J., 'A Note on the Attribution of the Literal Glosses in Paris, BnF, lat. 13368 to Peter Abelard', in *Arts du langage et théologie aux confins des XIe et XIIe siècle*, ed. I. Rosier-Catach (Turnhout, 2011), 606-46.

Martin, C.J., '*De Interpretatione* 5-8: Aristotle, Boethius, and Abaelard on Propositionality', in *Methods and Methodologies: Aristotelian Logic East and West, 500-1500*, ed. M. Cameron and J. Marenbon (Leiden, 2011), 207-28.

Martin, C.J., '"What An Ugly Child": Abelard on Translation, Figurative Language, and Logic', *Vivarium* 49 (2011), 26-49.

Matthews, G., 'Accidental Unities', in *Language and Logos*, ed. M. Schofield and M. Nussbaum (Cambridge, 1982), 223-40.

Meier-Oeser, S., 'Medieval Semiotics', *The Stanford Encyclopedia of Philosophy* (Summer 2011 Edition), E.N. Zalta (ed.), URL = <http://plato.stanford.edu/archives/sum2011/entries/semiotics-medieval/>.

Mews, C.J., 'On Dating the Works of Peter Abelard', *Archives d'histoire doctrinale et littéraire du Moyen Âge* 52 (1985), 73-134, reprinted in idem, *Abelard and His Legacy* (Aldershot, 2001).

Muñoz Delgado, V., 'La lógica en la Universidad de Alcalá durante la primera mitad del siglo XVI', *Salmanticensis* 15 (1968), 161-218.

Muñoz Delgado, V., 'Fernando de Enzinas (†1523) eminente lógico vallisoletano', in *Homenaje a Alfonso Candau* (Valladolid, 1988), 271-87.

Murè, D., '*Suppositum* between Logic and Metaphysics: Simon of Faversham and His Contemporaries (1270-1290)', *Vivarium* 51 (2013), 205-29.

Normore, C., 'The Necessity in Deduction: Cartesian Inference and Its Medieval Background', *Synthese* 96 (1993), 437-54.

Normore, C., 'Buridanian Possibilities', in *Logic and Language in the Middle Ages*, ed. J.L. Fink, H. Hansen and A.M. Mora-Márquez (Leiden, 2012), 389-402.

Nuchelmans, G., *Theories of the Proposition. Ancient and Medieval Conceptions of the Bearers of Truth and Falsity* (Amsterdam, 1973).

Nuchelmans, G., *Late-Scholastic and Humanist Theories of the Proposition* (Amsterdam-Oxford-New York, 1980), 94-102.

O'Donnell, J.R., 'The *Syncategoremata* of William of Sherwood', *Mediaeval Studies* 3 (1941), 46-93.

Orme, N., *English Schools in the Middle Ages* (London, 1973).

d'Ors, A., 'Las *Summulae* de Domingo de Soto: Los limites de la regla «Tollendo ponens»', *Anuario Filosofico* 16 (1983), 209-17.

d'Ors, A., '*Ex impossibili quodlibet sequitur* (Walter Burley)', *Archives d'histoire doctrinale et littéraire du Moyen Âge* 57 (1990), 121-54.

d'Ors, A., 'Sobre las *Obligationes* de Richard Lavenham', *Archives d'histoire doctrinale et littéraire du Moyen Âge* 58 (1991), 253-78.

d'Ors, A., '*Tu scis regem sedere* (Kilvington, S47[48])', *Anuario filosófico* 24 (1991), 49-74.

d'Ors, A., '*Ex impossibili quodlibet sequitur* (John Buridan)', in *Argumentationstheorie. Scholastische Forschungen zu den logischen und semantischen Regeln korrekten Folgerns*, ed. K. Jacobi (Leiden, 1993), 195-212.

d'Ors, A., '*Sortes non currit vel Sortes movetur* (Roger Swyneshed, *Obligationes*, § 137-138)', *Archives d'histoire doctrinale et littéraire du Moyen Âge* 60 (1993), 165-72.

d'Ors, A., '*"Non erat veritas", "Non erit veritas"*. Sobre las pruebas anselmianas de la eternidad de la verdad', in *Verdad, percepción, inmortalidad/Wahrheit, Wahrnehmung, Unsterblichkeit*, ed. S. Castellote (Valencia, 1995), 201-14.

d'Ors, A., '*Dubium proponitur*. Andres Limos and the Treatise on Obligations', in *Medieval and Renaissance Logic in Spain*, ed. I. Angellelli and P. Pérez-Ilzarbe (Hildesheim, 2000), 225-49.

d'Ors, A., 'Sobre hablar y enseñar. Un comentario de texto a propósito del "De Magistro"', in *Cómo se comenta un texto filosófico*, ed. J.J. García Norro and R. Rodríguez (Madrid, 2007), 81-96.

d'Ors, A., '*"Omnis volens ipsum suum velle vult"*. A propósito del *De libertate arbitrii* de San Anselmo', in *"Autotrascendimiento". Homenaje al catedrático de filosofía D. Ignacio Falgueras Salinas por su jubilación*, ed. J.A. García González and J.J. Padial (Málaga, 2010), 183-203.

d'Ors, A., 'Logic in Salamanca in the Fifteenth Century. The *Tractatus Suppositionum Terminorum* by Master Franquera', *Vivarium* 51 (2013), 427-63.

d'Ors, A. and M. García-Clavel, 'Sobre las *Obligationes* de Robert Fland. *Antiqua et nova responsio*', *Revista de Filosofía* 7 (1994), 51-8.

Panaccio, C., *Le discours intérieur. De Platon à Guillaume d'Ockham* (Paris, 1991).

Parsons, T., 'Comments on Stephen Read's "The Truth-schema and the Liar"', in *Unity, Truth and the Liar: The Modern Relevance of Medieval Solutions to the Liar Paradox*, ed. S. Rahman, T. Tulenheimo and E. Genot (New York, 2008), 129-34.

Pelletier, F., 'Sameness and Referential Opacity in Aristotle', *Noûs* 13/3 (1979), 283-311.

Pérez-Ilzarbe, P., 'Jerónimo Pardo on the Unity of Mental Propositions', in *Le langage mental du Moyen Âge à l'Âge Classique*, ed. J. Biard (Louvain-Paris, 2009), 185-204.

Perkams, M., *Liebe als Zentralbegriff der Ethik nach Peter Abaelard* (Münster, 2001).

Perler, D., 'Diskussionen über mentale Sprache im 16. Jahrhundert', in *'Res et verba' in der Renaissance*, ed. E. Kessler and I. Maclean (Wiesbaden, 2002), 29-51.

Pickard-Cambridge, W.A., *Topica*, in *The Complete Works of Aristotle. The Revised Oxford Translation*, ed. Jonathan Barnes, vol. 1 (Princeton, NJ, 1991).

Pironet, F., *Guillaume Heytesbury: Sophismata Asinina* (Paris, 1994).

Priest, G., *One* (Oxford, 2014).

Read, S., 'Formal and Material Consequence, Disjunctive Syllogism and Gamma', in *Argumentationstheorie. Scholastische Forschungen zu den logischen und semantischen Regeln korrekten Folgerns*, ed. K. Jacobi (Leiden, 1993), 233-59.

Read, S., 'Self-Reference and Validity Revisited', in *Medieval Formal Logic*, ed. M. Yrjönsuuri (Dordrecht-Boston-London, 2001), 183-96.

Read, S., 'The Liar Paradox from Thomas Bradwardine Back to John Buridan', *Vivarium* 40 (2002), 189-218.

Read, S., 'The Truth-schema and the Liar', in *Unity, Truth and the Liar: The Modern Relevance of Medieval Solutions to the Liar Paradox*, ed. S. Rahman, T. Tulenheimo and E. Genot (New York, 2008), 3-18.

Read, S., 'Inference', in *The Cambridge History of Medieval Philosophy*, ed. R. Pasnau (Cambridge, 2010), 173-85.

Rescher, N., 'The Equivocality of Existence', *Studies in Ontology*, ed. N. Rescher (Oxford, 1978).

de Rijk, L.M., *The Place of the Categories of Being in Aristotle's Philosophy* (Assen, 1952).

de Rijk, L.M., *Logica Modernorum: A Contribution to the History of Early Terminist Logic.* Vol I: *On the Twelfth Century Theories of Fallacy* (Assen, 1962).

de Rijk, L.M., 'Some new Evidence on Twelfth Century Logic. Alberic and the School of Mont Ste Geneviève (*Montani*)', *Vivarium* 4 (1966), 1-57.

de Rijk, L.M., *Logica Modernorum: A Contribution to the History of Early Terminist Logic.* Vol II: Part 1: *The Origin and Early Development of the Theory of Supposition / Part 2: Texts and Indices* (Assen, 1967).

de Rijk, L.M., 'Some Thirteenth Century Tracts on the Game of Obligation I', *Vivarium* 12 (1974), 94-103.

de Rijk, L.M., 'Some Thirteenth Century Tracts on the Game of Obligation II', *Vivarium* 13 (1975), 22-54.

de Rijk, L.M., 'Richard Billingham's Works on Logic', *Vivarium* 14 (1976), 121-38.

de Rijk, L.M., 'The Semantical Impact of Abailard's Solution of the Problem of Universals', in *Petrus Abaelardus (1079-1142). Person, Werk und Wirkung*, ed. R. Thomas, J. Jolivet, D.E. Luscombe, and L.M.de Rijk (Trier, 1980), 139-51; reprinted in de Rijk (1989), no. III.

de Rijk, L.M., 'Abailard's Semantic Views in the Light of Later Developments', in *English Logic and Semantics from the End of the Twelfth Century to the Time of Ockham and Burleigh*, ed. H.A.G. Braakhuis, C.H. Kneepkens, and L.M. de Rijk (Nijmegen, 1981), 1-58; reprinted in de Rijk (1989), no. VI.

de Rijk, L.M., *Some Earlier Parisian Tracts on* Distinctiones Sophismatum (Nijmegen, 1988).

de Rijk, L.M., *Through Language to Reality. Studies in Medieval Semantics and Metaphysics*, ed. E.P. Bos (Northampton, 1989).

de Rijk, L.M., 'Semantics and Ontology. An Assessment of Medieval Terminism', *Vivarium* 51 (2013), 13-59.

Robert, A., 'Les Deux Langages de la Pensée: A Propos de Quelques Réflexions Médiévales', in *Le langage mental du Moyen Âge à l'Âge Classique*, ed. J. Biard (Louvain-Paris, 2009), 145-68.

Roncaglia, G., *Palestra Rationis: Discussioni su natura della copula e modalità nella filosofia 'Scolastica' tedesca del XVII secolo* (Florence, 1996).

Roncaglia, G., 'Mesino de Codronchi's Discussion on *Syncategoremata* and Mental Language in his *Quaestiones on De interpretatione*', in *Aristotle's Peri hermeneias in the Latin Middle Ages. Essays on the Commentary Tradition*, ed. H.A.G. Braakhuis and C.H. Kneepkens (Groningen-Haren, 2003), 149-63.

Rosier, I., 'Les sophismes grammaticaux aux XIIIe siècle', *Medioevo* 17 (1991), 175-230.

Rosier, I., *La parole comme acte. Sur la grammaire et la sémantique au XIIIe siècle* (Paris, 1994).

Rosier, I. and B. Roy, 'Grammaire et Liturgie dans les "Sophismes" du XIIIe Siècle', *Vivarium* 28 (1990), 118-35.

Rosier-Catach, I., 'Roger Bacon and Grammar', in *Roger Bacon and the Sciences: Commemorative Essays*, ed. J. Hackett (Leiden, 1997), 67-102.

Rosier-Catach, I., 'La notion de *translatio*, le principe de compositionalité, et l'analyse de la prédication accidentelle chez Abélard', in *Langage, sciences, philosophie au XIIe siècle*, ed. J. Biard (Paris, 1999), 125-64.

Rosier-Catach, I., 'La tradition de la grammaire universitaire médiévale', in *Manuscripts and Tradition of Grammatical Texts from Antiquity to the Renaissance*, ed. M. De Nonno, P. De Paolis, and L. Holtz (Cassino, 2000), 449-98.

Rosier-Catach, I., 'Abélard et les grammairiens, sur la définition du verbe et la notion d'inhérence', in *La tradition vive, sur la définition des textes en l'honneur de Louis Holtz*, ed. P. Larded (Turnhout, 2003), 143-59.

Rosier-Catach, I., 'Abélard et les grammairiens, sur le verbe substantif et la prédication', *Vivarium* 41 (2003), 175-248.

Rosier-Catach, I. (ed.), *Les syncatégorèmes*, issue 25/2 (2003) of *Histoire Épistémologie Langage*.

Rosier-Catach, I., 'Priscien, Boèce, les *Glosulae in Priscianum*, Abélard: les enjeux des discussions autour de la notion de consignification', *Histoire, Épistémologie, Langage* 25 (2003), 55-84.

Rosier-Catach, I., *La parole efficace. Signe, rituel, sacré* (Paris, 2004).

Rosier-Catach, I., 'Les discussions sur le signifié des propositions chez Abélard et ses contemporains', in *Medieval Theories on Assertive and Non-Assertive Language. Acts of the 14th European Symposium on Medieval Logic and Semantics*, ed. A. Maierù and L. Valente (Florence, 2004), 1-34.

Rosier-Catach, I., 'Priscian on Divine Ideas and Mental Conceptions: The Discussions in the *Glosulae in Priscianum*, the *Notae Dunelmenses*, William of Champeaux and Abelard', *Vivarium* 45 (2007), 219-37.

Rosier-Catach, I., 'Discussions médiévales sur l'expression des affects', in *Le sujet des émotions au Moyen Âge*, ed. D. Boquet and P. Nagy (Paris, 2008), 201-23.

Rosier-Catach, I., 'Speech Acts and Intentional Meaning in the Medieval Philosophy of Language', *Bulletin de Philosophie Médiévale* 52 (2010), 55-80.

Ross, W.D., *Aristotle's Metaphysics*, 2 Vols. (Oxford, 1966).

Schepss, G., *Handschriftliche Studien zu Boethius De consolatione Philosophiae* (Würzburg, 1881).

Schreiber, S., *Aristotle on False Reasoning* (Albany, 2003).

Serino, G., 'Para una interpretación unitaria de la doctrina de los predicables', *Anuario Filosófico* 35 (2002), 183-219.

Sharpe, R., *A Handlist of the Latin Writers of Great Britain and Ireland before 1540* (Turnhout, 1997).

Sharpe, R., 'Anselm as Author: Publishing in the Late Eleventh Century', *Journal of Medieval Latin* 19 (2009), 1-87.

Shimizu, T., 'Word and *Esse* in Anselm and Abelard', in *Anselm and Abelard: Investigations and Juxtapositions*, ed. G.E.M. Gasper and H. Kohlenberger (Toronto, 2006), 179-95.

Sirridge, M., 'Robert Kilwardby: Figurative Constructions and the Limits of Grammar', in *De ortu grammaticae: Studies in Medieval Grammar and Linguistic Theory in Memory of Jan Pinborg*, ed. G.L. Bursill-Hall, S. Ebbesen, and K. Koerner (Amsterdam-Philadelphia, 1990), 321-37.

Slomkowski, P., *Aristotle's Topics* (Leiden-New York, 1997).

Smith, R. (trans. and comm.), *Aristotle: Prior Analytics* (Indianapolis, 1989).
Sommers, F., 'Do We Need Identity?', *Journal of Philosophy* 66 (1969), 499-504.
Spade, P.V., 'Roger Swyneshed's *Obligationes*: Edition and Comments', *Archives d'histoire doctrinale et littéraire du Moyen Âge* 44 (1977), 243-85.
Spade, P.V., 'Richard Lavenham's *Obligationes*. (Edition and Comments by Paul Vincent Spade)', *Rivista Critica di Storia della Filosofia* 33 (1978), 225-42.
Spade, P.V., 'Robert Fland's *Obligationes*: An Edition', *Mediaeval Studies* 42 (1980), 41-60.
Spade, P.V., *Walter Burley. On the Purity of the Art of Logic* (Yale, 2000).
Strobino, R., *Concedere, Negare, Dubitare. Peter of Mantua's Treatise on* Obligations, PhD dissertation, Scuola Normale Superiore, Pisa, 2009.
Strobino, R., 'Contexts of Utterance and Evaluation in Peter of Mantua's *Obligationes*', *Vivarium* 49 (2011), 275-99.
Stump, E., 'Roger Swyneshed's Theory of Obligations', *Medioevo* 7 (1981), 135-74; reprinted in her *Dialectic and Its Place in the Development of Medieval Logic* (Cornell, 1989).
Stump, E., 'Obligations: From the Beginning to the Early Fourteenth Century', in *The Cambridge History of Later Medieval Philosophy*, ed. N. Kretzmann, A. Kenny, and J. Pinborg (Cambridge, 1982), 315-34.
Suto, T., *Boethius on Mind, Grammar and Logic: A Study of Boethius' Commentaries on* Peri hermenias (Leiden, 2011).
Szövérffy, J., *Die Annalen der lateinischen Hymnendichtung. Ein Handbuch*, I. *Die lateinischen Hymnen bis zum Ende des 11. Jahrhunderts* (Berlin, 1964).
Thomson, R.M., *A Descriptive Catalogue of the Medieval Manuscripts in Worcester Cathedral Library* (Cambridge, 2001).
Uckelman, S.L., 'The Reception of Saint Anselm's Logic in the Twentieth and Twenty-First Centuries', in *Saint Anselm of Canterbury and His Legacy*, ed. G.E.M. Gasper and I. Logan (Toronto, 2012), 405-26.
Uckelman, S.L., '*Sit verum obligationes* and Counterfactual Reasoning', *Vivarium* 53 (2015), 90-113.
Valente, L., 'Langage et théologie pendant la seconde moitié du XIIe siècle', in *Sprachtheorien in Spätantike und Mittelalter*, ed. S. Ebbesen (Tübingen, 1995), 33-54.
Valente, L., *Phantasia contrarietatis. Contraddizioni scritturali, discorso teologico e arti del linguaggione nel* De tropis loquendi *di Pietro Cantore († 1197)* (Florence, 1997).
Valente, L., 'Fallacie et théologie pendant la seconde moitié du XIIe siècle', in *Medieval Analyses in Language and Cognition*, ed. S. Ebbesen and R. Friedman (Copenhagen, 1999), 207-36.
Valente, L., *Logique et théologie. Les écoles parisiennes entre 1150 et 1220* (Paris, 2008).
Valente, L., 'Il desiderio di filosofia nel pensiero filosofico e teologico di Pietro Abelardo', in *Il desiderio nel Medioevo. Atti del convegno Il desiderio nel pensiero medievale*, ed. A. Palazzo (Rome, 2014), 185-206.

Vecchio, S., 'Il piacere da Abelardo a Tommaso', in *Piacere e dolore. Materiali per una storia delle passioni nel medioevo*, ed. S. Vecchio and C. Casagrande (Florence, 2009), 66-86.

Walton, D., *A Pragmatic Theory of Fallacy* (Tuscaloosa, 1995).

Wedin, M., 'The Strategy of Aristotle's Categories', *Archiv für Geschichte der Philosophie* 79 (1997), 1-26.

Weijers, O., *Le maniement du savoir. Pratiques intellectuelles à l'époque des premières universités* (*XIII*^{e}-*XIV*^{e} *siècles*) (Turnhout, 1996).

Weingart, R.E., *The Logic of Divine Love. A Critical Analysis of the Soteriology of Peter Abelard* (Oxford, 1970).

Wetzel, L., 'Types and Tokens', *The Stanford Encyclopedia of Philosophy* (Spring 2011 Edition), E.N. Zalta, ed., URL = <http://plato.stanford.edu/archives/spr2011/entries/types-tokens/>.

White, N., 'Aristotle on Sameness and Oneness', *Philosophical Review* 80 (1971), 177-97.

Wyllie, G., 'Signification et forme logique dans le *De grammatico* d'Anselme de Cantorbéry', in *Anselm of Canterbury (1033-1109): Philosophical Theology and Ethics*, ed. R.H. Pich (Porto Alegre, 2011), 111-18.

Yrjönsuuri, M., *Obligationes: 14th Century Logic of Disputational Duties* (Helsinki, 1994).

Yrjönsuuri, M. (ed.), *Medieval Formal Logic*, (Dordrecht-Boston-London, 2001).

Index of Concepts

Index of Manuscripts

Index of Names

Contemporary authors are only included when the text contains explicit discussion of their views.